MW00677033

My First 90 Years
Plus 3

by

Ken Nelson

DORRANCE PUBLISHING CO., INC.
PITTSBURGH, PENNSYLVANIA 15222

The events, people, and places herein are depicted to the best recollection of the author, who assumes complete and sole responsibility for the accuracy of this narrative.

ISBN: 978-0-8059-7090-6
Library of Congress Control Number: 2005935632

Printed in the United States of America

First Printing

For more information or to order additional books, please contact:
Dorrance Publishing Co., Inc.
701 Smithfield Street
Third Floor
Pittsburgh, Pennsylvania 15222
U.S.A.
1-800-788-7654
www.dorrancebookstore.com

Dedicated to the memory of June,
my beloved wife.

Foreword

This book is the chronicle of my life, which began in 1911, and includes my first ninety years plus three.

I want to thank Jo Walker Meador, Christine Farnon, Lorraine Wilson, Dee Kilpatrick, Francis M. Scott, Kim McHugh, and Ralph Emery, who provided me with needed information. I want to thank my relatives and friends, acquaintances, artists, musicians, song writers, and recording engineers. If it hadn't been for all of these people, I wouldn't have had a life to write about.

Last, but certainly not least, if I could speak every language in the world, I wouldn't be able to find enough words to express my appreciation, gratitude, and heartfelt feelings for my daughter's patience, devotion, caring, and help.

Special thanks to Joel Whitburn for the information and vital statistics I garnered from his book, *Top Country Singles 1944-993 Billboard*. Also *special thanks* to Richard Weize of Bear Records, Hamburg, Germany, for reissuing and sending me CDs of many of the artists I produced.

Ken Nelson

My First 90 Years Plus 3

This is the unabashed autobiography of my life from the day of my birth, January 19, 1911, to June 2004. Each chapter covers a ten year period detailing every happening of that period— the good, the bad, the evil, and my sexual experiences. At the end of each decade there will be pictures of the events of that period.

My mother and father were not married. Mother took me to Chicago where I spent the first thirty-seven years of my life. During my pre-teen and teenage years I worked for music publishers, played the tenor banjo in orchestras, and sang on radio stations. At the age of twenty-two I became a radio announcer, and five years later I became musical director of a radio station. In the meantime I was married and divorced from a disastrous relationship. During World War II, I was drafted. After my stint in the army I returned to Chicago and my position as a musical director. I met the girl of my dreams and we married. With the exception of a few bumps here and there, we had a happy marriage.

In 1948 I was hired by Capitol Records to be the producer of the artists in their transcription library, and our family moved to California. In 1951, I became the director and producer of Capitol's Country Music Department. In my twenty-eight year career with Capitol, I produced transcriptions, popular and country music records, and albums of over two-hundred artists. I was elected a vice-president of Capitol.

I served two terms as president of The Country Music Association. I tell about many of the artists I have produced and about business associates and friends. My home base was Hollywood. My second home base was Nashville. My autobiography contains a great deal of music publishing and recording history.

In 1976, at the age of sixty-five, I retired. My wife June didn't want to travel anymore. We kept busy with family affairs and played a lot of golf. After June passed away in 1984 I searched for and found relatives on both my mother's and father's sides of my family who I hadn't seen or heard of since my childhood. My daughter, Claudia, and I traveled all over the world. In writing about our travels I have included many historical facts. In 2001, at the age of ninety, I was inducted into the Country Music Hall of Fame. Since 2002 I have been dealing with the miseries of old age.

1911-1920

I was born in the small town of Caledonia, Minnesota, on January 19, 1911. My mother, Susan Roster, and my father, Conrad Nelson, were not married. I don't know how they got together or why they didn't marry. Mother's religion was Catholicism, and I was baptized in the Catholic church as Kenneth Francis Nelson. Mother assumed the name of Mrs. Susan Nelson.

My father wanted to put me in a home for unwanted children, but Mother ran away with me to Chicago, where her sister, my Aunt Catherine, was living. She put me in St. Vincent's Orphanage. I couldn't have been more than six months old, but I vividly remember Mother handing me over to a nun, and as she held out her arms to take me I bit her thumb.

When I was about three or four years old, Mother put me in an orphanage called The Home of the Friendless, located on Chicago's south side at Fifty-First and South Park Avenue. Mother paid six dollars a week for my maintenance. It's strange, but I still remember the names and can visualize the principal, Mrs. Stocking, and our caretaker, Mrs. Barnett. I have many memories of the home, most of them pleasant. The home was for both boys and girls, ranging in age from about three to ten, but we did not mingle; we were in separate sections.

Our caretaker, Mrs. Barnett, was very strict, I don't recall her ever spanking or hitting anyone; our punishment was going to bed without supper. We had to make our own beds, and I recall scrubbing the stairs up to the second floor where the bedrooms were. During the day when we were in the playroom and needed to go to the toilet we had to raise our hand and indicate by our fingers, one finger for urinating and two fingers for defecating. I never could understand the reason for this.

Every Friday night was bath night. The bathtub was about three or four feet deep. Mrs. Barnett would bathe us, and she only changed the water after bathing about ten children. I don't recall how many children there were, but there must have been at least thirty. The janitor and maintenance man was Mr. Larson; he was very kind and gentle with the children. He had a large mustache and an accent, which I now presume was Scandinavian. I recall him killing a rat that was almost the size of a baby rabbit.

Our normal living and play areas were on the first floor, but during the summer and in periods of good weather we were allowed to play outside in a large cement area. There was a long stairway leading up to the kitchen on the second floor. For some reason or other, one of the cooks, a large Afro-American woman, took a liking to me and I to her. She would come down the stairs and I would run to her. She would hug me, press me to her huge bosom, and say, "Bless your little ol' heart," then we'd chat a bit. I've never forgotten her. I can still see her coming down the stairs, and I can still feel her warm embrace.

The orphanage had its own bakery, and the baker was a kind red-headed man. Every once in a while I would go in the bakery and he would give me some goodies. When I was about fifteen years old, I was walking down a street and I recognized him as he came toward me. I stopped him and told him who I was. He said "Oh yes, you used to come into the bakery. Are you still making up songs?" He said that even at that early age I was always singing and making up songs. I do recall one song in particular. From our outside play yard we could see the elevated trestle and sometimes only one car would go by. When that happened I would sing out, "I see one elevator, I see one elevator."

One of the scariest things that ever happened to me was, one night as I was sleeping, I was awakened by someone running their fingers over my neck. I was petrified. I realize now it had to be one of the other children, but to this day I must have a sheet or blanket covering my neck. Another scary event was when I was awakened by horrible screaming. I didn't find out until years later that it was two cats.

The orphanage had a huge auditorium, and on Christmas day all of the children, both boys and girls, were taken there. On the stage was Santa Claus. He would call a child's name, who would then walk up to the stage and receive a present. One year another boy and I were not called and didn't get a present. I'm sure now that it was an oversight and not done intentionally, but it did affect me for many years to come at Christmas time.

Two of my most pleasant memories of the orphanage were during the summer. A Mr. Gordon would come to the orphanage once or twice a week, and after lunch he would take us to Washington Park, where we would spend the afternoon playing games. He always wore a straw hat. I don't recall him ever having any trouble with us.

The other unforgettable and pleasant memory is, one day five of us decided to run away to see the outside world and we sneaked out. I don't remember how, but we got as far as the University of Chicago on the Midway. It had to be at least three or four miles. The police finally caught up with us there in the late afternoon. In those days the police had what were called "paddy-wagons." They were huge enclosed vehicles with a long bench-like seat on both sides. When they put us in the wagon we were scared to death, but a few minutes later they stopped in front of an ice cream parlor and bought us all ice cream cones and told us they were taking us back to the orphanage. Our only fear then was what Mrs. Barnett would do to punish us. It was Friday evening, and when we got back to the orphanage she was giving the children their weekly baths. She didn't say a word to us. We just undressed, had our baths, and went to bed without supper, and that was the end of it.

We went to a church about twice a month, I don't know what the denomination was, but I do know it wasn't Catholic, which was Mother's denomination. We went to a public elementary school called Burke. It was within walking distance of the home, and we were accompanied by an adult both going and returning.

One day in the boy's toilet, I became curious, I wanted to see what made the toilet flush. In those days the water was in a tank four or five feet above with a pipe leading to the commode with a chain that you pulled to flush it. I was standing on the toilet seat looking into the tank when a teacher walked in. He took me to the principal's office, where I was reprimanded. Mrs. Barnett was informed and I was sent to bed without supper.

Today I realize that was the wrong procedure. My curiosity should have been encouraged. A similar incident happened a few years later when I was ten or eleven years old and living with Mother. I took her alarm clock apart because I wanted to see what made it go. Mother was furious and slapped me several times.

Mother never gave me any affection, never hugged, held, or kissed me. She would come to visit me two or three times a month, and if I tried to hug her she would push me away. Every now and then Mother's sister, my Aunt Catherine Sasso, and her husband, Uncle Charlie, who lived in Chicago, would come and visit me. Both were kind, would bring me candy, and were tender and affectionate.

When I was six or seven years old, at the beginning of summer, Mother took me to Caledonia to visit her favorite aunt, Aunt Esche, who had a huge farm there. Before we went to the farm we visited my father's mother, my Grandma Nelson. I recall not going into the house; we just stood on the front porch, which covered a large area. Grandma Nelson cried when she saw me, and she hugged and kissed me and held me as she and Mother talked. After a while she told us to wait and went into the house. When she returned she had a beautiful gold watch with a diamond in the back of it. She told Mother it was for me when I grew up. I don't remember how old I was when Mother gave it to me. It is an Elgin, the kind that women wore on their breast, and it has a small lever on the side that you pull out to set the time. It still keeps perfect time. My wife, June, used it during our marriage, and now my daughter Claudia has possession of it and has promised to pass it on to my granddaughter.

Our visit to Aunt Esche's farm was during threshing season. I don't recall what Aunt Esche looked like, but I do remember her hugging me quite often. She used to give me a slice of homemade bread in a deep dish, sprinkle sugar on it, and pour pure cream over it. I can still taste it and her out-of-this-world homemade ice cream. I don't believe I've ever tasted anything like those two treats during my lifetime.

There was one very unpleasant incident. One day I went out to the field to watch the men work and operate the huge threshing machine. One of the hired hands had what looked like a candy bar. He took a bite out of it and asked me if I would like some. Of course I said yes, and I swallowed some before I realized how awful it tasted. It was chewing tobacco. When I started to regurgitate, one of the men caught a lizard, put it in front of me, and said I had vomited it up. I got sick. When Aunt Esche found out what happened she became very angry and ordered the two men off the farm immediately.

After we left Caledonia we went to Brownsville, Minnesota, bordered by the Mississippi River, to visit Mother's brother, my Uncle Andy Roster, and his wife, Aunt Lena. Aunt Lena was the local telephone operator and the switchboard was in the parlor of their house. The telephones hung on the wall were in wooden boxes with a crank on the side so that when cranked, it rang a bell to get the operator's attention. They had a huge organ in the parlor that had foot pedals that you pumped to get the sound. It gave me my first musical experience. Somewhere along the way I had heard the song "Smiles." I must have heard it several times because it stuck with me and I picked it out on the organ.

I used to play with a neighborhood boy and we would hunt for turtle eggs along the railroad tracks that ran along the Mississippi River. Uncle Andy took me fishing several times, but all we caught were carp, which we threw back because Uncle Andy said they were not good to eat. I don't know how long we stayed in Brownsville, but I enjoyed the stay and hated to leave.

From Brownsville, Mother took me to Minneapolis, where her sister, my Aunt Elizabeth, and her husband, Alfred Heinz, who was a barber, lived. Mother stayed a few days and left. I stayed with them. They had no children and treated me very well. It was in Minneapolis that I had my first criminal experience. I don't know why, but I stole pennies from a newspaper stand and took some milk bottles, for which there was a refund, and bought penny candies. It was unnecessary because Aunt Elizabeth and Uncle Al always bought me candy whenever we went to the store. I'm vague as to how long I stayed in Minneapolis and or how or when I got back to Chicago, but it must have been quite a while because we got there in the summer and left in fall or winter, because I remember me and a neighbor boy building a snow house alongside a cement wall that fronted our house which was on a hill. Outside of my initiation in crime, the stay was uneventful but pleasant.

Mother came and got me, and we went back to Chicago and stayed with Aunt Catherine and Uncle Charlie until she found a place to board me. In about a week or so she took me to a Mr. and Mrs. Hoffman, whose house was on Kedzie Avenue. They had two grown daughters, Helen and Louise; a grown son, Walter, who was a plumber; and in addition they were boarding two other children, a thirteen-year-old girl, Frances, and a six-year-old boy, Freddie. I was then eight years old, and that made eight people living in the house. I didn't think about it then, but I still can't understand why they boarded three children.

My stay there was a nightmare. Mrs. Hoffman was a mean bitch. For some reason or other she took a dislike to me. She would slap me for the slightest reason. Mr. Hoffman was a kind and gentle man. Occasionally when he came home from work Mrs. Hoffman would tell him that I had committed some kind of offense and that he should take me to the basement and spank me. He would take me to the basement and tell me to cry as if I was being spanked. I guess he knew his wife.

Many times when the other two children were outside playing, she wouldn't let me go out. Every Saturday morning I had to vacuum the rugs. I ate at the kitchen sink and had to help do the dishes every evening. I don't recall the other two children having to do anything.

Mother would come every couple of weeks and take me to a drug store and buy me an ice cream soda, and once or twice Mrs. Hoffman slapped me when Mother left, saying I was late for supper and I should have told Mother to bring me home on time.

The two daughters, Helen and Louise, were good to me, and Helen started to give me piano lessons on the upright piano in the living room. That started my desire to be a musician.

I had my first sexual experiences at the Hoffman house, although at the time I didn't realize it. One day when we three children were alone in the house, Frances, the thirteen-year-old girl, grabbed me, laid on the floor, pulled me on top of her, and moved up and down, simulating the sex act. Of course I thought she was just being playful. The other incident happened when Mrs. Hoffman sent me to the bakery, where I had been several times before and had become acquainted with the two sisters whose father owned the bakery. They were both around my age, possibly a bit older. This one particular day they asked me to come into the backyard. There was a long picnic table there, and they asked me to lay on it as they were playing doctor and nurse. I did, they opened my pants, I got an erection, and they stood by me and giggled, I'm sure it was just a matter of curiosity to them. I had had erections before, but I had no idea why or what caused them. I buttoned my pants, we played a little while, and I went home with the bakery goods and got slapped for taking so long.

One late afternoon Freddie and I were playing on the back porch. He had broken a little iron automobile, and he handed it to me, asking if I could fix it. Just at that moment, Mrs. Hoffman's son, Walter, a plumber, coming home from work, came on the porch and saw me holding the broken auto. He assumed that I had broken it and grabbed it out of my hands. As I backed away from him he threw it at me. It hit me on my left hip and left a bleeding gash.

Mrs. Hoffman sent all of us children to her church, which was Lutheran. I found out later that Mrs. Hoffman had promised to send me to a Catholic church and that Mother gave her a dollar a week extra for me to put in the collection box. Freddie, Frances, and I attended Sunday school every week. The church school decided to put on a play and wanted me to take part in it. I refused. A few days later—I remember it was on a Saturday morning—Mrs. Hoffman and I were standing in the kitchen, and she had been informed that I had refused to be in the play. She asked me why I didn't want to act in the play.

I said, "I don't want to." She said, "You will be in the play." I retorted, "I won't." With that she slapped me.

There was a knife on the table. I picked it up and said, "If you hit me again I'll stab you." She said, "If I had a nickel, I'd call the police." I replied, "I'll go get you a nickel."

She didn't slap me again, but she said, "You just wait until Mr. Hoffman gets home." I guess all of my hate and rebellion against Mrs. Hoffman had finally come to the fore.

Mr. Hoffman only worked half a day on Saturdays. When he came home and was told what I had done, he took me to the basement and said, "Kenneth, I've got to punish you for this." He took down my pants, turned me over his knees, and really gave me a hurtful spanking.

Mother came to visit the following Monday. Up to this point I had never told her of the horrible abuse to which I was being subjected; I guess I was too afraid. This time I blurted out everything. Mrs. Hoffman said I was lying. I replied, "Mother, if you don't believe me look at this!" I pulled up my shirt and showed her the scar that had been caused by Walter throwing the toy automobile at me.

That did it—that ended the nightmare. We gathered up my few clothes and belongings and went to Mother's place, which was the front half of an apartment consisting of a kitchen, a bedroom, and a living room. It was between sixtieth and Sixty-First Street; the living room and bedroom fronted Prairie Avenue. Three events that happened there come to mind.

Mother was a waitress, and in those days the usual gratuity was a nickel or a dime and every once in a while a quarter. Every evening when she came home from work she would put the dimes in a bank that was shaped like the Flat Iron Building in New York City and kept in a locked dresser drawer. I had made friends with a neighborhood boy, and one day he came to the apartment. I have no idea why but I told him about the bank. We decided to break open the drawer and steal it, and the still more puzzling thing is the fact that we didn't break the bank open but took it across the street and buried it in the front yard of an apartment complex.

When Mother came home it was dark outside and I was in my pajamas ready for bed. The minute she walked in the bedroom and saw the dresser drawer, she knew immediately what I had done. She didn't lose her temper but calmly asked me, "What have you done with my bank?"

I was never able to lie to Mother. I told her the truth about me and my friend and that we had buried it across the street. I expected some severe punishment, but all she said was, "Kenneth, you march right across the street and bring that bank back."

I was going to put on a coat, but no, she made me go in my pajamas—and believe you me, that was punishment enough. I never stole from Mother again, except maybe occasionally a dime from her purse.

One night Mother came home and told me an angry customer had thrown a glass and hit her in the back of her head. There was no serious damage except pain for a couple of days.

The third outstanding event occurred when my mother enrolled me in a Catholic school adjacent to a church. I seem to recall the name Saint Aneselems. It was located at Sixty-First and Michigan Boulevard. I was in the fourth grade. I don't recall what I had done or said, but one day our teacher, a nun, beat the daylights out of me. I went home crying and thought to myself, *She can't be a holy lady if she can beat me like this.*

When Mother came home I told her what had happened and said, "I'm not going back to that school." Mother tried to persuade me, but I absolutely refused. After much confrontation she saw how determined I was, and enrolled me in a public school.

The year was 1919, and school was out. Mother had become acquainted, and I guess enamored, with a World War I veteran who had lost an arm in the war. His left arm was severed at the elbow, leaving him with just a stump. He convinced mother to become his paramour and move to Peoria, Illinois, with me and live with him. We had a nice house with a large backyard. His name was Joe, and he had a large Airedale dog of which I became quite fond. We seemed to get along very well, but after about four or five days I got an unwanted surprise.

We lived near the end of the Elizabeth Street car line. About three times a week I would have to get on a streetcar with him. He wore his army uniform and carried a knapsack full of packages of needles. It was my job to pass out the needles. He would then follow me and collect twenty-five cents from each person or take the needles back from those who didn't want them. Of course, people assumed that I was his boy and that he, a veteran who had lost an arm in the war—which was true—was trying to support his family. Most people were sympathetic and would buy the needles that cost him five cents a package. I'm sure he made a good living.

Three other incidents during this sojourn have stayed with me. One, the house had a pot belly stove in the living room, and one day I must have done something that angered him. He tried to grab me, but I kept running around the stove and he never did catch me. A good memory was when Joe, I, and the dog went fishing and stayed in a tent all night. It was thrilling.

The third memory is of Mother and I sitting under a large shade tree. I laid on my stomach and put my head on her lap. She pulled up my shirt and squeezed blackheads out of my back. It was one of the rare times Mother showed me any affection; I have never forgotten the thrill of those few moments.

We were in Peoria for about six months or so when Joe left to go to St. Louis, Missouri. We had worked all the streetcar lines in town, and I presume he decided to move to virgin territory. I don't know whether he told Mother that he would come back or if we were to come to St. Louis later on. I also have no idea what happened to the dog. I never saw him again after Joe left. After he had been gone for about two or three weeks, I guess Mother hadn't heard from him. We were sitting at the dining room table one afternoon when Mother suddenly blurted out in a fit of rage, "He's down in St. Louis with all those whores." Of course at the time I had no idea what that meant, but I never forgot her saying it or her anger. We stayed in Peoria a few more days and then went back to Chicago.

I'm not sure, but I think it was at this time that Mother became a waitress at the Palmer House, a notable hotel in Chicago's Loop. One day a drunken waiter spilled a pot of hot coffee down her back and severely burned her. She was taken to a hospital, treated, and brought home. She was incapacitated for over a month. We moved in with Aunt Catherine and Uncle Charley so that Aunt Catherine could take care of her. I recall a man coming to the apartment and having Mother sign some papers. I presume he was an attorney for the Palmer House and the papers were releasing them of all responsibility. I don't know if Mother received any compensation. I don't think she returned to work there.

In the summer of 1920, when I was nine years old, Mother and I went back to Minnesota, this time to visit her brother and sisters and other relatives. We stayed at her brother Mike Roster's farm, which was about three miles north of Freeburg, Minnesota and about ten miles from Caledonia, the town where I was born. Uncle Mike's family consisted of his wife, Aunt Annie; his and my mother's mother, Grandma Roster; his son, Leonard, who passed away at the age of nineteen; and three daughters, my cousins, Cecelia, who had a speech impediment, Alvina, and Agnes. I never forgot them or the other relatives. With the exception of my three cousins, whom I didn't see again until I was eighty-three years old—more about that when I relate that period of my life—I never saw or heard from any of Mother's relatives again, with the exception of Aunt Catherine, who lived in Chicago.

The farm was huge; it lay in a valley. On one side was a hill that I and my two cousins, Alvina and Agnes, used to climb and hunt for Indian artifacts. In the back was a hill that was a heavily treed forest. It was called Meadow Brook Stock Farm. Uncle Mike raised and bred white Wyandotte chickens, shorthorn cattle, white Embden geese, white Holland turkeys, Chester-white hogs, and white Peking ducks, along with the usual farm grains and vegetables. During the harvest season, the surrounding area farmers would help each other with the harvesting and their wives or daughters would come and do the cooking. It was an exciting time. The family living quarters were a fairly large two-story house. There was no inside plumbing, no gas, and no electricity. At night kerosene lamps were used for light. Water was obtained from an outside well that had a large hand pump.

Every Saturday night Alvina, age ten, Agnes, age eight, and I took our weekly baths in a large wooden wash tub. All three of us had to bathe in the same water because it was heated on the kitchen stove that only used wood logs for fuel. All cooking and boiling of water was done on this stove. I don't know when other members of the family took their baths.

Mother and I slept in a bedroom upstairs. There was a large parlor that was kept locked and was only opened when company came or when Uncle Mike had a business conference. It was only opened once while I was there, for a family reunion of the Roster family of about twenty relatives.

Besides the barn, which was bigger than the house, there were four other buildings: a hen house, storage house, spring house, and outhouse. I recall a Sears, Roebuck catalog in the outhouse; the pages were used for toilet tissue. The spring house was a stone house built over the source of a creek that emanated from the hill at the side of the farm. It was very cool inside and was used to keep milk and other perishable foodstuffs. It housed the cream separator; right after milking the cows the milk was put in the separator, which you cranked to separate the cream from the milk. Several live trout were kept in there as pets, and they would come and eat out of your hand. Feeding them was one of my favorite pastimes.

I got into a lot of trouble on the farm. One day I saw Aunt Annie catch a chicken and chop off his head with a hatchet. I caught a lame chicken, got the hatchet, and chopped off its head.

Uncle Mike raised a special breed of cattle and had a vicious breeding bull in a pen by itself that no one dared approach. I got into the pen and started to pet the bull; for some reason or other he just stood there and let me pet him. Aunt Annie happened to see me and screamed, "Kenneth, get out of there right away." The bull didn't budge but I got out.

Another time I got on a horse and rode into the forest adjacent to the farm. I guess no one noticed that the horse and I were missing until dusk.

When it was finally noticed, Uncle Mike, Aunt Annie, and Mother ran into the forest and kept yelling, "Kenneth! Kenneth!" but they needn't have worried. I didn't know how to guide the horse and let him have free rein; he returned to the farm of his own volition. I was never punished for these and other mischievous acts I might have committed, just reprimanded.

One incident still holds a very vivid memory in my mind. Mother had just bought me a new pair of shoes, and I walked in the creek with them on. Mother, who was washing clothes at the time, saw me; she was furious and evidently lost her temper. She grabbed me and was beating me with the stick that was used to stir the clothes in a large tin wash tub. Aunt Lena, who was nearby, saw what was happening and snatched the stick away from her, and bawled her out. One of my cousins later told me that Grandma Roster, Mother's mother, also reprimanded her and said, "That is no way to treat a child."

One really pleasant memory: one day Aunt Annie asked me if I would like to ride into town with her. I was thrilled. She hitched up a one-horse shay and we went to the general store in Freeburg, which was about three miles from the farm. She brought along two huge crates of eggs, which she traded for the items she wanted. No money was exchanged. That ride was one of the highlights of my stay. We stayed at the farm for about a month and then went back to Chicago.

Me, at the age of 5, in Chicago's Home of the Friendless.

A gathering of the Roster family in Freeberg, Minnesota. My mother, Sue Roster Nelson, is the fourth person from the left on the top row. In the bottom row, me at age nine showing off, cousins Alvina and Agnes.

Crooked Creek Town Hall, Freeberg, Minnesota. My mother was baptized here.

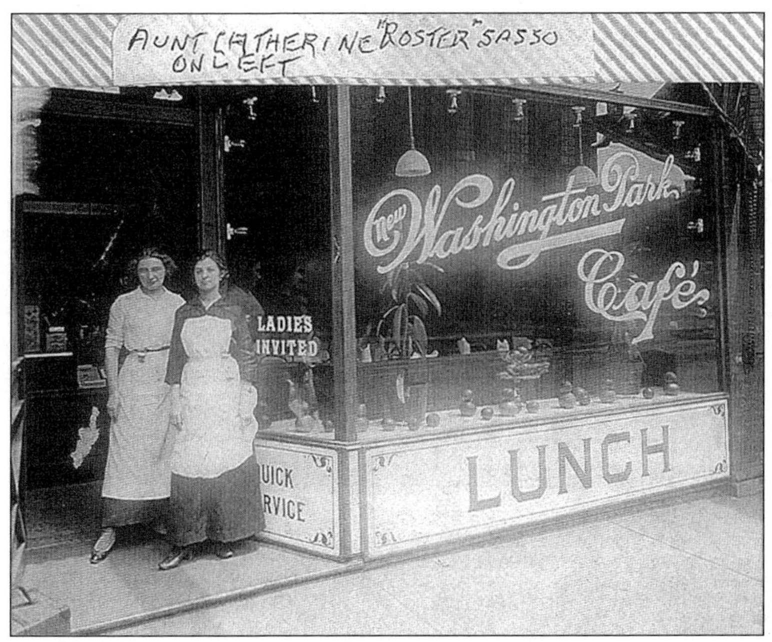

The waitress on the left is my Aunt Catherine. Note the sign on this Chicago restaurant.

The Nelson Lumber Yard in Caledonia. My father and grandfather.

1921-1930

THE FORMATIVE YEARS

Some of the events may not be in proper sequence, but all happened in the same period.

Mother and I moved to a two-room apartment, a kitchen and bedroom, at Fifty-Eighth and Prairie Avenue. I was enrolled in the fifth grade at Carter Practice Elementary school at Fifty-Eighth and Michigan. Our teacher was Miss Nisbett. I have never forgotten her because of two outstanding incidents. Miss Nisbett had a habit of yelling at misbehaving students. Every Friday morning we would have an arithmetic test. I made good grades on these tests.

On this particular Friday morning I was concentrating on a problem when Miss Nisbett started to scream at a student. I yelled out, "Shut up." She was stunned. Our classroom was a portable building with an enclosed entrance. She came over to me, yanked me out of my seat, and took me to the enclosed entrance. I realized what I had done and expected the worst. We both stood in the hallway, in silence, for about half a minute. Finally, after what seemed a lifetime, she spoke and said, "Kenneth, I was wrong in yelling, but you were wrong too. Don't you ever do that again." Oh boy, what a relief. She continued to yell at misbehaving students, but I always managed to maintain my silence.

The other outstanding incident: our classroom was overcrowded, and there was a desk on each side of Miss Nisbett's desk for extra students. At one of these desks was a boy named Joe Ribokowski. One day he broke wind quite loudly. I'm sure it wasn't intentional. All we students were trying to hold back our laughter. Miss Nisbett saw this and said, "Oh, let's all have a good laugh!" We all burst out in one big explosion of laughter, including Miss Nisbett. Although she did have a temper, she had a good sense of justice, and I'm sure we all liked her. I know I did.

I have many fond memories of Carter Practice. At that time it was the only grammar school in the city that had a swimming pool, and once a week we were given swimming lessons. Boys and girls were never allowed in the pool together. In eighth grade we had a music class once a week where we learned such songs as “America,” “The Star Spangled Banner,” “America the Beautiful,” “Row, Row, Row Your Boat,” “Goodnight Ladies,” “Juanita,” “Love's Old Sweet Song,” “Student of Cadiz,” and many others. Our teacher was Miss O'Connor. She directed us with a ruler but was always scratching herself with it below her stomach.

We had several Afro-Americans in our class, and for some reason or other the smallest one, Albert Harris, started to taunt me. I think he wanted to prove his prowess because I was so much bigger than he. Every day for about two weeks, when school was out and we were in the playground, he would challenge me. I had no desire to fight him because of the difference in our sizes; I was sure I would hurt him. I just laughed at him, which infuriated him. He finally gave up and we became good friends.

Our eighth grade teacher was Miss Farnsworth. She was very strict about word pronunciation, and one day when it was my turn to read aloud I said “pitcher” for “picture.” She stopped me and made me repeat the word “picture” about ten times, emphasizing the syllable “pic.” I've never mispronounced the word since. There were several other words that she was very adamant about the students pronouncing correctly, including “library,” “when,” “what,” “why,” and “where.” If a student said “wen,” “wut,” “y” or “wear,” she would make them say “who” first and then say the word. “Woe betide” the students who said “git” instead of get, “fergit” for forget, or “jist” for just. They would have to emphasize the syllable “eh” and “uh” several times.

One of my classmates was Joe Peter. We became close friends and remained so until his demise in 1999. He lived at Fifty-Seventh and Prarie, which was only a block away from where I lived. As my mother was working and didn't get home till late in the evening, I would go to Joe's home after school and help him with his chores. His father was a janitor and took care of several buildings, so there was always plenty for Joe and me to do. Joe's mother, father, and two sisters, Ann and Dolly, accepted and treated me as if I were one of the family. Mrs. Peter disciplined me as if I were one of her own. I can still hear her saying, “Kenneth, don't do that. Behave yourself.” As my mother was working and didn't have time to cook, she would buy me a meal ticket and I ate most of my evening meals in a restaurant, but every now and then Mrs. Peter would tell me to stay for dinner. The Peters were of Hungarian heritage and Mrs. Peter made the most delicious Hungarian goulash. She baked bread in a large dishpan.

Wanting to be grown up, Joe and I would wrap dried corn silk in toilet paper and try to smoke it. I don't remember how it worked out, but we tried it several times.

The elevated station was at Fifty-Eighth between Prarie and Calumet Avenues. The restaurant where I had my meal ticket was directly across the street as you came out of the El station. On the same side, on the corner of Prairie was Bob's Auto Shop. Radio was just coming into existence, and there was only one broadcasting station in Chicago, KYW. Bob had installed a large hanging speaker over the entrance of his shop, and when he turned it on a huge crowd would gather and listen in awe.

Across the street on Prairie was an ice cream parlor. A couple of doors down on Fifty-Eighth was Rudy's Hardware Store, and a couple of doors from Rudy's was a kosher meat market. On the north side of Fifty-Eighth, as you came out of the El station, was a cigar store, and on the corner was a drugstore. Across the street on the corner was another cigar store, and a few doors down was Lutka's Bakery, where delicious sweet rolls were twenty-four cents a dozen. I think the drug store was a Walgreen Store.

There were two gangs in the neighborhood. One hung out in front of the drugstore and the other in front of the ice cream parlor. There was never a thought of violence between the gangs, but there was friendly competition. I seem to recall them playing basketball in the yard of St. Edmund's Church on Indiana Avenue between Fifty-Eighth and Fifty-Ninth Street. There were, however, some unpleasant incidents. At that time there was much antagonism against Afro-Americans who were beginning to increase in number on the south side of Chicago. Some of the boys from the drugstore gang would throw milk bottles at any Afro-American driving a car through the neighborhood. I think this was the gang Ed Farrell wrote about in his book *Studs Lonigan*. I do remember that Jesse Binga's house was bombed. He was an Afro-American banker and his house, if I remember rightly, was at Sixtieth and South Shore Drive.

In the summer of 1921, when I was ten years old, Chicago held a "Pageant of Progress" exposition to show the latest achievements of artistic, industrial, athletic, naval, military, mechanical, and aerial progress. The pageant was held from July 30 to August 14 at the Municipal Pier, which was in two buildings extending three thousand feet into Lake Michigan. There were about twenty-five exhibits.

I have no idea how a man named Charlie knew my mother, or that I could sing. He had written or worked for the publisher of a song titled "Meet Me at the Pageant of Progress." He had a flatbed fenced-in truck with a piano on it. He was going to tour the city to sell sheet music copies and needed someone to sing the song. He asked Mother if she would let me go with him and do the singing. He promised to pick me up, bring me home, and buy my lunch and dinner. Mother consented. He would pick me up around 11:00 A.M. and have me back around 6:00 P.M. He promised me a penny a copy for each sold. I was thrilled and excited. I sang through a megaphone and drew really huge crowds, I guess because I was just a kid and had a good voice. I did this for about ten days. I know he sold hundreds of copies. When the pageant was over he handed me one dollar. I was abashed. He had the nerve to ask Mother for a date. He was a little man with rotting teeth. I saw him years later; he was a down and outer. I felt nothing but pity for him. I can still sing the song. The lyrics are as follows:

Oh, won't you meet me at the Pageant of Progress
Where Lake Michigan breezes blow.
You'll find good cheer down at the pier
And everybody's rarin' to go.
Meet me where the bands are playin'
And everybody's happy and gay,
So won't you meet me at the Pageant of Progress
And we'll all have a wonderful day.

In the summer of 1922, when I was eleven years old, I had been helping Bob in his auto shop and was wearing a pair of coveralls that had become slightly greasy. One evening after helping Bob I decided to go to an amusement park called White City. It was located at Sixty-Third and South Park Avenue. I didn't bother to change my clothes. As you entered the park, the Fun House was one of the first buildings you saw. In front of the Fun House was a stand where they were selling sheet music, ukuleles, and kazoos. The front of the stand was lined with sheet music; ukuleles and kazoos were hanging from the ceiling. A kazoo is a small tin tube with a protruding hole in the middle with a thin membrane. You hum a melody through it and it produces a buzzing sound. I think they sold for ten cents, and sheet music was fifteen cents a copy.

In the stand were a piano and two men, one of whom was playing the piano to demonstrate the sheet music songs. I don't recall what song he was playing, but I leaned over the counter and started to sing it. The piano player turned around and said, "Hey, kid, you got a pretty good voice. Come in here." He helped me into the stand. He wrote a parody to "The Sheik of Araby," which was a big hit at that time. Although it was not composed for the motion picture *The Sheik*, which starred Rudolph Valentino, who was the reigning heartthrob of the time, the song was written about it. The parody referred to a mental institution, which was located in the city of Kankakee, Illinois. The parody went thus:

I'm the sweep of Kankakee.
This broom belongs to me.
At night when you're asleep,
I sweep and sweep and sweep.

The rest of it slips my mind. I stood on a chair, holding a broom, a megaphone on my head and one to sing through. I drew a large crowd. The piano player who had written the parody was Marty Bloom.

The stand was owned by two brothers, Walter and Lester Melrose. They also owned a music store, which was directly across the street from the Tivoli Theater at Sixty-Third and Cottage Grove Avenue. Lester didn't come to the stand; he was taking care of the store. They had also started a music publishing firm called Melrose Brothers Music Company.

Walter asked me if I would like to come to the park and sing every night during the summer season. He would pay me a dollar a night. Of course I said yes. He told me to be sure to wear the same greasy coveralls. I always drew large crowds, and I learned many songs.

When summer vacation was over and it was time for me to go back to school, Walter asked me if I would like to work in his music store after school for a couple of hours and on Saturdays. I was thrilled. My job was to help around the store, run errands, and so forth. I really enjoyed it. Their music publishing firm, Melrose Brothers Music Company, emanated from the store. I learned how to package sheet music of the songs they published for shipment. Their first hit was "Someday Sweetheart."

In those days sheet music was the main source of a publisher's revenue. Phonograph records and piano player rolls were important, but secondary. Some of the phonograph records, I recall, were Victor, Columbia, Brunswick, Edison, Vocalion, Gennett, and Aeolian. Piano player rolls were Q.R.S., which Walter called "quite rotten service" because they were always late in delivering. Piano players were upright and were operated with foot pedals. All phonographs had spring motors that had to be wound up by hand. Victor, Columbia, Brunswick, Edison, Vocalion, and Sonora were the main brands. There were no 45s, 33 1/3s, or albums, all records were 78 rpms, were made of very thin shellac and were to be handled very carefully. The exception was Edison records which were 3/8ths to 4/8ths of an inch thick.

Two of my most prominent memories of the store are of Jelly Roll Morton, a popular jazz pianist, and King Oliver, one of the top trumpet players of the time. They used to come to the store, probably to discuss publishing interests of their songs, and would always invite me to the corner drugstore and buy me an ice cream soda. Jelly Roll had two front teeth made of gold with diamonds in them. He smiled a lot and you couldn't help but notice them. King Oliver was a huge man and had a bulging eye. They were both cheerful, warm, and treated me gently.

The other wonderful memory: In December of 1922 a new ballroom called the Trianon, which was patterned after Le Grande Trianon, a French palace built for Louis XIV, had its formal opening to the music of the world-famous Paul Whiteman orchestra. It was located on Cottage Grove Avenue between Sixty-Second and Sixty-Third Streets. Walter gave me four orchestrations, which were printed orchestra arrangements of "Someday Sweetheart," and told me to deliver them to Mr. Whiteman at the Trianon. I never could understand why he would send a kid to deliver music to this world-famous man. I guess he figured I'd have better acceptance than an adult. I told the doorman I had come to deliver music to Mr. Whiteman. He laughed, took the music, and said, "I'll see that he gets it, kid." He let me stand by an open door, listen to the music, and watch the dancers, many of whom were in costume. It was a thrilling sound and sight. I've often wondered if Mr. Whiteman got the music.

Radio was really in its infancy, and tube radio sets were just beginning to come into existence, so there was no universal way for the public to hear the old and new songs of the day except in ballrooms, theaters, vaudeville shows, or night clubs. Every music store that sold sheet music, including the music counters of Woolworths and S.S. Kresge, had to hire a piano player to demonstrate the songs of the day. Walter and Lester hired a beautiful young lady named Blanche. She invited me to the first birthday party I had ever attended. It was for her twelve-year-old sister. Both Walter and Lester fell in love with Blanche, and both wooed her.

She married Lester, and as a result the brothers broke off their partnership. Walter kept the store and the publishing company and retained the name Melrose Brothers Music Company. Lester started a record label. He signed and recorded only Afro-American artists, and in those days Afro-American recordings were called race records. I don't recall the name of the label. and I don't know how long he stayed in business. I do remember that he published one fairly good-sized hit, "A Chinese Honeymoon." I never heard of Lester or Blanche after the break-up. Walter kept the store for a few months and then sold it. He decided to go into the music publishing business exclusively. He became very successful. I went back to work for him when I was sixteen years old. I'll tell about that later.

There were two other younger Melrose brothers. Frank, a jazz piano player, was found murdered in an alley. The reason for the murder was never determined or solved; it was presumed a robbery. The other brother was a year or two older than me. He used to come into the store but never worked there.

Another classmate with whom I became good friends was Ed Smith (not his real name). He lived with his father, who was a detective. I never asked him about his mother, whether she had passed away or whether they were divorced. Occasionally I would spend the night at his apartment. One evening Ed and I went to a movie and got back to his apartment around 9:30. The front door opened into a hallway that gave you an immediate view of the parlor. Sitting in a chair, fully clothed, was his father. In front of him was a beautiful lady dancing completely in the nude. Nobody uttered a word; there was complete silence. Ed and I went directly to his room and never discussed it.

Mother and I moved from our two rooms on Prairie Avenue and rented a room with a Mrs. Bryan (not her correct name) a block east on Calumet Avenue. She had two sons, Tom and Roy. Tom was fourteen or fifteen and Roy was in his early twenties. I don't recall a Mr. Bryan. One day Tom, and

I were in the house alone, and I had to go to the bathroom. The door was slightly ajar and as I opened it Tom was standing over the toilet masturbating. I said, "Why are you hurting yourself?" he said angrily, "Get the hell out of here." That was my initiation to the art of self-pleasure.

We soon had to move from the Bryans because our twin beds were infested with bedbugs, and though Mrs. Bryan tried, she couldn't get rid of them. We moved about a half a block away on Calumet and had a room on the third floor facing the street.

The elevated tracks were in the alley behind the building and there was always a lot of activity going on. Besides the noise of the El trains, you'd hear the clip-clop of horses' hoofs, the vegetable man in his wagon shouting his wares, the bell of the scissors and knife sharpener announcing that he was in the area with his hand-pushed cart and its huge round pedal-operated stone wheel, the sing-song cry of the man buying secondhand and used clothing, "Any old clodees for saale," and, of course, the ice man. Electric refrigeration had not yet become a common household item. Most homes had iceboxes. Twenty-five to fifty pounds of ice were kept in the top compartment and the food in the bottom. The ice man, with his horse and wagon, had a daily route and steady customers. We kids in the neighborhood jumped on the back steps of the wagon and took chunks of ice, especially during the summertime. The ice man didn't mind and never chased us off.

This was some time in 1923, when I was twelve. It was here that I learned how to make crystal radio sets, and this is how I remember them. The sets consisted of a cardboard tube two and one-half to three inches in diameter, about seven inches long, wrapped in a thin copper wire with a tuner that you slid back and forth to get a broadcast station. You then connected your earphones and antenna to their inputs. The crystal was in a small round metal casing with a needle that you jiggled around to get the sound. You had to have an outside antenna on the roof with a wire leading down to the set. It was strung between two posts and was eight to ten feet long. I cased the sets in Kraft Cheese boxes and sold them for five dollars each, minus, of course, the earphones and antenna. I sold about four or five of them.

If some extraordinary event happened, the Chicago newspapers would publish an "Extra" edition. I would buy as many copies as I could carry, for two cents each, and go down the streets yelling, "Extra Paper!" and sell them for five cents each. These editions usually came out in the early evening and were gobbled up quickly. I'd make two or three runs a night. During this same period I delivered Sunday newspapers and also washed dishes in a restaurant for almost two weeks.

When I was twelve we moved again, this time between Fifty-Sixth and Fifty-Seventh on Calumet. Our landlady was Mrs. Glanz. She had a thick foreign accent and lived in the apartment on the first floor. We had the front room facing the street on the second floor. There were four other rooms rented out on our floor, with one bathroom. Ours was a large living room with two beds and a sliding door between us and a bedroom which was occupied by a beautiful young lady. Every now and then I would crack the door open very slightly to see if I could catch her undressing. I never did. One time I snuck into her room and on her dresser was a printed sheet with a dirty parody of the song "Ma, He's Making Eyes at Me." I didn't look in the closet or open her dresser drawers, just looked on top of the dresser. I recall one of her boyfriends had a sports car and wore a raccoon coat. We lived there for almost two years, until I graduated from grammar school in 1925 at age fourteen. All of the following events occurred during this period.

For a short period of time I worked in Letz's Jewish Delicatessen after school and on Saturdays. Mr. and Mrs. Letz were very small in stature. His wife didn't work in the store, but she would come in almost every day with their small child and they would continually argue for about ten to fifteen minutes, then she would leave. I really enjoyed working there. I always got a kick out of the way many of the Jewish people would answer a question with a question. As an example, I would say, "Good morning, Mrs. Levine. How are you today?" Her answer was, "How should I be?" or "What's the matter, I don't look so good today?" Those two phrases are still with me today.

The delicatessen was right next door to the Prairie Theater, which was at Fifty-Eighth on Prairie. On the other side was Gus' Candy Store. In those days the theaters didn't have popcorn, candy, or beverages available in the lobby, but you could smoke in the theater. The films were silent, and most theaters had an organ, but some only had a piano player to provide the musical background for the feature picture. As a means of promoting songs, music publishers would provide theaters with song slides which would project the lyrics on the screen, hoping the audience would sing along and buy the sheet music or records. To encourage the audience to sing, theater managers would hire two or three singers to be a part of the audience and sing. Mr. Siegal, who owned the theater, hired me as a singer and paid me fifty cents a night.

Once a week many movie theaters would have Amateur Night contests. The master of ceremonies would announce to the audience that anyone who would like to show their talent and perform was welcome to come up on stage and participate. There would be three prizes awarded: ten dollars for first place, five dollars for second place, and three dollars for third place. One night at the Prairie I decided to participate. I went up on stage along with about five or six other people. I don't recall what song I sang, but I won first place and ten dollars. The winner was decided by the MC holding his hand over the head of each contestant, and the one receiving the most applause was the winner. This was done two more times to determine the second and third place winners.

After the show Mort Greene, who was the MC, asked me if I would like to be in amateur shows at other theaters. I said, "Sure." Mr. Greene put on these shows at several other theaters on the south side of Chicago, and in order to assure a performance he assembled four or five amateur performers who sat in various sections of the theater and came on stage when he made his announcement. It was necessary to have this group because many times no one from the paying audience would enter the contest. Each of us in the group would receive a minimum of five dollars plus any prize money we might win. Of course, after we had performed on the complete circuit of theaters our services were no longer needed, because people might remember us as having performed previously.

Mr. Greene took a liking to me and one day invited me to his house for dinner and to listen to his new tube radio. Many households now had tube radios. There were no networks at that time, and a popular hobby was trying to get as distant a radio station as possible. All of the Chicago radio stations were aware of this and agreed to have a night of silence and to cease broadcasting at about 6:00 P.M. Monday was chosen, and every Monday was silent night. It was on a silent night that I was at Mr. Greene's house, and I've never forgotten the thrill of hearing a radio broadcast all the way from Schenectady, New York.

Ever since I had had piano lessons from Mrs. Hoffman's daughter, Helen, the desire to play grew within me. I had asked Mother several times if we could get a piano so I could take lessons again, but that was impossible because of the cost, plus the fact that living in rooming houses we had no place to put it. I was determined to play something, so with the money I earned from the amateur shows and Mother's help, I bought a four-string tenor banjo. It turned out to be a major event of my life, because many years later through the banjo I met Lee Gillette. Lee and I both had a great bearing and influence on each other's lives. Mother paid for my lessons every week for about two months. I learned very quickly; it only entailed learning the names of the notes, the key signatures, chord symbols, and chord inversions. Tenor banjos were part of every rhythm section of both big and little orchestras—even the world renowned Paul Whiteman Orchestra had a tenor banjo. The banjoist rarely had a solo part; all he did was play chords and beat out the rhythm. They became obsolete years later and were replaced by guitars.

I didn't have a case for the banjo, and that was the cause of me committing the first of four incidents that I have regretted all my life and that I wish I could undo. One day I saw a special delivery letter on the table in the front hall where the mailman put the mail for all the roomers. I surmised that it might contain money, and I stole it. There was a twenty-dollar bill in it, and along with an additional five dollars I was able to buy a banjo case. I didn't read the letter, but thinking about it a few years later I realized that it must have been money needed for some emergency.

The year was 1924, and I joined my first orchestra, The Southtown Syncopaters, as banjoist and vocalist. There were six members, Stan Jacobs, leader and pianist; Al Mirfield, E-flat saxophone; Paul Derringer, B-flat saxophone; Manuel Sanchez, cornet; Dave Davis, drums; and me, banjo and vocalist. Some of our favorite instrumental numbers were "Tiger Rag," "Bugle Call Rag," "San," "That's a' Plenty," "Charleston," and "Twelfth Street Rag." My favorite vocal numbers were "I'll See You in My Dreams," "That Old Gang of Mine," and "Oh, What a Pal Was Mary." We rehearsed once a week at Stan's house and occasionally would play a dance for two dollars apiece.

1925 was one of my most eventful years. I was fourteen years old and had just graduated from grade school. I enrolled at an all-boys high school, Tilden Tech. I continued playing banjo and had won a city sponsored contest for musicianship. As a result I did my first radio broadcast on the *Big Boy Merrill Yagel* show, over WBCN, the Southtown Economist's station. I continued to compose music; melodies just came to me, although I couldn't put them down on manuscript paper.

One of the first lyrics I wrote was an answer song to "Does the Spearmint Lose Its Flavor on the Bedpost Overnight." My answer song was called "Here Folks, Park Your Gum." I had acquired a ukulele and used it to accompany myself when singing, and because of that I was invited to neighborhood teen parties.

I recall two parties in particular. One of the parties was held almost every Saturday night and included practically the same people every week. The girls would leave their coats and purses in the bedroom, and usually there were always two or three purses rifled of money. This one guy was the first one to offer the girls carfare if they needed it. One night some of the boys decided to catch the thief, and one of them hid under the bed. Sure enough it was the good Samaritan who was the thief. A couple of the boys gave him a good shellacking, kicked him out, and, of course, he was ostracized from the gang.

At another party, which included some of the athletes from Tilden Tech High School, which I was attending at the time, there was quite a bit of heavy drinking going on. I happened to see this over six-foot-tall football player come out of a bedroom and look furtively about before closing the door. This aroused my curiosity. I went into the bedroom; lying on the bed was a girl completely passed out, her dress pulled up to her waist and a condom on her stomach. I was flabbergasted. I took the condom off her stomach, pulled her dress down, and threw the condom down the toilet. I sure lost my respect for that jerk, who was one of the stars of the football team. I realized later that had someone walked in the room while I was there I could have been accused of rape.

During this period I had my first sexual experiences. One afternoon after school a few of us neighborhood guys and gals met at one of the guys apartment. While I was talking to a couple of the fellows, one of them said, "Hey, there's Reba over there. She loves to screw—she'll screw anyone." A week or so later I met Reba walking down the street. I approached her and coaxed her into coming up to my room. She came willingly. I was a novice at this sort of thing, but we were soon both undressed and in bed. Being completely ignorant of a woman's sex functions I tried to enter her through the pubic hairs. She said, "You've got it in the wrong place," and guided me to the proper destination. She seemed to enjoy herself, and I know I did.

Another sexual experience, which was very strange, came shortly after my affair with Reba. This friend of mine brought two girls who were sisters up to my room. We were on separate beds and started necking almost immediately and were fondling each other's sexual organs. The girls wouldn't undress and wouldn't let us enter their vaginas. The girl I was with guided my finger and massaged it around her clitoris; I soon caught on. She masturbated me and we both reached a climax. That's how I learned about the clitoris, the seat of woman's passion.

At the beginning of summer vacation 1925, one of my schoolmates, whom I knew only "casually," came up to my room and said he was going to look for a job. He was driving a car and asked me if I would like to come along. Mother had gone to Cincinnati with one of the players of the Cubs baseball team, and as I had nothing to do I readily accepted. We were driving down Lake Shore Drive exceeding the speed limit when a motorcycle cop pulled us over. He then told us to follow him to the police station. I don't recall exactly but it was either the Thirty-Fifth or Thirty-Ninth Street Station. We parked in front of the station, and I stayed in the car, confident there was no problem for me, while my casual acquaintance went into the station with the officer.

All of a sudden the officer came out, opened the car door, yanked me out and said, "Get in here you son-of-a-bitch." I was put in a room, told to sit down, and the motorcycle cop and a plainclothesman started to interrogate me. I had no idea what this was all about and was pretty scared. The plainclothesman spoke first, "All right, tell us where you swiped the car?" Of course I had no idea what they were talking about, and I didn't know what my casual acquaintance had told them. The interrogation went on for about fifteen or twenty minutes. Finally, the motorcycle cop said, "Listen, you son-of-a-bitch, if you don't tell us where you swiped the car, I'll kick you right in the belly." I said "Go ahead and kick, I don't know anything about that car."

The plainclothesman, whom I presume was a detective, then asked me who my parents were and where I lived. I told him I had no father and lived in a rooming house with my mother, who was out of town. I gave him the name of our landlady, Mrs. Glanz. I didn't know her phone number, but luckily it was listed in the phone book. I was put in a cell and later Mrs. Glanz came to visit me. I assured her that it was all a mistake and that I had nothing to do with the theft. She said she would let Mother know what happened and where I was. I spent the night in a jail cell and the next morning was transported to the juvenile detention home.

In all this time I had not seen or heard about my casual acquaintance, and he was not at the detention home. I was in the home for two weeks and actually enjoyed it. I was big for my age and during the day had to work. I swept floors with a push broom and did some mopping and other chores. For some reason or other the guards took a liking to me. About the second or third day I was there, I saw two of the guards playing checkers. I had played checkers for a couple of years and was pretty good at it. I told them I was a good player and they invited me to play. I won a couple of games and from that time on played almost every day. As a result I was the fair-haired boy and ate supper at the guards' table every night.

I wasn't too popular with the other inmates and did get into a couple of heated arguments. The one saving grace was that I was not relieved of my daily duties. Mother came to visit me a couple of times. She understood the circumstances and didn't reprimand me.

After my second week in the detention home my trial came up and my casual acquaintance was also in the courtroom. He told the judge that I had no knowledge of, and had nothing to do with the theft of the car. I explained how I had come to be with him. The judge put me on six months probation. I don't know what sentence he received but during the trial it was revealed that he had a venereal disease, had stolen a bicycle and some clothing, and that his father was the Water Commissioner of the city.

The rest of the summer of 1925 was also quite eventful. I continued to play banjo and was playing with three different orchestras. One night we were playing at a Polish wedding, and I drank a little too much beer and was a little tipsy. I don't know what I did but one of the guests grabbed me by my right arm and pulled it behind my back. It really hurt. I guess he was trying to take me outside. Our drummer, who was a hefty and very strong man, saw what was going on. He came over and said, "Let that kid go. Anyone who picks on him has got me to reckon with." With that the man let go of me and punched the drummer. That started a melee. I think the groom hit his new father-in-law. The orchestra leader said, "Let's get the hell of here." We did—just as the cops were arriving. I was still on probation, and I shudder to think what sentence I would have received had I been arrested. I was pretty drunk. The drummer took me home, and of course we didn't get paid.

It was still 1925, and by this time there were many radio stations in Chicago. It was easy to get an audition, and if you had any talent at all you could get on. Of course, you weren't paid unless you had a sponsor. By August I was on a regular program on WGES, and by September I was also playing and singing on WSBC. I continued to play dances and earn a few dollars and also had a couple of theatre engagements.

In 1926 I was still singing on the radio and playing dances, and I won first place in a talent contest at the Midway Gardens, a popular dance hall on Chicago's south side. I had my first two heart pangs of unrequited love. I fell in love with a beautiful neighborhood girl named Juanita but she was going with a friend of mine and I knew it was useless to pursue her. However, I did write a song about her and whenever I want a good laugh I think of the lyric.

Juanita, Juanita, so beautiful and sweet
So lovely and so neat,
And in the night when the moon is shining
My heart sighs and starts to pining.
Juanita, Juanita, I love you, yes I do.

I later re-wrote the song with Lyle Smith, a saxophone player with George Olsen's Orchestra. It was renamed "Luna," and was one of the first songs I had published. My other unrequited love was Louise Brooks, a famous Hollywood movie star of the time. I thought she was the most gorgeous, beautiful girl I had ever seen, but I didn't think I had a chance with her.

One night I had just come out of Gus' candy store eating an ice cream cone, which in those days only cost five cents. Four of the boys from our Fifty-Eighth Street Gang saw me, surrounded me, and started pounding lumps on me. They knew that I usually had money and wanted me to buy them cones. Pounding lumps was not meant to hurt; you were hit very lightly and shoved a little. It was just a jocular way of getting you to do their bidding. We were standing in front of Gus' plate glass window and I was accidentally shoved against it. The window was shattered but left intact. Luckily no one was hurt or cut. We all ran. I ran to my room, put on a sweater, and came back to the store, thinking Gus wouldn't recognize me because of the change of clothing. I sat down, and Gus said, "I know who you are, and I'm going to call the police." I don't recall whether or not I made any denial of involvement. I did order an ice cream soda and Gus served it. The window was replaced the next day and we never heard any more about it. I presume he had insurance.

It was that year that I became aware that my mother and father had never married and I was an illegitimate child. It had a lasting effect on me. I felt inferior and inadequate because in that era both the mother and child were held in disdain. Mother never once during her entire life talked about or discussed my father. She never once during her life, except maybe when I was a baby, ever put her arms around me, kissed me, paid me a compliment, or said "I love you." She always pushed me away if I tried to put my arms around her. I was constantly trying to please her, I guess trying to get her acceptance. I'm sure she loved me but just couldn't express it. She never denied me anything within her power to give and helped me out of many a financial crisis.

I continued singing on radio stations and playing dances every now and then. I recall playing several dances in Aurora and at the Elgin Watch factory in Elgin, Illinois. I had saved enough money to buy Mother an ivory dresser set for Christmas. I always tried to surprise Mother with a gift on her birthday, August 8, and at Christmas time. She always thanked me but never with any show of affection.

In early 1927 we moved to the Northside. I don't remember the address, but I got off at the Wilson Avenue El station. Mother and I had the front end of the third floor apartment, and a man, his wife, and their child had the rear section. One afternoon I came home from an unsuccessful search for a job, put on my bathrobe, and was about to relax, when I heard this blood-curdling scream coming from the rear. I rushed back, opened the door, and saw this huge black man, his pants open, his penis out, tussling with the woman, trying to rape her. I yelled, "Get the hell out of here." He ran through the kitchen and down the backstairs with me after him in my bathrobe. As we were running down the street there were two men walking toward us. I yelled, "Catch that nigger!" As he approached them they parted and let him go through. I continued running, tripped, fell face down, my arms outstretched, and cut the palm of my right hand on a piece of glass. It was stupid of me to chase him. I don't know what I would have done had I caught him. He was a massive man and would probably have killed me. That was the only time I ever used the term "nigger" in my whole life because I had nothing but pleasant warm feelings and respect for any black person with whom I had ever been involved.

When I returned to the apartment the lady was naturally very upset, nervous, and shaking. I tried to calm her down. She couldn't thank me enough and told me that her eight-year-old son had just gone back to school after having lunch and this man had come to the back door and offered to wash the windows for a nominal fee, and that's why she had let him in. When her husband came home that evening, he too couldn't express his gratitude enough. My hand was bloody and hurting. He insisted on taking me to a doctor. The cut was pretty deep, and the doctor extracted a small piece of glass. He told me I was lucky I had not cut a tendon. Had I, I would have had a paralyzed finger. A paralyzed finger would have hindered any banjo playing. A couple of days later they bought me a new bathrobe, which I had for many years.

It wasn't long before I got a job at the Continental Bank in Chicago's Loop. I was hired as an errand boy to take memos or whatever necessary from one teller to another or to whomever he designated. I didn't stay there more than two or three weeks, but one incident still gives me a chuckle. About the second day I was there, one of the tellers told me to go to another teller and get the check stretcher and bring it back to him. I thought it was a device for printing the amount of money on the check. Each teller sent me to another teller saying he had the check stretcher. I guess I made the rounds of all the tellers and it finally dawned on me that this was a newcomer's initiation gag.

Mother and I moved again, still on the Northside near the Devon Avenue El station. We moved in with a couple, Bert and Jean, who let us have full run of the apartment. Bert was a commercial artist and he drew a miniature pencil portrait of me, which I still have.

I soon got another job as a mail boy at Crane Company's eight or nine-story office building at Ninth and Michigan Boulevard. The mail room was on the top floor and there were two of us mail boys. We stood in front of a table on which there were slots for the offices and people throughout the building. I learned the names and offices very quickly. The mail was brought to us by our supervisor, who was a crotchety old man. After sorting the mail we would deliver it. After each delivery I would come back to the mail room and go to the lavatory to check to see if my hair was in place, my tie straight, and that I looked neat and clean. I felt that I should always look presentable when delivering the mail. About the third week I was there, I took one morning off to go to my optician to get my new glasses.

On the way back to the office I stopped and bought a couple of candy bars. I arrived back in the mailroom about 11:00 A.M. My partner was sorting mail. I was going to join him but before I did I put my arm around his waist gave him a slight squeeze and offered him the other candy bar. He uttered a faint squeal and took the candy bar. The supervisor saw this and came over and started to berate me. He also said I was taking up too much time going to the lavatory. He obviously had false teeth and his voice was very crackling. I got mad and said, "Why don't you take the marbles out of your mouth." That did it, he was furious. He almost screamed, "You're fired. Go downstairs, get your paycheck and get out of here." I was pretty mad myself and thought, *To hell with him*. I went down to the office manager and told him the whole story and explained why I went to the lavatory so often. Then I said to him "If you had had a man like him for your boss when you started here you wouldn't have the position you have today." He looked at me, smiled, and said "Kenneth, you're the kind of person we want in this company. I'll find another position for you. Go get your paycheck. I'll call you as soon as I find something for you."

I thought, *Oh well, that's the end of that*, but when I got home he had already called. I returned his call and he told me to report the next day at the factory on Kedzie Avenue. I was to work in the stockroom until he found a more fitting position for me. One of my duties was to assist the stockroom manager to count and weigh metal ingots as they were taken out of a freight car parked at the factory. We would both write the weight of each ingot on a separate piece of paper, and after so many were weighed add up our totals, which were supposed to coincide; they never did. I'm sure I was the one who goofed. He had been doing this for several years, and I'm certain his figures were correct. He was a good-natured man and would grin and change my tallies to coincide with his. I worked in the stockroom for about two weeks when, true to his word, the office manager got me an advancement.

I was transferred to the factory office as an assistant cost clerk. My supervisor was figuring the estimated cost of valves for U.S. Navy ships and was to train me in the mechanics of cost estimating. After about a week or so I was getting the gist of it, and though I liked mathematics I became bored. One morning I came to the office, sat down at my desk, started to work, stopped, looked around, and said to myself, "What the hell am I doing here?" I got up and walked out without saying a word to anyone. That was unfair; my career at Crane Company was over.

I contacted Walter Melrose, who was now sole owner of Melrose Brothers Music Company. He hired me as a shipping clerk and song plugger. During the day I filled and wrapped sheet music and orchestration orders for shipment and tended the sales counter, mostly at lunch time. When I first joined the firm the office was in the George M. Cohan Opera Building but soon moved to larger quarters in the Loop End Building at State and Lake Streets.

The sales counter was to accommodate musicians and orchestra leaders who wanted to get orchestrations. If the leader was well known or broadcasting he would be given the orchestrations free; otherwise the cost was thirty-five cents. I recall giving Benny Goodman, who was just beginning to get a reputation, Tommy Dorsey, and several other well-known leaders free orchestrations.

A song plugger was a person who took professional song copies, which were printed solely for singers, and orchestrations to orchestra leaders and tried to convince them to perform the song. They took the music to theatres with vaudeville acts, to nightclubs, which were very important because remote broadcasting was becoming popular, and to radio stations. Many publishers had a pianist and a piano room in which to demonstrate and teach singers their songs.

Walter by now had an outstanding catalog and was considered a major Chicago publisher. He had acquired the publishing rights to "The Sweetheart of Sigma Chi," which was written by two students of a Michigan College, the rights to publish the orchestrations of all the Big Ten college football songs, and the right to publish the orchestrations of Scott Joplin's "Maple Leaf Rag." He had some fairly big hits "Tin Roof Blues," "Spanish Shawl," "Someday Sweetheart," "Wolverine Blues," and Copenhagen and Jelly Roll Morton's, "King Porter Stomp."

I was not a song plugger in the true sense of the word as I was told by Walter where and to whom I was to deliver music. I took orchestrations to Ted Weems and Lawrence Welk at the Trianon ballroom, Wayne King at the Aragon ballroom, Frankie Masters, Benny Meroff, and Paul Ash, who were masters of ceremonies of stage shows at Balaban and Katz's ornate theatres such as the Tivoli, the Oriental, the Marlburo, and others. I took orchestrations to Louie Armstrong at the Sunset Café at Thirty-Fifth and Calumet Avenue. Louie was very congenial, as were most of the leaders. When I took a song titled "Wear a Hat with a Silver Lining" to Ted Lewis, performing at the Chicago Theatre, he was very aloof and cold to me. When fronting his orchestra he wore a high hat. Within a few days, after looking the song over, he saw the showmanship value of it, put a silver lining in his high hat, and while singing the song would take off the hat and display the silver lining to the audience. He used the song for the remainder of his career.

Another experience, Walter told me to take an orchestration to the Frolic Café, on the near Southside, I think somewhere in the Thirties block area. I got to the Café around nine o'clock that evening. When I entered I saw Al Capone, a notorious bootlegger and gangster of the time, at a table with several other men. I started to walk to the backstage and Capone saw me. He said, "Hey kid, come here." I went to his table and he said, "What the hell are you doing here?" I replied, "I'm delivering music to the orchestra leader." He said, "Give it to him and get your ass out of here," and then he laughed, as did a couple of the other men.

I was still playing some dances and singing on the radio, and was now living by myself. Walter was paying me $12.50 a week plus streetcar and El fare when I delivered music.

After working for the firm about six months I asked Walter for a raise. He replied, "If you can do better someplace else, go there." I was stunned, hurt, and angry. I was happy in the job, I was loyal, I worked in the office during the day and often delivered music till ten and eleven at night. I had learned bookkeeping and kept records of sheet music and orchestration sales. This was another time that I did something dishonest. I thought, *Okay, you won't give me a raise, I'll give me a raise*. When I was alone at the sales counter, instead of putting the sales money in the cash drawer, I pocketed it. It sometimes amounted to one to two dollars a day, some days nothing. I did this for a couple of weeks and guilt overcame me, so I became honest again.

Marty Bloom, who was the piano player at Melrose's Music Stand in White City, where I first sang, had been in New York City representing the firm. Walter called him back to Chicago to be the professional manager. Marty seemed to like me and often invited me to his apartment for dinner with he and a beautiful blonde lady, who was very nice and gracious to me. I think she was his girlfriend. He introduced her to me as Grace.

It was in the early part of 1928 that Marty told me he had formed a music publishing firm with Gene Austin and Ted Koehler and asked me if I would like to work for the new firm, which was called Austin, Bloom, and Koehler. My salary was to be eighteen dollars a week. I was to take care of the office, fill music orders, and do the shipping and bookkeeping. I jumped at the chance. We both left Melrose. Our office was in the Woods Theatre building, located at Randolph and Dearborn Streets.

Gene Austin was the most popular singer and recording artist of the late 1920s. Up until 1925 singers and orchestras performed directly into a recording horn. In that year the condenser microphone, with the use of a vacuum tube amplifier and an electromagnetically powered cutting stylus was being developed. It increased the frequency range of recorded music by two and a half octaves, allowed singers and musicians to record in a spacious studio, and allowed singers with soft voices and crooners to record. Gene was one of the first crooners to record with this new technique. He sold millions. His Victor Record rendition of "My Blue Heaven" recorded in 1927, was the fourth biggest record seller of the pre-1955 era, with sales of over five million copies, topped only by Gene Autry's "Rudolph the Red Nosed Reindeer," which sold more than eight million, Vernon Dalhart's "The Prisoner's Song," which sold more than seven million, and Bing Crosby's "White Christmas," which has sold over thirty million and is still selling.

Ted Koehler was the songwriter who, in 1933, wrote the hit "Stormy Weather." One evening as I was leaving the office Ted invited me to have dinner with him. On the way to a restaurant Ted stopped in front of a building on Clark Street and said, "I'm going upstairs for a few minutes. Come along." We walked up a flight of stairs to a room on the second floor in which there were several young girls in chemises. Ted chose a girl and went into a bedroom. That was my introduction to a house of prostitution. I guess he expected me to do the same. I wanted to but I was too shy. While I was waiting in the room amongst all the other girls, a couple of other customers came in, chose their girls and disappeared. None of the girls tried to entice me. After about fifteen minutes Ted came out and said, "Let's go." He never mentioned anything about the incident, and neither did I.

The first song we published written by Gene, Ted, and Marty was "The Voice of the Southland." Although Gene recorded it, it did not reach any degree of popularity. Sheet music copies were not selling, and our only income was from Gene, who was in New York. Money from him was sent at infrequent intervals, and my salary was delayed. Luckily I was still playing dances, and with the help of a little financial aid from Mother I managed to survive. I also continued singing on radio.

It wasn't long before Ted Koehler decided to leave the firm and go to New York to pursue his song writing career. He did become a successful writer. Within a month or so Gene and Marty decided that, as New York was the hub of the music publishing business, there would be more opportunity and advantages for the firm by moving there and changing the name to Gene Austin, Inc. It was either June or July and Marty asked me if I would go to New York and continue working for the firm. I readily said yes, and he assured me that I would get the back salary I was owed. When it was time to leave I packed a small bag with what little clothing I had and brought my banjo.

We took the train, the Twentieth Century Limited, and were in a Pullman car which had sleeping berths. I was really thrilled on entering the city. One of the first sighting was a *Billboard* announcing the arrival of Paul Ash, the popular master of ceremonies from Chicago. We stayed in a hotel that night, and the next day I found a room in a rooming house for six dollars a week. The room was very small, on the second floor, and the hallway was lighted with a gas fixture. My room had a sixty-watt light bulb. We had a community bathroom which seemed to be in constant use. The room was kept clean, sheets changed, clean towels provided weekly, and the landlady was very pleasant.

Our office was in the DeSylva, Brown, Henderson building at 745 Seventh Avenue near the Earl Carrol Theatre. We were on the third floor. After I was there about a week Gene paid me the back wages I was owed, and noticing my scanty appearance, took me to a clothing store and bought me a complete new wardrobe, including a suit, shirts, tie, and shoes.

We were now represented in England by Campbell-Connelly, a major publishing firm in London, and by Allen & Co. in Australia. We soon acquired other songs, "Down by the Old Front Gate," "Then Came the Dawn," and the American rights to publish two songs of our English representative, "Peace of Mind" and "A Garden in the Rain," which was adjudged one of the most perfect songs. It was a hit. Three interesting incidents about "Then Came the Dawn." It was written by Harry Warren and Al Dubin; Harry was the melody composer and Al the lyricist. In the early thirties they left for Hollywood and wrote the musical score for many hit movies. One of their most memorable is "Forty-Second Street."

When we first took the song we had the orchestration done by the top orchestrator of the day, Frank Skinner. We were about to print his arrangement when Sonny Clapp, who was the composer of "Girl of My Dreams," which Gene had recorded, brought a young man to the office, extolled his merits as an arranger, and suggested that he arrange "Then Came the Dawn." Marty told him, "We already have an arrangement by Frank Skinner." The young man spoke up and said, "If you let me make the arrangement and you don't like it, just throw it in the wastebasket." Marty said okay. In a couple of days he brought the arrangement in and Marty took it to an orchestra. They played both arrangements; Marty threw Skinner's arrangement in the wastebasket. That young man was Archie Bleyer, who became a top orchestrator. In the 1950s he formed his own record company, Cadence Records, and produced many hits, most notably by the Everly Brothers.

Gene's record of the song had been released, and as a result we were getting orders for sheet music copies. Harry was always anxious to know how many copies were sold. I rarely left the office before eight or nine o'clock, and almost every evening after office hours he would come and ask what the sales figures were for the day.

From the stairwell on our floor the back of the Earl Carrol Theatre could be seen, and during extremely hot weather a back door was left open. Occasionally Harry and I would go into the stairwell and watch as a parade of beautiful naked chorus girls paraded by, presumably going to or coming from the shower.

I naturally had brought my banjo with me to New York. I put pennies on each side of the bridge, which softened the tone and allowed me to vibrate the strings, and thus I could sing with it without the harsh tone of the banjo. Marty arranged for me to sing on two or three radio stations. I even had my picture in the *New York Evening Journal* as a well-known singer and banjoist from Chicago. One afternoon Marty took me to a radio station which had an orchestra and they were going to play "Then Came the Dawn." He told me he had arranged for me to sing the song. When the orchestra played it I went to the microphone and sang the second chorus. The orchestra leader looked a little puzzled, and later a man came out of the control booth and said, "Who gave you permission to do that? Don't ever pull a stunt like that again." I was agape. I guess Marty hadn't got permission.

Gene had bought a yacht, at a cost of fifty thousand dollars, and named it after his hit record "My Blue Heaven." It was moored on the Hudson River. It had a defective motor and wouldn't run. I don't know how the problem was finally resolved. Whenever I went on the yacht I had to take my banjo because Gene got a kick out of the way I could make the strings quiver while I sang. I'm not clear as to whether or not the lady on board was his wife or girlfriend, but she had a Pomeranian dog and every once in a while it would either fall or jump in the river. I would have to dive in the filthy Hudson and retrieve him. I don't know what they did when I wasn't aboard.

Gene really enjoyed my singing and playing. He thought I had possibilities of being a successful recording artist and set up an audition for me with Columbia records. Columbia had been trying to induce him to leave Victor and come to their label as he was the top singer of the time. On the afternoon Gene took me to the Columbia Studio I became nervous and jittery, and as a result my performance was way below my normal standard. Of course I didn't get a contract, but Gene said, "Don't worry about it, Ken. All you need is a little more experience." I think I just needed more self-confidence. Becoming a recording artist never occurred to me again.

George Olsen's orchestra was appearing in New York. Lyle Smith, his young saxophone player, and I had become good friends in Chicago. Lyle came to the office one day and told me that some members of the orchestra had been invited to a party at the home of a well-known physician whose home was across the river in New Jersey. He said, "Why don't you come with me? The other party guests won't know that you're not a member of the band." I enthusiastically said yes. It turned out to be a very bad decision on my part.

The house was a three-story Victorian type, and when we arrived there were quite a few other guests, including the mayor of the town and several attractive young ladies, some of who were nurses. The doctor was a very gracious host. I liked him immediately. It was during the era of prohibition, but the liquor was flowing freely and I stupidly overindulged. After a couple of hours I was feeling pretty high. I sat down on the piano bench and was soon joined by an attractive lady. I judge she was between twenty-five and thirty years old. We talked a few minutes and then she took my hand and said, "Come with me." We went up to the second floor and she opened the door to a bedroom, but it was occupied. She took me up to the third floor and that bedroom was also occupied. We went back to the first floor and went into the bedroom where the guests' coats were on the bed and closed the door. We laid on the bed and covered ourselves with some coats. I was in seventh heaven and was about to make the grand entry when the door opened. It was the maid. I hollered, "Get out of here." She closed the door, and just as I started to resume my pleasurable task three men came in and yanked me off the bed and took me to the kitchen where there were a couple of other men. One of them was the mayor. They were dressing me down, calling me a cad, a no-good son-of-a-bitch, when the doctor, hearing the commotion, came in. He immediately started defending me. He said, "This nurse has done this before so don't blame this kid. I doubt that any of you can say you've never been enticed." They were debating the subject, so I felt it best that I leave. I have no recollection whatever of getting back to New York. Lyle didn't know what had happened until after I left. He told me the next day that even after I left they were still having a friendly argument, some defending me, some damning me.

One day there was a small fire in our office building and the fire department was called. Naturally a crowd gathered on Seventh Avenue. We weren't told to evacuate, so the publishing firm that owned the building and had their offices on the top floor decided to take advantage of the situation. The song they were trying to popularize at the moment was "Together." A window facing the street was opened and a man with a megaphone sang the song two or three times to the crowd below; some of the people applauded. The fire was quickly extinguished and all returned to normal.

Another 1928 memory was the presidential election. Calvin Coolidge, who was vice president under Woodrow Wilson and became president when Wilson died, announced that he did not choose to run in the 1928 election. This pitted Al Smith, who had been elected governor of New York four times, a Democrat, against Herbert Hoover, a republican. Much was made of the fact that Smith was a Catholic and against prohibition. Hoover had promised a chicken in every pot and two cars in every garage. He became our thirty-first president.

Because of his popularity many publishers would try to curry favor with Gene. One in particular was Mrs. Stasney of Stasney Music Corporation. She kept Gene well stocked with Canadian Scotch. It irritated Marty and me because, although Gene was not a heavy drinker, once in a while he would over-imbibe and become a little difficult to cope with.

We now had a catalog of about six songs, and in early 1929 Gene and Marty decided to send me back to Chicago to represent the firm. I rented desk space in the office of a local publisher, Ted Browne, located in the Woods Theatre Building at Randolph and Dearborn Streets. Most of the tenants in this nine-story building were local publishers, the local offices of New York publishers, and booking agents. I was soon to discover that the building was a favorite stomping ground for prostitutes, many who would give you oral sex for a dollar. I was usually in the office after everyone left, and one evening I succumbed. I was having difficulty reaching a climax and the girl became excited and bit the head of my penis. It wasn't a deep cut, but it was bleeding. I shoved her away and ran to a doctor in the twelve-story Capitol building across the street, which was purported to be the first skyscraper built in Chicago. When I told the doctor what happened he laughed, cauterized the wound, and said it was nothing serious.

Another incident in that vein: Again I was alone in the office when the door opened and a fairly young woman in a wheelchair came in—I never did figure out how she got in the building. We talked a few minutes and she came right out and asked me if she could give me oral sex. I was shocked and said no, but she pleaded with me and said that was her only form of sexual gratification. I felt sorry for her and consented. I did reach a climax. It was an awkward and unusual situation, and I still feel a little ashamed and guilty that it happened.

One other incident: One Saturday afternoon when there were very few people in the building, Irwin, the accountant for Ted Browne, Phil a song writer, and I, were in the office and drinking pure alcohol mixed with orange juice. We all got pretty high, especially me. Phil left the office and came back in about twenty minutes, said something to Irwin, and he left the office for about twenty minutes. When he returned he said, "Ken go to the front office. It's your turn." I didn't know what he meant, but I was pretty tipsy and went. When I opened the door the sight that greeted me was completely disgusting and turned my stomach. Here was this huge plump woman leaning over a desk, her skirts up and her bare buttocks showing. I took one look, closed the door, went to the lavatory and regurgitated. I went home immediately and was hung up for two days. That was the first and last time I ever drank straight alcohol.

Robbins Music Corp., a New York firm, also had their Chicago office in the Woods Theatre building. It was managed by Chick Castle. Chick was a very small man, I'd say not much taller than five feet. He was an immaculate dresser, and every afternoon around three o'clock, he would leave his office, go to his room which was across the street above Henric's Restaurant, and change his clothing and return to his office. His firm had several hits that he was working on at the time, "Pagan Love Song" and "Just You, Just Me." So I couldn't understand why one day he came to me and said "Ken, I need a hundred dollars for about a week. If you can lend it to me I'll pay you twenty-five dollars."

I said, "Chick, I'll lend you the money, but you don't have to pay me interest." At the end of the first week he gave me $25.00. I thought it was an installment. This went on for three more weeks, and I felt he had paid me in full. At the end of that time he handed me one hundred dollars. I said "Chick, you've already paid me." He replied, "I said I would pay you $25.00 a week interest, and I don't go back on my word." It was useless to argue with him, so I took the hundred dollars. Some time later he was found dead in his room. I don't know the cause of his death.

I worked tirelessly plugging our catalog and singing on radio, and although Marty was working just as hard in New York we only had one hit, the English song "A Garden in the Rain." Some of the other songs were selling fairly well, but not enough to sustain the business. At the beginning of summer Marty sent me my final paycheck and said that business just didn't justify keeping me on. Luckily I was still playing the banjo and had moved into an apartment with drummer Dave Davis. Dave would get two or three and sometimes four dance engagements a week. We also had an additional source of income. Our apartment was right above an undertaking parlor, and we would often be called upon to serve on a coroner's jury, which consisted of five people. We were paid five dollars each.

Some of the cases we judged were shootings or accidents. Two cases still stick with me. One was a shooting case where a man was shot in the head and stomach. We went into the embalming room, and on the table was the body of the man, his stomach cut wide open and a doctor sawing off the top of his head. He was trying to find the exact location of the bullets. We had to stand around the body, raise our right hand and swear to tell the truth about the cause of his death. I think we all turned green. I almost upchucked but didn't. The other case was when a six-year-old boy, killed by an automobile, was brought in. I can still hear the mother screaming when she saw the body.

One evening one of Dave's friends brought two girls to the apartment and said they were hitch-hiking to Detroit and needed a place to stay that night, could they stay with us? We said yes. One of the girls was a beautiful, gorgeous brunette; the other was fat, ugly and had bad teeth. Dave had a job that night and I didn't, so I was alone with the two girls. I kept promoting the gorgeous brunette with great anticipation. Dave got home about 1:00 A.M. We sat around and talked a few minutes and I went to the bathroom. When I came out Dave was in bed with the gorgeous brunette and the fat ugly girl was in my bed. I had no alternative but to climb in with her. She tried to entice me but I couldn't respond. The next morning I woke up with an erection and thought, *Oh heck, why not*! Just as I started to advance the alarm clock went off and that quelled all of my desire. How lucky can you get? Dave acquired syphilis from the gorgeous brunette, and I probably would have suffered the same fate had I given into my male instincts or if the alarm clock hadn't gone off.

Dave had organized a twelve-piece orchestra, and my grammar school friend, Joe Peter, with whom I had stayed in contact, was the tenor saxophonist and doubled on violin. One night we were on a job and one of the musicians gave us a marijuana cigarette, which was supposed to make you think slower and play better. Joe and I each took a puff, chickened out, and threw it away. To my knowledge neither of us ever tried it again, or any other kind of dope. I know I didn't and I'm sure Joe didn't.

Dave had booked us for a week in Keokuk, Iowa. When the date was finished the promoter had skipped town without paying us. That left us with a hotel bill that most of us couldn't pay. Some of the boys belonged to the Musicians Union, some didn't. Luckily Dave did and got the union to advance us enough money to pay the hotel bill and get back to Chicago.

Another unpleasant incident, which was of my own making, involved swimming, which was the only sport in which I excelled. I would go to the beach whenever I got the chance. I had become acquainted with a dental student, Maurie Wall. We became good friends. Maurie was quite athletic; he could do cartwheels and handsprings and was an excellent swimmer, as was I. One day in August we were both at Rainbow Beach when Maurie saw a girl he knew. He introduced me to her. I acknowledged the introduction and left the two of them and went swimming.

A couple of days later, on a Thursday, I went to the beach and saw her with another girl. I approached her, smiled, and said hello, assuming that she would remember me, but obviously she didn't. As I started to talk she said, "Get away from me." I started to explain that we had been introduced by Maurie, but she wouldn't listen and repeated angrily, "Get away from me." It frustrated me and I waved my hand and said "Aw, go screw," which was not a nice thing to say. With that she slapped me and that peeved me. I put her over my knee and lightly spanked her. I didn't hurt her but I did embarrass her.

She went to a lifeguard and complained. He just laughed and said, "There's nothing I can do, but there's a policeman over there, maybe he can help you." She and her girlfriend brought the policeman over to me; and she gave her version of what happened. The officer said, "I didn't see it happen so there's nothing I can do, unless you want to come to the police station and file a complaint." She turned to her friend and asked, "Should we?" Her friend hesitated a moment and said "Oh no." Smart-alec me said, "You better, or I'll turn right around and do the same thing to you."

That did it. The officer called a paddy-wagon. We all went to the station, she filed her complaint, and I spent the night in jail. The next day was Friday, and I appeared in court before Judge Borrelli. The girl wasn't in court but the officer who arrested me was. He showed the complaint, told what had happened, and then went up to the judge and whispered something to him. I explained my side of what happened, but to no avail.

Maurie, who had heard what had happened, was also in court. Just the week before he and some other beach goers had been before this same judge. They had jumped this same officer to stop him from shooting on the beach as he chased a suspect. All were exonerated, but because of this Maurie was reluctant to say anything in my behalf. The judge's son, who had been arrested a few days earlier for assaulting a girl, got off scot-free, but he fined me fifty dollars. I didn't have that amount of money with me. I told Maurie to get in touch with my mother and tell her what had happened and where I was.

It was Friday afternoon and I was carted off to Cook County Jail, which was for adult prisoners, to work off my fine. I'm sure that the police officer told the judge I was twenty-one years old. I spent Friday, Saturday, and Sunday there. I was put in a cell with a man with a foreign accent who was very nice. He got a kick out of my predicament but didn't tell me why he was there. The cell had a bunk bed; I slept in the upper and he in the lower. Our toilet was a tin can, and in the morning all of the prisoners took the cans outside and dumped the contents in a huge well. It was quite nauseating. We rinsed the cans, took them back to our cells, and went to breakfast. The meals were acceptable.

After breakfast Monday morning a guard came to my cell and said, "Come with me." He took me to the office, where Mother was waiting for me. I was being released. On the way home Mother told me that Maurie had told her what happened and where I was. One of her steady customers that she waited on was a judge. She had called him and told him what had happened and where I was. He was outraged. He had phoned Judge Borrelli and said, "How dare you send a young boy to Cook County Jail for an inconsequential incident like that when your son beat up a girl and went scot-free. Release him immediately." There was no fine paid. Mother did not reprimand me. Every newspaper in Chicago ran the story. One of the headlines was "Singing Over Radio Doesn't Excuse Spanking Girl Swimmer Over His Knee."

By 1929 radio sets were in practically every household and the radio industry was staging annual shows. From October 21 to 27 the eighth annual Chicago Radio Show was held in the Coliseum. Television was in the development stage, and RCA wanted to show the public what was in store for the entertainment media of the future. I was hired to demonstrate it because I had a chubby face, played the ukulele, sang, and came over the set very well. There was no color then; the screen was made up of brown horizontal lines. I sang upstairs and my image was transmitted to the audience in the South

Ballroom downstairs. RCA wanted me to go with the show to other cities but I didn't want to because I was still getting enough work playing and still singing on radio, which I didn't want to give up.

October 28 and 29 were known as Black Monday and Tragic Tuesday, the days of the big stock market crash, and the start of the worst depression in American history. Orchestra engagements diminished, so Dave and I gave up the apartment and rented a room on Michigan Boulevard across the street from the Automobile Club. The lady who owned the house operated a restaurant on the first floor which was open only at the noon lunch hour, primarily for the employees of the Automobile Club. She did not live there and rented a room upstairs to Dave and me. We were the only roomers. On Sundays and holidays the restaurant was closed.

On Thanksgiving Day Dave and I were fairly well short of money because there were no orchestra engagements forthcoming. As the restaurant was closed and no one was in the house, we decided to raid the kitchen. When we opened the refrigerator, all there was in it was a pumpkin pie which we devoured. We did not get any jobs for the rest of the month. I managed to subsist with Mother's help.

On Christmas day Dave had left and I was alone in the house. I decided to raid the refrigerator again, but lo and behold, all there was in it was a pumpkin pie. I became very depressed and disillusioned with life and decided to end it all. I went back to my room. Although it did have electric lighting it was an old house and still had gas fixtures. I laid on the bed and turned on the gas until I started to smell the fumes. I jumped up, turned off the gas, and thought, *This is stupid and a coward's way out. Things will turn out.* I guess I was feeling sorry for myself because I was alone. I don't know why I was just not with Mother on Christmas Day.

After the first of the year Dave and I gave up the room on Michigan Avenue and parted company. I was still dependent on Mother's financial aid, and with her help I was able to rent a room, back in my old neighborhood, with a musician with whom I had worked. His given name was Leonard; I don't recall his last name. He was from Joliet, Illinois.

Mother was a waitress at the restaurant in the Pittsfield Building on Wabash Avenue, and whenever I went to see her I would go to the Woods Theatre building just to keep up acquaintances and because of my hopes of becoming a successful song-writer. I knew almost everyone in the building. One day in early 1930, Izzy Ullman, who was manager of the local office of Joe Morris Music Co., asked me if I'd like a job as a song plugger, and I was thrilled. They were a well established New York firm and had many hits, their most notable being "My Melancholy Baby." Although first published in 1912, it had become a standard and was still selling. Everyone called Izzy "Cryin' Izzy Ullman" because of his high, squeaky, piercing voice. We had two new publications on which we were working on. One of them, "All That

I'm Asking Is Sympathy" caused a lot of laughter because when Izzy talked about the song it sounded like he was pleading. The other song was "Somewhere in Old Wyoming." Although we did get fairly good airplay, neither song did very well.

The Depression was beginning to take hold and the music publishing industry was beginning to feel the pinch. After we worked about six weeks on the songs and nothing happened, Izzy had to let me go. A few days later, while in the building, I was approached by Eddie Talbot, another song plugger who had been dismissed. He said "Ken, I'm now managing a new firm called Gold Star Music Publishing Co., and I'd like you to be our eastern representative." Eddie was a short rotund man, around forty years old, and very likable. I anxiously accepted. I was to go to St. Louis, Cincinnati, Detroit, and then on to New York. It was agreed that my salary and expense checks would be sent to me certified. We only had one song, titled "You're Tired of Me." it really was an amateurish song. I had no confidence in it, but a job was a job. All of the top hotels in those days had live orchestras, and most of them broadcast nightly. I was to contact the orchestra leaders and radio stations in those cities. I took enough orchestrations and professional copies with me to cover the first three cities and would be sent more material for New York.

It was when I left for St. Louis that I did one of the things that I have regretted and which has haunted me all my life. Leonard had been given a pocket watch that was engraved with his name and stating that he was an outstanding oboe player in his high school orchestra. To this day I can't understand why I stole the watch. Was it envy, jealousy, or what? I didn't need a watch; I had a wrist watch. When I got to St. Louis I pawned it for two dollars. I would give anything in the world if I could find the watch, locate Leonard, and beg his forgiveness. I should have had enough sense to mail it back to him and say I took it by mistake.

I was in St. Louis on a Sunday, and as a rule we never contacted orchestra leaders on that day. The bridge that crossed the Mississippi River into East St. Louis was near my hotel. That evening I decided to cross over and see what was on the other side. I was flabbergasted. I walked right into a red-light district. There were a row of houses and a girl on the porch of each of them urging you to come in for two dollars. My male inclination got the better of me when I saw this cute little blonde, and I surrendered. However, there were two upsetting incidents. When I was ready to leave she got on an earthenware pot and urinated in front of me. In the house was a child—she couldn't have been more than twelve or thirteen years old. I was told you could have her go to bed with you for four or five dollars. I'm sure she wasn't doing this of her own volition, and I guess she was kept there for pedophiles. I felt so sorry for her and left with a feeling of despair and disgust.

I worked St. Louis for a week without too much success.

There were two very famous orchestras playing at the two top hotels in Cincinnati, Paul Whiteman and Vincent Lopez. One of the hotels was the Sinton; I don't recall the name of the other. I went to see Mr. Whiteman one afternoon at rehearsal. He was really very gracious and amused when I told him about delivering music to him on the opening night of the Trianon Ballroom. He looked the song over, handed it back to me, and said, "It just isn't the type of song we play." I couldn't have agreed more, but of course I didn't tell him that. We talked a few minutes and I left with a good feeling about him. When I went to see Vincent Lopez it was just the opposite; he was rude and wouldn't even look at the song.

The main purpose of my going to Detroit, besides covering the orchestras and radio stations, was to try to get the Kresge listing. S.S. Kresge was the second largest chain store next to the Woolworth 5 and 10 cent chain. Both of them had sheet music counters, with an upright piano and a piano player to demonstrate the songs. Getting the Kresge listing meant that every one of their stores nationwide would order one hundred copies. Because of my lack of confidence in the song I had a feeling of uncertainty when I took sheet music copies and went to see the man in charge of that department, but Io and behold, I got the listing. He kept smiling as I talked. I think he was impressed with my youthfulness. The S.S. Kresge stores are now known as K Mart, and I believe have more outlets than Woolworths. Sheet music counters have long been gone.

I was a hero back in Chicago.

My final destination, New York City, is where I had one rewarding incident and where disaster struck. The first week there I had contacted several radio stations and orchestra leaders, among them Rudy Vallee, who was playing in a Chinese restaurant. He was really pleasant and likable and, much to my surprise, two weeks later played and sang the song on one of his radio broadcasts. Although I did have limited success with artists in other cities, this was my crowning achievement. This, along with the Kresge listing, made me a real hero back in Chicago.

Because of the amount of walking I did all of my socks began to have holes in them so I had to buy new ones. The socks I bought must have been of inferior quality because the dye in them caused blood poisoning in my right foot and it started to become difficult to walk. I went to a doctor who had been recommended to me by the hotel where I was staying. I do remember he was on Thirty-Fifth Street near Broadway. I explained to him that my paycheck hadn't come from Chicago yet but that I would pay him as soon as it did. He was going to have to see me a couple of more times, and knowing the hotel where I was staying, he said okay.

Up to this time all of my checks had been certified as I requested. This time, however, the check was not. I thought, *Oh well, somebody just forgot or wanted to get it to me on time and didn't have time to get it certified.* Having cashed three or four of my previous checks, the hotel cashed it. I paid my bill and had intended to pay the doctor the next day. That evening I got a phone call from Eddie. He said, "Ken, if you've cashed that last check we sent you get the hell out of town, it's no good. I'll explain when you get back here." I was panic stricken. My foot was still hurting, I wanted to see the doctor again but I didn't dare, and I had no idea what would happen to me if the hotel found out the check was no good while I was there. The next morning I checked out and took a bus back to Chicago. I felt more guilty about not paying the doctor, who had been so kind and helpful, than I did about the hotel.

I took the bus back to Chicago; it was a trip that seemed to have no ending. I slept on the bus. There was no lavatory on board, but there were frequent rest stops. I was miserable, my foot was still hurting, and I felt like an escaping criminal. When I got back to Chicago Eddie told me that the man who had financed the company had swindled a woman out of about fifty thousand dollars. He was finally exposed, put in jail, and all funding for the company stopped. That was the end of Gold Star Music Company. It took about two weeks for my foot to heal.

The Depression by now had really taken hold, and the music business was in the doldrums. I contacted some of my musician friends and was told there were hardly any orchestra engagements, maybe a wedding once in a while. It was impossible to get any kind of job, and those who had one certainly held on to it. I even tried to sell little packages of aspirin that were stapled to a cardboard stand that were supposed to be a hot selling item for saloons, but after soliciting about a dozen of them with no sales I gave that up.

It was shortly after I returned to Chicago that it was discovered that Mother had cancer of the uterus. The doctors put her in the hospital and were going to operate, but she needed a blood transfusion. I was tested and found acceptable. Plasma was either unknown or just in the experimental stage, and transfusions were given directly from donor to patient. I still have the scar on my right arm where the needle of the tube allowing my blood to flow into Mother was injected. The doctor told me after the operation that Mother had only about five more years to live. She didn't pass away till about thirty years later. I don't know whether or not Mother had insurance or how her hospital and doctor bills were paid.

I wasn't working I was broke and confused. It was then that I decided to go to Caledonia, confront my father whom I had never met, and ask for help. Aunt Catherine gave me the money for train fare, food, and extras.

My grandfather, H.B. Nelson, had established a lumberyard in Caledonia in 1894, and I presumed my father, Conrad A. Nelson, was now his partner. When I walked into the lumber yard office my father was sitting at a desk and Grandfather was standing nearby. There was no mistaking that I was a Nelson, all three of us had the same shaped body and the same stance, our fists on our hips with elbows extended, but what was really odd was my father and I were smoking the same brand of Turkish cigarettes, Murade. As I walked to my father's desk he turned around and I said, "I'm Kenneth. I guess you're my father." I don't recall his response, but he had a look of surprised fear on his face. He was married now and had two children. It's possible that his wife didn't know about me and I could cause problems for his family. Grandfather came over and I told both of them that Mother was in a hospital, I couldn't find a job, and I was broke, needed help, and my only hope was my father. That was the reason I come to see him. I am not calling my father Dad because Dad is a term of endearment, and I have no feeling one way or the other for him, so I will continue to call him Father. I found that Grandfather was a wonderful, warm, thoughtful, loving man so I will call him Grandpa, and after all these years he still lingers in my mind and heart, as does his daughter, my Aunt Lillian.

My conversation with Father was very short. He didn't ask me about myself or about Mother. He did say that he would help me. Grandpa took me by the hand and said, "Come with me, Kenneth." He took me to his house, where I immediately recognized the front porch where Mother and Grandma Nelson had conversed when I was six years old. He told me that Grandma had passed away and that his daughter, my Aunt Lillian, was living with him. When he told her who I was she threw her arms around me, held me close to her, kissed me on the cheek a couple of times, and said, "Kenneth, I've thought about you so often." Not being used to affection I felt embarrassed, but that was nothing to how I felt when Grandpa took me down to the basement to show me the new furnace he had just bought.

As we were walking down the stairs I hit my head on the first floor ledge. He grabbed me, held me in his arms, and kept rubbing my head and repeating "Did you hurt yourself, did you hurt yourself?" Here I was, this nineteen-year-old hulk, being held and comforted by this wonderful old man who must have been in his late eighties. If my head was hurting I wasn't aware of it because my feelings of helplessness and embarrassment were so intense. For some reason or other I can't recall where I stayed that night, but the next day when I saw my father again there wasn't too much conversation. However, he did comment about the fact that we were both smoking the same brand of cigarettes.

When I went to see Aunt Lillian, we had quite a long talk. She asked about my mother and me. I told her what I had been doing, that Mother was a waitress, and that we had been getting along financially until Mother's illness and the Depression hit. She told me that Grandma on her deathbed made my father promise to take care of me. She gave me pictures of Father and Grandpa in the lumber yard, Father in his army uniform, of him with a huge fish he had caught, and a picture of his two children, a boy about four or five with him holding his little sister who was about one year old. I still have the pictures, but wish I had had the presence of mind to ask for a picture of her and Grandma. Grandpa came in as we were talking, and when we were through he gave me a hundred dollars and said, "If things don't get better and you need more help, write Aunt Lillian." When we said goodbye I had feelings of love and relief. Aunt Lillian hugged and kissed me, and Grandpa hugged me for a long time.

A hundred dollars went a long way in those days. I could get along on about fifteen or eighteen dollars a week. After a month or so I still wasn't working and my funds were low. I wrote Aunt Lillian almost every week for the next three months, and she would send me a twenty dollar bill. In one letter she told me that Grandpa had sold fifty thousand acres of timberland that he owned in Canada. I often wondered who was sending the twenty dollars, my father, Grandpa, or Aunt Lillian. I saved all of her letters, but much to my disappointment, somewhere along the way they disappeared. I don't know when Aunt Lillian or Grandpa passed away, but I heard that he was ninety-three. By the end of 1930 Mother had fully recovered and was back to work at the Pittsfield restaurant. The Depression had really taken hold and I was still out of work.

My grammar school graduation. Second row from the top, me at the age of fourteen and my lifelong friend Joe Peter are in the middle.

At the age of sixteen.

1931-1940

I made the Woods Theater building my hangout and continued to write songs. I had become well acquainted with several writers, Johnny Burke, Tommie Mallie, Charles Newman, and Fred Rose. Johnny had gone to Hollywood with the intention of writing melodies for the movies, without success. He came back to Chicago very downhearted. I knew he had talent as a lyricist. I said to him, "Johnny, you're a good lyric writer, why don't you write lyrics?" I don't know if my saying that had anything to do with it, but in 1933 he had his first hit, "Annie Doesn't Live Here Any More," which he co-authored with Joe Young. He returned to Hollywood and wrote the lyrics for the songs in most of Bing Crosby's films.

I recall Tommie Mallie because both of his arms were cut off at his elbows. His biggest hit was "Jealous." Charles Newman's big hit was "Sweethearts on Parade."

Fred Rose was writing popular songs at the time. His big hit was "Honest and Truly." He later went to Nashville, Tennessee, and formed a publishing company with Roy Acuff. The firm, called Acuff-Rose, became the largest publisher of country music in the world. It held that position for many years. My relationship with Fred lasted until his death in 1954.

Archie Bleyer, who was now a well-known orchestrator, was with the New York publishing firm Charlotte-Irving & Co. He had come to Chicago with the express purpose of hiring a local representative. He remembered me from New York and hired me. My first assignment was to send the firm the names, including the middle initials, of all the broadcasting orchestra leaders. They had wallets and pocket notebook cases made of Russian leather for each leader, with his initials in gold. One was made for me, which I still have. They were well received. I had one song to work on written by Helmy Kressa, "That's My Desire." I got a lot of airplay but it just didn't catch on. Mind you, this was 1931. The song became a big hit in 1947 when Frankie Laine recorded it. It was his first hit and established him as a top artist.

I was now living at the Jackson Park Hotel at Sixty-Sixth and Stoney Island Avenue. My room was on the ground floor. The bathroom was communal, but each room had a wash-basin. I would get home from work around eleven o'clock at night. Almost every night, sitting on a couch in the lobby was this rather attractive girl. As I walked by her I would nod and say, "Good evening," and continue on to my room with the evening paper. I would prop myself up in bed and read till I fell asleep.

I never bothered to lock my door, and one night as I was reading, the door opened and in came this girl. I was shocked. She said, "You're going to lay me." I retorted, "I am not. Get out of here." She took off her clothes, handed me a condom, and got in bed with me. It was too much to resist. I gave in. We kissed and petted a few minutes, I put on the condom, and as I was ready to start intercourse she said, "Let me put it in." I did. As I started action I felt that the condom was broken. I stopped to check, and sure enough it was. She had another condom and we went through the same procedure. After I reached a climax I saw that the second condom was also broken. She got out of bed, dressed, and said, "You stuck up son-of-a-bitch. I've got the clap and I hope you get it too." She obviously had broken the condoms on purpose. I was mad and scared. I said, "Get out of here before I lose my temper." I got up and washed myself for about fifteen minutes with Lifebuoy soap, which had a medicinal odor. I still don't understand her reasoning. It must be that she was mentally ill and wanted attention, which I didn't give her. I never saw her again. The next day I went to a doctor and he gave me a shot to counteract any possibility of disease, so I'll never know whether or not she was infected.

The firm and I worked on the song about three or four months, and as it was the only song they had I was discharged. Luckily I was still playing banjo, getting engagements mostly on Friday and Saturday nights, and along with Mother's help I was able to get by. One Saturday night after the dance this very beautiful girl, her name was Evelyn, asked if I would take her home. I couldn't understand why a girl as pretty as she was didn't have an escort. I was flattered and consented. We took the streetcar to her house. I had intended to take her to the front door and leave, but she insisted I come in. We sat on a couch and talked a few minutes, when she suddenly threw her arms around me, was kissing me, and begged me to have intercourse with her. I was pretty worked up and wanted to but refused because it was a two-story house with stairs leading down to the parlor where we were. I visualized her parents coming down and seeing us and the embarrassment it would cause for all concerned.

It was difficult restraining myself. I explained my reason for refusing, gave her the address and my room number of the hotel where I was staying, and said, "Why don't you come and visit me at the hotel?" She said she would be there Monday evening after work. We kissed goodbye and I left, thinking she wouldn't come, but sure enough a little after six she came. She was a wonderful sex partner. We would spend one-half to three-quarters of an hour together, and then she would get dressed and leave. She wouldn't let me take her to dinner. The only money I ever spent on her was the seven cents streetcar fare the night I took her home from the dance. She came two and sometimes three times a week for almost a month, and then I never saw her again. I presume she found a better partner. I really missed her.

It was now 1932, and Mother and I were together again in a basement apartment in the old neighborhood. It was the year that I met the man whose life and mine would be forever interwoven. I had been playing several dances with Ted Toll's orchestra. Ted was the drummer. One night he had booked a date and couldn't make it. He called Lee Gillette, who was also a drummer, and asked him to fill in for him. That's how I met Lee. Ted later became a staff writer for Downbeat Magazine and soon after moved to Hollywood and became a staff writer for the ABC Network.

I was playing almost exclusively with Lee, as he seemed to be getting the most engagements. Our sax player, Jim Crotty, was a tall thin fellow. His father was an undertaker, and every once in a while he would drive us to a dance in a hearse. We got a kick out of seeing people's reactions when they saw us getting out of the hearse with our instruments. One night we played a Polish dance on Chicago's far south side. After the dance we packed and left our instruments on the stage and were on the dance floor talking with the manager and collecting our pay when this real tough-looking guy grabbed Jim's sax off the stage and started to walk away with it. Jim stopped him and said, "Hey, that's my sax." The guy retorted, "Whatta ya accusin' me of, stealin' it?" He was about ready to haul off and hit Jim when big hero me stepped in between them, took the full force of the blow, and was knocked down. Luckily I wasn't hurt. When Jim's father, who was a tall athletic man, heard about it, he was furious. The next day he went to the dance hall, got the guy's name, found him, and beat the hell out of him.

Another embarrassing moment. We were to play at a church dance and were setting up our instruments when this lady came up to us and was telling us where to set up our instruments, I noticed that she was telling other people what to do. There was a man standing near me, and I asked him who that bossy woman was telling everyone what to do. He smiled and said, "Oh, that's my wife." I wanted to sink through the floor.

We played a nightclub called Sam's Club for about three weeks. Prohibition was still in effect, but Sam was selling alcoholic drinks. Enforcement of the Volstead Act, the Eighteenth Amendment to the Constitution prohibiting the sale of alcoholic drinks, had become lax because President Roosevelt had signed a resolution nullifying the act. The next year, 1933, the Eighteenth Amendment became the only amendment ever to be repealed.

About the third night we were at the club, I saw Sam playing checkers with one of the waiters. I told him I was a pretty good player. He said, "Let's find out." I beat him, and almost every night after that he insisted I play with him. I won more games than he did. Lee was upset because the orchestra was without my banjo and singing sometimes for over an hour. One night after the club closed I had left and the other orchestra members were getting ready to leave when two armed men walked in and held up the club. They also took Jim's saxophone. Sam replaced it.

We also played a nightclub where Wesley Rose, the son of Fred Rose, was the coat and checkroom boy. Wesley, many years later, joined his father in Nashville and became the head of Acuff-Rose.

It was 1933, and I had written many songs. Among them was a comic novelty number called "Oh, For the Life of a Lifeguard." I showed the song to Charles Newman. He thought it would be good for Ben Bernie, who was playing at the College Inn in the Sherman Hotel. During my song plugging days I had contacted practically every big name orchestra but never Bernie. Charles said he would take me to him, introduce me, and I could show him the song. One afternoon we went to the orchestra rehearsal and I showed Bernie the song. In an overbearing voice he said, "Hey, kid, that's pretty good. So you wanna become a big song writer, eh? Okay, we'll make you a success." I was thrilled. I left him the copy, but I didn't like his attitude. Two or three weeks later, while reading the radio page, there was a story headlined "Ben Goes English," it stated that he was going to do Philip Craig's Bolero "My Word" and "Oh, For the Life of a Lifeguard." You can't imagine my excited anticipation and elation. When I tuned in, I was really brought down. All of my ideas were used, the melody was changed, and he introduced the song as being written by his piano player—no mention of me, not even as co-writer. I consider him a despicable, dishonest man.

It was in that year that we had formed a vocal trio and called ourselves the Campus Kids. I was the lead singer, Jim Crotty tenor, and Lee baritone. One day as we were passing the building on Wabash Avenue in which the studios of radio station KYW were located, I said, "Hey, guys, I know the staff pianist of KYW, let's go up and get an audition." The pianist was Mel Stitzel, whom I had first met when I was with Melrose Brothers. We published a song of which he was a co-writer, "Tin Roof Blues." I had also contacted him many times as a song plugger. He listened to us, liked what he heard, and said, "Wait here." He left the room and came back with the program director. He liked us and set up an audition with the orchestra which was directed by Rex Maupin. That audition was also successful, and we were soon doing three afternoon programs a week, sometimes with Rex Maupin's orchestra and sometimes with the other staff orchestra leader, Jules Herbeveaux. We also had a Sunday program with a girl singer, Dorothy Adams. We weren't paid because we didn't have a sponsor; however, we did get more dance engagements because of the publicity generated by our broadcasts. The station manager was Homer Hogan; one of the staff announcers was Lowell Blanchard, who later became the top country disc jockey in Memphis, Tennessee. Some of the sponsored acts were Fred Rose and Elmo Tanner, the whistler and singer with Ted Weem's orchestra (they were a duet), Uncle Bob, a kiddy's program, and Dream Daddy Harry Davis, another child's program.

Because we had to learn many songs Lee suggested I move in with him. His mother was a piano player and would help us. He said he had twin beds in his room and that he thought it would be okay with his folks. We spoke with his parents and they agreed; however, I would have to pay $4.00 a week room and board. What a deal. Lee got the dance engagements which more than paid my room and board. His mother enjoyed playing for us. Once again I left my mother, she didn't mind.

Mrs. Gillette, Lee's mother, had an old violin, and I decided I'd learn to play it. I bought a lesson book and practiced every chance I got. Lee had difficulty waking up in the morning. It was like pulling teeth to get him out of bed. A few mornings when we'd have an early rehearsal at the station, I'd stand beside his bed and practice the violin. That woke him up, but he'd get so mad at me that when we boarded the Illinois Central electric train to go to the studio he wouldn't stay in the same car I was in, in order to avoid talking to me. He was back to normal when we'd get to the studio. Between the studio and playing dances we were kept pretty busy.

Charles Newman, who had written the song "Sweethearts on Parade" with Guy Lombardo's brother Carmen, set up an audition for our trio with Guy, whose orchestra was playing at Al Quadback's Café, located at Sixty-Eighth and Cottage Grove Avenue. After the audition Guy thanked us and said we weren't what he was looking for. In the fall of this year we played a dance at the Pardeeville, Wisconsin, High School.

Lee's uncle, Dr. Gillette, was the local physician. When Lee and I went to his office to see him, he was in the process of removing a spider from a young man's ear, another memorable incident. It was a repeat of what had happened to me once before. After the dance this attractive young lady, a high school student, asked me to take her home. It was within walking distance of the school. I accepted her invitation to come in the house. We sat on the couch and talked a bit. She cuddled up to me, I put my arms around her, and we kissed and kissed. We both were overcome with passion. She wanted sex and so did I, but darn it, common sense overtook me again. Any girl under the age of consent was called jailbait, and she couldn't have been more than fifteen or sixteen. The other deterrent: we were in her home, and if her parents should catch us, what a mess. I could be prosecuted and sent to jail. I pushed her away and explained to her what the consequences would be if we were caught. She would be shamed, and I could be sent to prison. I kissed her goodnight and left. The following week Lee received a letter from her. She called me her knight in shining armor on a white steed. A few years later she moved to Chicago and we did get together for a short period.

In early 1934 I decided to leave the trio and become a solo singer. We were at the station when I told Lee of my decision. He didn't ask why, ask me to stay, or say, "Please don't leave the trio." I felt a little hurt that he had accepted it so casually. Fate has a strange way of working. As it turned out it was the best thing that could have happened, not only for Lee and me but for another young man, Hal Derwin. As Lee and I were standing in the hallway talking, Hal got off the elevator; he was holding some sheet music. Lee asked him if he was a singer. He said yes, he had come to get an audition. Lee got Mel, Hal sang, and they decided that he would fit right in, he had the same quality of voice as I. Hal agreed to join the trio. He later sang with Shep Fields and Les Brown's orchestras, formed his own band, was the house orchestra at the Biltmore Hotel in Los Angeles, and recorded for Capitol Records. It wasn't long after I left that Crotty left, I don't know why. The new tenor was Norm Heynie. He had an overbearing attitude and Lee didn't like him but put up with him because he was a good singer.

I moved in again with Mother. We had an apartment on Seventy-First Street, it was near the Illinois Central train station. I had changed my first name to Kennedye because I didn't like the harsh sound of the 'th' in Kenneth. Kennedye Nelson had a smooth, flowing euphonious sound. I put the 'e' on the end of Kennedye because I thought it gave the name a more distinctive look when seen in print. I continued to sing as a soloist on KYW until August or September, and I had begun singing on WAAF.

WAAF was the second oldest station in Chicago. They had started broadcasting in 1922. It was originally located in the stockyards and was owned by the *Drovers Journal*, a trade publication of the livestock and commodities business. It was a one-man operation run by Carl Ulrich, who was both engineer and announcer. During the day he periodically would broadcast the market and weather reports. There was no music until 1929, when regular commercial programming began with live talent and recordings. Their broadcast license restricted the station to operate only from sunup until sundown; in the fall and the winter, they signed off at 5:00 P.M. In spring and summer it varied from 5:00 to 9:00 P.M. Now Carl could devote himself to engineering exclusively.

In May of 1934 a huge fire in the stockyards melted the metal in the transmitter tower into ingots and destroyed the phonograph record library. In July they started broadcasting again in a new studio on the top floor of the Palmer House, one of the main hotels in Chicago's Loop. The manager was Art Harre. There were two studios. The larger one, A, was used for live talent and plays; the smaller, B, was used mostly for talk shows and rehearsals. In between the studios was a small booth with a turntable on each side of the announcer's desk, which held the daily log, the commercials and announcements to be read, and the records and transcriptions to be played. It was the announcer's responsibility to operate the turntables. In addition there was also a small alcove that encased the engineering equipment. If two people were in the booth at the same time it was crowded. The other components of the complex were the manager's office, the record library, the program director and staff writer's office, where the United Press News machine was located, and a large reception area.

I had conceived a program, written a theme song for it, and called it "The Song Salesman." I would put together a group of songs that were related and told a story. Jesse Alexander, with whom I had graduated from grammar school, was a scriptwriter for the station. We'd get together, he'd write a script, and then we'd decide what sound effects to use.

There were two union musicians at the station, Jimmie Kozak and Estelle Barnes. Jimmie was a flashy pianist. Estelle was my accompanist; she was very gifted and could play any piece of music at first sight.

I was still singing on KYW and thought it was best to use another name on AAF. I concocted what I thought was an original romantic name, Warren Gaylord. Many years later I read of a person with that same name. I did get quite a bit of fan mail.

I had written a song titled "When I Join the Easter Parade." I sang it over KYW with the full orchestra. I sang it on my AAF program. Eddy Simmons, who was not only program director and announcer at AAF but was also the producer of the "Saturday Night WLS Barn Dance," heard me singing it and liked it. He had it broadcast with the full orchestra and chorus on the Barn Dance. I was on cloud nine until a few days later, when I walked into Lyon & Healys, probably the top music store in Chicago and saw a song on the sheet music counter called "Easter Parade" by one of my favorite composers, Irving Berlin. I hadn't heard the song because it was not played on radio. This number was from a show playing on Broadway, called "As Thousands Cheer," and many songs from musical shows were restricted from airplay by the publisher until the show had run its course. I rewrote the song as a semi-classical waltz. It turned out to be a beautiful melody but of no commercial value. I called it "When You Look in the Heart of a Rose."

One day one of the announcers told me he had been hired by a station in Des Moines, Iowa, and was leaving AAF. I decided to apply as his replacement, even though I had no experience as an announcer. I competed against two other applicants and got the job. I was to start broadcasting at 6:00 A.M. and my last program would be 12:00 noon to 1:00 P.M. which meant I had to be at the station no later than 5:30 A.M. in order to turn on the engineering equipment and get things ready. During the five years I worked there I was only late once, and that was because of a traffic accident. My salary was to be fifteen dollars a week. I could get along on this because I was still living with Mother and occasionally played a dance job on Saturday night.

My schedule was as follows. I was the sole announcer from 6:00 A.M. to 9:00. I was relieved until 10:00, then broadcast until 11:00. My final program of the day was from 12:00 noon until 1:00 P.M. My first hour was devoted to livestock and commodities reports and country music, which at that time was called Hillbilly music. My last hour, 12 noon to 1:00 P.M., was the *Symphonic Hour*, which had previously been arranged and broadcast by the University of Chicago but was now the station's full responsibility.

As I had no knowledge of classical music, I bought *The Music Lovers Encyclopedia*, edited by Rupert Hughes. It was a pronouncing dictionary of musical terms, composers, their works, and epithets. I also bought an English book to catch up on my grammar. I soon realized that my announcing was in a monotonous monotone with no inflection in my voice. I started to exercise my jaws, learned to twist my tongue, and analyzed the alphabet. It was quite obvious that every letter, with the exception of O had an *E* or *eh* sound. Aee, Bee, Cee, Dee, Eee, ehF, Gee, aeecH, Iee, Jayee, Kayee, ehl, ehM, ehN, 0, Pee, Keyu, aheR, eS, Tee, eeU, Vee, doubleeeU, ehX, Yee, Zee. I would pronounce single words, then put them in a half sentence and then a full sentence. "To-day I am go-ing," then "To-day I am go-ing to the store." I did this with the commercials I had to announce.

I studied my English book and reviewed the meaning of nouns, pronouns, verbs, adverbs, adjectives, and so forth so that I could put the right emphasis on the proper words. I studied the music dictionary and tried to be very careful in pronouncing the composer's names and musical terms. I was pretty pleased with my progress until one day I received a phone call after the *Symphonic Hour* broadcast, from a Mrs. Dubois, a French lady with a slight accent. She said, "Mr. Nelson, we think you have a lovely voice, but many of your pronunciations are incorrect." I explained to her that I had very little knowledge of classical music, and although I had bought a musical dictionary, I probably did mispronounce some musical terms and composers names. I also told her that it was the last hour of my daily broadcast schedule and was my responsibility. She obviously was a dyed-in-the-wool classical devotee. She said, "Would you mind if I came to the studio and helped you?" I was delighted and said, "I would be most appreciative if you did." She came to the studio every day for over three weeks, and we would go over the program before each broadcast.

She pointed out to me that in many foreign languages, especially Italian and Spanish, "e" is pronounced *a*, "a" is *ah*, "i" is *e*, and "w' in Russian and German is *v*. I never did fathom French. As a result of the tutoring I soon became proficient and was recognized as a classical authority, which of course I wasn't. It was now my responsibility to select the selections to be played on the program.

Occasionally I would announce the program of the Chicago Symphony Orchestra, and I was invited to one of their board meetings. I felt I would be out of place, but I went anyway. Most of the discussions were over my head—business, finances, attendance improvement, etc. I enjoyed the meeting; it gave me an insight as to what goes on behind the scenes of a symphony orchestra. As I was leaving, Dr. Frederick Stock, the German-born conductor, said to me in his thick accent, "Mr. Nelson, always leave the audience singing." What he meant was, end the program with a familiar, melodious singable selection. I did that whenever I could, but it wasn't always possible because of the length of the program. That, of course, is good advice for any musical performance.

At that time the record companies were not sending free promotion records, the stations had to buy them. I was given that task. We had a trade deal with a furniture company. In return for a given number of commercials, we were allowed to purchase up to four-hundred dollars worth of records a month, for which they were billed. I would go to the Cable Piano Company store on Wabash Avenue and buy the new releases. I also purchased records from England, HMVs, His Master's Voice, which were imported by RCA Victor. Our daily broadcasts were a plethora of variety, news, and music, such as Waltztime. Showtime, and fifteen to thirty minute segments featuring a top singer or orchestra of the day. There were talk shows, such as Bob Hawk's *Man on the Street*, in which he would actually interview people on the street. We even had a program featuring live canaries singing to the background of recorded Hawaiian music, sponsored by Hartz Mountain Canary Birdseed. We kept the canaries in Studio B. I don't remember who took care of them, but it wasn't me.

Some of the other announcers during my period of employment were Harry Creighton, who left to become a sportscaster on WGN and later the distributor for a large brewery company; Joel Douglas, a pitchman who later became a top commercial announcer in Los Angeles; Virgil Irwin, who purportedly had an offer from Warner Brothers studio; Jack Russell; Eddie Simmons, the program director; and others that I don't remember.

Before a newscast we would tear off the news being wired to us over the United Press machine and read it over the air, sometimes without a chance to look it over. On one newscast, Eddy Simmons was reading a story about a horse that had pitched and tossed the governor. Eddie goofed and said the horse pissed and tossed the Governor. Of course we all mispronounced words at times, but none quite so hilarious, Eddie never lived that one down.

Another memory: During the Great Depression there was much labor unrest, and every May Day, May 1st which was considered Worker's Day, we had a police officer spend the day, guarding against possible labor union terrorists taking over the facility in order to expound their dogma. I presume the other stations had the same protection.

From 7:00 A.M. to 9:00 A.M. I had a variety program that featured popular artists and orchestras of the day called "The Woodlawn Express." It was sponsored by the Woodlawn Businessmen's Association. Woodlawn was a large area on Chicago's Southside between Stony Island and Cottage Grove Avenues, from Sixtieth Street to Sixty-Seventh Street. A short walk from the area on Sixtieth Street would take you to White City, the amusement park where I had started my singing career. The promotion and publicity man for the organization decided that the members of the committee should meet the announcer of their radio program. He was going to pick me up in a couple of days, so I had time to prepare a short speech. On the way to the meeting I told him what I intended to say. In introducing me to the committee he gave my speech almost verbatim. I felt like an idiot. I don't remember what I said, but I ad-libbed my way through it somehow. After the meeting most of the members shook my hand and said they were pleased with the program and my announcing. In my opinion that promotion man was a class-A jerk.

After being at the station over a year, I decided I should have a raise. The owner, Mr. Hutchinson, seldom came to the station. On one rare occasion when he did, I met with him and said, "Mr. Hutchinson you have an announcer working here who has opened the station for over a year, has never been late, purchases records, plans programs, and does newscasts. Don't you think he deserves a raise?" He looked at me, smiled, and said, "Yes." I was now making twenty-five doallars a week. A year and a half later I was making sixty-five dollars a week.

In 1935 I joined the Chicago Musicians Union, whose president was James C. Petrillo. He made it mandatory that only union musicians could operate the turntables, that is play the records and transcriptions. He was lenient with the smaller stations, and as we had two pianists we only had to have one record turner. When this ruling came I was allowed to be the record turner and continue announcing. Our manager was happy with this arrangement because it saved an announcer's salary. At the larger stations the record turners could not announce and could only work five hour shifts five days a week.

On September 3, 1939, I announced the following bulletin from United Press via Western Union at 6:31 A.M.: "LONDON—PRIME MINISTER CHAMBERLAIN HAS JUST PROCLAIMED THAT A STATE OF WAR EXISTS BETWEEN GREAT BRITAIN AND GERMANY."

I still have the telegram. That was quite an exciting news day!

Soon after I left the Campus Kids Trio, which now consisted of Lee Gillette, Hal Derwin, and Norm Heynie, they got a sponsor. The Prohibition Amendment had been repealed, and their sponsor on KYW was Seagrams Liquor. In addition they were also singing with Harry Sosnik's orchestra at the Edgewater Beach Hotel. Then they were selected as a vocal group for the *Fibber McGee and Molly* show, which originated in Chicago. It became so popular that the network decided to move the show, including the

Campus Trio, to Hollywood. I don't know how long they stayed with *Fibber McGee and Molly*, but after they left they joined Buddy Rodgers' Orchestra. Buddy Rogers was a movie actor who was married to a very popular movie actress, Mary Pickford, who was known as America's Sweetheart. I understand that Mary objected to Buddy being an orchestra leader, so he disbanded the organization and the trio were out of a job.

They came back to Chicago and Lee and I renewed our friendship. He was always interested in radio and was surprised to learn that I was an announcer. He said that was one of his ambitions. It was 1940 or 1941, and one of the announcers was going to leave. I met with Lee, gave him a few pointers, and told him to audition for the job. I had previously spoken to Art Harre, our manager, and Eddie Simmons, our program director, about Lee. He auditioned and was hired. Lee and I were now working together again.

When I was staying in Lee's home in 1934, he had been dating a girl, Charlotte (not her real name) who had a sister, Myra (not her real name), who was beautiful and sexy. We double dated about three times and Lee stopped going with Charlotte. Up to this point in my life I had never had a girlfriend, had no experience whatsoever with dating or courtship. All of my relationships with the opposite sex had been short sexual encounters.

Myra was very aggressive and glommed on to me. I was like a babe-in-the-woods and fell victim to her wiles. I never did feel completely at ease with her, and a couple of times when I tried to break up she waited outside where I was living and caught me when I came out. I think it was the fact that she paid so much attention to me that kept me under her spell. For over a year I refused to have sex with her, although we did a lot of heavy necking and petting. One day she said if I didn't have intercourse with her she would find someone who would. I should have said goodbye right then and there, but I didn't.

It just so happened that that weekend my friend Joe Peter's folks were out of town, and there was a bedroom in the basement of the apartment building where he lived which and his father maintained. He agreed to let me use it. Myra and I spent the night together and I was really hooked. She was great, the best bed partner I ever had. I should have realized that Myra was emotionally all mixed up, but I didn't. Her father was an alcoholic, and her mother would pick up a couple of men and call Myra to come join them. When Myra was sixteen she helped her mother have an abortion; she had become pregnant but not by her husband. I don't know how, but Myra said she used a coat hanger.

Motels were not in existence then and I didn't want to go to a hotel because we would have had to register as man and wife. We always found some place for our love-making. I was still living with Mother and many weekends she would stay with a friend, so Myra and I would be together all Saturday night.

In 1936 the station gave me a Christmas bonus, and my salary was now $65.00 a week, which was a mighty good wage at that time. I must have been out of my mind but I let Myra talk me into getting married. The details of the wedding are sketchy, but on January 1, 1937, I vaguely recall taking the electric train to Milwaukee, Wisconsin, and being married by a justice of the peace. I do recall one of the announcers at AAF, Jack Russell, and his girlfriend came along. Jack was best man and his girlfriend was witness. I do vividly recall thinking to myself over and over again, *This is wrong, I shouldn't be doing this*. I can't even recall where we spent our wedding night. I still can't understand how I let myself fall into this quagmire. The only good thing about the marriage was the sex.

We rented a furnished apartment at Seventy-Eighth and South Shore Drive. I bought a Baldwin acrosonic piano for $295; it was a half size upright piano. This was a new type that hadn't been on the market very long. Myra didn't like my practicing and would leave the apartment when I did. Some evenings we would go to her mother's for dinner; they both liked to play gin rummy. I enjoyed the game too but was still opening the station and would have to leave early, they would coax me to play a little longer. I'd give in and would be tired the next day.

I had not been circumcised and sometimes having sex, which we were having quite frequently, was painful, and I decided to have the operation. This meant I could not participate in the act for two or three months until I healed. This upset Myra but I tried to satisfy her desires until things got back to normal.

Our apartment on South Shore Drive did not have a bedroom. We slept on a Murphy bed, which folded up into the wall behind closed doors. We decided we wanted a bedroom and our own furniture, so we rented an apartment at Seventy-Seventh and Marquette, furnished it completely, and bought a console phonograph. Myra's favorite singer was Nelson Eddy. We went to one of his concerts, and for some reason I've never forgotten him singing "Shortnin' Bread," I can still visualize and hear "Mammy's Little Baby Loves Shortnin' Bread." Her favorite popular song was "Careless." We also went to see Gilbert and Sullivan's *Pirates of Penzance*. We became acquainted with the young couple next door. They had a grand piano and she played beautifully, I envied her. Two songs I recall her playing frequently were "Cocktails for Two" and "You Go to My Head."

Things were going fairly smoothly until Myra decided she wanted to get a job. Although we had never taken precautions she hadn't become pregnant, and staying at home all day was rather boring, so I agreed. She was hired as a salesperson at Sears Roebuck. She seemed to be happy, and I felt that everything was okay until a couple of months later she started to come home late, sometimes one or two hours, about twice a week. She always had an excuse, she worked late or stopped off at her mother's. Her sexual enthusiasm was not up to par, but I attributed it to the fact that she was working. I did not question her but I did become suspicious.

My suspicions were confirmed on January 13, 1940. Charlotte, Myra's sister, whose husband also worked at Sears, Myra, and I were invited to a party at another Sears employee's house. We were all enjoying ourselves and drinking moderately. After an hour or so Myra was not in the same room that I and the other guests were. I assumed that she had gone to the lavatory, but after she didn't appear for about twenty minutes I went looking for her. I found her in another room dancing with a man and biting his ear. I was furious. I lost my temper; I grabbed her and slapped her. The man hightailed it out of the room.

Myra ran into a closet. I opened the door and said, "I'm getting a divorce." I left the party immediately. I presume Myra and her sister went to their mother's apartment. Four days later I received a letter from Myra begging my forgiveness, blaming her over-indulgence on the liquor, stating that nothing like that would ever happen again, and pleading for me not to get a divorce. I guess her letter really touched me. I phoned her and said, "Okay, let bygones be bygones, come on home." When she came back I kissed her and said, "Let's not talk about it anymore." Although our sex life was not quite the same, things were going along fairly well until May.

One day I came home from work early. When I went in the bedroom, Myra was passed out, lying on the bed with her dress up to her neck and semen all over her stomach. It was the same scene I had witnessed when I attended a party as a teenager. The difference was there was no condom this time. I have never forgotten my reaction. I had a feeling of complete release and relief, almost ecstatic, as if a big burden had been lifted off of my shoulders. I cleaned her stomach, pulled her dress down, and when she sobered up I said, "You know what this means." She said, "Yes," and without further ado she moved in with her mother till the divorce. I let her file for the divorce, which was granted on grounds of cruelty, July 9 1940.

Charlotte, Myra's sister, a very sensible and intelligent girl, knew that Myra was having an affair with one of the Sears employees, and as I had no desire to expose Myra's lewd conduct; she agreed to testify that on several occasions I had struck, beaten, and kicked Myra. The only time I had ever hit her was when I caught her biting the guy's ear at the January party. I did not appear at the trial but had previously agreed to all the terms. I would pay ten dollars a week alimony for one year only, pay the attorney's fee of one hundred dollars, pay one hundred fifty dollars for tuition at a beauty school, and let her retain all of the furniture we had bought, with the exception of the piano, which I kept. Believe me, it was a cheap price to pay for the wonderful feeling of relief and freedom that I had.

Lee soon got the hang of things at the station and really enjoyed the job. Although he too belonged to the musician's union, our station was required to have only one union record turner, and I was it. All the other announcers were allowed to operate the turntables. I don't know what Lee's salary was.

In 1914, Victor Herbert, one of the top composers of the day, and a group of other authors, composers, and publishers formed The American Society of Authors, Composers, and Publishers (ASCAP). Its purpose was to license and ensure that a fee was paid for every public performance of their music. This was legally within their jurisdiction because they owned the copyrights. Of course at that time there were no radio stations. When radio broadcasting did come into existence, every station was required to get an ASCAP license. The fee was based on the station's income. The stations had no alternative but to pay because ASCAP controlled practically all popular music published. It was a tightly held organization, and almost impossible to become a member. I tried and was turned down, even through I had the correct qualifications.

In 1940, after eighteen years of paying increasing fees to ASCAP, the radio industry rebelled and all stations refused to play ASCAP songs. The industry established its own performance society, Broadcast Music, Inc. (BMI). This made it extremely difficult for all of us making up programs because BMI was only in the process of signing up publishers and writers. All we could program was music whose copyright had expired and was in the public domain. As most classical music was in public domain, it didn't affect the *Symphonic Hour*.

The public was drenched with Steven Foster melodies, "Beautiful Dreamer," "Camptown Races," "My Old Kentucky Home," "Carry Me Back to Old Virginia." if Steven, who died penniless, were alive he would have made a fortune in performance fees. There was one popular song we could program, the theme song from the film *Intermezzo*, which starred Hedy Lamarr, and it sure got programmed. Nine of the top orchestras recorded it. Its copyright was controlled by the European Society (SESAC).

It was in 1940 that I made my second appearance on television. Balaban and Katz, the theatre chain, had an experimental TV station in the State Lake theatre building. There couldn't have been too many TV sets because I don't think sets were publicly available; however, they were broadcasting. They called Art Harre, our manager, and asked if he would send over a couple of announcers to broadcast the election returns, so I had the privilege of announcing the election results of President Roosevelt and his Republican opponent Wendell Wilkie. Roosevelt was elected to his third term.

1933, The Campus Kids, Ken Nelson, Lee Gillette, Jim Crotty. The girl, Dorthy Adams, was not a member of the group but occasionally sang with us on our KYW broadcasts.

1941-1950

ASCAP was a very close-knit organization and would accept only popular and musical show tunes. To become a member you had to have had at least five songs, usually hits, published by an ASCAP publisher. They did not accept hillbilly or race music writers, and even though their songs were played over radio they didn't receive performance fees. BMI changed all that. It opened the door and accepted publishers and writers of all types of music, and they would now receive performance fees. Three of the first BMI songs I recall were "I Hear a Rhapsody," "There I Go," and "High on a Windy Hill." Because of BMI, country music and rhythm and blues came into their own.

It was either 1940 or 1941 that I first met Reg McHugh and his wife-to-be at a gathering one afternoon at Harry Creighton's apartment. We took a liking to each other immediately and became lifelong friends. He had no connection with either radio or music, but he did have quite an interesting career. Because of a knee injury while playing football in college, he was not drafted. When I first met him he was working as a metallurgist in a Southside steel mill. He was let go from that job when the mill hired all female metallurgists because the army had drafted most of the men. I don't know whether or not I influenced him, but I kept telling him that he had all the qualifications of an outstanding salesman—voice, looks, personality, and a definite attitude. He enrolled in a class on salesmanship at Northwestern University, got a degree, and later taught on the subject there. He also taught at the University of Illinois, the Chicago YMCA College, Field Sales Management Institute, and the School of Bank Marketing.

He worked for Dow Chemical Company as a salesman, but because of the war it was difficult to sell their products. While working for Dow he met Jan Phillips who had a company called Phillips Marketing Ways. Its business was to teach how to market products. He joined the company as vice president. After two years he left Phillips and joined Apex Railway Products as sales manager, selling steel buildings, steel framing, and mobile homes. He was at Apex for about two years when he ran into Jan Phillips, and they decided to form a company and call it Sales Training Dynamics. They mailed letters to banks explaining their function and received a call from one of New York's largest banks, Bankers Trust. They were interested. Reg went to New York and gave his program, which was how to provide and improve the sales skills of their contact personnel. The bank was impressed and bought the program. Reg eventually gave seminars at hundreds of banks, including Lloyds of London and a bank in Hong Kong. Later, Reg and Phillips separated and Reg formed his own successful company; when he retired his son took over.

In 1942 I had three more songs published, including "Lazy Mississippi Moon," for which I received my first royalty check in the amount of twenty-nine cents. I didn't cash it; I still have it. I did receive more royalties later, but no performance fee; the publisher was a SESAC firm. "Cotton Pickers Jamboree" was published by Peer, a BMI firm, but nothing happened. I made the mistake of letting Eddie Chase, who had a program called *Make-Believe Ballroom* on our station, publish a song, written by me and Alan Surgel, titled "No Need to Be Sorry." He got his BMI license with our song and put his name on the printed copies as one of the writers, which he wasn't. It was recorded by Lawrence Welk and Sammy Kaye, but we never received one penny in royalties. I should have sued him, but I was naïve in such matters. I didn't realize until a few years later that, being a writer, I should have applied for membership in BMI.

Eddie Chase was the announcer for the program *Make-Believe Ballroom*. Actually, he was what is now called a disc jockey or DJ, but the term was not coined until 1941 and came into full use around 1942. The title *Make-Believe Ballroom* was conceived by Martin Block of a Detroit radio station. I presume he copyrighted it because I understand he franchised it, and Chase was the franchisee for the Chicago area. It was the height of the big band era, and the two-hour program featured fifteen to thirty minute segments of the top bands of the day. Chase was supposed to assemble his own program but was negligent in doing so and would leave it up to Gillette and me.

It was still my responsibility to purchase records, and I had to make sure we had all of the latest by the name bands. Lee and I would assemble his programs, and Lee was his record turner. Chase kept reiterating over and over, "I'm going to take care of you boys." When the time came to take care of us he gave us the magnanimous gift of a half-pint of Gordon's gin to share. We really didn't expect anything, but this was not only funny but ridiculous. Of course we continued doing our job.

After my divorce I moved into a one-bedroom furnished apartment located at Seventy-Fourth and Phillips Avenue. It had a kitchen and a fairly large living room that accommodated my piano. It was directly across the street from the apartment building where Lee's folks, Mr. and Mrs. Gillette, now lived. Although I wasn't actively singing I didn't want to give it up, so I started taking vocal lessons. My teacher was Mr. McBurney, whose studios were in the Fine Arts Building. Mary, a fellow student, was an adopted child. She wasn't overly attractive but had a nice figure and a pleasant personality. She lived only a block away from me. We would occasionally ride home together and became quite friendly, but I had no designs on her. One day she invited herself up to my apartment. She went almost immediately to the bedroom, undressed, took a diaphragm out of her purse, inserted it, and lay down on the bed. What could I do but partake of the pleasure? She would come to my apartment at least once and sometimes twice a week, once in a while give me oral sex, and occasionally stay all night. She never asked or demanded anything of me. This went on for quite a while. I had no love feeling for her but I liked her; she was a good sex partner and satisfied my male instinct. I did occasionally take her to dinner. She never said she loved me but was very considerate and loving. I just think she was oversexed and being adopted was looking for acceptance, which I gave her.

In 1941 the Atlas Brothers, who owned Radio Station WJJD, with studios in the Carbon Carbide Building in Chicago's loop, which was the downtown district of the City, decided to make WJJD the good music station of Chicago. They also owned WIND in Gary, Indiana.

The former manager of WAAF was now the sales manager for JJD. He suggested they hire me because of my five years of planning and announcing the *Symphonic Hou*r on WAAF. Al Hollander, the program director of JJD, contacted me, and when we met I told him I would only leave AAF if I was hired as union contractor and musical director. Every station in Chicago was required to have a musician's union member as contractor, and his salary was more than the average musicians and record turner. Hollander got back to me the next day and said okay. I learned later that the man who was the union contractor wanted to quit, so I wasn't the cause of him losing his job.

I was assigned an office and a secretary who was in another office. The station had a country music program called *The Supper Time Frolic*. All of the artists, musicians, and singers were live talent, including Uncle Henry's Kentucky Mountaineers, Bob Atcher, Karl and Harty, and several others who I don't recall. I was now the overseer of about fifteen people, including an organist and four record turners.

Just before I took over, a harmonica player and guitarist calling himself Rhubarb Red, who was a featured artist on the *Frolic*, left the station. His real name was Les Paul. He went on to New York, auditioned for Fred Waring's Pennsylvanians and was their guitarist for five years. He later became a popular recording star in his own right, had his own studio, and was one of the first to do multiple recordings when tape was introduced in America in 1949. He hired a girl to sing on his recordings. They later married, and became famous as top record sellers as Les Paul and Mary Ford.

My announcing days were over; my time was devoted to building a classical library, planning programs, and overseeing the musical staff. My basic salary was one hundred 23 dollars a week plus overtime. Union hours were five hours a day, any time over that was overtime. There was so much to be done that it was impossible to accomplish what had to be done in a five hour day, so with my overtime I was earning around 800 dollars a month.

I had to build the classical library from scratch. I had to buy dozens of albums; my secretary would type file cards, from which I would make up the programs. They were broadcast simultaneously over WIND by remote control. I also bought pop and records for other programs. Long playing 33 1/3 rpm's albums, created by Columbia records, and seven inch 45 rpm records, created by Victor records, were introduced around 1948 or 49. Prior to then albums consisted of twelve and ten inch 78 rpm records. There was dissension between Columbia and Victor over the single records. Columbia wanted to issue them at 33 1/3 rpm the same as albums, Victor wanted them at 45 rpm. Columbia had to capitulate when Victor put a machine on the market that would play only 45s. All records by all companies were 33 1/3 for albums and 45 for singles from then on until the advent of compact discs and CDs around 1979.

The Supper Time Frolic, a two-hour five day a week evening program, was very popular, not in Chicago but in rural areas, and especially throughout the southern states.

There was an announcer at the station who was one of those crude men who had no respect for women and thought nothing of using the vilest language in their presence. One day I was going to enter the record library but found the door locked. I had a key, and, when I opened the door quite a sight greeted me. He was having intercourse with one of the secretaries on the table. I closed the door and waited till they came out. They didn't say anything and neither did I. I never told anyone at the station about it.

Another time this oaf was the announcer for a woman's talk program, whose hostess was an attractive middle-aged lady. They were sitting across from each other at a table that was about one and one-half feet wide and two and one-half feet long. At the end of the program he reached under the table, put his hand up her dress and tried to pull her pubic hairs. She got up raving mad, slapped, punched, pulled his hair, and was screaming at the top of her voice. He was laughing like the idiot he was. I could never understand why he wasn't fired for this. One day he came to the studio with his face a bruised mess; he obviously had insulted the wrong lady and her boyfriend had beaten the daylights out of him. We were all happy about it. When he left the station he went to New York and became the announcer for one of the networks top comedy shows.

Bob Ellison, a well-known sportscaster, had his daily program on our station. An announcer recently hired would often have his girlfriend meet him at the station, and one day while waiting for him Ellison made the mistake of asking her for a date. Her boyfriend was a little irked and vowed to even the score. What he did was outrageously hilarious. He invited several announcers from other stations and most of the male members of JJD. We were told what was going to happen and sworn to secrecy. On the appointed day we lined the studio walls, sitting on the floor. Bob thought we were there to honor him. Half-way through the program a beautiful young lady came in and started to strip-tease. She was down to nothing but a G-string and went over to Bob, tantalizing him with her bare breasts. It was difficult to withhold our laughter, but we did as we watched him squirm, confused and unsure of whether or not he was on the air. He looked at the studio clock and, as it was his broadcast time, kept on going and finished the program. After it was over we all burst out in laughter. Bob took it good-naturedly and joined in the hilarity. He later became a navy officer at the Great Lakes Naval Training Center.

One evening my secretary was working late and Mr. Ralph Atlas, one of the owners, gave her a ride home. When his secretary, who was in charge of hiring the female employees, became aware of it, she told my secretary she was fired. This was not only unfair but ridiculous. She was an excellent worker and I didn't want to lose her. I went to Mr. Atlas spewing my anger. He said, "Calm down, nobody's going to be fired." He didn't know what his secretary had done. An interesting aside, my secretary saw a movie with a musical score by the great musical show composer Jerome Kern. All of the songs had lyrics but one; she wanted to find out the name of this instrumental number so she wrote Mr. Kern. He replied by sending her the autographed copy of the original manuscript. I envied her.

It was while I was at JJD that I wrote "Waiting and Praying for You," a war song. When I showed it to one of the top Chicago publishers he liked the song, with the exception of the lyric of the bridge (the middle part of the song). He had Fred Rose rewrite the bridge, and I expected Fred to claim part authorship. I would have been proud to have my name linked with his, but Fred said he did it as a favor. Although he did not have anything to do with writing the song, Bob Atcher, a singer's name, was printed on the song as a co-writer. It was commonplace to give a name, artist or orchestra leader, credit for writing, and sometimes even to cut them in on the royalties in order to get them to perform the song. The song wasn't a hit, but it did earn some royalties.

During September of 1939, the German dictator, Adolfh Hitler, declared war on Poland, Great Britain, and France. In 1940, because of Hitler's conquests, President Roosevelt signed the selective service and training act, which required all male citizens up to the age of thirty-five to register. It was the first peacetime military draft in United States history. Over sixteen million received registration cards, including me. On December 7, 1941, Japan bombed Pearl Harbor, our Hawaiian naval base. The next day we declared war on Japan.

On December 11, 1941, Germany and Italy declared war on us. It was truly a World War. The Office of Price Administration (O.P.A.) put into effect the rationing of food, clothing, gasoline, and other articles. Everyone had war ration books with coupons that had to be used when purchasing rationed goods. When you used all your coupons you got a new book at the local O.P.A. Board. Al Hollander, our program director, was one of the first to enter the service. He was called to New York to join the staff of the Office of War Information (O.W.I.) O.W.I. was responsible for radio programming and entertainment. I wrote Al and asked if I could volunteer my services for O.W.I. He wrote me and said they could certainly use me but were unable to accept my offer because they were only permitted to take straight 4-Fs, but if I was put in as 4-F to let him know immediately.

On September 11, 1943, I was inducted into the army and, after passing the physical examination, was to report for active duty, October 2 at Camp Grant, Illinois. As soon as I received my notice Art Hare and I went to the station manager and recommended that Lee Gillette be hired as my replacement. He was not only well qualified but his chances of being drafted were slim because he was now married and the father of two baby boys, Phillip, born in 1940, and David, in 1941. He was hired and was now musical director of WJJD. Incidentally, Lee and Edith Bergdahl were married in 1937.

It was a short train ride for about twenty of us new recruits to the camp, where we were fitted with uniforms and shoes and assigned to our branches of service. Because of my poor eyesight I was not eligible for active duty and was assigned to the medical department, but I still had to take the basic military training. When we heard that we were going to Camp Barkeley in Abilene, Texas, for our training we were all elated, thinking that Texas was always warm. Boy, were we wrong. On a couple of bivouacs, when we were out all night, I was never so cold in my entire life, and that was something having lived in Chicago where the temperature often fell below, way below, freezing.

About fifteen trainees were assigned to each barracks. At the foot of each cot was a locker for your personal belongings. Every Saturday morning the captain, sergeant, and sometimes a major would come into the barracks and inspect not only the soldiers but also the cabin, the beds, the windows, and the floors. The camp was on sandy ground and the floors were hard to keep clean because it was sometimes very windy, but we managed. We had to make sure we had on clean shirts. There was a communal laundry room where everyone did their laundry.

About the second day I was there the captain called me to his quarters and said he noted that I was a musical director and told me that he played the trumpet. He was not actively playing but still practiced. I told him I would get him some orchestrations. He said his sergeant was a piano player, so I said I'd get him some professional piano copies. I told him about my singing and announcer career, and as a result I did some singing and announcing with the camp orchestra. I wrote all of my publisher and song plugger acquaintances in Chicago, and they all responded with scads of music. I was the fair-haired boy from then on with both the captain and the sergeant.

One time we were on a field training exercise where we had to carry supposedly wounded soldiers on stretchers. As I was passing a bush someone yelled, "Hey, Nelson, come here." I went behind the bush and sitting there, well hidden from view, was the captain holding a pint of whiskey. He said, "Sit down have a drink. The sergeant's in charge—let the other guys do the work." I had one drink, he had two. We sat there quite a while, discussing music. When it was almost time to go back to camp and the coast was clear, we rejoined the group.

Each barracks at the camp took turns at doing Kitchen Police (K.P.) duty in the communal kitchen. It was necessary to get to the kitchen an hour earlier then regular reveille to get things going. The first time it was our barracks turn for K.P. we were in the kitchen about two hours when the sergeant came in. When he saw me he yelled "Who in the hell put Nelson on K.P? Nelson, come with me!" When we got outside I said, "Sergeant, I've got to live with these men. Please let me go back, I don't mind doing K.P." I went back and always did my regular turn from then on.

Once when we were on a long march on the highway, I was near the front of the line when a car pulled up in front of us. An officer got out, ordered us to halt and yelled, "Private Nelson, step out." He told me we were going to the WAC's camp in Sweetwater, Texas, to entertain the girls there. As we passed the men I jokingly thumbed my nose at them. They got a kick out of it. It wasn't too long a ride, and our Camp Barkeley orchestra was there when we arrived. If someone had a gripe at camp they would usually say, "blow it out your barracks bag." I took the saying literally and wrote a song about it. It was one of the songs I sang for the girls. I found out later that what it really meant was blow it out your ass. I don't know whether or not they knew the true meaning, but they did laugh a lot while I was singing it. I also did a short sex skit with one of the girls; she was a beauty and really tried to arouse me, knowing, of course, that it could lead nowhere.

In our barracks was a young man from New Jersey. He said his father owned a New Jersey baseball team. He had a rather thick accent and one of his favorite sayings that I still get a kick out of was, "Ah, it is spring and the boids are on the wing. How absoid, the wings are on the boids." Another member of our barracks was from the Appalachian Mountains in Kentucky. He could neither read nor write. I read his mail to him and wrote his answers for him. The Appalachian Mountains were, and I guess still are, one of the poorest areas in the nation. Even though he sent his wife most of his pay, she was constantly complaining about the hardships she was having because of the lack of money. One day after I read her letter he said, "Ken, I'm going to desert. I've got to make more money." I said, "John, if you do that they'll find you and put you in prison, and then where would your wife be?" I told him he could make more money right here at camp. "Most of the men, including me, hate doing their laundry and would be willing to pay for having it done. I'll be your first customer." "He took my suggestion and was soon doing laundry on his days off and every spare moment he had. He sent the extra money to his wife; her letters were more cheerful, and he seemed to be happier.

I recall Joe Lewis, who was then the World's Champion Heavyweight Boxer, coming to camp and putting on a boxing exhibition. I think he was enlisted in special services to put on exhibitions and give speeches throughout the nation and probably overseas. He was terrific.

The toughest part of my basic training was doing calisthenics and the obstacle course. I was now thirty-two years old and had never exercised, with the exception of swimming during the summer months. The obstacle course was really rough, especially crawling under a wire about two feet off the ground, on my belly, with full gear. After about a month or so the aches and pains disappeared. I lost about twenty pounds and I began to enjoy the challenges of the exercises.

An army regulation was that if you had sexual intercourse with a prostitute you must report to the medical center and have an antibiotic injected into the channel of your penis to prevent a social disease. I presume there were houses of prostitution in Abilene because many of the men would go there on the weekend. I never did, but the medical center was sure one busy place on weekends.

After two months of basic training a group of us were transferred to Fitzsimmons General Hospital in Denver, Colorado, for our medical training. We arrived late at night, had roll call, were assigned our barracks, our bunks, and as we had eaten on the train called it a day. In the morning when we went outside for roll call and calisthenics, I was flabbergasted by the beauty of the snow-capped mountains. We attended class daily. Blood plasma and penicillin were relatively new discoveries, and the military services were one of the first to use them. There was a tremendous lack of female nurses, so we were taught how to give penicillin and other shots by injecting each other with a hypodermic needle of sterile water. Our instructions included how to give plasma, catheterize, resuscitate, other medical procedures, and about the various medications. In essence we were male nurses and were jokingly called ninety-day wonders, or bedpan commandos.

Entertainments for the hospital, the trainees, and soldiers from a nearby camp were held frequently in the hospital auditorium. I sang there two or three times. Once when I sang "Blow It out Your Barracks Bag" some of the men in the audience yelled out the title line with me. There was usually a famous orchestra or performer on the program. One that I particularly remember was the world famous violinist, Jascha Heifetz. The audience loved him and wouldn't let him go; he had to play several encores.

We finished our medical training about the middle of March. At a graduation ceremony we were told that the top students were to get a special privilege. That privilege was we were given the honor of going on duty that night. I and several others were chosen. Two of us were assigned to orthopedic Ward C, which was one of the ward buildings outside the main hospital. We were told to report to the nurse in charge at 6:00 P.M. Our shift was from 6:00 P.M. to 6:00 A.M., and we would take turns relieving each other during the long night. When we got to the ward our lieutenant nurse was standing by the bedside of a patient with a hypodermic needle. We told her our names and that we were reporting for the night shift. She handed me the needle and said, "Give him his shot." He was lying on his stomach with his buttocks exposed; it had been punctured so many times it looked like a sieve. These were penicillin shots that were to be given every three hours, as he had osteomyelitis of the knee. I started to put the needle in as we had been taught, at an angle to avoid hitting the bone. The nurse said, "Straighten that needle." I said, "But we were taught...." She interrupted, saying, "I don't care what you've been taught, straighten that needle out." I did.

She showed us the kitchen, told us the penicillin was kept in the refrigerator, and showed us the cabinet where the medications for the other patients were kept. When she left she said she was in charge of other wards and would be back periodically to see how things were going.

Many of the patients were from the ski training camp, Mount Hood, in the Cascade Range in Oregon. I don't recall how many patients there were. Most had broken legs, knees, arms, and so forth; a few were ambulatory. There were private rooms for officers. We spent a couple of hours meeting the patients, learning what their medications were and at what intervals to give them. About eleven o'clock I took a three-hour nap and then relieved my partner, I don't remember his name. He told me that he had given the osteomyelitis patient his twelve o'clock shot.

I went to the kitchen to prepare for his 3:00 A.M. shot. The penicillin bottle was empty. I got a new one, punctured the rubber cap with the syringe and filled it. As I withdrew the needle the penicillin oozed out onto the floor. I was panic stricken. I had done something wrong, and I would be late in giving the shot. I started to cry. I cried and cried and cried; I couldn't stop, I was scared to death that someone would come in and see me. I finally got hold of myself, successfully filled the syringe, and gave the patient his shot. I never had a bit of trouble after that.

I really enjoyed what I was doing. Most of the male nurses did not. I got along famously with the patients. If one of the men said he hadn't eaten much for supper, I'd get him something to eat. All visitors were supposed to leave the ward at 9:00 P.M. I'd let them stay till close to ten when our nurse, who was quite punctual, would come to check on us. Once when I opened the door to a captain's private room to give him his medication, he was in bed with a woman. I presume she was a prostitute. I should have said, "Second or snitch." I didn't say anything. I closed the door and when she left I took him his medication. He begged me not to mention this to anyone. I assured him I wouldn't and I didn't. There was a picture of a woman and two children on his dresser. I presume it was his family.

For quite some time I was having an odd feeling in the pit of my stomach that caused me to be nervous, especially just before I was to perform. I thought it was the anticipation of performing, but it became quite consistent. I went to the doctor in the main building. He gave me an X-ray barium test. It showed that I had stomach ulcers, and that was the end of my six month army career.

I was discharged April 9, 1944. After the X-ray he gave me a medication called Sippi Powders, and on the day I left he said, "I noticed that you're from Chicago. Dr. Sippi's son has a practice there. You should go and see him." He gave me his address. I would have preferred staying in the service because I liked what I was doing and felt useful and needed. On my return to Chicago I stayed with Mother for about a week and then went to visit my former landlady to see if I could get my old apartment back. All she had available was a ground floor kitchenette apartment with a Murphy bed. I took it.

I called Dr. Sippi and was given a 4 P.M. appointment. I was still wearing my army uniform, and when I got to his office there were a couple of patients in the waiting room ahead of me. As I was waiting a couple more people came in. The doctor asked me if I would mind waiting until he finished with them. I said I didn't mind. It was a little after five, and everyone had left but the doctor and me. I went into his office and told him that the army doctor suggested I see him because he was Dr. Sippi's son and that I had been taking Sippi's powder for my ulcers. He said, "Those powders aren't worth a damn, they're nothing but an antacid. I don't know how the army even came to use them." He asked me a few questions about myself and then started to tell me about his troubles, which included family and finances. I made an effort to console him. I left his office thoroughly confused; he hadn't given me one bit of advice about my ulcer. It was obvious that he was downcast and wanted someone to listen to his problems. A story in the next morning's newspaper was a real shocker. Dr. Sippi had committed suicide by carbon monoxide poisoning. He left his car running in his closed garage. I've often wondered if there was some way I could have helped him.

If a person left his or her job to enter the military, their employer was obligated, upon that person's release from the service, to re-employ them in their former position. Lee Gillette who had taken over as musical director of WJJD when I left and was now married and had two children. I was single and had no obligations. I decided to let Lee keep the job and go to California. When I told the station manager of my decision, he said, "Ken, you can't do that because I need you here. We have a new type of broadcasting called FM (frequency modulation) and I need you to take charge of it." After some serious thought, I consented. FM sets were installed in the Chicago buses and in some department stores in the Loop. AM sets could not receive the broadcasts, and I don't think FM sets were available to the public as yet. There were no commercial announcements, so all I had to do was plan the musical programs for the day. It was shortly after I took charge of the FM station that Lee went to California and I was again musical director of WJJD. When he was in Hollywood singing on the *Fibber McGee and Molly* show, every program was recorded for the cast to listen to. It was recorded in a studio owned by Glenn Wallichs. Lee was the one who always picked up the recording. He and Glenn became good friends. In 1943, two well-known song writers, Buddy De Sylva, Johnny Mercer, and Glenn Wallichs formed a record company which they originally called Liberty Records, but they soon changed the name to Capitol Records. Glenn was president; he came to Chicago on business and looked up his friend Lee Gillette. When they met and Lee told him that he was musical director of a radio station, he said, "You're just the man I'm looking for to head our transcription department." Transcriptions were sixteen-inch discs with five selections recorded on each side. I think of them as the forerunner of albums. It was a service rented to radio stations, providing programs, scripts, and guaranteed to issue so many musical selections a month. Capitol was the forth major service to enter the field. There was World, owned by Decca Records, Standard, and Langworth.

Lee left for Hollywood but didn't take his wife, Edie, and the two children with him. He wanted to make sure the job was to his liking.

After about four months he came back to move his family to California and to do some recording for the Western Hillbilly section of transcriptions. There was no doubt he was in seventh heaven. He would be producing all types of music, including such stars as Nat King Cole, Duke Ellington, Pee Wee Hunt, The King Sisters, Gene Krupa, Peggy Lee, Alvino Rey, Tex Ritter, Stan Kenton, Merle Travis, and many others.

One evening before he left, we were in the kitchen of his apartment drinking scotch, Edie was in the living room listening to the radio, and the children were asleep. Knowing that I had written many songs he asked me if I had any country songs. I said, "No, but give me a title and I'll write one." He jokingly gave me the title "My Brother's Will." I wrote the entire song in less than a half-hour. He recorded it with Wally Fowler. He and his family moved to California, and he bought a home in the San Fernando Valley.

While in the army I had no contact or relationship with a woman, and when I got out, my male instincts were bulging at the seams. Radio stations still had to purchase phonograph records, and when I went to the Cable Piano Company store to buy them, I became infatuated with a petite, pretty saleslady, whose name was Nuwana. She was a piano student. She knew who I was because she used to listen to me when I was announcing the Symphonic

Hour of WAAF. We became quite friendly, but although I wanted to I never asked her for a date.

A few weeks later the girl who was my secretary left to get married. I asked Nuwana if she would like the job. I told her what it entailed and she accepted. I was thrilled. She learned the details of the job quickly. Some days after hours she would go in one of the studios and play the piano. I would sit beside her and my heart would go thump, thump. I never made any advances or told her of my feelings, but I think she surmised. I guess I was waiting for her to make the first move—she never did. It wasn't long before I realized this was just an infatuation and this girl was not for me.

It was the month of October 1944 when I met the wonderful, beautiful, talented woman who was to become my wife and change my whole being. Oddly, it was through Nuwana that I met her.

Her name was June. She was a student at the Sherwood Music School, an accredited college, and had earned a bachelor's degree in music, majoring in voice. She worked part time at the Cable Piano Company and became friends with Nuwana.

Nuwana's piano teacher had died. She asked for the day off to attend the funeral. June was to meet her at the studio and go with her. June arrived at the studio before Nuwana, and the receptionist called me and told me that she was waiting in the foyer. I went out to tell her that Nuwana had not yet arrived.

She made an immediate impression on me. I asked her if she would like something to read; she declined. When Nuwana arrived and they were about to leave, I invited them both to dinner that evening, and they accepted. It was a very pleasant evening. We talked about the war, music, and various other subjects. June was also a listener of the *Symphonic Hour* and knew who I was. Her mannerisms, poise and intelligence really impressed me. One of my most embarrassing moments was when I went to pay the tab. I was about five dollars short. June lent me the five and said as her school, which was in the auditorium building, was a short distance from the studio, she would come up and I could repay her.

I never in all my life had asked a girl for a date, but when June came to collect her loan, I did ask for a date. She turned me down. I wasn't in love or even infatuated, but there was something about her that made me want to know her better. I called the manager of Cable Piano and got her phone number.

She was surprised when I called and again turned down my request for a date. I called again and was turned down. For some reason or other I couldn't get her out of my mind. The third call was successful. She said she was under the impressions that I was dating Nuwana, which I vehemently denied. I told her I had thought of dating Nuwana but had lost all interest in doing so.

About six weeks later, Nuwana seemed to lose interest in her job. She started coming in late and leaving early. I had asked her several times to please be on time and not to leave until she was supposed to. She continued the same pattern, and as this was setting a bad example for the other employees, I had to let her go. I think she wanted to leave.

I don't recall when June and I went on our first date. We soon started going out quite frequently—dinners, movies, concerts, and football games. After the third date, she let me kiss her goodnight—that was in the foyer of the apartment building at Seventy-Eighth and Colfax, where she lived with her parents. Sex never entered my mind. She invited me to meet her parents, Dr. and Mrs. Fred Felcher, and to join them for dinner on Thanksgiving Day. I accepted. It was a pleasant day. I learned that Doctor Felcher was a dentist and had a ceramics factory where he manufactured false teeth. I learned later that Doctor Felcher's parents were born in Czechoslovakia and were of the Jewish faith. Mrs. Felcher, Bernadine, was of English heritage, whose ancestors came over on the Mayflower. They were married in 1921, and June Rebecca Felcher was born September 7, 1923.

June had been dating a distant relative who was a farmer. He had asked her to marry him. She told me she had her last date with him in December, told him she had no desire to become a farmer's wife and that she would not be dating him anymore. She didn't tell me his reaction. I invited her to dinner and to see the play *Voice of the Turtle* on New Year's Eve. It was an enjoyable evening and I did get to kiss her at midnight.

I had joined the American Federation of Radio Artists (AFRA), which later became (AFTRA) American Federation of Television and Radio Artists. In 1945 AFRA held a formal ball in the Drake Hotel. I, of course, was wearing a tux and she was ravishing in her evening gown. While we were dancing and I held her close to me, I knew right then and there that this was the girl I wanted to hold in my arms forever. I had never had a feeling like this before, a feeling of calmness, contentment, a feeling of this is right. I knew that for the first time in my life I was in love. It was a wonderful evening. We took a cab to her apartment. I didn't express my feelings, but when I kissed her goodnight in the foyer, I'm sure I held the kiss quite a bit longer than usual.

The next few days were hectic. I was in a mental turmoil. I was sure I wanted to marry her, but I was twelve years older than her and had been divorced. Would she laugh at me, think I was a fool, turn me down? I finally overcame my feelings of inferiority and insecurity and decided to propose. A few days later I invited her to the College Inn, a popular nightclub in the Sherman Hotel, which featured the top orchestras of the day. This night it was Les Brown's orchestra. We had dinner but I ate very little. I was nervous, jittery, unsure of myself. I kept drinking, trying to work up enough courage to pop the question. I was pretty inebriated and finally did ask her to marry me. I don't know how I phrased the proposal. She lowered her head and didn't say a word. I think she surmised what I was going through. We left almost immediately without either of us uttering a word. The taxi ride to her apartment was also in silence and I didn't kiss her goodnight. The next couple of days I was miserable. I knew that I had bollixed the proposal. I felt she was disgusted with me and would never want to see me again. I couldn't get her out of my mind. She was the one I wanted to be my wife, and I felt I would be a good and loving husband.

It was three or four days, on a Friday, before I got hold of myself and phoned her. I apologized for my behavior and asked if she would have dinner with me that evening. She was pleasant, seemed unperturbed by my behavior, and accepted my invitation. We had dinner at the Morrison Hotel, and each of us had only one glass of wine. I told her that I thought she was beautiful, talented, a wonderful person, that for the first time in my life I was truly in love, and that if she married me I would do my best to make her happy. I held her hand and said, "June, will you marry me?" She smiled and said, "Yes. I didn't answer you the other night because I didn't know whether it was you or the liquor talking," but she didn't say, "I love you, too." I was thrilled, excited, anxious, on cloud nine. During the cab ride home she snuggled in my arms and we talked of wedding plans. I told her I wanted to meet with her parents. I felt it was only right that I ask their permission. June already knew that I was twelve years older than she and of my previous marriage, but I felt her parents should know and that I should be the one to tell them. She agreed.

When I met with them (her father, Doctor Fred Felcher, a dentist, and her mother, Bernadine), I told them of our age difference, of my disastrous marriage, that as a musical director of a radio station, I was earning an adequate salary. I told them that I truly loved June and together we would have a good life and a happy marriage. I then said, "I hope you will grant me permission to take your daughter's hand in marriage." We talked for about a half hour, and then Dr. Felcher said, "Our main concern is June's happiness, and if marrying you is her desire, we're sure she's made the right decision and we accede to her wishes." Mrs. Felcher agreed. I left feeling happy and relieved. June, her mother, and I met the next day to make plans.

I don't recall why or who picked the date of March 6, but that was it. It was the middle of January and there was a lot to do. Mrs. Felcher would make arrangements for the wedding ceremony and reception at the Presbyterian church which she and June attended and also take care of the catering. We had to send out announcements and get a medical examination. When we took the examination, the doctor (Dr. Greene) told us that June would have difficulty in becoming pregnant, that it would take a long time, possibly ten years. My evil mind thought, *Oh boy, smooth sailing*. Before we took the medical exam we had discussed the subject of children and decided we would like to have two, but would wait two or three years.

June chose one of her classmates from her music school as bridesmaid, and I chose my friend Reg McHugh as best man. We went to a jewelers where I purchased a palladium tailored star sapphire ring with a center stone and a mounting set with four diamonds for her engagement ring and a white gold fishtail wedding ring set with seven large diamonds. It was to be a double ring ceremony. My ring was a dove-tailed white and yellow gold ring. I still wear it.

It was February and June gave a vocal concert at her school which was well attended, including me. I was impressed by her stage presence and beautiful voice. She had won first place in an amateur singers contest on radio station WGN, singing "The Lord's Prayer." The orchestra was conducted by Victor Young, who later became famous in Hollywood for his musical film scores and his conducting. I still have the acetate recording which I transferred to tape. She had informed me that she intended to continue school and earn her masters degree. I readily assented.

I went to a tailor and had him fit me for a tailor-made suit of Oxford Grey for the wedding. June bought a suit, which I didn't see until the wedding. I still have both suits.

I was still living in the one-room kitchenette, not ideal living quarters for a couple. You'd be constantly bumping into each other. About three weeks before the wedding we started looking for an apartment. The war was still raging, and apartments were almost impossible to find. We went to three real estate offices before we struck pay dirt. We told the lady in charge that we were about to get married and were having difficulty in finding a place to live. At first she said she had nothing available. We were about to leave when she said, "Oh, just a minute, I have an apartment that I was going to take myself, but I'll let you have it as a wedding present. It's a four-room apartment on Yates Avenue between Seventy-Seventh and Seventy-Eighth Streets. It's on the first floor, and the rent is $48.00 a month." We would have taken it sight unseen, but she insisted on taking us to see it. The rooms were small but adequate. The living room had a closet for a Murphy bed, but the bed had been removed. We went back to the office and signed the lease. She gave us the keys and we thanked the lady profusely.

June had the task of buying the furniture and the necessary utensils, which I'm sure she enjoyed. She accomplished this feat in less than two weeks. It seemed like it would never get here, but finally our wedding day, March 6, arrived, along with a snowstorm of blizzard proportions. It wasn't a sumptuous wedding, but in spite of the snowstorm it was fairly well attended by many of June's friends and relatives and a few friends of mine from the broadcasting industry. Lee was in Hollywood but Edie hadn't yet joined him, and because of the storm she didn't attend. I guess my mother didn't show up for the same reason. The ceremony went smoothly in spite of my nervousness. Reg was best man and Doctor Felcher, June's father, gave the bride away. After the ceremony the reception was held in the large entertainment room in the church basement. June was kissed by quite a few friends and relatives, but nobody kissed me, they just shook my hand. The catered food was excellent. Meat was scarce because of the war, so we had fish, side dishes, a delicious cake, and a non-alcoholic punch. After about an hour June and I left, leaving the presents to be taken care of by Mrs. Felcher.

I had previously made our wedding night reservations at Chicago's largest hotel, The Stevens, which had been taken over by the army but had recently been conveyed back to civilian use. Our room was $12.00 for the night. We took a taxicab to the hotel. I felt I was the luckiest man n the world. Outside of holding hands, hugging, and kissing, I had never had any sexual experiences with June, so I guess it was normal that I was anxious and anticipating. I'm sure she was, too. Because of the snowstorm, traffic was slow and it seemed like forever before we got to the hotel and checked in. When we entered our room there was a lovely bouquet sent by some of the staff of JJD. I tipped the bellhop, he left, and we were alone at last. I could tell June was shy and a bit apprehensive. We talked for almost a half hour. We both calmed down, and then came the time to consummate the marriage. She went in the bathroom and put on her nightgown. I got into my pajamas. When I saw her in her nightgown, I was breathless. How could this beautiful, wonderful, intellectual person marry insignificant me? We got into bed and, not wanting to rush her, we made love for quite a while and then consummated the marriage. We both reached a climax and then went to sleep with her in my arms. Just holding her was an ecstatic feeling that I had never had before.

We had planned to stay in the hotel just for our wedding night and then to leave for our five-day honeymoon destination the next day, so we had brought sufficient clothing. I had made reservations at the lodge in Starved Rock, an Illinois state park which was a short train ride from Chicago. Starved Rock got its name from a legendary incident that had occurred in the 1760s.

A small group of Illinois Indians lived in the area. One of them murdered the chief of another tribe. Seeking to avenge their chief's death, the tribe attacked the Illinois village, wiping out half the tribe. When the avenging Indians went to regroup, the Illinois realized they were in dire straits and decided to seek refuge on top of the great rock. When the avenging Indians returned they surrounded the rock. If an Illinois Indian tried to sneak off the rock at night, he was killed. Eventually all of the Indians on top of the great rock starved to death, and ever since the site has been called Starved Rock.

Just being together made our stay at the lodge most enjoyable. The rooms were pleasant, the services good, and the food was excellent. I recall it was the first time I had grilled salmon, and it's still one of my favorites.

The weather turned mild and we were able to go outside, enjoy the beautiful scenery, and hike along the Illinois River. In the evening there was usually a social gathering of guest in the lobby. June had lost some of her shyness and, like most newlyweds on their honeymoon, we wanted to make sure our marriage was legal, so we re-consummated our marriage several times.

As all good things must come to an end, our honeymoon was over. We took the train back to Chicago and to our apartment. I unlocked the door and carried her over the threshold of our home. We unpacked and checked the apartment. We had informed the electric and gas companies when to start service, so we had lights and gas. We talked a while and then went out to dinner. As it had been a long day, we came home and went right to bed. We were sound asleep when, at 5 A.M., we were awakened by people walking in the bedroom above us. This happened almost every morning. We usually went right back to sleep, so we learned to live with it. We found out that there were two elderly ladies living above us. The next morning we went out for breakfast, then I went to work. June went shopping to fill the larder and to wait for the iceman to fill the icebox and have him start our weekly delivery service. He always came at the same time, so we had to be sure someone was there to let him in. The grocery store we shopped at, an Atlantic and Pacific (A&P), was about four blocks away on Seventy-Seventh Street. It was not a self-service store. The grocer stood behind a counter, and behind him were shelves lined with various food items. You pointed at, or told him, what you wanted. He would put the items on the counter, then total the sum with pencil and paper.

Clarence Saunders of Memphis, Tennessee, noticing that the present way of grocery shopping was a waste of time and man hours, conceived the idea of shoppers serving themselves. In spite of predictions of failure, he opened his first self-service store in 1916 and called it Piggly Wiggly. It became an immediate success. He formed the Piggly Wiggly Corporation, secured the self-service format, and issued hundreds of franchises to grocery retailers throughout the nation to operate under the Piggly Wiggly name. You entered through a turnstile, took a basket, did your own shopping amongst open shelves, went to the cashier, paid, and left through a turnstile. I don't know when other self-service stores began to appear, but for many years Piggly Wiggly was the only one in existence.

June and I were happy in our togetherness and our new home. We had made friends with a couple who lived across the court from us. It was with them I learned to play bridge. I enjoyed the game, and many evenings we would go to their apartment or they would come to ours and we would play.

June and I were both smokers. She told me when she was a teenager her mother had forbidden her to smoke and she had never smoked in her presence. I said, "June, you must smoke in her presence because she has to accept the fact that you are no longer a teenager but an adult who makes her own decisions." When her parents came to visit us one evening, I offered June a cigarette. She took it, I proffered a light, she puffed away, and neither parent made a comment. She had broken the ice.

We had been married a little over a month. It was April 12, 1945. I was at the station when the tragic news came that stunned the nation. Our president, Franklin Delano Roosevelt, age sixty-three, died of a cerebral hemorrhage in Warm Springs, Georgia. Our station immediately stopped all commercials and live music programs. It was all news, interspersed occasionally with moderate tempo classical recordings. This went on for two days. It wasn't easy going through our library finding recordings that weren't too funereal or too spirited, but I did. I presume the other stations followed the same pattern.

Harry S. Truman was now our thirty-third president, and the war was winding down. Deposed Premier Benito Mussolini was captured April 28 by Italian partisans and shot by a firing squad. On April 30, Hitler and his mistress Eva Braun committed suicide in a bunker in the bombed-out Reichstag building. Totally defeated, Germany capitulated May 6 and signed articles of surrender on V.E. Day, May 8.

The atomic bomb was developed by British and American scientists, and an experimental bomb was successfully exploded at Alamogordo, New Mexico on July 16, 1945. It was now President Truman's decision whether or not to use the bomb. He chose to do so, and on August 6 he ordered the bomb dropped on Hiroshima, Japan. It completely wiped out the city. Then, on August 11, a second bomb destroyed Nagasaki. Japan sued for peace and surrendered (September 1, September 2 Tokyo time, V-J Day) aboard the *U.S.S. Missouri* in Tokyo Bay.

Sometime in May a bomb was dropped on the Nelson household. June was pregnant. We were a little shocked because Doctor Greene had told us that it would be extremely difficult for June to become pregnant, so we had taken no precautions. Though the news was totally unexpected, it was not unwelcome. The doctor said he too was surprised and gave no explanation. June's parents were elated my mother was non-committal. June continued going to school until three months before the big event and our lives were quite normal. I do recall, about three or four weeks after June became aware of her pregnancy, a pharmaceutical laboratory called and asked if she would be willing to sell her urine. They told her a pregnant woman's urine was a necessary ingredient in a medical product. We discussed it and, because it was for a good cause, she agreed to do it. Once a week a bottle was placed on the back porch to be replaced by another bottle. I don't know how she filled it, but she did. I don't recall how much she was paid. I think it was five or ten dollars a week. Doctor Greene must have given her name to the laboratory. We bought a baby crib, signed up with a diaper service, and bought all the necessary essentials, so we were well prepared for the coming event.

On November 28 I got home from the studio about six o'clock. June had just taken a shower. She told me she thought she was having labor pains and that we had an appointment with Doctor Greene at eight o'clock. I called the doctor and told him of June's feelings. He replied, "Oh, they're probably just premature labor pains, bring her to the office at eight o'clock." Around 6:30, June's parents came. Her mother talked to June for a couple of minutes and said to me, "This girl is about to have a baby." She called Doctor Greene and in no uncertain terms told him June was about to give birth. He said, "All right, if it makes you feel any better, take her to the hospital." We packed a small suitcase with the necessary clothing and toiletries for June, and I, anticipating a long wait, took along some magazines and a carton of cigarettes. Doctor Felcher, June's father, drove us to the designated hospital, Michael Reese. We arrived about 7:45 and registered. I assured June's folks I would call the minute I heard anything and that I would wait all night if necessary. They talked with her awhile and left. She was in a wheelchair. I kissed her and said I would be in the waiting room.

I was trying to read and puffing away on a cigarette when I saw Doctor Greene rushing by. About fifteen minutes later a nurse came in and told me I was the father of a beautiful baby boy and that my wife had come through the delivery without any problems. I learned later that he was born a little before 8:30. When the staff found out that the birth was imminent they had called Doctor Greene and tried to delay the birth until his arrival, but it was too late; the baby arrived before he did. It was over a half hour before I was allowed to see my son and June. He was already in the nursery, and a nurse brought him to the window for me to see. June was in a semi-private room—she was still kind of groggy. I told her how thrilled I was, how much I loved her, what a beautiful baby we had, and that I would see her tomorrow. Knowing how tired she must be, I kissed her on the cheek and left. I went to the lobby and phoned June's parents. They insisted on coming to the hospital and driving me home. When they came they saw the baby, but didn't go into June's room because she was asleep by this time. When I phoned my mother to tell her the good news, I was shocked and hurt. She was curt and non-committal. I couldn't understand why. Maybe I woke her up out of a sound sleep.

On the way home I jokingly said, "Gee, I bet we've got folks counting on their fingers. Our baby was born eight months and three weeks before the usual nine months pregnancy period." I don't think either parent liked the remark too much; they made no reply. I was only trying to ease the tension and excitement of the evening. We already had a name for our son. June had bought a book of names. We had decided on Gregory if a boy and Claudia if a girl.

I could only visit her in the evening, but Doctor and Mrs. Felcher would visit during the day and she had a roommate to converse with. She was recuperating nicely and was anxious to get home. In about five days I brought my family home. I had previously done the grocery shopping, which was so much easier now because on November 23 the rationing of meat, butter, sugar, and other commodities had been lifted. As June was not going to breastfeed the baby, I had to make sure there was enough milk.

One evening, about a week later, June's parents dropped by. We were talking when I suddenly remembered we were out of milk. I excused myself and went to the store. When I came home her parents were gone and June was standing by the crib crying. I was scared to death. I said, "Honey, what's the matter?" She sobbingly replied, "My mother said I wasn't taking care of the baby properly." I was furious. I took her in my arms and tried to calm her. I went to the phone and called her parents. Her father answered. I said, "Don't you ever again come in my house and tell my wife she's not taking proper care of our baby." I hung up without giving him a chance to reply. This, of course, was undiplomatic, but I was angry at seeing June so upset. I realized later Mrs. Felcher probably was only trying to be helpful. For the next month or so they managed to visit June and the baby when I wasn't there, and as far as I know Mrs. Felcher gave no more advice. We shortly resumed normal relations and no mention was made of the incident. How Christmas was spent slips my mind, but it had to have been with the Felchers and my mother.

It was now 1946. I recall hiring a blind man who charged six dollars for tuning the piano and a cleaning woman who came once a week for five dollars a day plus carfare.

June was still determined to get her master's degree and attended school two evenings a week. I became quite proficient in taking care of Gregory. If occasionally she had a day class, Mrs. Felcher would baby-sit.

Things were going smoothly at the station, so I thought. Karl and Harty, a singing duet on *The Suppertime Frolic*, brought a young man in his early twenties to meet me. They said he was a great guitar player who had come to town with the Red Foley radio show, appearing at a local theatre.

His name was Chet Atkins. They asked me to contact Gillette and ask if Capitol Records would be interested in signing him. I got in touch with Lee and his reply was, "We already have a great guitar player–Merle Travis." It so happened that Merle was Chet's idol.

I was soon to have my first experience as a record producer. Lee had come to town to record some artists for the transcription department. He had recorded them all with the exception of Uncle Henry's Kentucky Mountaineers. The day before the session, Glenn Wallichs, the president of Capitol, called Lee and told him he had to leave immediately and be in New York the next day. Lee said, "But I have a session set for tomorrow." Glen replied, "I don't care what you've got set, you must be in New York tomorrow." Lee came to me and told me of his conversation with Wallichs, that he had the session set up. It was too late to cancel and he would have to pay the musicians and studio regardless. Would I do the session? I said, "Uh, okay, but what do I do?" Lee replied, "You've worked with this group, you know them, it's no problem." He showed me how to fill out the union contracts and session reports, so I did it. I was nervous, but it turned out okay. It was my first album. I was later called upon to do more emergency sessions.

It was shortly after that, that the walls came tumbling down. The station manager called me into his office, told me that with the exception of myself and the five record turners I was to discharge all other musicians. There would be no more live music. *The Suppertime Frolic*, the station's most popular program, was to be taken over by disc jockey Randy Blake. I sadly gave the musicians their two weeks notice.

Our library had a limited number of country records, which were used only on weekends. I really had to scramble to fill the needs of a daily record country show. All records were 78s. There were no tapes or 33 1/3 albums at that time. We had subscribed to the Capitol Records transcription library, which had a few country artists, and that was of some help.

The president of our local Chicago Musicians Union, James C. Petrillo, had now been elected president of the National American Federation of Musicians. The increasing use by radio stations of recorded music caused a devastating decline in the employment of live musicians. Mr. Petrillo tried to stem the tide by forcing the stations to replace canned music with live musicians. He called a nationwide strike. His efforts were stymied when Congress passed the Lea Anti-Petrillo act, restricting his powers. It was signed by President Truman and later upheld by the Supreme Court.

I was called and told to inform my record turners that we were on strike. After a few days I went to see Mr. Petrillo. I told him that two of my record turners were financially strapped and it was my understanding that the local had a strike fund to help those in need. He said, "Who told you that?" I replied, "Mr. Benkert, the secretary treasurer." His answer, "He don't know what the hell he's talking about, there is no such fund."

The strike was soon over and things got back to normal. I had built a sizeable library of country records, including Decca, Victor, Columbia, and a new label, King Records of Cincinnati. The program became more popular than ever because of the greater variety of artists and the showmanship of the D.J. Randy Blake. The fan mail increased two-fold, especially throughout the southern states. At the time the station was transmitting on 20,000 watts. The owners were intent on getting greater power and were granted a license to broadcast on 50,000 watts. In doing so they .had to turn the transmitter in a different direction to avoid interfering with another station. As a result their signal could no longer reach the huge audience they had in the southern states. This happened after I left, so I don't know whether or not they retained *The Suppertime Frolic*.

June and I decided we were going to build our home outside the city. We chose the suburb of Highland Park. In an area called Clavey's Corner we found the lot of our dreams. It was about half an acre, the only one in the vicinity with trees. They were aligned on one side the full length of the lot.

We paid three thousand dollars for it, which was a lot for a lot in those days. We now planned to spend ten thousand dollars for the home itself; at that time a good-size house could be built for that amount.

June continued going to college and on March 18, 1947 gave her graduation recital, which I proudly attended. She had earned her master of music degree. A few months after her graduation we decided that we should have another baby so our son Gregory would have a playmate and we stopped taking birth control precautions.

In addition to producing transcriptions, Gillette was also given the task of producing the country artists. One of the first people he met on joining Capitol was Cliffie Stone, a country music disc jockey, master of ceremonies of a popular country music television show in the Los Angeles area, and a bass player. Cliffie helped Lee in finding talent and musicians to back up the artists. He played bass on most of the sessions and did some recording and producing. Lee and Cliffie became good friends. They decided that because there were so many excellent songs available without publishers they should form a publishing company. Because Lee was an employee of Capitol and Cliffie a close associate, they didn't want Capitol to become aware of it.

Lee, knowing of my past and long involvement in the publishing business, suggested that they take me in as a partner. It would also give the company a Chicago address, and although I had done a couple of sessions for Capitol, I was not an employee.

The year was 1947. I was still musical director of WJJD when Lee phoned and asked if I would be interested in forming a publishing company with him and Cliffie Stone. I had met Cliffie when he and his wife, Dorothy, came to Chicago. I remember taking them to the Field Museum. I liked him. I jumped at the chance.

I incorporated the firm in Illinois and, wanting a distinctive trademark and name, June and I came up with Century Songs Inc., using the Alla Breve for Century, the treble clef for Songs and the bass clef for Inc. Each of us put in three hundred dollars for operating expenses. I bought a filing cabinet and a typewriter. Our first office was in the empty Murphy bed closet in the living room of our apartment.

Because Lee and I had worked together for so many years we felt my name should not be connected with the firm either. When June and I explained the situation to her father, Dr. Felcher, he agreed to let us use his factory at Seventy-Ninth and South Chicago Avenue, where he manufactured false teeth, as our mailing address. He also agreed to become president, to sign all contracts and correspondence, to open a bank account for Century, and to sign all checks. He did everything he possibly could to help us.

As he only lived a couple of blocks from us, he'd bring us our mail, and if there were contracts, checks, or correspondence to be signed he'd do that. I had songwriter's contracts and stationery with our logo printed. From my past experiences I knew how to copyright, have lead sheets made, sheet music printed, and to set up the bookkeeping for writers' royalties. June did all of the typing and became quite adept at bookkeeping. We were in business. The first song we published was "The Gods were Angry with Me." It was recorded by Eddie Kirk on Capitol and by an artist on Decca records. We applied, were accepted, and became a BMI publishing firm. Lee would send songs that he had recorded and, along with several of my songs that he had recorded, our catalog began to grow and we were soon on the way to financial stability.

The contract between all record companies and the American Federation of Musicians was due to expire at midnight, December 31. Negotiations had been going on for several months, but an amicable agreement could not be reached. During the negotiations the record companies, anticipating a strike, were recording as much as they possibly could. Capitol, knowing that I had previously done so, called and asked me to do some sessions for them. I produced my first hit record, "Buttons and Bows," with the Dinning Sisters, accompanied by the Art Van Damme Quintet. The record reached the number five position on the *Billboard* chart and remained there for sixteen weeks. I also produced an album by Art Van Damme's Quintet. He was an outstanding jazz accordionist and was well-received sales wise. I did several sessions for Capitol's transcription library, including the concert orchestra conducted by Rex Maupin who was one of the orchestra leaders on KYW where Lee and I used to sing. I snuck in two selections of mine, "The June Waltz," which I had written for my wife, and "When You Look in the Heart of a Rose." There were only a couple of recording studios in Chicago at that time and I had to scramble to get space. I was told that I had to be out in three hours whether I was finished or not because the studio was booked solidly and the next group would be waiting. It was hectic, but I managed to complete all the sessions on time.

It was before Thanksgiving that we discovered that June's physician, Dr. Greene, didn't know what the hell he was talking about. He had told us that it would take a long time for June to become pregnant. He was wrong the first time, and boom, here she was with child again. We were both overjoyed and hoped it would be a girl.

On January 1, 1948, James C. Petrillo, president of the musicians union, called a strike and said, "We're never going to make records, ever." The strike lasted fifteen months.

I soon fell back into my normal routine at the radio station, but with all the anticipation and anxiety I had had doing recording sessions, plus managing the publishing company, my ulcers were acting up. I was quite uncomfortable at times and would feel a nervousness in the pit of my stomach. I went to a specialist and he advised me to have a vagotomy performed—an operation that severs the vagus nerve. The vagus is a nerve that stimulates the hydrochloric acid that digests the food in your stomach. Anxiety and nervousness causes it to over-stimulate the acid, causing ulcers. I decided to have the operation but kept procrastinating because I had so many other things on my mind.

I continued writing songs and in 1948 I composed music to "The Pledge of Allegiance." The original text was written in 1892 by Francis Bellamy. In 1954 Congress approved adding "Under God" to the text. We had already published the original text, had mailed printed vocal arrangements to schools throughout the country, and Tex Ritter had recorded it. In 1955 I rewrote the melody. We published the new version and Tennessee Ernie Ford recorded it. In 1972 John Wayne included it in his album *America and Why I Love Her*. The song earned several thousand dollars, but I didn't feel that I should profit from something that belonged to America so I gave the royalties to the Meharry Medical College, which is basically an Afro-American school in Nashville, Tennessee.

Along with the melodies, I always had the title and the idea for a song, but most of the time I had trouble developing the lyric. The first lyricist I wrote with was Alan Surgal, who was a writer for *Broadcast Magazine*. I'm sure he could have become a top lyricist, but somehow we lost contact. I think he moved to New York. I don't recall how we met, but in 1947 I found myself writing with Billy Fairman. We wrote quite a few songs together, and he was the last lyricist I wrote with. He had a good sense of humor. Gillette recorded two of our songs, "Bats in Your Belfry," with Tex Ritter and "You Cooked Your Goose with Me" with Karl and Harty. I gave "Bats" to Ritter's publishing firm and Century published "Goose."

Lee and Cliffie continued to send songs. Along with the studio and publishing company, I was kept pretty busy and before I knew it the big event was here. It was Sunday morning, June 6, 1948. I had taken our son, Gregory, for a streetcar ride. When we got home, no one was there. June was in labor and Dr. and Mrs. Felcher had taken her to the hospital. I prevailed upon our bridge neighbor to drive me and Greg to the hospital, which he willingly did. When we got there my daughter, Claudia, had already been born. When I saw her I became panic stricken. I thought, *My God, what have I done?* Her hair, her face, the exposed parts of her body looked as if they had been painted with red ink. My fears were soon allayed when the nurse explained that several babies had been born that morning preceding Claudia. They had run out of the usual after-birth antiseptic, so they doused her with mercurochrome. It looked like red ink and was a widely used antiseptic at that time, but it is no longer available. It turned out that she was, and still is, a beautiful redhead. I tease her and tell her they never got all the mercurochrome completely washed out of her hair. June and I were now the proud parents of two beautiful children. We had decided that Gregory's middle name should be my name and Claudia's middle name Lee, my friend Gillette's nickname.

It was a couple of weeks later that I received a phone call from Glenn Wallichs, the president of Capitol Records. He told me that the country music department was expanding and Lee was to be in charge of that department exclusively. Because of my radio and programming experience, Lee had suggested that I be hired to take over the transcription department. He told me Capitol would pay all moving expenses for me and my family. My starting salary would be six hundred dollars a month, which with my overtime was actually less than I was making at the station. He said my salary would be raised to eight hundred dollars in six months. I told him I would discuss it with my wife and let him know.

When June was around eight years old, Dr. Felcher had moved the family to Los Angeles to join his brother in a joint dental practice. They were there for two or three years when the Depression struck and he moved the family back to Chicago where he had left an established dental practice. When I told June of Capitol's offer, she said her childhood memories of California were happy ones and that it would be a better environment in which to raise the children. I told her that if Sue, my mother, consented, I would want her to come with us. June had no objections.

Mother had retired and was now on social security. When I asked her she seemed pleased and readily consented. It was all settled—we were going to move to California. I phoned Mr. Wallichs and told him that I would be willing to take over the transcription department. He said he would like me to be there by the first of August. I told him I would be, but that my family would have to follow later. This meant that June would be burdened with the task of making all travel arrangements, having the furniture and household goods, the files, accounting books, and printed materials of Century Songs moved to the coast. With the help of Doctor and Mrs. Felcher she managed. Of course, she had to wait till I established residency.

Realizing that moving and the responsibilities of a new job would create a lot of tension and nervousness, I thought it best to have the vagotomy before I left. The operation was performed at Billing's Memorial Hospital, a division of the University of Chicago. Five days later I was on my way to the coast. I'm sure I was a guinea pig because the vagotomy was a comparatively new operation and for several years I was requested to fill out a questionnaire as to my present state of health. I did have diarrhea for a few weeks, but the nervousness and tensions in my stomach had disappeared. The operation has long been obsolete.

With the exception of my frequent trips to the lavatory, my three-day train ride was pleasant. When I arrived in Burbank I was met by Lee, who drove me to his home in the San Fernando Valley where I was to stay in his guest house until I found a place of my own. I was warmly greeted by Edie, his wife.

The next day I went with Lee to Hollywood and met Mr. Wallichs and Jim Conkling, the head of A&R, the artists and repertoire department.

Capitol's offices were on the northwest corner of Sunset and Vine above the Wallichs' Music City store. Behind a drugstore, across the street on the southwest corner, was an old Hollywood residence which Capitol had furnished and used to accommodate out-of-town artists and guests during the war. It was called the Chateau and had now been converted into the headquarters of the transcription department. The shipping department was on the first floor and my offices on the second. In addition to the shipping clerks, there were two other people working with me, one was my secretary, Caroline. I don't recall her last name, but she later married Hal Cook. The other person was John Seeley, a script writer.

Two days after I was ensconced in my office, Jim Conkling assigned me the task of getting Duke Ellington to cancel his transcription contract. We already had seventy selections by Duke. His contract had two more years to run and at a very high cost. I met with his manager and told him that we thought we had a sufficient number of selections by Duke and would like to terminate his contract. He said he'd discuss it with Duke and get back to me. When we met again he told me that Duke said transcriptions had become quite burdensome and he was willing to cancel the contract. We agreed to a $25,000 termination fee. Believe me, the company saved a bundle.

During my first week I did my first Hollywood session at Radio Recorders, where Capitol did most of its recording. I produced a Christmas album with the Starlighters, a vocal group. It was done *acapella* because the musician's strike was still in effect. John Palladino was the recording engineer. He did many of my later sessions—he was tops. He was not only a musician but had a fine sense of balance.

One evening when Lee was working I went into the main house. The children were asleep. Edie was in the living room very upset and on the verge of crying. She told me she had found out Lee was having an affair. When she confronted him he said he had been trying to break it off but the girl kept after him. He told Edie he loved only her, that he had succumbed in a moment of weakness and that he had no desire to break up his family. Edie suggested that if an outsider was to talk to the girl, he could get her to see the futility of the affair. When she told this to Lee he agreed, and I was the chosen outsider.

I phoned her, told her I was a friend of Lee's, and made a dinner appointment. When we met I could see why Lee had strayed from the path of righteousness. She was very attractive and well mannered. I told her Lee's wife knew about her, that for the sake of their two children she had forgiven him, and for the same reason, Lee had no desire to break up his marriage. I told her it would be useless to pursue the affair any further. She cried, said she loved Lee but understood the situation, and agreed not to pursue him any further. When we parted she thanked me and I thanked her. She kept her word and stopped pursuing him. The Gillette household got back to as normal as it could be, and as far as I know Lee never strayed again.

It was imperative that I find a house for my family, as June was already making preparations to move. In our Chicago apartment, no matter what window we looked out of all we could see was a brick wall. I had vowed that when I bought a home any window I looked out of I would see the sky, trees and flowers. I chose the San Fernando Valley because Lee lived there and it was still fairly pristine. After being shown houses for four days, I found one I fell in love with. It was in Studio City on Sunshine Terrace and only a block away from Ventura Boulevard. It was a Spanish style two-story house with three bedrooms. One bedroom with bathroom downstairs would be for my mother. The master bedroom, on the second floor, had an enclosed porch where the baby would sleep and a connecting bathroom to our son's room. The dining room had a fireplace; the kitchen was large with a breakfast nook. I think what really got me was the thirty foot long high-ceiling living room and the orange and lemon trees in the spacious backyard. There was also a utility basement with a furnace and a garage that was quite a distance from the house. The price was $19,000. I excitedly called June, described it to her, said it would be a perfect home for us, and asked for her permission to buy it. She said she would like to see it before I bought it. I, in my eagerness, said, "But it might be sold before you get here." She said okay reluctantly. Actually it turned out for the best because I was not yet driving a car and the bus for the twenty minute ride to Hollywood was only a couple of blocks away. I was really excited. I had always dreamed of owning a home, having a family, and taking care of my mother. I put a down payment of $1,782.00 on the house. I still have the receipt, and if I recall rightly, the interest rate on the mortgage was 5 percent.

As the musicians were still on strike, I was not doing any recording, but I was kept busy bringing the catalog up to date, planning programs, and anxiously awaiting the arrival of my family. Lee was surreptitiously recording country records. There was portable equipment in the office building, and at night the artists and musicians would sneak in and record.

Jim Conklin, our A&R chief, went to Paris, France, and recorded some concert music for the transcription library. Lee also went to Paris and took orchestra arrangements with him to be recorded as background music for vocalists. I remember him telling me that because of a fuel shortage the studios were extremely cold and everyone wore overcoats. The musicians all wore gloves and took them off only when it was time to play.

It was late in September when escrow closed, I called June, and she said she would wind things up in Chicago and let me know when she would be here. She called a few days later and told me that she had alerted my mother and that the furniture would not get here for three or four weeks after her arrival because it was coming by truck. This posed a problem. Where would the family stay in the interim? The problem was soon solved by Herb Monte, with whom I had become quite friendly. He was a partner in the music firm Johnstone, Monti. The firm was financed by Jim Kennedy, whom I had met several times. He owned six nightclubs in San Diego, and as it was a naval base, all of the clubs did an incredible business.

Herb told Jim of our problem and he said, "Have them come down here and stay, there's plenty of room." It worked out fine. Jim was in his fifties and his wife, Ona, was in her late twenties. She and June really hit it off and became close friends. Ona had a girl's baseball team made up of the waitresses from the clubs and June played on it while she was there.

There was plenty of room in the house. Mother and the children slept in one room, and June's room was where I slept when I came on weekends. It was a beautiful Spanish-style house overlooking the valley, and to us it was a mansion. It even had an elevator from the first to the second floor. Staying there was like being on vacation.

Our furniture arrived in a little over three weeks and June, the children, and Mother came to Studio City and stayed in a close-by motel until we could put the house in order. We had to buy additional furniture, a washing machine, and household accessories. We soon moved in lock, stock, and barrel. Our next big project was to buy a car. Most of the automobile factories had been converted to war-time production and were not yet back to their normal operation; however there were two cars available. It was either Plymouth or Pontiac, I don't recall which, or Studebaker. The Studebaker was the first really modern looking car, and June chose it.

Now that I was a full-time employee of Capitol, I felt we should disband the publishing firm because it might be considered a conflict of interest. Lee and Cliffie both disagreed, saying we already had a catalog, were becoming financially stable, and that many other producers had publishing interests. They convinced me not to disband. After several so-called stockholder meetings, we made important decisions. It was decided that Cliffie, who was well known in Hollywood as a country music disc jockey, was master of ceremonies of the popular country TV show *Hometown Jamboree*, was a recording artist, and played bass on recording sessions, was not a salaried employee of Capitol, so therefore there was no conflict of interest. He could openly be known as the owner of Century Songs, negotiate and sign contracts, and handle other business affairs. We elected him president and opened an office at 4527 Sunset Boulevard in Hollywood. June and I would continue to do all of the basic work, copyrights, bookkeeping, ordering lead sheets, printing, wrapping, and shipping sheet music when ordered, issuing royalty statements, and paying all the bills. We hired our first full-time employee, Cliffie's cousin, Buzz Carlton. When we transferred our bank account from Chicago to Hollywood, we elected him secretary-treasurer and gave him two shares of stock. June's father, Dr. Felcher, as president of the company, had signed all checks while we were in Chicago. He was most cooperative in transferring our account to our Hollywood bank and sent the mail still received at our old address. He owned a share of stock and we retained him as vice president.

Both Cliffie's and Buzz's signatures were now required on all checks. They would sign a large book of checks and Buzz brought them to our house. As go-between the Hollywood office and our Studio City home, he daily made the trip bringing us the correspondence, contracts, orders, and bills. He would pick up our mail, orders, promotion records, and send them from Hollywood. Buzz was invaluable; we couldn't have operated without him. I had the interior of our garage remodeled and converted it into an office and shipping room.

A 1948 historical event I recall is Harry Truman running for his second term as president. His opponent was the Republican governor of New York, Thomas Dewey. Most political writers and polls predicted Dewey the winner by a large margin. On election night the *Chicago Tribune*, one of the nation's largest newspapers, printed its most embarrassing headline. In oversized letters it read "Dewey Defeats Truman." I recall the picture of Truman smiling, holding up the paper after his overwhelming victory of 303 electoral votes to Dewey's 189.

We were now fairly well adjusted to our new environment, and June was happy with her new car. I had never driven a car, and one day when we were in an isolated area I asked her to let me try. I almost ran into a pole. She took over, and even when I learned to drive, years later, she always drove when we went out together. She was an excellent driver, so I didn't mind.

In January of 1949 a rare event occurred in the San Fernando Valley: it snowed. Being from Chicago this was nothing unusual for my family, but it was for the Valley families. There was a fairly thick layer of snow on the ground after midnight, and many parents, fearing the snow would melt before morning, got their children out of bed so they could see and play in it. Our street was a scene of frivolity with children and even grownups laughing and throwing snowballs at each other at one o'clock in the morning; however, the snow lasted for about three days. I, thinking the oranges on our tree would freeze, picked them. They weren't even ripe enough for juice, so I wound up throwing them away. Our lemons did freeze.

My grandfather passed away and my father was now sole owner of the lumber company. Remembering that Aunt Lillian had told me that Grandma had asked Father to promise to take care of me, I decided to write him and ask for a loan of $3,000.00. I explained that I had been hired by Capitol Records to take charge of their transcription department, which required me to move to California. I told him I was married, the father of a boy aged three, a baby girl ten months old and that we had bought a house and a car. I explained that

I was running short of cash and needed a loan for about a year to tide me over and would pay him interest. He never answered my letter.

With my father ignoring my request, we decided to sell our Highland Park, Chicago suburban lot. We ran an ad in the *Chicago Tribune* for two weeks, listed at the $3,000.00 price we paid for it, with no response. Being desperate, we relisted it for another two weeks at $1,500.00 and still got no response. Five years later we received a phone call from a Chicago real estate agent offering us $5,000.00. We took it.

In March of 1949 the musicians strike ended and I was back in the recording booth. As I had twenty-five artists, groups, and orchestras to record along with planning programs, I was kept pretty busy. I wrote musical themes for some of the programs and some special holiday songs. I put some with Century and some with Capitol's publishing firm. Lee, Cliffie, and I wrote several songs together using the pseudonym George S. Novak, which we had concocted from our names, Gillette, Stone, and Nelson. Lee recorded them all.

Magnetic tape recording technology had been invented by the Germans around 1939 or 40 and had been used in their radio broadcasts since 1941. We were still recording on acetate discs and had done some recording on wire, which was impractical because if it broke it couldn't be repaired. John Mullen, a United States major and an electrical engineer stationed in England during World War II, was a classical music fan. He would listen to the Berlin Philharmonic radio broadcasts and soon realized that the Germans had a sound recorder far superior to the acetate discs being used in America. He got the chance to examine captured electronic equipment in France. When he left the army in 1946 he got official permission to bring two of the recorders and tape back to America. Mullen improved his two German machines and demonstrated them to other engineers in May of 1946. In 1947 Bing Crosby heard about the machines and arranged an audition. He was so impressed he hired Mullen as his chief engineer and in 1947 began recording "Philco Radio Time" on tape. Two years later Mullen headed the Bing Crosby Enterprises, the team that built Ampex, the world's first working videotape recorder. It wasn't long before all recording was done on tape. If I recall rightly, Bing Crosby Enterprises was also responsible for the development of frozen orange juice.

In 1949 we formed an ASCAP firm and called it Snyder Music Company. Snyder was Cliffie's legal name; Stone was his professional name and most everyone knew him only by that name. Cliffie was now managing Tennessee Ernie Ford and we formed the company to publish songs he wrote and later the arrangements for the hymns he recorded for which he is still noted. Our first big hit was Ernie's "Shot Gun Boogie." This meant extra work for June and me as we were now handling the business and shipping of two companies.

I had some well-known artists I was producing on transcriptions, including Buddy Cole, who played piano for Bing Crosby on his broadcasts; tenor, Clark Dennis; orchestra leader, Frank DeVol; The Mellowmen Quartet, who did backgrounds on Walt Disney cartoons; Jan Garber's orchestra; Les Baxter's concert orchestra; and many other artists.

I produced a ballet suite "Festival of the Gnomes," by Camillo Ruspoli Di Candriano. He was an Italian prince who had been decorated for bravery in World War I and had served in the Italian parliament. He was a composer and devoted his musical career to the creation of music which would further the understanding and respect for his native country, Italy. When he died, his wife, Princess Di Candriano, moved to Cuba and bought an orange grove. Being determined to make her husband's music famous, she came to Hollywood, somehow got in touch with Les Baxter, and brought her husband's suite to him. He liked it and asked my permission to record it. I said okay. The princess was charming. She came to the sessions, and we became quite friendly. Knowing she had few acquaintances here, I invited her to our house for dinner. She thoroughly enjoyed the evening, especially the children. June and I visited her apartment and she showed us pictures of her husband, he was really handsome, and herself on their huge yacht. She kidded us about our small California oranges, saying that her Cuban oranges were the size of grapefruit. We took her to Cliffie's *Hometown Jamboree*. We went back stage; I introduced her to Cliffie and some of the artists. She was overwhelmed and said she had never seen a show like this, enjoyed it, and would never forget it.

The princess was impressed with our transcription recording and was so intent on having it released as a commercial album that she paid all expenses for the pressing and packaging of the album. It was released under the Capitol label. After she left Hollywood I never heard from her again and I often wonder what happened to her after the Castro regime took over Cuba in 1959.

A year or so before I took over the transcription department, Lee had a session with Pee Wee Hunt's Dixieland combo. They had finished recording what was planned for the usual three hour sessions and were about to put their instruments away when Lee in the recording booth opened the microphone and said, "Hey guys, we've got a few minutes left, why don't you jam something and I'll record it." They jammed four minutes of "Twelfth Street Rag." Lee didn't intend to release it because of its length, but one day he was assembling a Pee Wee Hunt disc and found he was short a selection. He reluctantly included it as the fifth selection on one side of the transcription disc. When it was released, the demand by record buyers for Pee Wee Hunt's "Twelfth Street Rag" was overwhelming. It was decided to release a record of it but it could only be three minutes of music because if it was longer it would be distorted. Lee decided not to have Pee Wee re-record it because it might lose the relaxed, devil-may-care, feeling this version had. This meant the four minute version had to be reduced to three minutes, which was no easy task because it was recorded on an acetate disc; however, Lee and our top engineer, John Palladino, accomplished it. When it was released, the record sold over a million copies. This made Capitol become aware of the value of air play, and we were now sending promotion records to practically all the radio stations. Since the beginning radio stations had had to buy any records they wanted and for awhile Victor had printed on their record labels *Not for radio broadcast*, but now all record companies were sending promotion records to the stations. This eventually put all transcription companies out of business. The stations reasoned, *Why should we pay for music when we get it free?*

This was the end of variety programming on radio because the transcription companies would send scripts along with various types of musical programs. The stations were now playing only the records sent to them by the record companies. Disc jockeys became the fair-haired boys and programs such as the top forty hits of the day became all the rage.

During my army days I entertained troops at Fitzimmons General Hospital in Denver, where I was stationed.

On November 19th, 1944 while attending The Aftra Ball at Chicago's Drake Hotel with June. I knew for the first time of my adult life, I was in love.

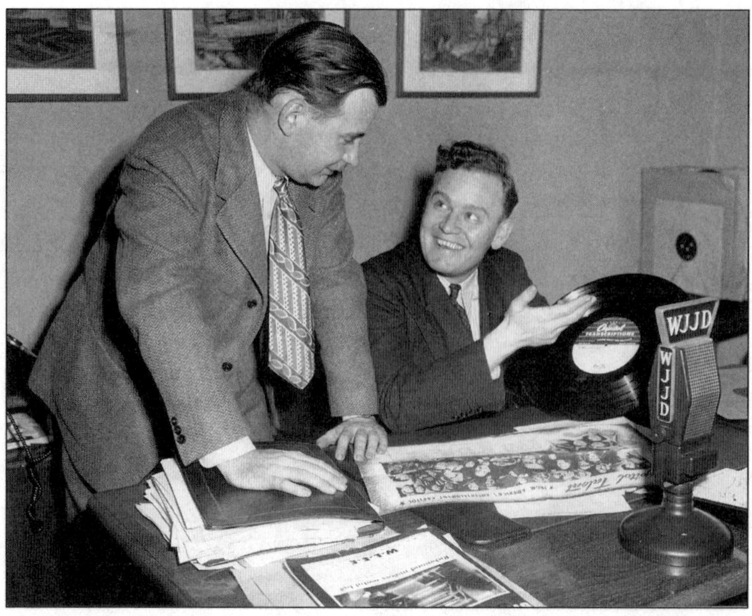

When Gillette moved to California to manage Capitol Records transcription department I resumed my position as musical director of WJJD. This photo shows Lee extolling the merits of Capitols transcription service. I bought the service.

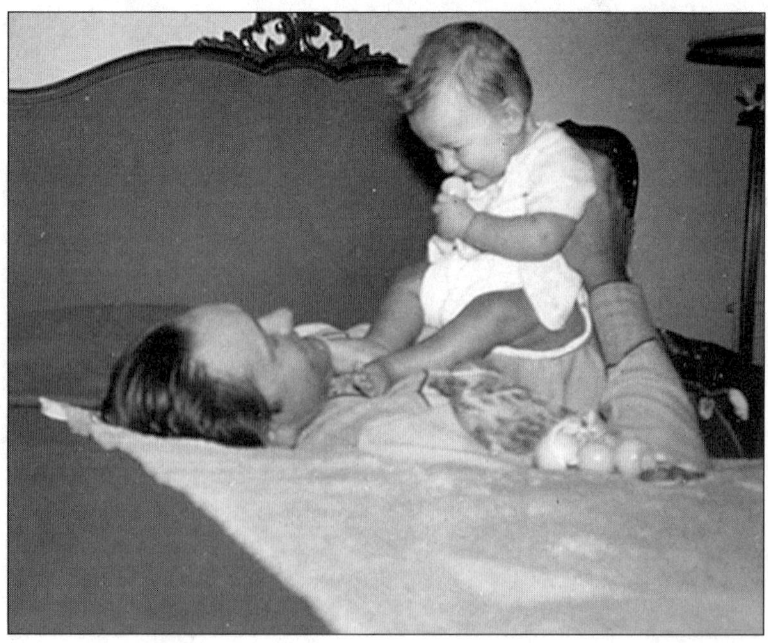

Tex Ritter and 7 month old son Tommy in 1947.

The only long time friends I had who were not involved with music, radio, TV. or recording were Reg and Elaine (Tina) Mc Hugh.

1951-1960

In 1951 Capitol decided that Lee should produce the popular artists exclusively and I should take over the artists who at that time were called "Hillbillies." All the record companies issuing records by artists of that type were listed under the category of "hillbilly music." All of the artists and everyone connected with that category, including me, felt it was a degrading term because it depicted a poor, unintelligent mountaineer with a jug of whiskey. Later the term "Country and Western" was used. When the Country Music Association was formed, we established the name "country music," which is now used world-wide. I will use the term "country" when writing about my artists.

This was my reply to a letter published in the *Los Angeles Mirror* newspaper titled "Hillbilly Junk" in August of 1951:

> August 16, 1951
> Editor of "Mail Bag"
> Los Angeles Mirror Newspaper
> 145 South Spring
> Los Angeles, California
>
> Dear Sir:
>
> This is in reply to a letter by Julia Kent in your column of August 13th entitled "Hillbilly Junk." Bigotry, no matter in what form, is ignorance and lack of understanding. All music no matter in what form is enjoyed by some groups of people. Therefore, we have no right to condemn any type of music just because we don't like it.
>
> Greatness, whether it be in medicine, science, art, or music, is that which does the most amount of good and is enjoyed

by the most amount of people. Hillbilly and Western music is a part of America. It was born in America and is pure, expressive American music. It has a greater audience in America than classical music because there is a larger number of people who understand and enjoy it.

In the words of Voltaire—"I may not like the music that my fellowman listens to but I will defend to the death his right to hear it."

Signed,
Kenneth F. Nelson (a Hillbilly)
11455 Sunshine Terrace
North Hollywood, California

My roster included Tex Ritter, who was the first country artist signed by Capitol, Hank Thompson, Merle Travis, and Tex Williams, who gave capitol its first country million seller, "Smoke, Smoke that Cigarette." Others were Leon Payne, Leon Chappell, Big Bill Lister, and the Statesmen, a gospel quartet. Lee kept producing two country artists, Tennessee Ernie Ford and Jimmy Wakely.

Cliffie Stone, who had brought Lee's attention to many artists, did some producing. Dee Kilpatrick, who started as a salesman and later became manager of our Atlanta branch, produced records by Hank Thompson, Leon Payne, Leon Chappel, James and Martha Carson, the Statement Quartet, and Big Bill Lister. Now I was to be the producer of all country artists, with the exception of the two Lee had decided to keep. This meant traveling, and travel I did. I did sessions in Dallas, Houston, Austin, Shreveport, Sioux City, Cheyenne, Minneapolis, Las Vegas, Lake Tahoe, New York City, Philadelphia, Atlanta, San Quentin Prison, London, England, and Tokyo, Japan.

Nashville, Tennessee, became my second home. I would be there for two and three weeks at a time throughout the year. If I had to go to Texas or Shreveport I would leave from Nashville and take a bus because most of the records on jukeboxes, throughout the south, were country. I wanted to hear what artists and songs were being played the most; it was a good education.

I was now an artist and repertoire producer (A & R man). My responsibilities were to find new artists and negotiate their contracts. If they didn't write their own songs or bring me suitable ones, I would find songs for them. I approved all songs to be recorded. If the artist didn't have his own orchestra, I would hire the background musicians. I would set the time, book the studio, and designate the recording engineer. In the recording booth I would sit next to the engineer and between us we would make sure the balances of the orchestra and voice or voices were correct.

At the beginning of each recording I would open the microphone and give a master number. We would re-do the record until both the artist and I were satisfied with the performance, although I had the final say. I had to make out a session report, which included the master and take numbers, the song title, the composers and publisher of the songs, sign the musician's contract, and turn it in for payment. The next day I would be sent acetates of the session. If I felt the equalization, the highs or lows, was not right, I'd get with the engineer and correct them. When the master was finalized I would set a release date and get with the promotion department. With albums, I would assemble them, six tracks on each side, meet with the art department, approve the album cover, and many times I would write the liner notes.

During the time I was a producer, to my knowledge there were no monetary advances or guarantees paid to an artist. The cost of their sessions would be deducted from any royalties earned. Only the cost of the musicians was deducted, not the cost of the studio or recording engineer. I started a new artist at a 3 percent royalty rate, and if their record sold one hundred thousand or more raise it to 5 percent which was the top royalty rate then. The royalty was based on the retail list price of a record or album.

After a period of time, if the sales of an artist's records were not sufficient to cover the cost of their sessions, I would be sent a report of their financial standing and a suggestion that I drop them from the label. If I really had faith in an artist I would ignore the suggestion, but after recording for at least another year, if there was still no sales reaction, I would drop them. A few times I let artists go who went to another label, had hits, and became well known.

We producers worked on a straight salary and didn't receive a bonus or royalty, no matter how many records our artists sold.

The Andrew Jackson Hotel, in Nashville, owned by Dinkler of Atlanta, was to become my home away from home for many years. The rooms were $6.00 a night and suites were $10.00 a night; I usually booked a suite. One time I had booked a suite for a three week period. After my second night, the manager, Leon Womble, told me I would have to move to a single room because of a convention being held so he needed the suite. I became upset and moved to the recently new Capitol Park Inn and though it didn't have suites, I was much happier there because it had a swimming pool. It became my home away from home for the remaining years of my career with Capitol, anytime I had to be in Nashville.

On my first arrival in Nashville, I met Joe Allison, who then was a country disc jockey. I have never forgotten Joe and still hold a warm spot in my heart for him because he took me in hand and showed me around town and introduced me to many important people in the business. I'll tell more about events in Joe's career in the time period in which they occurred.

The first artist I signed was Eddie Dean, who was a sidekick of Gene Autry's, and made several movies with him. Eddie had a beautiful voice but it wasn't country enough. After several releases I had to let him go because there was no sales response. Other artists I signed my first year were Jimmy Heap, whose big hit was "Release Me" and Skeet McDonald. His hit was "Don't Let the Stars Get in Your Eyes."

The most notable artist I signed my first year was not country. He was Stan Freberg, a comedic satirist who had a popular TV show *Time for Beany*. Cliffie Stone brought Stan to a session on which he was playing bass. Stan told me of his idea of a satirical version of a soap opera in which two lovers kept repeating each others' names in various passionate voices. He also had a satirical version of the song "When You and I Were Young, Maggie." I was impressed and said, "Okay, let's record them after this session." We had decided that we would only use an organ and a violin as background music. Billy Liebert, an all-around musician, was the organist, and Harold Hensley was the violinist. Stan did a little of "John and Marsha" for Billy, and he immediately sat down at the organ and composed a musical background for it. When we were finished I thought the record had great possibilities.

I had him come to my office the next day and sign a five-year contract. When I played the record for Jim Conklin, who was head of A & R, and Alan Livingston the producer of children's records and later president of Capitol, they were enthused. When I played the record for the head of the sales department, Hal Cook, who later became editor of *Billboard Magazine*, he was standing in front of a couch. After it was over he plopped down on the couch with arms folded and said, "What the hell are you throwing the company's money away for?" The record cost about $300.00 to produce.

Capitol had rented and was now recording in the abandoned radio station KHJ studios. It had a huge auditorium on the second floor with several hundred seats. I don't know how we got the audience, probably by giving away free records. When there were several new records to be released, usually about four or five, an audience was gathered and asked to vote for their favorites in sequential order. When "John and Marsha" was played the auditorium was filled with laughter and it was unanimously voted number one. It didn't sell a million but well into the hundreds of thousands.

I produced many hits with Stan and Billy May's orchestra, most notably an album *The History of the United States of America*. The only record of his I didn't produce was his biggest hit, which sold over a million, "St. George and the Dragonet." It was a takeoff on the very popular TV show *Dragnet* and was to be a rush release. The reason I didn't produce it was because Hank Thompson came to town and I had to record him on the same day and time I had scheduled Stan, because he was leaving the next day.

It was at that session that I produced Hank's and my first million seller. Billy May and his orchestra had been called for Stan's date, and if I canceled it we would still have to pay Billy and the musicians. I called Alan Livingston, told him of the problem, and he agreed to do the date.

Stan had written a satirical version about the commercialism of Christmas titled "Green Christmas." It turned out to be an hysterical record. A day or two after I put it on release, Glenn Wallichs, our president, called me into his office and told me the record should be taken off release because the board of directors had heard it and had objected to it because it ended with the orchestra playing hymns with a cash register ringing in the background. They were afraid that religious denominations would resent it and find the record offensive. I replied, "Glen, I think just the opposite, they will welcome and endorse it because it shows how commercial Christmas has become." He was standing directly in front of me, looked me straight in the eyes, and said, "Ken, do you really believe that?" I looked him straight in the eyes and said very emphatically, "Yes, I do." He replied, "Go ahead and release it." We received many letters and plaudits commending the record and it had excellent sales.

Stan's sessions were always a cause for anxiety. He was rarely on time for the session to begin, and that meant we would have to go overtime, which we usually did anyway. He was a stickler for perfection and would stay at home until the last minute checking and changing his script. Another problem was Billy May. He usually came to a session without having completed all of the orchestral arrangements, however, he always managed to get them done during the session. I also recall that almost every year I had to record Stan on the night of my wedding anniversary.

Because of the popularity of his album *The United States of America* I urged Stan to create a second album which would continue from the historical spot where it left off. He said he would but continued to procrastinate. I went to his home a couple of times and practically got on my knees and begged him, but to no avail. He had lost all interest in making records because he was now making TV commercials at which he became, and still is, very successful. Years later he did make the second album for another label, Rhino Records, which was released in 1996.

When I first went to Nashville, the Castle recording studio was the only one in town. It was owned and operated by three engineers who worked for radio station WSM, Carl Jenkins, Aaron Shelton, and George Reynolds. It was located in what was once the dining room of the old Tulane Hotel. During the two or three-year period, I recorded both Owen Bradley, a piano player, and Chet Atkins, guitar, who played on many of my sessions. Both Owen and Chet are mainly responsible for Nashville becoming the world center of country music, and both later became, without a doubt, the most talented and outstanding producers in the industry. Owen became head of and producer of Decca records in Nashville and Chet the same for RCA Victor.

It was in 1951 that Capitol invested a huge amount of money in a portable windup phonograph that was supposedly going to be a big and profitable seller. It was a big flop and caused the company a slight financial crisis. All employees were asked to take a 10 percent salary cut. June and I had my salary pinpointed down to the last penny. We had monthly mortgage and car payments, and along with the other household expenses, there was not a cent that wasn't accounted for. The publishing company was not yet in a position where we could draw a salary from it, so a 10 percent salary cut would have been disastrous. I made a list of all our expenses and took it to our president Glenn Wallichs. He looked at it smiled and said, "Don't worry, Ken, you won't have to take the cut." At Christmas that year the 10 percent cut was repaid and normal salaries resumed. I felt a little guilty and foolish.

In the early. years Capitol was a fun place to work. We'd have yearly picnics, and the A & R department and some executives along with the president would go on fishing trips. We also had sales conventions in various cities throughout the country and even had one in Puerto Rico.

In 1952 we enrolled our son, Gregory, in Carpenter Avenue grade school. There were several movie studio bit players whose children went there also, and about once a year they would put on a very professional play for the benefit of the P.T.A. Some of the student's mothers formed a mother's chorus, and June was chosen as director.

June's father, Doctor Felcher, had written a book, *Porcelain in Dentistry* that was reprinted in several languages and used as a textbook in dental schools. He spent six months in South America teaching the subject.

He had invented and patented a new method for making false teeth and had opened a factory to manufacture them. The factory was the original address of Century Songs. Doctor Felcher's dream of becoming a prominent figure in the manufacture of false teeth soon came to an end. At the time there were only two firms manufacturing them, and they were determined to maintain their monopoly. When he started to make inroads on their business they concocted a nefarious scheme. They had a firm in South America order thousands of sets of teeth. He hired extra help and worked night and day to fill the order. Thinking that because he had taught there and was well known in dental circles the teeth would be well accepted, he agreed to send them on consignment. In about a month they were all returned, and this, of course, left him financially strapped. He sold the factory and decided to move to California and open up a dental practice here so he and Mrs. Felcher could be near their daughter and two grandchildren.

When they came they stayed with us for about a month until they found a home. My mother had to move in with Gregory while the Felchers took over her room. She was not pleased and showed her displeasure in many ways. June had told me that while coming to California on the train, Mother had not been a very social person to be with and that although she had helped with the children, she had done so reluctantly. Doctor Felcher found a home about a mile or so from us and eventually resumed his dental practice in the valley. Mother moved back to her room but was still surly and morose.

Another problem soon arose. BMI had issued a license to a Century Record Company; there was also a Century Music Company in New York that dealt exclusively in classical music. We felt this would be confusing and decided to change the name of our company, but we wanted to keep our logo. We hit upon "Central" and after some research found there was no other publishing or record company with that name and we adapted it. It was a much better name anyway. We moved our office to 1483 N. Vine Street in Hollywood.

Of the artists I signed that year four would become popular and well known, Faron Young, Sonny James, The Louvin Brothers, and Merrill Moore. In Shreveport, Louisiana, radio station KWKH had a very popular country program, *The Louisiana Hayride*. Quite a few artists got their start there. Record companies were allowed to use their facilities to record. I was in Dallas and had to go there to record Leon Chapel and then return to Dallas. One of the musicians with whom I had worked said he had friends in Shreveport that he wanted to visit and would be happy to drive me there and back to Dallas when I was through. I finished on a Friday, and on Saturday as we were driving back to Dallas I turned on the car radio and heard this singer who I thought was terrific. I said, "I wonder who he is? I'd sure like to sign him." After his song ended the announcer came on and said, "You are listening to the Webb Pierce Program." Oh well, nice thought, but forget it. Webb records for Decca. A little later on the announcer said, "And now Webb Pierce will sing." It wasn't the same voice. I anxiously awaited the ending of the program to hear if they would announce the name of the unnamed singer. They didn't. I told the driver, "Turn around and go back to Shreveport. I've got to find out who that singer is." We checked into a hotel, and on Sunday afternoon I went to the station. I introduced myself to the disc jockey on duty, and after some casual talk I said, "By the way, who is that other singer on the Webb Pierce program?" he said, "Oh, that's Faron Young."

I didn't want to tip my hand because I had heard that if the station manager heard an artist was getting a record contract he would try to get him to sign an artist's contract. I didn't know if this was true or not, but I didn't want to take a chance. I had become quite friendly with Hubert Long, who at that time had his office in Shreveport. I liked and trusted him. He was the manager of Hank Snow, Johnny and Jack, and I'm sure some others. As I had to leave town, I decided to ask Hubert if he would get in touch with Faron and, if he wasn't with another label, to get him to sign with Capitol. He agreed. He then told me about a girl singer, the wife of Johnny Wright of Johnny and Jack. He said she was a terrific country singer and asked me to sign her. I thought, *Oh boy, he wants me to sign the wife of one of his acts*. I told Hubert that

I had no interest in signing girl singers because they were simply not selling. That was true at the time.

The girl was Kitty Wells, and she signed with Decca. Ironically, her first record "It Wasn't God Who Made Honky Tonk Angels" was a smash. It was the answer song to my first million seller, Hank Thompson's "The Wild Side of Life." Kitty was the girl who broke the ice for all country girl singers. Hubert not only got Faron to sign a Capitol contract but also signed him to a management contract. Hubert eventually moved to Nashville.

I did my first session with Faron in March of 1952. He continued to be an outstanding seller until he left us in 1962. His first release was "Tattle Tale Tears." His first hit was "Goin' Steady," which he wrote and which was published by Central Songs. If an artist recorded a song he had written and had not yet placed it with a publisher, I would suggest, but never insist, that they place it with Central Songs because it was an up-and-coming honest firm and, being in Hollywood, I could see to it that their record and song got the proper promotion. If Central or any other publisher had a song that I felt was for a specific artist, I would submit the song to him or her for their approval. Rarely did they refuse to record it.

Faron was a feisty and outspoken person and had no compunction about using foul language no matter who was present. He always treated me with respect, and if the occasion called for it he could be a perfect gentleman.

I had become quite friendly with Jack Stapp, the producer of the *Grand Ol' Opry* and although he didn't have a hit record, Jack agreed to give Faron a chance on the show.

When Faron came to Nashville for his first performance, his girlfriend Billie Jean, who was an exceedingly beautiful girl, came with him and they checked into the Andrew Jackson, where I was staying. On the night of his performance he called me and said he had to be at the Opry early for rehearsal and asked if I would bring Billie Jean over to the Opry later; I agreed. Around seven o' clock Billie and I walked to the Ryman Auditorium where the Opry was held. I felt a bit awkward conversing with her. We went backstage, and as usual it was bedlam with artists and musicians roaming all over the place.

In the producers booth, which was also backstage, were Jack Stapp, the engineer, Hank Williams, and a couple of other people. As we passed it Hank came out of the booth, stopped us, and said, "Hi, Ken. How about introducing me to your girlfriend?" I said, "Hank, she's not my girlfriend, she's Faron Young's friend," and I introduced them. I stayed with Billie Jean until after Faron's performance, which was very well received by the audience. He later soon moved to Nashville and became a regular on the Opry.

Hank and Faron had met previously. I don't know if it's true, but I understand they switched girlfriends that night. A short time later Hank and Billie Jean got married, but not for long because Hank died in December of '52. His death was tragic and unnecessary. I understand he had become addicted to morphine and on his way to a performance he visited a doctor and complained of back pain. The doctor accidentally gave him an overdose of morphine. He died in the backseat of the station wagon he and some of his musicians were traveling in. He was one of country music's all time greats.

This same year our country was still at war with Korea and Faron was drafted. Although he had no hit record up to this point, his career was beginning to take off because of appearances on the *Grand Ol' Opry* and the management of Hubert Long. Just before he left to report for duty Hubert and I met with him; he was pretty downcast. Hubert assured him his career would resume after his discharge, and I told him I would continue to release his records, to let me know when he was on leave and could come to Nashville and I would record him.

The military was always on the lookout for talent to entertain the troops and for recruiting purposes. After auditioning he was assigned to special services. He fronted a band called "Circle A Wranglers" that was sponsored by the army and heard over hundreds of radio stations.

In January of '53, I released "Goin Steady," which he wrote and which was published by Central Songs. With its exposure on the army show, it became his first big hit, reaching number two on the *Billboard* chart. While in the army he met his wife-to-be, Hilda, a beautiful, lovely, demure young lady. If I remember rightly, her father was a military officer.

After his discharge from the army in 1954 his next big hit was "If You Ain't Lovin, You Ain't Livin'." It was written by Tommy Collins and published by Central. It too reached number two on the *Billboard* chart and stayed there for 27 weeks. That was followed by his first number one hit, "Live Fast, Love Hard, Die Young," and that he did. The song was written by Joe Allison and also published by Central Songs.

His popularity soon led him to Hollywood in one of his several pictures he played the local sheriff. He liked the name and adopted it, calling himself the "Young Sheriff" and renaming his band "The Country Deputies."

Whenever he was in Hollywood he would occasionally come to my home. On his first visit I was a little concerned about his rough mannerisms and language; I needn't have been. His behavior was impeccable, as it was also at a luncheon held at the Hollywood Brown Derby, hosted by our president Glenn Wallichs. Present at the luncheon were Faron, Minnie Pearl, Tommy Collins, Hank Thompson, Merle Travis, and me.

Faron had good business sense. He published the first national country music publication *The Music City News*, which he later sold for a handsome profit. He also built a race track, Sulphur Dell speedway, and the first office building built by a country singer in the music row area. He also got me, Jim Reeves, Don Gibson, Porter Wagoner, and some other artists to invest in an oil well venture that caused me one of the most embarrassing moments of my life.

Miles Caraway, with whom Faron had gone to school, had this property in Shelby County, Texas, that he had had surveyed. He said it had great oil potential but he needed investors so he could start drilling. Faron assured us that Miles was an honest man and that from all indications this was one of the best investments of this type that he had seen and even the lawyers who drew up the escrow agreement were considering investing in it.

The plan was that after the first well came in each of us would invest in the second well and when that came in the third well and so on so forth.

A few weeks before I was asked to invest in this oil plan, while I was in his office, our president Glenn Wallichs received a telegram. He read it, smiled, and said: "My Oklahoma oil well just came in!" Remembering this, when I received the documents for the Caraway oil project I took them to him and asked if he thought this was a good investment. He looked them over and said "Ken, I think it is a good investment. Why don't you invest in the first well, I'll invest in the second, you in the third, I in the fourth and so on." I was pleased to hear this and agreed.

I hadn't met Miles Caraway but I wrote him about Glenn's interest. He answered my letter and said he was coming to Los Angeles and would like to meet me and Mr. Wallichs. Glenn said he would be happy to meet with him. At the meeting he told of the tremendous possibilities of the oil field and was so convincing that Glenn invested $25,000.00 in the venture. A few months later it turned out that Miles Caraway was a con man. I wrote to an attorney in Shreveport and asked him to look into this matter. He wrote back that he could not make any headway regarding this matter. He had on numerous occasions tried to have Mr. Caraway come to his office to discuss the matter. He'd promise to come but never showed up. A woman that he had swindled out of $28,000.00 had him put in jail but released him saying, "It wouldn't do any good because he's as slippery as can be." He had invested in many transactions and was heavily burdened with debts in every section. Many creditors were clamoring for his skin.

It is impossible to describe my feelings of remorse, knowing it was my fault that Glenn got involved with this con man to the tune of $25,000.00. I was feeling guilty, ashamed, and embarrassed. When I went to his office and apologized profusely, he put his hand on my shoulder looked at me and simply said, "Ken, I'm over twenty-one." I had to choke back the tears. It was a moment I'll never forget. I don't know what Glenn did about Caraway and I don't know what happened to him or the so-called oil field. I do know there were so many creditors ahead of us it was impossible to get our money back from him. I never discussed it with Faron.

Faron was well-liked by his fellow artists and had helped many novices further their career. He had a good sense of humor, and I still laugh when I think of the gag he pulled on me at a gathering of several of my artists, in my suite at the Andrew Jackson, unbeknownst to me, Faron was to present me a plaque of appreciation. In his presentation speech he extolled my many merits, what a great guy I was, a pleasure to work with, an outstanding producer, a good friend, and a pillar of country music. I felt embarrassed and was thinking, *Aw shucks, I don't deserve this.* When he unveiled the plaque it had two woman's breasts on it with the inscription, "To Ken Nelson, the second best closet man in Nashville." Everyone, including me, burst out laughing. The room was filled with laughter for about ten minutes. I asked Faron who the number one closet man was. He said "Chet Atkins." Closet man meant that if you were having an affair, it was a well kept secret and no one knew about it.

Faron's last hit on Capitol was "Hello Walls," written by his friend Willie Nelson. In 1962 he left Capitol, I don't remember why. He signed with Mercury Records. Faron became a heavy drinker and smoker, and when he was inebriated he was abusive to his wife and children. In 1986, his wife Hilda divorced him. In 1996 at the age of 63, his career was gone, he had emphysema, he was alone without his family and despondent. He committed suicide by shooting himself in the head. Hilda and the children rushed to the hospital and were at his bedside when he died. I always liked Faron, and was glad to see him inducted in "The Country Music Hall of Fame" in the year 2000.

My longtime friend Fred Rose called me one day and asked if I would sign the Louvin Brothers to a Capitol contract. He had been producing them on MGM records but was not satisfied with their sales or promotion. Having complete confidence in Fred, I signed them; it proved to be a good decision. Ira and Charley Louvin were not only good performers but also good song writers; they excelled in gospel music. Their records were enjoying good sales, and in 1955 they phoned me and asked if I could get them on the *Grand Ol' Opry*. I called Jack Stapp, with whom I had become quite friendly, and he agreed to audition them. They were accepted and became a popular addition to the Opry. They and their families moved to Nashville.

Ira had quite a temper and would fly off the handle at the slightest provocation, but he was always courteous, respectful, never showed his temper to me, and would usually accede to my suggestions. Charley was even tempered and, when Ira had a tantrum, would just stand by and wait until the storm subsided.

Charley, in writing about me many years later made several statements that were not true. He said that I had offered them a deal with Central Songs. He claimed that I had said, "You record any Central Song and later if we put a hundred songs in Central. When we become non-exclusive with Acuff Rose, I will give you 60 percent of the publisher's royalties instead of the usual 50 percent." Fred and Wesley Rose were two of my oldest acquaintances from our Chicago days and I would never try to persuade a writer to leave them or any other publisher. If I thought a song published by any publisher, including Central, was an artist's type, I would submit it to them for their approval. During my career, I never once made a deal with an artist to record a Central or any other song. If an artist had an unpublished song I would suggest, but never insist, they put it with Central.

The only Central songs I recall them recording were "Praying," "Wait a Little Longer Please, Jesus," and "My Baby's Gone." They also recorded a song Charley doubted that I wrote, "My Brothers Will." I did write it and it was published by Capitol before I joined the company. They both liked it because it was suitable for the album we were recording, *Tragic Songs of Life*.

Charley also stated that I had objected to their recording secular songs. I did not; some of their most successful recordings were secular. He also said that I had insisted Ira no longer play the mandolin on the recordings. I don't believe I made such a request because the mandolin was an integral part of their sound. I'm quite sure it was Ira's decision because the mandolin was difficult to keep in tune and this always upset him. He stopped playing the mandolin on their recordings in August of 1958 but resumed playing it on their records in October of 1960. Their last session as a duet was September 12, 1963. I don't know why they parted. I presume it was because of Ira's temper. I decided to record them individually. Ira's last session was May 17, 1965, and one month later, almost to the day, June 21, he and his wife were killed in an automobile accident. Charley stayed with us until 1969. When his sales did not warrant retaining him, I had to drop him from the label.

In 1944, Johnny Mercer signed and produced Capitol's first country and western artist, Tex Ritter. Tex was a movie star who had made about eighty films as a singing cowboy and was very popular. Gillette was producing both transcriptions and country record artists. He and Tex became close friends, and when I took over the country music department, I did too. Lee and I would often visit him at his ranch in the San Fernando Valley. Sometimes I would take my children, Gregory and Claudia, with me. Tex had two boys about the same age, Tom, who had polio but became a successful attorney, and John, who became a well-known and popular TV and movie star. Tex was very proud of them. Tex's beautiful wife, Dorothy, was formerly an actress and was his leading lady in some of his movies but was no longer acting. She had a cocker spaniel that had a litter of eight puppies and gave one to June and me. June named him Pokey Dot and he was a member of our family for many years. When I'd take the children to the ranch they'd play with Tom and John. Many times Tex would bring out White Flash, his famous movie horse. We'd take pictures of the children sitting on his back and Tex would have him do some of the tricks he had taught him.

Tex Ritter was one of the kindest, gentlest men with a good sense of humor that I ever knew. He'd give you the shirt off his back if he thought you needed it. In 1952 Tex recorded the soundtrack for the Gary Cooper movie *High Noon.* The song was "Do Not Forsake Me, Oh My Darling" and was used throughout the film. Because the film was not to be released for several months we were reluctant to record the song until it was released, and besides we had Tex's next record all set. I had not heard the soundtrack, and when we decided to record it we did it without the all important drive of the drumbeat. After the record was released I heard the soundtrack and realized I had goofed. Tex had gone to England so I couldn't get him back in the studio to re-record it. I called our mutual friend Lee Gillette, who was a drummer, and we over-dubbed the drums. We recalled the drumless version, but in the meantime it had been recorded by the very popular Frankie Laine. His record reached number five on the charts, and after his record started to fade Tex finally reached number twelve, but not on the country chart. However, it had excellent sales, almost a million. After seeing the film and hearing our record without drums, which had not yet been released in England, an English producer asked permission to re-record it. We gave it to him and Tex agreed. The background he used was a guitar, an accordion, and two tom-toms. It was a hit in England, and I'm sure if that version had been released here, it would have been number one.

In 1954 Tex sold his ranch in the Valley and moved to Toluca Lake. A year later I was again deceived. Hill and Range, one of the leading country music publishers, brought me a song titled "Let Me Go, Devil" and promised that if I recorded it they would not show it to any other artist until our record was released. However, they changed the title to "Let Me Go, Lover," and it was recorded by four female vocalists including Peggy Lee, Teresa Brewer, Patti Page, and Joan Weber, whose version of it became a number one pop record. These records came out about the same time as Tex's, which didn't have a chance.

In 1964 Tex was elected president of CMA, the Country Music Association, and served a two year term. He was also inducted into the Country Music Hall of Fame that year. In 1965, Tex, Dorothy, and Tom moved to Nashville. John was already involved in movies and television, was on his way to a successful career, and stayed in Hollywood. Tex became a regular member of the *Grand Ol' Opry*.

An amusing but scary incident happened in 1968, Tex and 39other passengers were on the inaugural flight of a TWA plane from Nashville to Miami when it was hijacked and ordered to Cuba. The plane landed without incident and returned to Miami the next day. Tex made the headlines in many newspapers.

In 1970, Tex was persuaded to run for state senator in Tennessee. He was well qualified because he had spent two years as a law student in college. He was defeated.

On January 2, 1974, Tex died as he had lived, helping his fellow man. One of the musicians in his band had gotten into a brawl on New Year's Eve and was arrested. The day after New Year's Tex went to the jail to bail him out and while he was there died of a heart attack. Tex was admired by all who knew him and many who didn't.

It was December 11, 1951, that I did my first session with Hank Thompson; it produced two hits, "The Wild Side Of Life" and "Waiting in the Lobby of Your Heart." "Wild Side" quickly reached number one on the *Billboard* chart, stayed on the chart thirty weeks and sold over a million copies. "Lobby" reached number three and stayed on the chart fifteen weeks.

Jimmie Heap and his Melody Masters of Taylor, Texas, had recorded "Wild Side," which he and his piano player, Arlie Carter, had written, using the melody of two standards, "The Great Speckled Bird" and "Thinking Tonight of My Blue Eyes," for Imperial Records. Imperial was a new company and had no distribution. Jimmie wanted to get on a major label and sent me a recording of his band. I liked it and signed him. Hank's wife had heard Jimmie's record and was impressed by the line "I Didn't Know God Made Honky Tonk Angels" and persuaded Hank to record it. I was impressed with the story of the song. It's still one of my favorites.

I kept Jimmie on the label for four years. He wanted to form his own record company, so by mutual agreement I released him. The song "Release Me," by the way, was Jimmie's biggest hit. In 1967 it reached number five on *Billboard* 's chart and sold over seven hundred thousand copies. In 1990 "Release Me" was recorded by two pop artists and became a hit again, one record reaching number five on the *Billboard* chart and the other number one. Jimmie died in a boating accident in 1977.

Hank would come to Hollywood twice a year to record because he wanted guitarist Merle Travis to play with his band. Merle had a playing style that was unique. He was the idol of country guitarists and many tried to emulate his style. I produced a couple of instrumental albums by him that were well received.

Merle was born in Rosewood, Kentucky, a coal mining town in Muhlenberg County. Although he never worked in the coal mines, his father did, so he was well aware of the problems miners faced. He wrote many coal mining songs such as "Dark as a Dungeon," "Nine Pound Hammer," and "Sixteen Tons," a million-seller for Tennessee Ernie Ford. He was the writer of Capitol's first million-seller, "Smoke, Smoke, Smoke That Cigarette." It was recorded by Tex Williams. Some of his folk songs, such as "John Henry," have become standards. All of these records were produced by Lee Gillette.

Merle had a pleasant, easy-going personality, but unfortunately he took to substance abuse. He was never obnoxious but sometimes he would come to a session a little befuddled and Hank and I had to be very patient, but Merle would eventually play the right licks and chords. The one time he really upset me was when he didn't show up for a session. Thinking he might have forgotten about it, we sent someone to get him. When he came to the session it was quite obvious that he was in no condition to play, so we had somebody take him home. The next day he phoned me and said, "Gee, Ken,

I'm sorry I didn't make the session yesterday." He didn't even know he had been there. I didn't tell him.

Merle later moved to Nashville, married Dorothy, Hank's ex-wife, made an album with Chet, performed at Carnegie Hall, and was in the film *From Here To Eternity* with Frank Sinatra. He was inducted in the Country Music Hall of Fame in 1977. He died at the age of sixty-six in 1983.

Hank Thompson was born in Waco, Texas, served in the navy during World War II, and attended Southern Methodist University of Texas. He was a well-educated man who knew what he wanted and how to get it. Ernest Tubb had arranged for him to become a member of the *Grand Ol' Opry*, but he didn't like the restrictions or the salary. As an example, drums were not allowed on any Opry show. His first pay check amounted to a little over nine dollars, so after the first week he decided to leave. Someone said to him "You got on the Opry and you're going to leave? It's everybody's dream to get on the Opry." Hank showed him the check and said "Yeah, but I can't live on dreams." He went back to Dallas, and with Billy Gray as band leader he formed the western swing band Hank Thompson and the Brazos Valley Boys. He was the first artist to sign with Jim Halsey of Tulsa, Oklahoma, who was to become one of country music's top booking agents.

In 1961 he had booked Hank in to the Golden Nugget casino in Las Vegas and suggested we record a "live on stage" album there. Hank and I liked the idea and we did it. Voyle Gilmore, who was head of A & R at the time, had done a couple of live albums with pop artists in Vegas, so we knew it was feasible. As far as I can determine this was the first live country album ever recorded. Along with the recording engineer, John Kraus, we set up microphones to get the audience reaction and took a portable recorder to get the various gambling sounds such as slot machines, wheel of fortune, and others. The room Hank performed in was well insulated to ensure that the music would not disturb the patrons gambling in the casino. The sales of the album proved well worth the time and effort.

We did two more live albums in 1962 one at the rodeo at the Cheyenne Frontier Days in Wyoming. The band was on stage out in the open, and because there was no isolation it was difficult to record. I added sound effects, such as the announcer, announcing the events, the chuck wagon race, and cows mooing. The album didn't sell as well as *The Golden Nugget*, however, it came in second at the National Academy of Recording Arts and Sciences (NARAS) for technical work and originality. The third live album was *The State Fair of Texas* in Dallas. Here, too, was the problem of the band on an outside stage with no isolation. I also added sound tracks, going down the midway with our portable recorder in a little red wagon getting the hawkers announcing their games, their wares, and the side-shows. We pulled our little red wagon around the football field to get the sounds of the Oklahoma-Texas game being played during the fair. Later John Kraus and I went to Hank's home and recorded voice tracks for the album but it didn't get the acceptance we had hoped for.

Hank was responsible for my signing my two most widely known female country artists, Jean Shepard and Wanda Jackson. Hank was with Capitol from 1948 to 1964, he always enjoyed good airplay and profitable sales. Through the years I had produced about ninety sessions with him and felt a great loss when he left. He and his manager, Jim Halsey, decided Hank's Capitol compensation was insufficient. Jim came to me and said that unless we would guarantee Hank a yearly advance of $40,000.00 he would leave the label. At that time Capitol was not giving yearly advances and the finance department turned down the request. Hank left and went first to Warner records, then to Dot, ABC, and MCA. He was inducted into the Country Music Hall of Fame in 1989.

In 1994, Hank paid Capitol a great compliment. He said, "I'd play one of those MCA, DOT records. I'd then drop the needle on one of those old Capitol's and, my gosh, it was all the difference in the world in the presence and quality of Capitol's."

Chet Atkins had been playing on most of my Nashville sessions and wasn't as yet the producer for RCA Victor. It was the spring of '52 that he called me and asked if I would come to his house and listen to a young Korean veteran friend of his who had a good voice and was anxious to get a recording contract. The young man's name was James Loden. As a youngster he had sung with his four sisters in the Loden family group and as a teenager had had his own radio show in Birmingham, Alabama. He also performed while in the service. He accompanied himself on guitar and sang three songs for me. I liked what I heard and agreed to sign him; however, I felt the name James Loden was not euphonious. In discussing it with him he said, "My folks used to call me Sonny." I said, "That's it, Sonny James." He agreed and adopted it as his professional name.

Sonny's first records were well received by disc jockeys and enjoyed good sales. It was in '53 that Fred Stryker, a local publisher, brought me the song "I Forgot More Than You'll Ever Know" and said I would have it exclusively, which meant if I promised to record it he wouldn't show it to any other record producer. I liked the idea of the song but the melody of the middle part didn't seem quite right, so I asked Fred if he would object to my changing it. I wouldn't expect writer credit. He said that would be okay. I told him I was going to Nashville the following week and would record it with Sonny James. Sonny liked the song, but when we started to record it we both realized the lyrics in the middle part didn't make sense.

Knowing of his writing ability, I phoned Fred Rose, told him of the problem, and asked if he could come to the studio and see what could be done. He came immediately and within ten minutes had the lyrics making sense. Fred did not want writer credit either, he did it as a favor to me. When I returned to Hollywood I played the record for Stryker and told him I planned to release it in the fall. He asked if he could have a dub so he could have the revised version copyrighted, and I gave it to him. He obviously immediately sent it to Steve Sholes, who was head of and producer of country artists for RCA Victor. He recorded it immediately with a girl duet, the Davis Sisters. Both records were released almost simultaneously. I have to admit that the Davis Sisters was an outstanding record that completely overshadowed Sonny's version. It was on *Billboard* 's chart for twenty-six weeks and was a number one record, sending Sonny's version into complete oblivion.

This same publisher, this same year, again broke his promise. I had signed Rod Morris, who had a pleasant but not outstanding voice. He was a prolific writer and never recorded a song he didn't write. In October of '53 we recorded the song "Bimbo," which is what he called his baby boy. The song was published by Styker and he promised not to show it to any other artist till our record was released. I was in the studios of KWKH when I saw an Abbott recording of "Bimbo" by Jim Reeves, and by December of '53 it was number one on the *Billboard* chart. I released our record, but Reeves was too overpowering. Rod continued to write good songs but never happened as an artist.

It was around this time that I became acquainted with Bill Lowery. He was manager and announcer at the radio station where I was to record The Statesmen, a gospel quartet. He interviewed me on his radio program. You couldn't help but like Bill; he had a pleasant, affable personality. We became immediate friends and have remained so to this day. In one of our conversations he mentioned that he had just been diagnosed as having cancer and was concerned about the future of his family. I suggested to Bill that he start a music publishing company because there was no publishing firm in Atlanta and there had to be a great deal of latent talent in the area. He took my suggestion and formed the Lowery Group of Music Publishing Companies. His company eventually expanded to four recording studios, a management firm, several production companies, a booking division, and MGM South Records. He discovered many songwriters and stars, including Ray Stevens, Jerry Reed, Roy Drusky, Joe South, Billy Joe Royal, and Tommy Roe. His success covered a wide spectrum of the music business. He served on the board of the Country Music Association for many years, was president of the Country Music Foundation, and served as president of NARAS, The National Association of Recording Arts and Sciences, from 1973 to 1975 and also as president of the local chapter. As I heard no more about it I presume his cancer was eradicated.

In October of 1956, while I was in Nashville, Bill brought me a record he had produced and said that RCA Victor was interested in buying but because of our friendship he wanted me to hear it. If I was interested I could have it for Capitol. I don't recall the title of the song. I listened and said,

"Bill, do me a favor, give it to Victor." I don't know why but I turned the record over; it was a song titled "Young Love." I played it and said, "Bill, There's your hit. I'm recording Sonny James next week, and with your permission I'll record it with him." He said okay.

Sonny was not overly enthused about the song but agreed to record it. That session was one of the rare times I ever raised my voice to an artist. We only recorded two songs, "You're the Reason I'm in Love" and "Young Love." When we had finished the third take on "Young Love," I said, "That's it." I felt the background was perfect, and Sonny had the right emotional appeal. When I played it back for him he wanted to do another take and was quite insistent. I too was insistent and in a determined voice said, "That's it, period."

I had so much faith in the record I put it on rush release. We recorded it in October, disc jockeys received it in November, and in December it was number one on the *Billboard* country chart. In those days it was quite common for record companies to cover a hit record, that is, to rush out their own version in hopes of cashing in on it. Randy Wood, owner of Dot records, immediately covered the song, recording it with Tab Hunter, a movie actor. He copied our arrangement to a tee. In 1957 both records became number one on the country charts at the same time. Sonny's version also became number one on the pop chart and Hunter's version number six on the pop chart. Both records combined sold about five million copies.

Wade Pepper, who lives in Atlanta, was at the time manager of Capitol's Atlanta branch. He later became the promotion man for our Country Music department. He was also a good friend of Bill Lowery's. Bill played him the record that RCA Victor was interested in; he liked it and thought I should have taken it. When I turned it down, he let me know he thought I had made a wrong decision. When "Young Love" hit, he wrote me a memo apologizing for his having doubted my judgment. An outstanding promotion man, Wade was responsible for much of the success of our country department. We have remained friends and are still in contact with each other today.

Many artists had more number one records than Sonny. He had twenty-three, but no orchestra, no singer, country or pop, not even Bing Crosby, the Beatles, or Elvis Presley had more consecutive number one records. From February of 1967 to May 1972 he dominated the country charts with sixteen Capitol consecutive number one records. In 1972, after twenty years with us, he signed with Columbia Records. I guess they offered him a lucrative contract. His last release on Capitol and his first on Columbia both charted number one.

1952 was the year my San Diego friend, Jim Kennedy, asked me to listen to Merrill Moore, a boogie-woogie piano player who entertained in one of the five night clubs he owned. I liked what I heard and signed him. His biggest hit was "House of Blue Lights." His records were well received but did not attain the popularity they did in Europe, where his records are still being played. He made personal appearances there almost until the day he passed away in 1999.

Although June had been brought up as a Presbyterian and I a Catholic, we were both agnostics. We wanted our children to have the knowledge of religion. In 1953 we found the ideal denomination, Unitarianism. It allows you to form your own religious philosophies. Periodically ministers, preachers, Buddhist monks, and speakers from other denominations, were invited to come and speak to the congregation. The church later joined with the Universalists and became known as Universalist-Unitarian. Our church was named Christ Memorial and was located in Studio City. We enrolled our children, Claudia and Gregory, in the Sunday school class, and they loved it. This created a problem with my mother, a staunch Catholic, who attended church two and three times a week. We would occasionally find her trying to make the children pray. June was one who never complained and kept her feelings to herself, but I could see that my mother's aloofness and actions were beginning to take their toll. I would get together with the two of them and, even though I knew June wasn't at fault, try to resolve the problems, but to no avail.

It was this year that I released the first recordings of Roy Acuff, Tommy Collins, Ferlin Husky, and Jean Shepard, artists that I had signed the previous year.

Wesley Rose, the son of Fred Rose, was a CPA (Certified Public Accountant). He and his father didn't get along when they lived in Chicago. When Fred first asked him to come to Nashville and join Acuff-Rose he refused but later at Fred's urging he assented and was now managing the firm. Wesley asked me to sign Roy Acuff, who was the other half of Acuff-Rose. Roy was one of the mainstays of the *Grand Ol' Opry* and was known as the "King of Country Music." I was more than happy to do so. I did my sessions with Roy Acuff and the Smokey Mountain Boys in the Castle Studios in the Tulane Hotel. I released several singles and an album of his most popular songs. Our promotion and sales department either didn't like this type of music or didn't realize the potential of this great artist, so did very little to promote the sales of his records or the album that I released in 1955. Because of the lack of promotion and sales, Wesley asked me to release Roy from his contract. I reluctantly did so. Without any help his album sold over eighty thousand. Later, at one of our A&R meetings, noticing the sales figures, I was asked why I had let Roy go. I said, "Because you idiots let your musical prejudices get in the way of your better judgment and you failed to accept or recognize the potential of this talented man." The album is still selling in re-issues.

Roy was one of the most respected men in the business, ran unsuccessfully twice for governor of Tennessee, was inducted in the Country Music Hall of Fame in 1962, and was given a Lifetime Achievement Grammy award in 1987. Roy passed away at the age of eighty-nine in November of 1992.

Hank Thompson was playing a one-nighter at the Nobles Melody Ranch in San Luis Obispo, California, when a young girl got up on the stage and sang with him. The girl was Jean Shepard. Hank was impressed and said, "Young lady, would you like to have a recording contract?" Naturally she said yes. He replied, "I'll see that you get one." Three or four months went by, and when she didn't hear anything she forgot about it. When Hank returned and played the same club again, he asked her if she had heard from Capitol records. She said, "No, sir. I haven't." He replied, "You will." Actually, Hank hadn't told me about Jean until the second time he met her.

Girl country vocalists had almost no sales at that time and I wasn't too interested, but on Hank's recommendation I went to see her. She was playing at the American Legion Hall in San Luis Obispo, it was on the second floor. As I walked up the stairs I heard a girl singing and her voice got my attention immediately. When I walked in the hall I saw this mite of a girl singing while playing a stand-up bass that was taller than she was in an all-male band. She had formerly played in an all-girl orchestra called the Melody Ranch Girls, but one by one the girls got married and were replaced by men. I listened to her sing several songs before I told her who I was. Her singing and outgoing personality really impressed me.

I introduced myself and told her I would give her a contract, but signing her was not all that easy. Although Jean was eighteen years old at that time, she was still considered a minor and all minor contracts in California had to be approved by a judge.

The reason for this was, back in the silent movie picture days, a child star, actor Jackie Coogan, had filed a lawsuit trying to retain his earnings. His mother and stepfather were spending his money without regard for his future. The suit had failed, but as a result the California senate passed the Coogan Act, known as the "Child Actors" bill. All contracts involving a minor had to be court-approved and their earnings put in a trust fund until they became adults, which at that time was twenty-one. A judge in San Luis Obispo said he knew nothing about the recording industry and refused to approve the contract; however, the judge in Jean's hometown, Visalia, did approve it. Today, age eighteen is considered adult.

Jean's first two records featuring Speedy West on steel guitar didn't do too well, but we broke the ice with her next release. I had heard a pop song, "I'd Rather Die Young" that I thought would be a hit for Jean. Fuzzy Owen and Lew Tally, two Bakersfield musicians that had played on some of my sessions, brought me a song, which included a recitation, titled "A Dear John Letter." They had recorded it with Bonnie Owens with Fuzzy doing the recitation. I liked the idea and decided to make it the B side of Jeans first hit. I had just signed Ferlin Husky and asked him to do the recitation. He agreed but said it wouldn't be necessary to pay him for doing it. I was sure "I'd Rather Die Young" would be a hit, but I sure was wrong. "A Dear John

Letter" took off like a scared rabbit, and before you could say Jack Robinson it was number one on the country charts and number four on the pop chart. When I saw what was happening I immediately arranged for Ferlin to receive one-quarter cent royalty for each record sold. It sold a million. Their follow-up record, "Forgive Me, John" was also a hit but didn't make the million mark.

In 1955 Jean became a member of the *Grand Ol' Opry* and her future as a top performer and recording artist was assured. Hawkshaw Hawkins had joined the Opry at the same time. They worked many road shows together, eventually fell in love, and decided to become man and wife. The wedding took place November 26, 1960 in Wichita, Kansas. Hap Peebles, the agent, gave the bride away, and I was given the honor of being best man. It wasn't intended to be a spectacle, but with a crowd of thirty-five hundred well wishers it turned out to be just that. They were an ideal couple, got along like two peas in a pod. Jean said she had never been happier, but her happiness was short lived. On March 5, 1963, tragedy struck. Hawkshaw, Patsy Cline, and Cowboy Copas were returning to Nashville in a plane piloted by booking agent Randy Hughes, who had only recently learned to fly. He had been warned not to take off because of weather conditions, but he said, "It's only about a half hour flight, so I don't see any problem." The plane crashed and everyone on board was killed. Jean was devastated. She was pregnant with her second child and went into seclusion for several months. Opry officials finally coaxed her back and she resumed her performing and recording career. She did eventually remarry. She was still performing in the 1990s, and the last I heard she has twenty-seven grandchildren.

Ferlin Husky was born December 23, 1925 in Missouri. During World War II. He spent five years in the Merchant Marine and was a popular entertainer with his shipmates, playing guitar and singing. After the war he played and entertained in clubs in Bakersfield, California. He made recordings for Four Star records under the alias Terry Preston. I don't recall how he was brought to my attention It may have been Cliffie, but I seem to recall him playing guitar on a couple of my sessions. I liked his voice and style, and as he was not under contract to Four Star, I signed him. I didn't like the name Terry Preston, it sounded too sissified for a country singer. I told him his given name, Ferlin Husky, had a good masculine country sound and he should record under that name, but he insisted on using Terry Preston.

Shortly before his first session, he, his father, and I were riding in a car and I told Mr. Husky about my objection to the alias. He turned to Ferlin and said, "Ferlin, you'll never be successful until you use your given name." Ferlin gave in to our wishes; however he did use an alias "Simon Crum" for his comedy records. That was okay. An interesting aside, unbeknownst to me, some of his Terry Preston Four Star records had become very popular in England, so the British officials decided to release his Capitol records under that name. I didn't become aware of this until after I retired. Oh well, Terry Preston has a more British sound than Ferlin Husky.

Ferlin had a long and varied career. He became a regular on the *Grand Ol' Opry*, and one summer when Arthur Godfrey, a popular CBS talk show host, went on vacation, he chose Ferlin to substitute for him. He appeared in dramatic roles on the *Kraft TV Theatre*, and made several movies. He co-starred with Jane Mansfield and Mamie Van Dorn in *Las Vegas Hillbillies*. In the movie *Hillbillies in a Haunted House*, he co-starred with three of the great actors of the previous generation, Basil Rathbone, John Carradine, and Lon Chaney, Jr. The film also featured Merle Haggard and Sonny James.

His records were consistently on the charts and always had excellent sales. His recording of "Gone" was number one on the country chart for twenty-seven weeks and was number four on the pop chart. "On The Wings of a Snow White Dove," produced by my assistant, Marvin Hughes, was number one on the country chart for thirty-six weeks and reached number twelve on the pop chart. His Simon Crum recording of "Country Music Is Here to Stay" reached number two and was on the chart for twenty-four weeks. "Gone" and "Dove" both went over a million.

Ferlin was married six times and had seven children. At an artist gathering in my hotel suite he became slightly inebriated and signaled me to come into the small side room. He closed the door, put his arms around me, his head on my shoulder, and started to sob. "I'm going to be a grandfather and I'm afraid when it becomes known it'll ruin my career." I consoled him as best I could and assured him his talent would prevail, which of course it did. He was still performing well up into his senior years.

Tommy Collins, whose legal name was Leonard Raymond Sipes, was born September 28, 1930, in Oklahoma City. He served a hitch in the United States Marines and upon his discharge moved to Bakersfield. Ferlin Husky was the one who suggested he call himself Tommy Collins. He adopted the name and used it throughout his professional career. He performed on Cliffie's *Hometown Jamboree* and I'm not sure whether it was Cliffie or Ferlin who brought him to my attention. He was a prolific songwriter and wrote hits not only for himself but for other artists as well. His songs always had a philosophical undertone. Two of my favorites were "What Difference Will It Make a Hundred Years from Now" and "If That's the Fashion."

I loved the profound opening lines of that song, "Each day there's someone who pays for another's mistake, the guilty go free and the hearts of the innocent break." His first record was "You Gotta Have a License." His second record "You Better Not Do That" was number two on the *Billboard* chart and stayed there for twenty-one weeks. He wrote Faron's hit "If You Ain't Lovin', You Ain't Livin'" and many songs for Merle Haggard. Central published most of his earlier songs. It was through Tommy that I became acquainted with Buck Owens. Buck played guitar on all of Tommy's sessions.

He had an introductory musical theme that was used on each of Tommy's records which immediately identified him. The first thing Tommy did when "You Better Not Do That" hit, was to buy a Cadillac. I had gotten him a one-time appearance on the *Grand Ol' Opry* and he decided to drive to Nashville. Of course. Buck had to go also because of his identifiably guitar sound. They suggested I go with them and rather than take the plane I did. It was a trip filled with fun and laughter that I've never forgotten.

Tommy's records enjoyed consistent sales. In 1958 we made and released an album of standard religious songs. Without my knowing it he must have been studying for the ministry, because one day he announced he was giving up his musical career to become a full-time minister. I tried to dissuade him, but to no avail. He became the minister of a small church in Oakland, California. I visited him two or three times, begging him to record, but he refused. His congregation was small, and after three years, he realized he wasn't amply supporting his family. He decided to resume his musical career. He left Capitol and signed with Columbia Records, where he had one hit, "If You Can't Bite Don't Growl," but the momentum of his earlier career was gone.

He moved to Ashland City, Tennessee, and became very successful at what he could do best, writing songs. He wrote twenty-two songs for Haggard, and Merle wrote and recorded a tribute song called "Leonard," which was Tommy's legal name. Tommy was inducted into the Songwriters Hall of Fame on September 19, 1999, and he passed away on March 4, 2000, at the age of sixty-nine.

The original Jordanaires excelled in gospel and religious music and coined their name from the biblical land of Jordan. I first engaged them as background singers for my country artists in 1951. They were capable of doing all types of music. The original personnel were Bill Matthews, Monty Matthews, Bob Hubbard, and Cully Holt, with Gordon Stoker as their pianist. In 1953 I signed them to a contract. The personnel had changed; they now consisted of Gordon Stoker, who was now singing, Neal Matthews (no relation to Bill or Monty), Hoyt Hawkins, and Cully Holt. In '54, Hugh Jarret replaced Cully Holt, and in '58 he was replaced by Ray Walker. That group remained intact from 1958 to 1982 when Hoyt Hawkins passed away and Louis Nunley joined them. Their versatility enabled them to provide vocal backgrounds for every type of music, religious, country, rock & roll, and pop.

Between 1951 and 1980 they provided background voices for practically every top country artist, both male and female, and such pop stars as Julie Andrews, Carol Channing, Connie Frances, Roy Orbison, Pat Boone, Tennessee Ernie Ford, and countless others too numerous to mention. It would take three or four pages to name all of them. The most notable, of course, was Elvis Presley.

They recorded with Elvis from 1955 to 1970 and were in twenty-eight of his movies. While they were in Hollywood making a movie I invited them to my home for a Sunday of swimming and relaxation. They all came, but no Elvis. I asked why. Elvis had asked them if I had teenagers, and when they said I had two he was concerned they would tell the neighborhood kids of his visit and in their anxiety to see him would cause a problem. Ironically he went to a movie that afternoon, was recognized, and had to leave the theatre.

When I first signed the Jordanaires, Nashville singers were unaware of (AFTRA) The American Federation of Television and Radio Artists, the union of which all singers in Hollywood, Chicago, and New York were members. They were being paid way below union scale. I thought this was unfair because all the recording musicians belonged to the musician's union and were paid union scale. I gave Gordon AFTRA's address and urged him to have the group join. They did and later were responsible for the establishment of the offices of AFTRA and SAG (The Screen Actors Guild) in Nashville.

I recorded the Jordanaires as a solo group from 1953 to 1961. During that period we released seven or eight religious albums which did very well and several pop records which did so-so. I engaged them for backgrounds for the remainder of my career. I was always amazed at their ability and speed learning a song they had never heard before. They rarely used printed music. The artist would sing or play a dub of the song to be recorded and as they listened they would make a chart of the chord changes.

I and the Jordanaires had two firsts in Nashville. In 1956, when I was going to record "Gone" with Ferlin Husky, I decided the song needed a different sound, a choir sound, and asked Gordon to add a high soprano voice to the group. I think he was a little reluctant, but he engaged Millie Kirkham who had occasionally sung with the Anita Kerr singers. The second first was using an echo chamber. An echo chamber is a room with reflecting walls used for producing hollow or echoing sound effects. A microphone and a loudspeaker are placed in the room and the sound fed back through the mixing board. We had been using them in Hollywood but Nashville didn't have one. An echo chamber would give the choir sound that I wanted. When I explained the problem to Mort Thomeson, the recording engineer, he solved the problem by putting a mike and speaker in a room that had a concrete floor and walls. This was the first time an echo chamber had been used in Nashville. It produced the desired effect.

"Gone" was number one on the country and number four on the pop chart. It sold over a million. Millie Kirkham continued to sing with the Jordanaires for some thirty years and still sings when needed. She was the feature voice on Elvis Presley's recording of "Blue Christmas" that became one of the most programmed Christmas recordings of all time.

At one time Gordon urged me to get Capitol to give the group more promotion because their ambition was to become a star act in their own right. I replied, "Gordon, today you might have two or three hit records, and by tomorrow be completely forgotten. No group can top you in background singing, and if you can stay in that field it will be a long and lasting career." They took my advice, but they did become a star act in their own right. Today they are known worldwide, were members of the *Grand Ol' Opry* for thirteen years, and were recognized in England as one of the world's "Top Ten" vocal groups. Their numerous awards include a special award from RCA Victor for their backgrounds of the Elvis Presley recordings, Nashville Music Associations Master award, and NARAS award for having sung on more top ten recordings than any other group. In 1998, they were inducted into the Gospel Music Hall of Fame, in 1999 into NACAI (North American Country Music Association International), and in 2000 into the Rockabilly Hall of Fame. They were nominated for two Grammy awards for collaborative albums, *The Lightcrust Doughboys* and the *James Blackwood Gospel Album*. It is estimated that the recordings sold with Jordanaire backgrounds vocals is 2.6 billion. For many years, until the year 2000, Millie and the Jordans made yearly appearances in Las Vegas. In 2001 they were inducted into the Country Music Hall of Fame. I don't know why it took so long. I think everyone will agree that the Jordanaires became stars in their own right.

My wife, June, was a person who kept her feelings to herself. She showed no emotion or affection, either for me or the children. She never hugged, kissed us, or said I love you, but she was a loving, caring mother and wife. She showed this in many ways. She never pushed me away as my mother did, if I put my arms around her or kissed her; she never denied me sex. I knew she loved me because she was always buying presents and making shirts, robes, and jackets for me. She was very attentive to the children, was receptive to their affection, and knew how to discipline them without being harsh. I not only loved her but admired her. She was not only beautiful but intelligent; her manners and dress were impeccable. I always felt a sense of pride when introducing her as my wife at social gatherings. I never understood why she married me.

June was now director of two choirs, the Carpenter Avenue school's Mother's Chorus and the church choir. The church, being located in Studio City, had quite a few professional actors and singers in the congregation, and they would occasionally put on musicals and plays such as *Oklahoma*, *The Gay 90s*, and others.

Central Songs and Snyder Music were coming to the fore. We had had several hits and were well on our way to financial stability; this, of course, meant spending more time in our office at home. When I wasn't working or out of town I spent much of my time with the two firms, but this didn't lessen June's burdens. Along with the children, the school, and the church, with Central Snyder she was kept pretty busy, but she never complained.

My mother was of no help; she continued her unfriendly attitude toward June. If June and I had to go someplace together and asked her to stay with the children, we were taking advantage of her. If we hired a sitter, we didn't trust her. Because of June's inability to express her feelings outwardly, she was becoming depressed and not feeling up to par. She went to her doctor. He found her physically fit and asked her if she was having domestic problems with her husband. She said no but told him of my mother's demeanor. The doctor phoned me the next day and said "Mr. Nelson, you have a choice. Your mother or your wife. If the present situation in your home continues, your wife may become very ill."

I was stunned! What could I do? I wanted to make a home and good life for my mother and still had deep feelings for her but my feelings for June were deeper. I didn't tell either one about the doctor's call. I thought possibly if Mother went on an extended trip she would come home refreshed and with a different attitude. I asked her if there was some place she would like to go for a vacation. I was surprised when she said "Yes. Havana, Cuba." I made all the hotel and travel arrangements and away she went. For three weeks, there was peace and tranquility in the Nelson household. When she came home she told us enthusiastically about her trip, treated June fairly well for about two weeks, and then fell into her old pattern. I was beside myself. I kept hoping and thinking things would improve but they didn't.

The year was 1955, Reg and Tina McHugh, my friends from Chicago, came to visit. One morning when the children were in school, Reg, Tina, June, and myself were sitting in the breakfast nook talking when all of a sudden my mother appeared, her chin quivering. I said "What's the matter, Mother?" She said, "The four of you are sitting there talking about me." I replied, "That's ridiculous, we're not talking about you." Then, pointing a finger at June, she screamed "And that goddamn Jew." I went berserk, lost complete control of myself, jumped up, grabbed my mother, took her into her bedroom, sat on the bed, turned her over my knee, and spanked her. I then got her suitcases out of the closet, opened her dresser drawer, and said, "Pack your bags. Get out of here and don't ever come back. If you need money let me know."

I was aghast at what I had done and have never forgiven myself. There was no excuse for my violent reaction, I should have realized Mother was emotionally unstable and resented the fact that June was part Jewish. She went to a neighbors' house with whom she had become friendly and then rented a room from one of the parishioners of the church she attended.

With Mother no longer living with us, June soon regained her composure. Mother showed no physical affection toward the children but she was fond of them, and June, not being one to hold a grudge, agreed to let her visit the children on Saturday afternoons. She would usually take them to Kiddie Land, an amusement park in the Valley. The children really looked forward to her visits. In 1957 Mother became ill and we hospitalized her for three weeks and then transferred her to a nursing home. When I was in town June would come with me to visit her every week, for which I was grateful. Mother never apologized but June showed no animosity, and they did have limited conversations.

In August of 1959 Mother passed away at the age of 73. I cried, not so much because she had died but because I had wanted her to be happy, to have a good life. I had wanted to do so much for her, but she wouldn't let me. June, I, and the children attended a requiem mass for her and her internment at San Fernando Mission cemetery, where she had requested to be buried.

1954 was a banner year for country music record companies and producers. Owen Bradley, who was now the producer for Decca Records, and his brother, Harold, a guitarist, knowing the need for better recording facilities in Nashville, bought a house on 16 Avenue. They added a quonset hut and converted it into a recording studio. It was an immediate success. All of the major record companies, Capitol, Columbia, Decca, and RCA Victor, recorded there. It was an excellent studio and provided a central place to record. It wasn't long before music publishers, booking agents, and music publications moved into this area, and it became known as "Music Row." Owen Bradley and RCA Victor Producer Chet Atkins were responsible for Nashville becoming known as Music City, U.S.A. There is now an Owen Bradley Park as well as a Chet Atkins Street near Nashville's Music Row. There is no doubt that these two men were two of the most outstanding country producers.

Owen Bradley learned to play piano as a youngster. He was basically a pop musician and had fronted pop dance orchestras, but being a native Tennessean, he was well aware of country music and proved it by the many, many hits he produced by such country artists as Kitty Wells, Webb Pierce, Patsy Cline, Red Foley, Ernest Tubb, Burl Ives, Conway Twitty, and Loretta Lynn. I always admired him and his ability. I regretted that I didn't get to know Owen better. We met several times at meetings and award shows but were never on a personal basis. Owen was inducted into the Country Music Hall of Fame in 1974 and passed away in 1998, at the age of 83.

I first met Chet Atkins when I was musical director of WJJD in Chicago. Karl and Harty had brought him to me, told me of his great talent, and asked if I could get Lee Gillette to sign him to Capitol. Lee wrote me and said, "We already have a guitar player, Merle Travis." I didn't see him again until I started to record in Nashville in 1951. Chet played on most of my sessions for two or three years. We became good friends.

The last time I saw him was in 1993. He was still doing stage shows and appeared at a theatre in Ventura, California. The house was packed. The audience amazed me, it was mostly youngsters. Chet sang and played and got encore after encore. We met and spent a couple of pleasant hours reminiscing.

Chet, too, was a native Tennessean. I consider him a musical genius because he was self-taught and could play all types of music–classical, jazz, pop, rock 'n roll, or country–equally well. Other guitarists shared my opinion.

I met Laurindo Alameida, one of the world's leading classical guitarists, when he was recording at Capitol. It so happened they were both in town at the same time. Laurindo Alameida knew about Chet and Chet was a fan of his. I knew they would like to meet each other and arranged a meeting at my home. I was a little disappointed that they didn't bring their guitars, but they hit it off immediately. It was an exhilarating afternoon for all of us.

In 1957 RCA Victor built their own studio on Music Row. Chet was put in charge of Nashville operations and later made a vice president of the company. His natural musical instincts and abilities served him well as a producer. Some of the artists included in his roster were Floyd Cramer, Waylon Jennings, Dolly Parton, Elvis Presley, Charlie Pride, Jim Reeves, Hank Snow, and occasionally Perry Como, who would come to Nashville to record with him.

Chet was the most unassuming person I ever knew. You couldn't help but like and admire him. He was elected to the Country Music Hall of Fame in 1973 and also won several Grammy awards. His fame was worldwide. He retired from RCA in 1981 and made personal appearances throughout the country for several years. He passed away in 2001.

Don Law of Columbia Records also produced country artists in the Bradley studio, and in 1962 when Owen built another studio, The Bradley Barn, Don convinced Columbia to buy Owens's original studio. I continued to record there. Don's roster included such stars as Johnny Cash, Lefty Frizzell, Marty Robbins, Flatt & Scruggs, and Carl Smith. Although I was well aware of his outstanding achievements, in all the years I worked in Nashville I regret to say I never met him. He was inducted into the Country Music Hall of Fame in 2001. Don passed away in 1982 at the age of 80.

It was early in my career as a producer that I had been offered George Jones. I turned him down because I heard that he was a heavy drinker and I didn't want to get involved with someone I thought would be a troublemaker. Instead of a troublemaker, George Jones turned out to be a hit maker. I learned to disregard rumors and never since then have concerned myself with an artist's personal life.

I'm going to digress a moment and tell of an embarrassing incident that happened to Gillette and me. One night when we were both working in the Melrose Avenue studio, after we were through, we decided to go across the street and have a nightcap. Sitting at the table with our friends was a man Lee and I both thought was Virgil Irwin, an announcer at WAAF in Chicago when we worked there. When Virgil, a tall handsome man, left the station, he said Warner Brothers Studio was paying all of his expenses to Hollywood to audition him for the movies.

There was no doubt in our minds that the man at the table was Virgil. We approached him, slapped him on the back, and said "Virgil, how the heck are you?" He looked up at us and said, "My name isn't Virgil." I said, "You mean to tell us you're not Virgil Irwin, who we worked with at WAAF in Chicago?" He said, "You're mistaken! My name is Victor Mature." Realizing our mistake, we apologized and slunk away. Victor Mature was a popular movie star. He and Virgil could have passed for twins!

I had signed Freddie Hart in 1953, and in 1954 we recorded "Loose Talk," which he and Ann Lucas wrote. I was sure it would be a hit and it was, but not for Freddie. Carl Smith, a very popular Columbia Artist, heard Freddie's recording and decided to cover it. It hit number one almost immediately and stayed on the chart for thirty-two weeks. It completely buried our record. I kept recording Freddie for three or four years, but our promotion department couldn't get him off the ground, so I let him go. In 1959 he signed with Columbia without much success, and in 1965 switched to Kapp Records, with the same results. In 1969 Buck Owens brought him back to Capitol, and within a year his recording career was off and sailing with his hit "Easy Loving." It even made the pop charts. He continued to be a disc jockey favorite with excellent sales until he left Capitol in 1979.

Two other artists I signed in 1954 were Hylo Brown and Dallas Frazier. The strange thing about Hylo Brown, a "blue grass" type singer who was brought to my attention by Joe Allison, was that his records never got on the *Billboard* chart, but his record sales were very consistent until 1960 when his sales became inadequate and I had to let him go.

Dallas Frazier was a very talented lad. At the age of fourteen he was the youngest artist I had ever signed. He was raised in Bakersfield, worked with Ferlin Husky, and also appeared on Cliffie's *Hometown Jamboree*. I'm not sure who brought him to my attention, Ferlin or Cliffie. In 1954, Lou Busch, a ragtime piano player known as Joe Fingers Carr, wanted to record two Christmas songs with Dallas, "My Birthday Comes on Christmas," and "Jingle-O-the-Brownie." I thought it was a good idea until we got in the studio and started to record. The tempo Lou set was way too fast. I kept telling him this and asked him to slow down, but he kept insisting fast was the right tempo. What could have been a good record didn't turn out so because of the fast tempo.

I have no record of recording him between 1954 and 1965, the year he first appeared on the *Billboard* chart. In 1969 he switched to RCA. He moved to Nashville and became a successful songwriter with many hits to his credit.

In October of 1954, I gave the following speech at our National Sales Meeting.

The Phonograph Record—By Ken Nelson, 7-54:

All of us in the repertoire department have been asked many times just what we think of when we go into a recording booth to make records. To tell you what I think of, I have to go back a few years.

When I was musical director of a radio station in Chicago, we had a staff of fifteen musicians. One day the manager of the station came to me and said, "Ken, fire all of those musicians." I was astounded. I said, "But what are we going to do for music?" His reply was, "Phonograph records—go out and get phonograph records." So I found myself buying all the phonograph records I could get my hands on, setting up a filing system, and making out record programs. I soon got bored with the job. I felt I was playing nursemaid to a batch of damn phonograph records.

It wasn't long after I was fortunate enough to be hired by Capitol, and instead of nursing the records, I was making them. Soon my whole conception of phonograph records changed. It happened one day as I was taking a tour of our factory in Scranton. It suddenly dawned on me that here were hundreds of people who depended on the phonograph record for their livelihood—who depended on it to support their families, to clothe and feed them, and to send their children to school.

When I got back to my hotel room that night, I decided to figure out just who else depended on phonograph records and to what extent. Naturally, all of us with Capitol and the other record companies—factory workers, technicians, office help, salesmen, branch managers, distributors, and executives—we all depend on the phonograph record for our living. I thought next of the recording artists, the musicians, and the song writers whose dreams, whose hopes, whose ambitions, whose very career and future depend on the phonograph record. The performing rights societies ASCAP and BMI and the hundreds of music publishers would find it difficult to exist today without the phonograph record.

Next to come to my mind was the phonograph and radio manufacturers, the juke box manufacturers, and the juke box operators who depend solely on the phonograph record. I thought of the hundreds of record stores and record dealers throughout the nation and the people who work for them, who depend so much on the phonograph record to keep them in business. I thought of the disc jockey, who depends on the phonograph record to entertain and to hold his audiences—where would he be without records?

I realized that practically every independent radio station in America today depends almost 100 percent on the phonograph record to keep them in business. They would find it difficult to exist without records because talent costs would be prohibitive. I thought next of the thousands of radio sponsors and advertisers all over America who depend on the phonograph record to sell millions and millions of dollars worth of their products over the radio every day. In thinking about the many other industries that depend on the phonograph record for some portion of their income, I couldn't help but realize what a tremendous effect the phonograph record has on the whole economic situation in America today.

Last, but please believe me, not least, I thought of the public—how they too depend on the phonograph record. Practically every person in America today, whether he knows it or not, depends on the phonograph record for entertainment for a hobby, for relaxation, for pleasure, for education, and most important of all for an emotional outlet. When I summed all this up, I could no longer look at the phonograph record as a piece of shellac. I look at it now as a living, pulsating, breathing disc—a disc that contains the creativeness, the thought, the work, and the effort of so many, many people. A disc with hope, with ambition, with anxiety, with disappointment, with joy, with every human emotion running through its grooves, and with so much dependent upon it.

Well, those are some of the things that all of us in repertoire think of when we go into a recording booth to make records.

We all feel proud and privileged to be connected with such an important industry as the making of phonograph records and we are prouder still to be with the best and most progressive company, and the company that has the finest sales force in the world—Capitol.

December 1, 1954 was a sad and regrettable day for country music and for me. Fred Rose, a guiding force and stalwart of the industry, passed away at the age of 57. I lost a friend. Fred and I had both sung on the same radio station, KYW in Chicago, in 1933 and even then he was always available with wise counsel and help. I always knew him as a popular songwriter and was quite surprised to learn he had moved to Nashville and formed a country music publishing firm with Roy Acuff. I was more than pleased to know that when I came to Nashville, I had a friend there. I also knew Wesley, his son, from Chicago. He, too, was a big help to me. They built the firm into the largest country music publishing firm in the world and guided countless top artists on the road to success.

It would be interesting to know how many songwriters Fred helped in writing their songs. In 1961 Fred was one of the first three to be inducted into the Country Music Hall of Fame. Wesley insisted that Fred's office remain intact, exactly as Fred left it, and never be occupied by anyone else. Wesley was inducted into the Hall of Fame in 1986 and passed away in 1990.

Bill Lowery's music publishing firm in Atlanta was growing and he was becoming quite adept at finding talent in the area. In 1955 he played me the dubs of two artists he thought I might be interested in–Jerry Reed and Roy Drusky. I was impressed with Jerry; he was a good writer and I liked his style, but he was only eighteen years old. I didn't want to sign Jerry because he was too young, but Bill kept insisting so I gave in. Jerry's first record was "If The Good Lord's Willing and The Creek Don't Rise." Another song I recall, "Rocking In Baghdad," featured an oboe player from the Nashville Symphony Orchestra.

I was sure it was going to be a hit. Although Jerry's records sold well in the Atlanta area, none ever made it onto the *Billboard* chart. Jerry's last session was in 1958, after which he joined the Army. A few years later, a more mature Jerry Reed signed with RCA Victor, was produced by Chet Atkins, and was on the *Billboard* chart for sixteen years. His biggest hit was "When You're Hot, You're Hot." Several of his records made the pop charts and Jerry went on to become an actor, appearing on television, and in important parts for several major movies.

Although I thought Roy Drusky was a good singer, I turned him down and he signed with Decca Records, then with Mercury. He had a very successful recording career. I had been hearing and reading about a young singer named Elvis Presley, who was recording for Sun Records in Memphis, Tennessee. I found out that his manager, Bob Neal, was a Memphis disc jockey. I decided to try to get him for Capitol. I went to Memphis and met with Bob, and he told me that Elvis's contract was not for sale. A few weeks later, I read that RCA Victor had signed Elvis and his manager was Colonel Tom Parker, the dean of all booking agents. I understand RCA paid $35,000.00 for the contract. I met Elvis several times and was always impressed by his gentlemanliness.

In 1956 we sold our Studio City home and bought a home on Devon Lane in Sherman Oaks. Our new home was like an estate. The site was comprised of two lots, with the house being built on the hillside and having three levels, and on either side there was a vacant lot, which we also owned. The full price was $36,000.00. The second level was a basement with a laundry room, a furnace room and another large room that we converted into an office for Central and Snyder. There was also a poolroom for the swimming pool, which was on the first level. On the second level, one of the lots had a patio with a barbecue pit. We set up a ping-pong table for Greg and Claudia—they loved it!

It was also in 1956 that Capitol moved into its new headquarters, the thirteen-story Capitol tower in Hollywood. The architect suggested it be in the shape of a record. It was purportedly the first round office building built. At that time, because of earthquake possibilities, the Los Angeles building code stated no building could be more than thirteen stories high. It wasn't long after that the restriction was lifted and the sky was the limit. The studios were at street level. The executive offices were on the thirteenth floor and the A&R offices on the twelfth floor. Just a year later, Capitol Records was sold to an English corporation, English Musical Industries (EMI). We were all relieved to learn that there would be no changes in the modus operandi. EMI brought us The Beatles!

The catalogs of Central and Snyder Music were growing by leaps and bounds. We had quite a few hits and the workload was getting quite heavy, especially every six months in February and August, when we had to send royalty statements and checks to the writers. Every writer and every song title had to be posted on individual bookkeeping sheets, and as computers had not yet come into existence, the royalty earnings had to be totaled on an adding machine and a statement typed. June and I were still doing all the work. The financial status of Central, Snyder was in tip-top shape, and now besides our go-between, Buzz Carlton, Lee, Cliffie, June, and myself were now drawing salaries from both companies.

In addition to her company responsibilities and directing the mothers' chorus and church choir, June was now occasionally directing the June Nelson Singers on recordings. Her singers were all professionals. She did backgrounds for Tex Ritter, Nelson Riddle, Tommy Sands, Tennessee Ernie Ford, and others. Her group did the background for two of Ernie's religious albums, which were million sellers that won several awards, became standards, and are still selling on cassettes and CDs today. No matter how busy she was, the children always came first and she never complained.

1956 was the year I signed Bobby Bare, Wanda Jackson, Wynn Stewart, and Gene Vincent. Bobby Bare was with us for two years and then he was drafted. After his stint in the Army, he had a successful career as a writer and recording artist for RCA Victor.

When she was sixteen years old, Hank Thompson brought Wanda Jackson, who had already recorded for Decca Records, to my attention. I was still reluctant to sign a minor and waited until she turned eighteen years old. She had been touring with Elvis Presley when he was on his way to stardom. He convinced her that she should sing what are now called rockabilly-type songs. She followed his advice and her first recording sold fairly well, but only one, "I Gotta Know," made the *Billboard* chart. She was a hit in Europe and especially the Scandinavian countries. One record, "Fujiyama Mama," was a smash hit in Japan.

In 1961 Wanda returned to the more standard type of country songs with "Right or Wrong" and "In the Middle of a Heartache," both making the pop charts. She was on the *Billboard* charts consistently for the remainder of her seventeen years with Capitol. She and her husband, Wendell Goodman, whom she married in 1961, decided they wanted to enter the religious field and wanted to record gospel songs only. We recorded one gospel album, but when Wanda wanted to do another, I put my foot down and explained that Capitol was *not* a gospel label. I reluctantly released her from her contract.

Today Wanda appears on religious television programs and has performed in churches throughout the country; however, when she frequently goes to Europe, it's a different story. She is still in demand as a rock 'n roll and country performer, although she manages to do a couple of gospel songs during her performances. She records in Sweden on the Tab label. It was always a pleasure to work with Wanda. She and her husband live in Oklahoma City and we still keep in touch with each other.

In 1956 Skeets McDonald brought me Wynn Steward, a guy he had been working with, and I thought he had good possibilities so I signed him. Skeets, who played bass on Wynn's first session, brought along a young man whose ambition was to become a songwriter. His name was Harlan Howard. Harlan and I were in the control booth when Wynn recorded his first song, "You Took Her Off My Hands," now released as "Take Her Off My Mind." Harlan was the sole writer but in appreciation of the efforts on his behalf, Wynn and Skeets were considered co-writers and claimed royalties of the song. As Harlan did not have a publisher, I suggested Central Songs. All of his first songs were published by Central.

Being enthusiastic and anxious, Harlan would come into the office every day and ask about the progress of his songs. This irritated Buzz Carlton, our go-between and office manager, who was a blustery man with no understanding of talent. He told Harlan to stop bothering him. When I found out about this, I wanted to slug him, but I didn't dare as he was bigger than I was. Harlan moved to Nashville and became one of the most prolific writers of country songs with hit after hit. He was inducted into the Songwriters Hall of Fame and, in 1997, to the Country Music Hall of Fame. I signed him to a recording contract, but without much success. His forte was writing. I also signed his wife, Jan Howard, without success. She later went with Decca Records and had a moderate recording career.

I recorded Wynn Stewart for two years, but he only had one chart record, "Waltz of the Angels," a Central publication. In 1958 he went with Challenge Records and had several "charters." Challenge was owned by Joe Johnson and Gene Autry. Joe was managing Autry's publishing firm. In 1964, at Cliffie Stone's urging, I re-signed Wynn. He and Cliffie got together and decided to form a publishing company, which would be a subsidiary of Central. We called it Freeway Music.

We had several hits with the firm; the biggest being "It's Such a Pretty World Today," written by Dale Noe. Wynn was the most aggravating artist I ever had. He was difficult to contact. I'd phone and there would be no answer. If I did get someone and leave a message, maybe he'd respond in two or three weeks. A few times I had to reschedule a recording date because he didn't show up. This happened in October of 1966. I had scheduled a session in Nashville and had to leave two days after the session when Wynn didn't show up. I told Marvin Hughes, who was manager and producer of the Nashville office, which I opened and was overseer of, to do the session if and when Wynn showed up. The day after I left, Wynn showed up and Marvin produced his biggest hit, "It's Such A Pretty World." Wynn left Capitol in 1971 and recorded for RCA Victor for two years. Despite his penchant for not answering phone calls and not showing up for sessions, Wynn was likeable. He died in 1985 at the young age of 51.

When I was home, I always attended church with June and the children. Our minister would have a member of the congregation act as an associate, who gave the church news of coming events. Most of them muttered and were difficult to understand. I used to say to June, "It would be nice to know what he's saying." One time when I was out of town, Herb, our minister, asked June if she thought I would be willing to be his associate. June, knowing of my constant griping about the associates, said yes and that she would let him know when I was back in town. When I came home, June told me that she had told Herb I would be his associate.

I was always nervous in front of an audience and I blew my stack. I said, "You've got a lot of nerve telling him that. Call him and tell him I won't do it!" That night when I went to bed, I got to thinking,

Why do I get nervous and jittery in front of an audience? Because I'm afraid of what they will think of me? I'm not thinking of the audience. I'm thinking of me. I'm a former radio announcer. They will be able to understand me. They will be able to hear clearly what I'm saying. I will be giving them news and information.

I leaned over to June, kissed her, apologized for my anger, and told her I would tell Herb I would be his associate. I was the associate several times and always went on the podium with the thought and attitude—I'm giving!

Capitol now had distribution branches in every major city and market in the country, and every year or so would hold a sales convention in various cities. It was always attended by our president, Glenn Wallichs, along with the head of artists and repertoire (A&R), all members of the A&R staff, branch managers, salesmen, and promotion men. Members of the A&R staff were Lee Gillette, Voyle Gilmore, Dave Cavanaugh, Dave Dexter, Alan Livingston, and I. There were usually two or three artists attending also.

In 1953 we held our convention at Lake Placid, New York. One of the artists was Mel Blanc, the comedian, who was riding high on his record "Tweety," the canary. Mel's hobby was collecting antique watches. His prize possession was an extremely rare French pocket watch. When the back was opened, it had the figures of a naked man and woman fornicating with each movement of the second hand.

At these sales meetings, members of the A&R staff usually spoke about their artists and future releases. I spoke at every one of these meetings. Country music was still being called "country-hillbilly," and there were some sales and promotion men who didn't believe in the potential of country music. This is the speech I gave at Lake Placid.

> First of all, I want to tell you something I think you all know. For the past few months, the sales of our country-hillbilly records have increased tremendously. We've had the number 1 hit song of the Nation. This is due largely to the efforts of you salesmen, and we in Repertoire want to take this opportunity of thanking each and every one of you.
>
> Believe you me, we know without you this would not have been possible. We want to thank Gene Becker and Marvin Townsend of our promotion department, who have done such a wonderful job, and we want to thank Lloyd Cook for his great help. Lloyd, you know, lives and works out of Nashville, Tennessee, the hub and heart of the Hillbilly country. Lloyd has been a great help, not only promotion-wise, but has been finding us new talent and new material. You men have been selling country-hillbilly records where they've never been sold before. You've been proving not only to us but also to yourselves that country-hillbilly music can be sold anywhere in the nation even in such remote areas as New York City, Chicago, and Los Angeles.
>
> No matter where you go in America today, you'll find people who buy country-hillbilly music and records. Everyone at the home office is aware of the great sales potential of country-hillbilly music and is bound and determined that Capitol Records will have the outstanding country-hillbilly Division artist-wise, material-wise, and sales-wise. Everyone is cooperating in this determined effort.

Last spring our President, Mr. Glenn Wallichs, went down to Nashville, Tennessee, to meet all the people connected with WSM's *Grand Ol' Opry*, which is an important factor in the sales of country-hillbilly records. We now have an open door to the *Grand Ol' Opry* and already have two of our artists, Faron Young and Martha Carson, on their permanent roster. There will be more of our artists on the *Grand Ol' Opry* in the very near future.

We are constantly building our talent roster—weeding out the unproductive, adding new potential stars. We have at present the greatest talent roster in the history of our division headed by Hank Thompson, Tennessee Ernie, Faron Young, Jimmy Wakely, and Martha Carson. Some of the newer names, which have already proven themselves, are Rod Morris, Billy Strange, Skeets McDonald, Ferlin Husky, and many others.

We are constantly on the look out for new talent and will go anywhere to find it. It used to be that I could stay in Hollywood and do all of the Hillbilly recording sessions, but not so now. Only 25 percent of our hillbilly-country records are now made in Hollywood. I'm out on the road a great deal of the time. The majority of our hillbilly records are now made on the home ground in Tennessee, Texas, Kentucky, Alabama, Georgia, Louisiana, and other states.

You men can be a big help as far as talent is concerned. If you hear of anyone that you think is good, let me know. If you hear of any material that is good, let me know. Believe me, I need all the help I can get in this respect, and today you never know where your next hit is coming from.

We are also getting more and more into the religious field. Here is another source of sales we haven't even begun to tap. I think right about now is the time to tell you of our big country-hillbilly campaign, which starts August 4th with Release 329. It is made-up entirely of country-hillbilly records, which we feel are the strongest we've had in a long time: Tennessee Ernie, Faron Young, Jimmy Wakely and Rod Morris. Release 329 will consist only of these five country-hillbilly records.

Our Promotion Department has come up with some wonderful aids to help you in selling these records, although we know they will sell themselves up to a certain point. For the remainder of August, there will be no other country-hillbilly releases. This means that you have an entire month to concentrate on these five strong country-hillbilly records. There is no doubt in our minds that these records are so great that all five of them could, and in all probability will, hit the *Billboard* charts, not only as the most played by Disc Jockeys but as the best selling records in the country field. Now, I know you fellows can and will do it.

Our Promotion Department has come up with some wonderful things to help in this great drive. We have 100 percent publisher cooperation, which means that the publishers of these songs will take out Billboard ads, will service disc jockeys, juke box operators, and will do everything in their power to help us put these records over.

Two other items the Promotion Department has come up with that I think are great are the special country-hillbilly record sleeves which will immediately identify a record as country-hillbilly and will advertise only records of the country-hillbilly division. Another terrific item is the country-hillbilly browser box. All I can say is, "Brother, it's going to help you sell country-hillbilly records like they've never been sold before!"

Two other promotion items that will be of great help are soft sheets on each record in the release and finally, we are having printed 20,000 booklets of our country-hillbilly artists for free distribution to all Dealers who want them." This drive on country-hillbilly records will be the talk and envy of the entire industry.

In closing, I'd like to talk a little about musical traits. Right here in this room there is a great divergence of opinion as far as music is concerned. Some of you like classical, some Dixieland Jazz, some popular, and a great many, like myself, country-hillbilly music.

A few of you know this: At one time I was considered an authority on classical music. I ran a program for years in Chicago called *The Symphonic Hour*. I used to announce the Grant Park Concerts, and also the programs of the Chicago Symphony Orchestra. Well, it so happened that the station I worked for also had live talent hillbilly programs and it was part of my job to hire the hillbilly musicians, and I soon found myself just as interested in hillbilly music as I was in classical.

I think you will agree that greatness—be it in medicine, science, or music, is that which does the most amount of good for the most amount of people. It is common

> knowledge that country-hillbilly music is understood, played, sung, and enjoyed by more people in America than any other type of music. Therefore, it has a greater sales potential than any other type of music.
>
> I just want to leave you with a slight variation of a popular saying by the great French writer Voltaire:"I May not want to hear the music my fellow man wants to hear, but I will defend to the death his right to hear it."
>
> Thank you.

• • •

I got a French lesson from Dexter at our New Orleans convention meeting. Ten of us had gone to this fancy French restaurant for dinner and were seated at one long table. Dexter was seated next to me, and when we were almost finished eating, Dave said to me, "Ken it's always courteous to say, "*L'addition sil vous plait*" to the waiter. I motioned the waiter and when he came, I said "*L'addition sil vous plait.*" He smiled and handed me the check. Of course, that meant "The addition, please." Everyone had a good laugh, including me. It didn't matter, because the bill went on my expense account."

Central and Snyder continued to grow, and we bought a building on Ventura Boulevard for $25,000, thinking we might move our home office operation there, but it turned out to be impractical. There was a men's clothing store next door, whose owner wanted the building for expansion. We sold it to him for $50,000. We found out later, the owner's brother was an attorney with Capitol.

In 1956, when I was planning a trip to Nashville, I listened to a dub sent to me by Disk Jockey Sheriff Tex Davis of radio station WCMS, in Norfolk, Virginia. It was a Rock 'N' Roll song called, "Be Bop A Lula" sung by Gene Craddock. I was impressed by the singer and the song and felt that Rock and Roll was to become an important part of the music industry. I immediately called Davis and said, "If you can have Gene and his band in Nashville by May 4, I'll record them." He assured me he could and he did; however, on my way to Nashville I began to wonder if I had acted too hastily. After all, I had only heard one song by the group, but when they were in the studio and recorded their first song, my misgivings were immediately dispelled. I felt we had a winner!

There is a misconception about that first date. It's been said that because I wasn't sure of the group I had hired some of Nashville's top musicians to standby in case they were needed. Nothing could be further from the truth! If there were Nashville musicians in the studio, they had just finished a session and were hanging around. I wasn't about to pay the extra cost of standby musicians for a new, untried artist.

During the first session we recorded four songs, "Race with the Devil," written by Sheriff Tex Davis, and Gene; "Be Bop A Lula," also by Tex and Gene;

"Woman Love," by Jack Rhodes; and "I Sure Miss You," by Tex and Evelyn Brown. I brought "Woman Love" to Gene, which was published by Central, and as they had no publisher for the other three songs I suggested they put one in Central and the other two in my friend, Bill Lowery's firm, Lowery Music Company in Atlanta, Georgia. "Race with the Devil" went to Central and the other two "Be Bop A Lula" and "I Sure Miss You," went to Lowery Music.

I was sure "Woman Love" was going to be the hit; I made it the "A" side and backed it with "Be Bop A Lula" as the "B" side. "Woman Love" was banned by many radio stations and completely in England because of a line, "a huggin' and a kissin' and smokin' all the time." They said it sounded like, "a-fuckin' and a kissin'." I was usually very careful about pronunciation and language but I sure blew this one!

Gene had a rather soft voice, and when we started to record, the band was so overpowering it was difficult to hear him. In Hollywood we had portable isolation booths which could be moved anywhere in the studio and had three panels. The middle one had a glass window and the other two were on hinges. Bradley's studio, being relatively new, didn't have one. The problem was solved by putting Gene in the hall of the quonset hut.

I felt the name Craddock was too harsh a sounding and I suggested he replace his last name with his middle name, Vincent. Gene Vincent had an easy, flowing, euphonious sound. Gene agreed and has been known by that name ever since.

When Gene signed his Capitol contract, I learned he had signed a previous contract with the owner of the radio station where he broadcast. The radio station contract also granted the owner a percentage of any royalties he might receive from recordings if he signed with a recording company. I thought this was taking undue advantage of a young man, without any knowledge of contracts or the music business. I was determined to break this contract. I don't recall the details of how the meeting with the owner of the radio station, whose name I forget, was set-up, but I met with him in his hotel suite in New York and told him he was taking advantage of a young, inexperienced artist. He countered with, "It was through his broadcasting over my station that he was gaining popularity and I think that's a form of advertising for which I'm entitled to some compensation." I had to laugh at that remark and said the contract is illegal because Gene was only twenty years old and still considered a minor when it was signed. He was still reluctant until I said, "I'll just turn the matter over to our attorneys at Capitol and let them handle it." He cogitated a couple of minutes and then agreed to forget the contract. We parted on a friendly note.

Gene was really a likeable young man but was emotionally immature, although I never had a problem with him. Since he had no manager, I called Ed McLemore, a Dallas business man, who besides managing artists, owned parking lots, had the first syndicated televised wrestling hour, and ran the Big "D"

Jamboree. At the time he was managing Sonny James and he agreed to add Gene to his talent roster. A few months after that he called me and said "Ken, I'm dropping Gene. I can't handle him. He's too much of a problem. He's erratic and constantly asking for money." I'm not sure who became his manager.

In 1952 at the age of seventeen, Gene joined the navy and was discharged when he got in a motorcycle accident and injured his left leg. The leg was in a cast for the remainder of his life, But it didn't impede his stage performances and, in fact, gave him a certain distinction.

When "Be Bop A Lula" reached the million mark, I went to Chicago to present him, on stage, with his gold record. He was playing in an auditorium that seated thousands. The place was jam-packed. After the show I urged Gene to leave by the back entrance to avoid the crowd, but he insisted on going out the front. When we got to the street, we were completely surrounded by hundreds of teenage fans. A riot ensued and the police were called. One of the musicians panicked and was up against a wall screaming. We surrounded Gene to try to protect him. Even I was messed up. It took a little while for the police to calm things down and we finally left. It was a harrowing experience.

I produced my last two sessions with Gene and The Blue Caps in August of 1959, and in December of that year they toured England. In January of 1961, my then-assistant Karl Engeman, produced two sessions by them, and in October of that year, their last Capitol session in America was produced by Nick Venet. It's an odd paradox that Gene never attained popularity in the United States but became a worldwide rock 'n' roll idol who sold millions of Capitol records. These are still in demand today on CDs. His band, The Blue Caps, which was named by its outstanding drummer Dickie "Be Bop" Harrell, occasionally still tour Europe.

In 1956 I wrote a song using the pseudonym Billie Willie, with Jack Rhodes and Freddie Franks, titled "Five Days, Five Days." It was the only song of mine that Gene recorded. I have received royalties on the song almost every year since we recorded it. The last check I received was in the year 2000. Around 1965 Gene's musical ability began to wane, but his records continued to sell. Sometime in 1970 he came to my office and wanted to record again for Capitol. I felt sorry for him and sad that I had to turn him down. In October of 1971 he died from a bleeding ulcer. In 1998 he was inducted into the rock 'n' roll Hall of Fame, which he richly deserved.

Jack Stapp and I became good friends. I guess he thought I was kind of a Guru. He not only would ask my advice but would bring other people to me for advice. Mr. Dinkler, whose first name I don't remember, was the owner of the Andrew Jackson and another hotel that I knew of in Atlanta. He and Jack were friends. Whenever Dinkler came to Nashville, he stayed in the larger top floor suite. On one of his visits Jack told me he wanted to meet me. When we met the three of us chatted awhile, and then Dinkler asked me if I thought he should put a television set in every hotel room. I said I thought it would be a wise move and gave him reasons why. He then told me his wife had written several songs and when I come to Atlanta, he would like me to meet with her. I presume that was the reason he wanted to meet me.

When I went to Atlanta a short time later, I called Dinkler and met with him and his wife. She was beautiful, stunning, statuesque, and obviously a socialite. He introduced us and left, closing the door behind him. I felt awkward, embarrassed, and ill at ease, and I probably showed it! I looked the songs over and it was obvious they had no merit whatsoever. I didn't tell her that but fibbed and said I would show them to some artists. I returned them later and wrote her that the artists turned them down. I don't know when or why, but I understand that Mr. Dinkler either committed suicide or fell out of a window in his Atlanta hotel.

Jack was divorced and became quite a ladies man. Twice he called me and suggested we have dinner together, once at the Andrew Jackson and the other at the Maxwell House, the hotel Maxwell House Coffee was named after. When I entered the dining room, Jack was sitting at a table with two women. He probably thought I wanted female companionship, which I didn't. I was too much in love with my wife, although once I almost fell by the wayside, which I'll tell you about later. I don't know what my unsolicited dates expected, but I would make sure they saw my wedding ring and I'd talk about my children. After dinner I signed the check at the Andrew Jackson and Jack took care of the Maxwell House tab. I excused myself after the checks were taken care of; I don't know what they did after I left!

One evening, in response to a knock on my door, I opened it and there stood a pretty young girl. She couldn't have been more than fifteen or sixteen years old. She said Jack Stapp told her to come to my suite. I was a little shocked but told her to come in and sit down. I couldn't understand this—was she a prostitute? Had Jack paid her to come to me?

As we talked, she seemed to be ill at ease but she even told me who her father was, which I'm not going to divulge. Was Jack holding something over this girl that made her do his bidding or what? I really felt sorry for her and I wasn't about to take advantage of the situation. After about twenty minutes, I told her to go home. As she left, she seemed relieved. I was a little miffed at Jack but didn't discuss it with him and he never mentioned it either.

During World War II, Jack was assigned to the Office of War Information (0WI) in London, England, headed by Louis B. Cowan, who later became the owner and producer of television shows. His most famous television show was *The $64,000 Question*. He and Jack became friends and remained so after the war, even though Jack lived in Nashville and Cowan in New York. Stapp became manager and program director of WSM's *Grand Ol' Opry* and, seeing the potential the Country Music publishing business, persuaded Cowan in the early 1950's to form a publishing firm with him. They named it Tree Music.

In 1955 Tree Music published its first hit, "Heartbreak Hotel." In 1956 it was recorded by Elvis Presley and was his first RCA Victor recording. It quickly became number one on both the County and Pop charts. Cowan and his attorney, Mr. Fleischman, couldn't understand why they hadn't received any royalties after the record was out a couple of months. I was in Nashville and mentioned to Jack that I was going to New York. He told me about Cowan and his attorney's concern about not receiving royalties. He asked me if I would meet with them and explain how and when royalties were paid. I agreed. He gave me Cowan's address and phone number, and said he would let them know to expect me. When I got to New York, I phoned them and set a date and time to meet.

I arrived at their office, on the top floor of the building, around 5 o'clock. I introduced myself and Cowan and I exchanged a few pleasantries. He then turned to his secretary and asked if she had made dinner reservations. She said "Yes." I said, "Can't we go someplace and just have a couple of beers?" Cowan seemed relieved and told her to cancel the reservations.

We went to the 21 Club. As we entered, it seemed that everyone knew him and greeted him with, "Good Evening, Mr. Cowan." I didn't know at the time that this was one of the most exclusive clubs in New York. We were seated in a rather isolated booth. I ordered a beer and don't recall what Cowan ordered. We chatted a few moments and he asked me where I was from. I told him I grew up in Chicago, and he said, "So did I. What part of Chicago?" I replied the south side. He asked me where on the south side and I told him Fifty-Eighth Street and Prarie. He looked very surprised and said, "You didn't happen to go to Carter Practice Grammar School did you?" I replied, "I sure as hell did!"

It turned out Cowan lived right across the street from the School on Michigan Avenue and had graduated a half year before I did. There was an immediate bond between us. We reminisced about the old neighborhood and knew many of the same kids. He told me that he married a daughter of the Spiegel family, which was one of the leading catalog merchandising companies. He wanted to make good on his own and he did.

We each had a sandwich and left the club around 7:30. He walked with me to my hotel, which was a short distance away. He told me his wife was on the French Riviera at the family chateau. We made an appointment for the next day to meet with him and his attorney. When I met with Cowan and his attorney, Mr. Fleischman, a very nervous man, I explained that record royalties were paid twice a year on February 15th and August 15th, and that because "Heartbreak Hotel" was released in February, there would be no royalties until August and possibly not until next February.

They had no knowledge whatsoever of what was involved in music publishing, so I gave them a brief synopsis of copyrights, writers contracts and payments, getting a song recorded, performance fees, promotion and the business in general. I got the feeling that Fleischman was totally uninterested and would rather not be bothered with the company. Cowan didn't seem to be too enthusiastic either. I had dinner the next evening with Louis, and he sort of indicated he was too busy with his production company to worry about the publishing company. We enjoyed reminiscing about our days in Chicago.

The next day he took me to the studio and introduced me to the master of ceremonies and the production staff of *The $64,000 Question*, which was probably the first TV game show of its type. I don't recall the year, but there was quite a scandal regarding the show. Some of the contestants had been given the answers to the questions. Cowan, being the owner of the show, was the executive producer but was not actively involved in the actual production. It was assumed that the producer who gave the contestants the answers either wanted to make the program more exciting or possibly may have been splitting the prize money with them.

At dinner that night, he made me promise to let him know when I came to New York and if I informed him of the time of my arrival, he would have his chauffeur pick me up at the airport. I never took advantage of that offer, but I would let him know I was in New York and if possible, we would get together. After three or four years we lost contact.

On my return to Nashville, I told Stapp what had transpired and of their seemingly disinterest in music publishing. I told Jack it's possible that Cowan might be willing to sell him his interest in the company. He said he didn't know if he could afford it. I said make a deal whereby you pay him with the BMI performance fees and a percentage of profits after company expenses are paid. I don't know the details, but it wasn't too long after that when Jack Stapp became the sole owner of Tree Music Publishing Company, Inc. He hired Buddy Killen, who played bass on the *Grand Ol' Opry*, to acquire songs, get artists to record them, and build the catalog. He brought Buddy to my suite and asked me to tell him what to look for in a song. I could only tell him how I judged a song. Does the song have an understandable, interesting lyric, a singable melody, and emotional appeal?

Buddy became very successful at finding good songs, getting them recorded, and was bringing hits to the company. When I saw what Buddy was doing, I told Jack he had better make him a partial partner in the Company or he would lose him. He did. If he hadn't, I would have had Cliffie hire him for Central Songs. Jack passed away in December of 1980 at the age of 68 and was inducted into the Country Music Hall of Fame in 1989. I don't know if Buddy became the sole owner of Tree Music, but I do know he built it into a major publishing firm and sometime around 1996 or 1997 the company was purchased by Sony for forty million dollars.

The time I made an unsuccessful attempt to stray from the straight and narrow, I had been away from home for an unusually long period. I was staying at the Andrew Jackson and Mae Axton, who was a successful writer of country songs, including "Heartbreak Hotel" had the room next to mine. One evening she came to my room, wearing only green silk pajamas. She looked ravishing, along with the aroma of her perfume; my biological urges were aroused and I lost my head.

Because of my early sexual experiences, I assumed she had come for sex, but boy was I wrong! We talked for a few minutes and I made my move. I put my arms around her and kissed her on the neck. She pushed me away and said, "Ken, I came to chat and discuss songs and nothing else."

I immediately regained my composure and, realizing what a fool I had made of myself, I apologized. We talked for almost an hour, and when she left; I again apologized for my unwarranted behavior. She said, "Forget it Ken. I understand." We remained friends. I respected her and was glad she saved me from the depths of degradation, but I always had a feeling of guilt and shame whenever we met.

• • •

Gillette always dreamed of owning a radio station, and in 1956 he learned that a 250 watt station, KRKS in Ridgecrest, California was for sale, the price $12,500.00. Lee, Cliffie and I were well-steeped in radio broadcasting, and as our publishing companies could now easily finance it, and even though its signal reached a very limited area, we bought it and named it Gilson Broadcasting Inc. Ridgecrest which was near the China Lake Naval Test and Training Center, about 125 miles north of Hollywood and about a 2-1/2 hour drive. Lee was acquainted witti a man who formerly managed a radio station in Alaska and he agreed to manage and be salesman for KRKS. We hired one of Lee's musician friends as our engineer. Our staff also included two announcers and a secretary, whose duties were to type the daily logs, take care of the record and tape library, and type the statements and a list of all records and songs broadcast. All stations were now licensed by both BMI and ASCAP and were required to send them a monthly list of songs broadcast. The writers were paid performance fees based upon the number of times a song was played, which was assembled from these lists. The daily log included the name and time of a program, the name and time a sponsored announcement was made and the name of the announcer on duty, who was required to initial and write the time a commercial was read.

The manager's office, the studio, and transmitter were located on a 17 acre plot that was about a half mile from any housing or businesses. I felt we should also own the land. Lee and Cliffie agreed. We contacted the owner and he agreed to sell us 17 acres for $17,000.00. We paid for it from our Snyder Music account. We purchased another turntable and an Ampex tape recorder, as a result we had to enlarge the announcers booth and modified the studio. This was paid for by Central Songs. All of this meant more responsibility and work for June and me.

I had a classical library of about three hundred albums and decided to do a weekly *Sunday Symphonic hour*. I would assemble six weeks of programs along with the taped announcements so that when I had to leave town, there would always be a program.

Lee, Cliffie, and I would go to the station whenever we could; usually one of us made it at least once a week. Gillette, who produced most of Dean Martin's recordings and was friendly with Frank Sinatra, asked them to make KRKS station breaks, which they did as a favor to him.

A trade deal was giving a sponsor equal air time to cover the cost of any merchandise purchased. We allowed our manager to do this for his personal needs.

The station was making a meager profit of a little over one hundred dollars a month after expenses were paid. This didn't bother us; we felt as the area grew so would the station's profitability. The things that disturbed me were the logs, the statements, and checks were always mailed to us late and the office and studios were always unkempt. We expected promptness, and although we didn't have a cleaning service, it would not be a difficult task to keep the place neat and clean. When we would speak to the manager about this, he'd say his neglect was caused by his being so busy. During the next three years the station's profit increased slightly but we still received the mail late and the office and studios were still not as clean and neat as they should be. During this time we received about four statements signed by the manager stating he was unable to collect.

One Saturday afternoon, Lee and I drove to Ridgecrest. We entered town around noon and decided to stop in a restaurant for lunch. When I picked up the menu, I said, "Hey, Lee, this is a place that refused to pay its bill. Let's find out why." We introduced ourselves to the manager and asked him why he refused to pay his broadcasting bill. He replied, "What do you mean? Just a minute." He went in the kitchen and came back with a paid in full receipt, signed by our manager; he was paid in cash. We were embarrassed and apologized for our mistake. Our manager's lack of efficiency always disturbed me and I was glad we had a legitimate reason to discharge him, which we did post haste. We hired one of the announcers as the new manager, and with our permission he discharged the secretary and hired his wife to replace her. Together they always kept the office and studios neat and clean, the logs were typed neatly, and the statements, checks and bills were mailed to us promptly. We were pleased. After a couple of months, the roof fell in! There was no more profit. We weren't even making expenses for which Central and Snyder were responsible. Our new Manager was obviously not a salesman.

In 1961, after several months of no financial gain, realizing that a station of KRKS's size should have an on-site owner, we decided to sell and luckily sold it for $20,000.00. Lee wanted to sell the land too, but Cliffie and I wanted to hold onto it because the new owner would be paying rent and the City would eventually expand to that area. We each paid lee $2,600.00 which covered the cost of his third of the property. We then each paid eighty-five hundred dollars to Snyder Music Co. And had the title transferred to us as joint ownership. We held the property until May 1979, when we sold it to Eastside Properties for $34,000. I don't recall what the down payment was, but they were to pay five hundred dollars a month or more in principal and interest.

In 1982 Cliffie asked me to buy his half of the note which I did for $8,000. In 1984 Eastside Properties paid the note in full, which was $16,760.00 plus interest of $97.00. I'm sure the property is worth a great deal more today than what we sold it for, but I didn't make out too bad collecting rent and interest all those years.

In 1957 two of the music industry's very important organizations were formed The Country Music Association (CMA) and the National Academy of Recording Arts and Sciences (NARAS).

CMA was born at a meeting held in Miami, Florida by the Country Music Disc Jockey Associates (CMDJA), whose President was Connie B. Gay. Connie had invited Wesley Rose, Dee Kilpatrick, who was then manager of the *Grand Ol' Opry*, Hubert Long, the Wilburn Brothers, and a couple of other people to discuss the lack of interest in the organization, whose cash on hand was less than $1,000.00. After a three hour discussion by Connie, Wesley, Dee, and Hubert, it was concluded that the problem was the CMDJA was only one segment of country music, and that in order to be successful the organization must encompass all segments of the industry, radio and television, music publishers, record companies, artists, managers, bookers, and trade papers. It was decided to form a Country Music Association with headquarters in Nashville. This concept was presented to the disc jockeys, and they voted to donate the remaining money in their treasury to help start the new organization. With the assistance of two (2) Nashville attorneys, Ward Hudgins and his assistant, Dick Frank, who donated their legal services, the State of Tennessee Corporation Committee, on September 26, 1958, granted CMA it's charter on November 20 and 21.

The first officers and directors were elected: Connie B. Gay, president; Eddy Arnold and Harold Moon, vice presidents; Wesley Rose, chairman of the board; Hubert Long, treasurer; Mac Wiseman, secretary; Vic McAlpin, representing song writers; Cracker Jim Brooker, representing disc Jockeys; Bob Burton director at large, representing Artist Management and Bookers, Oscar Davis; representing Radio and Television, Dee Kilpatrick; representing Trade Magazines, Charlie Lamb; representing Record Companies, Ken Nelson; and representing Artists; Ernest Tubb.

Even though its treasury was skimpy, the Board voted to hire a Secretary. I don't know who suggested Jo Walker, but whoever did deserves a medal. She was hired for a salary of three hundred seventy-five dollars a month. Without her aptitude, devotion and dedication, I don't believe CMA would have survived!

I designed CMA's first logo, a note with a world map imprinted on it with the words "Best Liked Worldwide." The large flag of the note was imprinted with "Country Music Association." The drawing was made by Marvin Schwartz of Capitol's Art Department.

Early in 1957 the Hollywood Walk of Fame Committee invited five top recording executives, Sonny Burke (Decca), Lloyd Dunn (Capitol), Dennis Farnon, (RCA Victor), Jesse Kaye (MGM) and Paul Weston (Columbia), to lunch and asked them to select a group of artists whose names would be inscribed on the walk along with other entertainment stars. At a later meeting, these record men decided that since the movie industry had a National Motion Picture Academy, and television had a National Television Academy, the Recording Industry should have a National Recording Academy to honor artists and technical achievements in the industry. They requested Jim Conkling, who was formerly head of the Artists and Repertoire Department of Capitol Records and had recently retired as President of Columbia Records, to take on the role of Chairman. He accepted the responsibility.

In June of 1957, top recording artists, producers, songwriters, and others met to appoint a steering committee and nominate its governors. At its first meeting the Los Angeles Chapter of NARAS elected Paul Weston its President and Lee Gillette its Vice President. Several months later the New York Chapter elected Guy Lombardo its President. Within three years chapters were founded in other major cities, including Chicago, Nashville, Atlanta, San Francisco, and Memphis. A national organization was formed and Paul Weston was elected the first national president.

Christine Farnon, a young lady who started in radio and later was with Capitol Records, was asked by the founders of the Academy to provide staff support during the creations of the organization. They couldn't have made a better choice. She became the bulwark of the Academy. Her achievements were unlimited. She assisted in development of the National and Chapter structure development of the Grammy Awards, categories and award rules, and of the television awards shows. Along with her other official responsibilities, I can't figure out how she had time to breath!!

In 1959 the Academy held its first Grammy Awards presentation at the Beverly Hilton Hotel. The New York chapter was lack-a-daisical in organizing and didn't get as many nominations and awards for its East Coast artists as it expected. Most of the Academy's voting members were on the West Coast, and as a result Capitol Records dominated the Ads with ten out of twenty-eight winners. The closest rivals were RCA Victor, four, and Decca and Liberty, three each. New York soon realized the importance of the Academy and became very interested and active. It wasn't until 1971 that the Grammy Awards presentations were televised. The show is very popular and has been televised worldwide ever since. In 1961 Ms. Farnon was appointed Los Angeles chapter executive director and also alternated as national executive director with the New York executive director.

In 1971 the National Board of Trustees voted that Los Angeles be recognized as the official national office and Ms. Farnon became the sole National Executive Director. In 1986 she was named Executive Vice President. In 1992, after playing a major role in the development of the organization and forty-five years of complete dedication, she decided to leave the Academy.

Having known each other from our Capitol Record days, Chris, as I've always called her, and I renewed our acquaintance and became friends. She entered art school and every now and then sends me photos of her paintings. It's quite obvious that she devotes the same verve and veracity to her paintings as she did to the Academy. Her paintings are flawless and very realistic.

Francis M. Scott III, known as Scotty, was Vice President of Business Affairs at Capitol Records, and in 1960 the Academy elected him its National Treasurer. He played a major role in the organization when it was struggling with financial problems, but he kept the boat afloat. In 1965 the Academy elected him its National President. His executive expertise so impressed the trustees that they wanted to elect him for another term but couldn't because the National Constitution limited the Presidency to one term only. Soon after the Trustees changed the Constitution to allow a President with the same expertise that Scotty had shown another term. Scotty later moved to New York, and after several years as president of Time Life Records, he returned to California and is still an active member of NARAS.

On one of my trips to Houston, Texas, Biff Collie, a popular country disc jockey, asked me to talk to a young man, Tommy Sands, who had made a couple of records for RCA Victor. Because of the lack of interest in them, his contract had just been terminated. Tommy was feeling rather depressed and Biff thought I might be able to cheer him up. He couldn't have been more than sixteen years old. I listened to his recordings, and though his voice was immature, I heard good possibilities in his style. We left the studios in his old Ford and had a couple of hamburgers. I told Tommy that the songs he had recorded were not the right type for him, but if he came to see me in a couple of years I would give him a contract.

In 1956 Tommy moved to Hollywood and was appearing on Cliffie's TV show. He told him of my promise. Cliffie brought him to my office and said "Ken, you promised to give him a contract if he came to see you in a couple of years, and here he is." I was a little taken aback but I remembered my promise—and a promise is a promise—so I signed him.

The first song we recorded on his first session was "Teenage Crush" written by Joe Allison and his then-wife, Audrey. I was quite enthused by his performance and hadn't yet set a release date. In the interim Tommy was chosen for the lead part in a forthcoming one-time network television show, "The Singing Idol" a *Kraft Theatre Hour Production*. The producers wanted Elvis Presley, but Colonel Tom Parker, his manager, turned them down. The Colonel had at one time managed Tommy and recommended him for the part. The producers sent me a song and requested that I have Tommy record it, release it, and they would use it on the show. I told them that the song was not suitable for Tommy and I had already set the release date for his first record. I sent them a dub of "Teenage Crush" and said this is the song I'm going to release. The record was released about the same time the show was televised. I was pleasantly surprised the music was used as a theme throughout the show and Tommy's performance was tops! A couple of days later' the producer called me and thanked me for my decision. The record quickly reached number two on the pop chart, was over a million seller, and Tommy became a teenage idol. A few weeks later, Ralph Edwards of TV network show "*This Is Your Life*," with Ralph Edwards and Tennessee Ernie Ford watching, I presented Tommy with his million seller Gold Record. His future seemed assured.

He was in demand for personal appearances, and when he was to perform at the Roxy Theatre in New York City, I went with him to bolster his confidence. It was an experience I've never forgotten. Each performance played to a full house of screaming teenagers, mostly girls, police officers were placed in front of the stage to prevent them from climbing onto it. Tommy's dressing room was at the rear of the theatre, near the backstage entrance. It was a little less than a story high and had a window facing the alley. After each performance, girls would rush to the rear hoping to see him. Tommy would usually wave to them. One day a girl tried to climb up to the window and fell. She laid on the ground and hysterically kept yelling, "Tommy, Tommy." He and I went down to her. He held her hand and tried to console her. In a few minutes the police came and took over. We heard no more about the incident so we assumed she was not injured.

A couple of days later, Tommy and I were joined by Capitol's promotion man, Don Ovens, in between shows, and things had calmed down outside his dressing room. Tommy decided he needed a haircut. We hailed a cab and went to a barber shop. On our return we noticed there were several groups of teenagers around the stage entrance. I said, "Let's go in the front entrance," and instructed the driver to do so. Some of the kids evidently saw us and started to run after the cab. We had no alternative but to go in the front entrance. We got out of the cab with the girls about a half block behind.

We had intended to rush by the ticket taker, but he demanded tickets. I said, "This is Tommy Sands." He replied, "I don't care who he is, where's your tickets?" Just then the group of girls rushed into the theatre. The ticket taker, seeing what was going on, let us through, but he couldn't stop the girls running after us. An usher, seeing the chase motioned us to follow him. We ran up a flight of stairs with the girls right behind us. He led us to a backstage entrance door. Before we got to the door, Don got in the way of another rather hefty girl. She punched him and knocked him down. He recovered quickly. The usher unlocked the door, the three of us got in, and he slammed it shut before the girls could enter. Don was not hurt. We thought it was quite frightening but an amusing happening and had a good laugh.

His reputation as a rock 'n' roll teenage idol was becoming well-established, and he starred in several movies. His albums including "Steady Date with Tommy Sands," "Sing Boy Sing," which was the title of one of his films, and an album recorded live at the Sands Hotel in Las Vegas, "Sands at the Sands," which enjoyed above average sales. His records and albums were now popular in Europe and Australia, and he was well on his way to becoming an international star.

In 1958, Tommy brought me a list of 12 standard love songs and said he wanted to record an album with Nelson Riddle's orchestra. I told him I thought it would be a mistake and could hurt his career because these were not the type of songs his fans expected or wanted from him. He was very insistent and, as his royalty account was well in the black, I foolishly consented. Nelson hired my wife's group, the June Nelson Singers, for the choral background.

During the three hour sessions, which we completed in three days, Tommy kept making irrelevant suggestions to Nelson, and when we finished the album, made some disparaging remarks about the vocal background. I attributed his behavior to his feelings of insecurity. Nelson came to me and said "Ken don't ever ask me to record with him again." The album was not accepted by disc jockeys and had very limited sales. His rock 'n' roll records continued to do well.

Exactly one year later he brought me another twelve standard pop songs and said he wanted to record another album with Nelson Riddle. I protested vehemently, but as his royalty account was still in the black, I again foolishly consented. I expected Nelson to turn me down, but much to my surprise, he didn't. He wanted to use the "June Nelson Singers" again, but I wouldn't let June do it. The sessions went smoothly and Tommy made no suggestions. This album too had little acceptance. It wasn't until 1960 that I realized why he wanted to record with Nelson Riddle. I didn't know he was going with Frank Sinatra's daughter, Nancy; he probably wanted to prove to her that he could attain the same stature as her father by recording with Nelson Riddle's orchestra, which did all of Frank Sinatra's Capitol records. Had I been aware of this, I'm sure I would not have let him talk me into it. When his five year contract was up, I didn't renew it.

Nancy and Tommy were married in 1960 and divorced three or four years later. After the divorce Tommy moved to Hawaii and for a long period of time gave up entertaining. Many years later he did resume making personal appearances and in 1990 appeared in a rock 'n' roll festival in England. I was fond of Tommy and felt badly about the reversal of his promising career.

Three other artists I signed in 1957 were Del Reeves, Ray Stevens, and Buck Owens. Del and Ray were with me for the short period of two years. I don't recall whether they left of their own volition or if because after releasing four records by Del and six by Ray there didn't seem to be any disc jockey interest and no sales I let them go. Del later signed with United Artists records, joined the *Grand Ol' Opry* and had a well established career.

My friend, Bill Lowery, brought Ray Stevens to my attention. I had to drop him from the label because of poor disc jockey and sales response. Almost immediately after he left Capitol, he had a hit record, "Alley Oop" on another label. He became known for his novelty recordings and appeared on many TV shows, including his own for a season. Although he was considered a country artist, many of his records including two number ones were on the Pop charts. He continues to enjoy a successful career.

I missed the boat with Ray, but I hit the jackpot with Buck Owens!

Alvis Edgar Owens was born in Sherman, Texas. It was during the Depression of the 1930's that the family decided to move to California. They started the trip in the family's old Ford, but it broke down in Mesa, Arizona. As a result, they settled there, and that's where Buck spent his childhood and teen years. He had learned to play guitar and had done some singing on a local radio station. It wasn't until 1951 that Buck and the family moved to Bakersfield, California. I first met Buck when Tommy Collins hired him as a guitarist for his recording sessions. There was no doubt that he was an exceptional musician. I had him play on every session where it was up to me to assemble the orchestra and even on some of my pop and rock 'n' roll dates.

As I hadn't yet learned to drive a car, many times after a session Buck would drive me home. I really liked him. It seemed to be mutual, and we became friends. He kept asking me to audition him as a singer.

My attitude was, "get away from me boy; you bother me." But he kept bothering me, and one day after a session I finally gave-in and said, "Okay, let's hear you sing." He didn't even get through the first 32 bars of the song, when I stopped him and said, "Okay, that's enough!"

His voice and style struck me immediately. I didn't have to hear anymore. He came in the booth, thinking I had turned him down. I said, "Buck, you've got a contract!"

Buck later told me he was negotiating a contract with Columbia Records and he thought that was the reason I agreed to listen to him sing. If he did, I couldn't have cared less because, at the time, I thought of him only as an outstanding rhythm guitarist.

Buck Owens became one of the truly greats of Country Music. His talents and accomplishments were unlimited. His musicianship, his voice, his stage presence, the songs he wrote were all tops! And he had a phenomenal sense of business.

Our first session on August 30, 1957, got little attention, but our second session produced "Second Fiddle," his first charter that reached twenty-four on the *Billboard* chart.

That same year "Under Your Spell Again" was his first hit. It reached number four on the *Billboard* chart and stayed there for twenty-two weeks. In 1960 he had three charters, and after that, until he left Capitol in 1975, he had five and six records on the charts every year, including twenty Number Ones. Many of his records also made the Pop charts.

The Beatles were fans of Buck's and requested I send them dubs of our sessions. They recorded his hit, "Act Naturally."

Buck soon formed his own band. When he told me he was naming it The Buckaroos, I objected because I had remembered a song titled, "My Little Buckaroo," which was about a child. I thought buckaroo meant little child. When I looked the word up in the dictionary, I found out it meant "cowboy" or "broncobuster." I withdrew my objection.

The band members were Tom Brumley, Steel Guitar; Willie Cantu, Drums; Doyle Holly, Bass; Don Rich, Fiddle; and of course, Buck, Rhythm Guitar. Because of Buck's other interests, Don Rich, a very talented musician, was the leader of the band taking care of rehearsals, instrumental arrangements, and so forth.

Buck Owens and the Buckaroos also became well-known as an instrumental group and we released albums, which were very successful and single records by them. One of the singles, "Buckaroo" became number one on the Country charts and was also charted on the Pop chart.

In 1963, Buck retained Jack McFadden as his manager and booking agent. Buck not only became a National celebrity but an international celebrity as well! We, made several live performance albums; one at the Golden Nugget in Las Vegas and, in 1966, a live performance album in New York City's "Carnegie Hall."

In 1967 we recorded a live performance album in Tokyo, Japan's "Kosei Nenkin Hall." In Japan we received a royal welcome at the airport. Geisha girls in traditional Japanese gowns, greeted Buck and the Buckaroos with bouquets, cameras were flashing and reporters bombarded Buck with questions. A press conference was held later and many photos were taken with the Geisha girls.

The hall was packed, as were all of Buck and the Buckaroos live performances. Even though he couldn't speak their language, the audience was more than enthusiastic! Buck spoke to them through Tetsuo Otsuka, a Tokyo radio announcer who acted as Master of Ceremonies.

We also made a live performance album at the "London Palladium" in London, England. The Beatles wanted to attend but were out of town. However, their manager came and sat in the recording booth with me during the show.

When Buck was to appear on the Jackie Gleason Show in Florida, he asked me to go with him to make sure the mixer got the correct sound and vocal balances during their performance. I thought the mixer might resent my presence, but he didn't and followed my suggestions.

Buck had a song titled, "I Wouldn't Live in New York City" (If They Gave Me the Whole Dang Town). We decided to record it on the streets of New York in order to get some of the City's sounds. We got up at 4 A.M. and, with portable equipment, recorded it around 5:30 A.M., when the City was just beginning to stir. It wasn't a smash but turned out okay reaching Number 9 on the Country chart and even making the pop chart.

Buck Owens Enterprises was formed and comprised all of Bucks many business ventures, including Blue Book Music Publishing Company and Buck Owens Production Company. All of his decisions were implemented by his sister, Dorothy Owens. I admired Dorothy, not only for her astute capabilities but as a person. We became good friends.

A building was built to house Buck's office, the three newspapers, the studios of radio station KUZZ, and a TV station that the enterprise now owned. A radio station in Phoenix, Arizona, was also purchased to be managed and programmed by Buck's two sons, Michael Owens and Buddy Allen Owens. When an old theatre in Oakdale, a suburb of Bakersfield, was bought by the Enterprises and converted into a recording studio with all the latest equipment installed, we did most of Buck's sessions there.

Blue Book Music Publishing was formed by Buck and Harlan Howard. When Harlan moved to Nashville, Buck took over the company completely. His Mother was put in charge of business operations. I advised her on copyrights, contracts, royalty statements, and other details. The firm became highly successful, publishing not only Buck's songs but most of Merle Haggard's, Red Simpson, and other writers. I'm sure Buck surmised that I was part owner of Central Songs, but he still would occasionally give a song to Central. His recording of "My Heart Skips a Beat" backed with "Together Again" was a unique happening; both sides became number one on the chart. He had given "Together Again" to Central. It's still one of my favorites!

Buck had his guitar and all of the promotion items that he sent to disk jockeys, and friends, colored Red, White and Blue. These items included an old fashioned dial telephone; a cigarette lighter with a picture of him and the Buckaroos on it; a lapel pin in the form of a Red, White and Blue guitar with the word "Buck"; a money clasp with a guitar and his name on it; a miniature golf bag; and a wrist watch with a picture of him with his guitar in the middle along with the words "Buck Owens."

President Ronald Reagan, then the governor of California, was a country music fan, and he and Buck became friends. I saw a newspaper picture of Mr. Reagan wearing a Buck Owens watch.

For about three years in the early 70's Buck sponsored the "Bakersfield Buck Owens Shotgun Golf Invitational." I played in all of these along with top professional golfers, local businessmen, music executives, artists, and movie stars. Willie Shoemaker, the famous Jockey played in one of the golf tournaments. I remember him because he was so small. With his specially-made clubs, he looked like a little boy playing; he could hit the ball a mile! John Wayne attended one of the games but didn't play; he just watched. I can still picture Buck's Father firing his long shotgun to begin each tournament game.

In 1968 Buck co-hosted, television's *Hee Haw* show with Roy Clark. It was probably the longest running show in television history, running from 1968 to 1986 for a total of eighteen years.

When Buck's contract expired in 1970, he signed a new Capitol contract that guaranteed Capitol Records would release a certain number of albums and records that Buck produced of himself or other artists he might sign. It also included another unheard of clause that, after a certain length of time, the production company would retain ownership of any masters it made and also become owner of the master's Buck had previously recorded. The legal and financial departments approved the contract even though I opposed it, because it meant we no longer had a say in who or what was to be recorded or when it was to be released. It also loused up my release schedule of other artists because I had to release Buck's artists whether I wanted to or not. Actually, it was a smart business move and I later realized that this type of contract would become common and many artists would produce their own records and lease them to record companies.

Don Rich joined Buck in 1959 and became the backbone of the Buckaroos. He played fiddle and also sang duets with Buck and Buck's son, Buddy Alan. Don had a most intriguing personality. I seldom saw him without a smile on his face; you couldn't help but like Don. In 1974 tragedy struck! Don was riding his motorcycle at night and was killed. Buck was devastated; they had felt a brotherly kinship towards each other.

In 1975 Buck left Capitol Records and signed with Warner Records. In 1988, his duet with Dwight Yoakam, "Streets of Bakersfield" charted number one on the Reprise label.

I don't know when Buck's Mother and Father passed away, but in 1995 his sister and my good friend, Dorothy, upon whom he depended to carry out his business decisions, died. I attended her memorial service. Buck gave a most inspiring eulogy.

In 1996 Buck was inducted into the Country Music Hall of Fame. In 1997 he opened his night club, The Crystal Palace, where he still occasionally performs. There had been an archway with the word "Bakersfield" spanning the highway at the entrance to the City. The City decided to take it down. Buck either bought it or had it given to him, and he had it erected at the entrance of the club. The opening was attended by the Mayor and other dignitaries and myself. During his stage performance, Buck insisted I come on the stage and be introduced. I was embarrassed as he gave me too much credit for his success; with his many talents, he couldn't help but be successful. There is no doubt that Buck Owens was one of Bakersfield's most notable and respected citizens; because of him the City of Bakersfield is now known worldwide. I usually visit him and we have lunch at least once a year.

By 1958 Central Songs had hit after hit. The catalog was growing by leaps and bounds, and Central Songs was now recognized as a major Country Music Publisher. Doing all of the internal work was becoming too much for June and I to handle. It was imperative that we get help. Lorraine Wilson and her husband, Stu Wilson, who was formerly a popular Los Angeles radio announcer and then real estate agent, were parishioners at our church. One Sunday I happened to hear Lorraine say she was working part-time for the gas company. I decided to ask her if she would like to work for Central Songs. I explained why we operated from our home, what the job entailed, and that I would give her a key to the office and she could decide her own hours.

Lorraine was quite an actress, being one of the mainstays of the plays sponsored by our church. She had been in many movies from 1939 to 1948 and still occasionally got a call. She was also now doing television commercials. The idea of no set hours appealed to her because it gave her freedom to accept any television or movie calls she might receive. She became an integral part of the Company, was meticulous in everything she did, and always got done what needed to be done. Along with her, Buzz Carlton, our go-between, June and I, and later our two children, kept our home office running smoothly.

Since I was a teenager I had been smoking. One day in 1953 I decided to quit because I was tired of the lousy taste in my mouth and my smelly breath. I came home, threw the package of remaining cigarettes on the counter and said, "I quit." I don't recall having any withdrawal symptoms, but I would occasionally smoke a cigar during a recording session. I didn't touch another cigarette until 1958.

June and I were playing bridge with our friends. I was dealt a "grand slam" hand, trying to be nonchalant, I picked up a cigarette as I bid and smoked it. Everyone knew I had quit smoking and that something was up. I made the slam, but for some reason I started smoking again. About a year later I decided to quit again, but this time I was going to taper off. I would only smoke once an hour, but that didn't work. I'd light up a cigarette and tell myself not another one for an hour. In about twenty or thirty minutes, I'd light up again and go through the same routine.

I was in my office, lit a cigarette, and told myself not another one for an hour. After about twenty minutes, I started to light up again, when I suddenly realized I had become a clock watcher, spending more time thinking about the damned cigarettes than about our business. I threw the package in the wastebasket and again, with no withdrawal symptoms, I quit. I haven't smoked a cigarette since. I started to smoke a cigar at home on weekends, but when June said the curtains and drapes were beginning to stink, I gave up cigars too.

When the Finance Chairman of our church resigned, our minister, Herb Schneider, asked me to take the position. After discussing it with June, I accepted. The following was my inaugural speech.

> "When I was first approached about accepting the position of Finance Chairman, my first reaction was "Oh boy! Who needs this?" Then, as any good Unitarian will do, I got to thinking about it. It occurred to me that I really didn't know what the money I was pledging and contributing each week to my Church and denomination was being spent for, or exactly what I was getting for my money. Oh yes, I knew we had to keep up the building, pay the utilities, the minister's salary, and all the other expenses, but this seemed so cold and mechanical. Surely there was something else. Well, what better way to find out than to accept the position of Finance Chairman. So I did—and here's what I discovered.
>
> Our Church is used free of charge by many community organizations, such as, the boy scouts, the girl scouts, narcotics anonymous, youth groups, senior citizens groups, divorcees anonymous, teenagers, and any responsible community organization can use the facilities of the Church for a meeting-place free of charge. Many people who do not themselves attend Church send their children to Sunday School. My weekly pledge and contributions make me an active participant in community affairs.
>
> When the Minister of the Church is in the pulpit on Sunday morning or is helping and counseling a troubled member of the congregation, visiting someone who is hospitalized or sick, presiding at a funeral or wedding, attending a community or denominational meeting, my weekly pledge and contributions means that I am with him in spirit and thought and am actively participating in helping the individual.
>
> The Religious Education Department is responsible for the curriculum of the Kindergarten, Sunday School, and

Parent and Adult Education. It selects and buys pamphlets, books, and all educational material used in our Church. It arranges for speakers of pertinent subjects relating to community, civic, and world affairs to appear before our congregation. It brings us speakers and ministers of other religious faiths to speak and present their viewpoints. My weekly pledge and contributions mean that I am an active participant in furthering and broadening the education and understanding of my fellow man.

This year the congregation voted to include our financial responsibility to the Unitarian-Universalist Association in the budget; therefore, it will be included in our personal pledges. I would like to suggest that you pledge, if you can, one dollar a month additionally, to meet this obligation.

"It would be impossible, at this time, to enumerate all of the activities of our denomination; however, I will talk of a few of the more important ones.

"The Unitarian-Universalist Association maintains several theological schools for the education of new ministers, thereby assuring the continuation in the growth and development of our belief in the Freedom of Religious Thought. The Association has observers at the United Nations so that we can constantly be aware of the many social problems the world is faced with. Its members attend meetings to help promote better racial understanding. The U.U.A. is constantly sending food, clothing, medical supplies, doctors and social workers to many parts of the world to help the sick and under-privileged.

"My pledge and contributions mean that I am actively participating in keeping alive and bringing to the world the ideals, ideas and democratic principles of such famous Unitarians as Isaac Newton, Thomas Jefferson, Henry Wadsworth Longfellow, Oliver Wendell Holmes, Ralph Waldo Emerson, Horace Mann, Daniel Webster, Florence Nightingale, Albert Schweitzer, and so many, many others. I could be here all night naming them and never get through.

"The summation of my weekly pledge and contributions to the Church and denomination means that I am sharing and experiencing new inter-personal relationships from which I have formed lifelong friendships. I have become more tolerant and understanding of my fellow man's viewpoint, and have become actively involved, and am participating in community, national and world affairs.

I am growing in knowledge and experience. In other words, I have become actively involved in life itself and am helping other people do the same.

"Am I getting my money's worth from my weekly pledge and contributions to my Church and Denomination? I'll let you be the Judge of that!

• • •

Gene Vincent, in 1958, brought me a demo tape of a rock 'n' roll singer by the name of Esquerita. His piano playing and vocal style was very impressive, so I signed him. Esquerita was an African American. He and his back-up band came to Nashville and I recorded them at the Bradley Studios. He loved to perform before an audience, so when he recorded I would get a few people in the studio to watch him. His actions while performing were fun to watch, and the audience loved it!

I released two singles and an album by him but had limited airplay and sales response. I think he may have been a little "ahead of his time," though oddly enough his album and records did very well in France and England. After his album was dropped from the Capitol Catalog, it became a collector's item. Esquerita passed away in 1986, and in 1990 Capitol reissued his album on a CD. He should be considered one of rock 'n' roll greats.

When I took over Capitol's Country Department, my roster included Martha Carson, a gospel singer, who later became known as "The First Lady of Gospel Music." When you listen to her sing her songs of faith, you can't help but feel the joy and happiness she was expressing in her faith even the musicians were uplifted by her singing. Although gospel music was not Capitol's forte, her sales were always way above average. Our first sessions were held in the old Tulane Hotel Studio. Chet Atkins was the lead guitarist, Harold Bradley, rhythm guitar, and Marvin Hughes, piano. We recorded Martha's biggest hit, "I'm Satisfied," on one of these early sessions. Our recording of "I'm Satisfied" was placed in the archives of the Smithsonian Institute in Washington, D.C. It has become a standard and has been recorded by various artists over 180 times.

When Voyle Gilmore was head of the A&R department, he was always impressed by Martha's singing and thought she could become a popstar. I told him that, in my opinion, he was wrong. He insisted that I have her come to Hollywood and he would produce her pop records. He being my boss, I had no alternative. X. Cosse, Martha's husband and manager, was elated with the idea and brought her to Hollywood. They met with Voyle and worked out the details and set the date. The orchestra was comprised of studio musicians and, of course, they would be playing orchestral arrangements for her background. I don't recall the leader. The session did not turn out as Voyle had anticipated. The spirit, the freedom, the joy of her gospel recordings were not there. Her singing was restricted because she had to follow the strict beat of the orchestra, whereas in Nashville the musicians unimpaired by arrangements, followed her, allowing her free spirit to flow forth.

After listening to the recordings several times, both Voyle and I agreed that Martha sounded too stilted and that they would hurt her gospel popularity and career if released. When we told her manager, X. Cosse, of our decision not to release the records because we felt they would hurt Martha's career, he gave us an ultimatum. Either release the records or release Martha from her contract. I couldn't believe my ears! I pleaded with him, but to no avail. He was quite adamant! So I, unwillingly and with sadness, released Martha.

In 1958 June and I booked passage on the Matson cruise ship Lurline for the five-day trip to Oahu, Hawaii. A small group of friends, mostly Church members, including Stu and Lorraine Wilson, came aboard to wish us *Bon Voyage*. The trip was most romantic and enjoyable from beginning to end. We were invited to sit at the captain's table for dinner. June learned the *hula*, and another dance, I think it was called the *huki lau.* There was always some activity in which one could participate.

As we were about to enter the harbor to dock, a speedboat with Tennessee Ernie standing up and waving kept circling the boat. He knew we were coming and wanted to greet us. As we disembarked, we got another shocking but pleasant surprise! Stu and Lorraine Wilson greeted us on the dock; they had flown over!

A little before noon, with the landing festivities over, June and I went to our hotel and checked in but were informed our room would not be ready until after three o'clock. With plenty of time to kill, we took a walk along the beach and stopped at an open-air restaurant. Having had a late breakfast, we weren't hungry but decided to have a refreshing drink. On the menu was an alcoholic Hawaiian drink called "Mai Tai." We decided to try it—it was delicious! I had two but June had three. She really got sloshed! It was the first and last time I ever saw June inebriated. She was not a drinker; her limit was one drink. At three o'clock I managed to get her back to the hotel. We spent the rest of the day and night in our room. The hotel was about two blocks from the beach. We were on the fifth floor and there was nothing to obscure, our view of the ocean. At night, from our room, we could see the full moon shining. It was so romantic! Of all the many times we visited Hawaii, none of our visits were as thrilling or romantic as that first visit!

It was just a year later that Gillette asked June and me if we would go with him and his wife, Edie, to Kona, another one of the Hawaiian Islands. We were delighted! This time we flew to the Islands. At that time there were no jet passenger planes so the flight took about twelve hours. I think it was on this trip that the TWA plane we took had sleeping quarters, and

I distinctly remember climbing upstairs into a cocktail lounge. It was a fun trip.

The highlight of this trip was when Lee and I hired a charter boat and went fishing for Marlin. Our boat left the dock at 6:00 A.M. and it was almost two hours before we were out far enough to cast our lines. Nothing happened until about 1:00 P.M. when I hooked up with a huge Marlin. I immediately got in the angler's swivel chair, with Lee manipulating it left and right according to the direction the fish went. I would reel it in, almost up to the boat, and it would jump up in the air, dive in and zoom off, like a torpedo, out to sea again. This went on until about 6:00 P.M. and I still couldn't get it close enough to get it onboard.

The Skipper of the boat came to me and said: "Why don't you let my mate take over. He'll bring it in, in short order." As Lee and I were both "bushed," we said "Okay"! It was the Skipper's birthday and he was to attend a party that evening. But, he was determined to bring that fish in because he thought it might be a world record Marlin catch. His mate took over and by 9 P.M., even he couldn't get the fish in. Just about that time a ship came searching for us. Our ship's radio was not working and we had been gone 15 hours. The folks on the Island were worried that we might have had a mishap. The search ship radioed that we were okay and on our way back to port. The Skipper, still determined to bring in the Marlin, decided to drown it by slowly maneuvering the ship towards shore until the fish couldn't jump up in the air anymore, and it would be fairly easy to get it onboard. Searchlights guided our way to the pier. Besides June and Edie, it looked like the whole town was out to greet us and see this possible record Marlin catch. I don't know if the catch was a record, but it was eleven feet three inches long from tail to snout and weighed four hundred eighty-five pounds pounds!

The Skipper insisted that I be given full credit for the catch because I was the one who hooked it, struggled with it for five hours, and even his experienced mate could not bring it in. A picture was taken of the fish hanging by its tail, dwarfing me. I was standing beside it with my anglers rod, and a *Billboard* showing its length, weight and stating that Ken Nelson of Hollywood, California was the angler who made the catch. I still have the 8x10 photo.

The Skipper invited us to his birthday party, but Lee and I were too exhausted. Lee had been wearing sandals when he was working the angler's chair and his feet became so sunburned that he had difficulty walking for a couple of days We spent the remaining days on the Island sightseeing.

Around 1956, Marvin Hughes, a pianist, who was the orchestra leader of WSM's morning broadcasts and played piano on many of my local sessions, had sent me a dub of a singer who wanted to get on Capitol Records. His name was Bobby Darin. I thought he was great, but he wasn't a country artist. I played the dub for Dave Cavanaugh of the Pop Department, and he, too, was impressed. Knowing that I was going to New York the following week, Dave asked me to look him up and sign him.

I called Mr. Darin at the hotel where he was staying and made an appointment. I went to his room, introduced myself. I explained that I was the Country A&R man, but that Dave Cavanaugh of the Pop Department would like to have him on the label. I told him that we started new artists at a 3 percent royalty rate and when his records reached the one hundred thousand level, their royalty would be raised to 5 percent. Bobby objected, saying he should be signed at 5 percent. I said, "Why should we pay you our top royalty rate when you haven't proven a darn thing yet?" Bobby retorted, "No, but I will!" I liked his confident attitude. As I was about to leave, he said, "I'll tell you what. If Capitol guarantees to put a full-page Billboard ad on every one of my records released, I'll sign."

I told him I personally could not guarantee that, but when I got back to Hollywood, I would present his offer and let him know. When I returned to Hollywood, I told our then President, Allan Livingston, of Bobby's request. He said, "Ken, we can't do that because if we did it for one artist, we'd have to do it for all artists." I wrote Bobby and told him his request for a full-page Billboard ad on every released record had been turned down.

He signed with Decca Records and in 1959, at the first Academy Grammy Awards presentation, June and I were standing in line waiting to be seated when all of a sudden I felt an arm encircling my waist. I turned around and it was Bobby Darin. He smiled and said, "See, I told ya!" He was to be awarded a Grammy for his record of "Mack the Knife."

Meredith Wilson, who was riding high on the success of his musical show, "The Music Man," in 1959 asked me to record an album with Curt Massey and Martha Tilton. I agreed. I was familiar with the name Curt Massey, but wasn't sure in what area. I vaguely recalled him being with a country group. Martha Tilton was a pop singer with several hits to her credit. The album turned out to be basically pop and sold fairly well. I surmise Meredith was a friend of Curt's and wanted to help him further his career. In appreciation of my making the album, he gave me a pair of gold cuff links, inscribed with the notes of the hit song from "The Music Man," "76 Trombones" on the back of the links was engraved, "To Ken from Meredith."

Rose Maddox had been singing with her four brothers, known as the Maddox Brothers and Rose. When the group disbanded in 1959, I signed her. Her Mother attended our first session. I had heard that she was a domineering person and directed the group with a heavy hand, even at recording sessions. When we started to record, she began making suggestions to Rose and the musicians. I made it quite clear to her that I would *not* tolerate any interference at my sessions. She never came to another session. I'm sure Rose was relieved and her recording career sailed along smoothly. She also recorded successful duets with Buck Owens, "Loose Talk" and "Sweethearts In Heaven."

One day in 1964 when Rose came to the studio, it was quite obvious that she had taken some kind of drug. We tried to record, but it was impossible. Her tempo was off and her lyrics were incoherent. I rescheduled the session and the next time she was okay. However, the following session she gave the same impossible performance. It was apparent she was taking some addictive substance. Rose was having family problems, and was taking something to relieve her depression and agony. I pleaded with her to come to the sessions without taking anything beforehand. She promised she would but the same impossible performances happened at the next two sessions and I was beside myself. I liked Rose but when her option was due, I had no choice but to let her go. I was debating with myself, whether or not I should tell this part of Rose's career, and I wouldn't have except for the fact that Rose was a strong-willed person and a year or two later overcame her problems and resumed her personal appearances, but not her recording career. Rose passed away in 1998.

It was the year I gave up smoking for the second time when I caught my son, Gregory, now 14 years old, smoking. I still cannot understand why I reacted the way I did, especially when I had been smoking since I was about 12 years old. Instead of sitting down and reasoning with him, telling about the dangers of smoking, I completely lost my temper. It was the one and only time I ever struck my son. I slapped him and don't remember what I said but it was the most stupid thing I could have done. No amount of talking or punishment, especially when his peers are smoking, will stop a teenager from smoking until he reaches maturity and hopefully he becomes aware of the pitfalls and dangers of smoking. I have always and still do regret this incident.

Central Songs published its biggest hit in 1959, "He'll Have To Go," written by Joe and Audrey Allison. It was recorded by Jim Reeves on the RCA Victor label and became his biggest hit. It was Number One on the *Billboard* Country chart and stayed on the chart for 34 weeks. It was Number Two on the Pop chart and was well over a million seller. I recorded the answer song, also written by Joe and Audrey, "He'll Have To Stay" with a girl artist I had just signed, Jeanne Black. Her record only reached Number Six on the Country chart. It stayed on the chart twelve weeks and was Number Four on the Pop chart. It, too, sold over a million. Central also printed and sold thousands of sheet music copies. That same year, we published "Under Your Spell Again," which was Buck Owens first notable hit, and Cliffie hired Joe Allison as our professional manager.

One day, Glenn Wallichs, our President, called me into his office. With him was Alan Livingston, now our A&R Chief. They thought I should move to Nashville because it was the center of the country music industry, and I had so many artists there. I pointed out that I had just as many artists in Hollywood and if I moved, I would be spending the same amount of time traveling between the two cities as I had been. I also said I have no desire to disrupt my wife and children, who were well-established and happy here.

They looked at each other and both shrugged their shoulders as if to say, "Well, that's that." I pointed out that because my roster was expanding, I should have an assistant. They agreed. Had they insisted I move to Nashville, I would have had to resign because Central Songs and Snyder Music were highly successful firms and it would have been impossible to move the operation to Nashville.

In all my years at Capitol, I had a completely free hand; my decisions were never questioned.

Jim Conkling, now head of Warner Brothers Records, knowing of the many artists I was handling, asked if I would consider hiring a young man, Karl Engeman, for which he had no place in his Company, as an Assistant Producer. I got permission from Mr. Wallichs and hired him. He was personable and intelligent, but he was with me only a short time when Allan came to me and asked if I would object to him being transferred to another department that would give him more responsibility and a better salary. Of course, I consented. A few years later when Voyle Gilmore left the Company, Karl was appointed head of A&R. One of the first things he did was get me a $10,000 a year raise, several of us, including Karl, were made Vice Presidents. I was now Vice President in charge of the Country Music Department.

I don't recall who recommended him or how I met Paul Wyatt, but I hired him as my Assistant.

Jimmie Davis, a native Louisianan, was born in 1899. In the early 1920s he attended three colleges: Louisiana Pineville College, a business college where he earned a Bachelor of Arts degree in History; and Louisiana State University where he graduated with a Master's Degree in Education and Psychology. In the late 20's he taught history at Dodd College. His musical career began while singing with his college quartet. In 1934 he signed with a then fledgling Decca Records. His first hit was "Nobody's Darlin' But Mine," recorded in 1935. During his lifetime he has written well over 300 songs, but none more popular than "You Are My Sunshine," written with co-writer Charles Mitchell. He recorded it in 1940 and it was an instant hit. It became a standard, recorded by many country and pop artists.

Jimmie and the song became so popular that in 1943 he was persuaded to run for Governor of Louisiana. With his educational background, he was well-qualified. He easily won the election and served one term from 1944 to 1948. During his Governorship, he continued to record and had several hits. I don't know why, but it wasn't until 1959 that he ran for Governor again. During the interim, he continued making personal appearances and starred in movies. His popularity hadn't diminished and he again won the election. Hubert Long had been his booking agent and I met Jimmie several times. He was a warm and affable person. He invited Hubert and me to his 1960 inauguration at the Capitol in Baton Rouge. It was a gala affair. I had the honor of introducing him as the Keynote Speaker for the WSM Disc Jockey Convention at a breakfast at the Maxwell House in 1961. Jimmie never lost his homespun touch. He was inducted into the Country Music Hall of Fame in 1972. He passed away November 5th in the year 2000 at the age of 101.

When Wanda Jackson was appearing in Las Vegas, at the Golden Nugget, I went to see her. She had just hired a front man who was a guitarist, banjoist, singer and comedian. He was formerly with Jimmy Dean. His name was Roy Clark. His instrumental wizardry was incredible and I thought overshadowed his other talents. I signed him basically as an instrumentalist and shortly after Wanda came to Nashville to record I also recorded two instrumentals with Roy – "Under The Double Eagle" and "Black Sapphire." While we were recording, Owen Bradley came into the control booth and said, "Ken, where the deuce did you find him? He's fantastic!" Disc jockeys gave the record a lot of airplay, but it had minimum sales. We next released an album, "The Lightning Fingers of Roy Clark." It sold very well.

Roy kept asking me to let him record vocally. I finally consented. Joe Allison, who was well acquainted with Roy and was now working for Central, brought me a song not published by Central, that he thought could be a hit for Roy. It had been recorded a couple of years earlier by Bill Anderson, "Tips Of My Fingers." He asked if I would let him choose the background musicians. Thinking he would use country musicians, I said OK. When I entered the studio, I thought I was in the wrong studio! There was an orchestra of thirty (30) of Hollywood's finest musicians. Joe said he felt the song needed that kind of background and hired Hank Levine to make the arrangements and lead the orchestra. I was shocked and dumbfounded but there was nothing I could do but go ahead with the session. Because whether I used them or not, I would have to pay them! When the session was over, I was sure we had a hit in "Tips Of My Fingers." It was and did reach number ten (10) on the Country charts and number forty-five (45) on the Pop chart. It had a better than average air play and sales. I later recorded Roy's first vocal album, "Tips of My Fingers," it had good sales as most of his later albums also did.

Jim Halsey, Manager of Hank Thompson, Wanda Jackson, and several others, was now managing Roy. After the success of "Tips of My Fingers," they asked me if I would let Joe produce Roy's records. I consented. In 1965 Roy had only one chart record, "In The Eyes Of A Fool" and in 1965 only one, "When The Wind Blows in Chicago." I was finding it difficult to release his vocal records because of the lack of enthusiasm by disc jockeys and our promotion and sales departments. I'm sure the problem was he was recording songs that had already been hits by other artists. I should have intervened, but I didn't.

In 1966 when Roy's career was just beginning to really take-off, he and Halsey met with me and said they wanted off the label because Capitol was releasing too few of his records and when we did release one, were not giving them proper promotion. I tried to get them to change their minds, but they were determined so I reluctantly let him go. In 1968 he signed with Dot Records and became a consistent charter, both single and album-wise, for many years.

He had an unusually varied and successful career. In 1967, he occasionally acted on the popular Beverly Hillbillies TV Show, co-hosted the Johnny Carson Tonight Show several times, guest starred with the Boston Pops Orchestra, under the direction of Arthur Fiedler. He was the first and possibly the only American Country Artist to tour Russia. From 1969 to 1986, he co-hosted Hee-Haw, with Buck Owens. In 1973 he won two Entertainer Of The Year Awards, the Country Music Association, and the Hollywood based Academy of Country Music.

In 1963, he opened the Roy Clark Celebrity Theatre in Branson, Missouri and that was the beginning of Branson becoming one of the entertainment meccas of America, not only for Country artists but pop artists as well. I'm sure there are many other facets of his career I'm not aware of. The last time I saw Roy and Jim Halsey, was at the unveiling of his star on the Hollywood Walk of Fame.

Martha Carson was known as "The First Lady Of Gospel Music." Her recording of "I'm Satisfied" was placed in the archives of the Smithsonian Institute, in Washington, D.C.

CHET ATKINS

Before becoming a producer and manager of RCA Victor's Nashville office, Chet was a studio musician. He played on most of my early Nashville sessions.

One day Chet phoned me and asked if I would come to his house and listen to a young singer who wanted to become a recording artist. I came, I listened, I signed. Many artists have had more number one hits than Sonny James, but he is the only artists, country or pop who has had 16 consecutive #1 hits.

Knowing of his innate sense of recognizing talent, when Fred Rose asked me to sign The Louvin Brothers, Ira and Charley, I did. They became a popular duet singing both country and gospel. When Ira died in an automobile accident, Charley continued his successful career as a soloist.

When Wesley Rose, Fred's son, asked me to sign Roy Acuff, I was happy and thrilled to do so, because Roy was known as "The King of Country Music."

THE JORDANAIRES

Leaning on the piano (L-R) Hoyt Hawkins, Ray Walker, Neal Matthews, sitting at the piano, Gordon Stoker. I signed the world famous Jordanaires in 1953. They provided vocal backgrounds for every type of music, country, rock n' roll, popular, gospel, you name it, they sang it.

This is one of my favorite photos, Tommy Collins' daughter, watching daddy during a recording session.

Faron Young, me, Jean Shephard. I discovered Faron in Shreveport Louisiana. Hank Thompson brought Jean to my attention.

Gene and the original Blue Caps, 1956
(Clockwise left to right); 'Wee Willie' Williams, 'Galloping' Cliff Gallup, 'Jumpin'' Jack Neal, Dickie 'Be-Bop' Harrell and 'The Boss'.

In 1956 disc jockey Sheriff Tex Davis of Norfolk Virginia, sent me a dub of a rock n'roll group singing "Be-Bop-A-Lula." I was impressed. I felt that this type of music was the coming trend. I signed Gene Vincent and the Bluecaps. Their records are still selling world wide today.

My daughter Claudia, Gene Vincent, My son Gregory and me, Ken.

WANDA JACKSON
CAPITOL RECORDS
1956

A month after signing Gene Vincent, I brought Wanda Jackson to Capitol. She was also brought to my attention by Hank Thompson. Wanda was unique. She sang country, rock n' roll and gospel. She became famous in Europe as a rock n' roll artist and has gone there to perform for many years. She had a smash hit in Japan "Fuji Yama Mama."

In 1957, 0n the Ralph Edwards TV show “This is Your Life,” I presented Tommy Sands his gold record of “Teenage Crush.” From L-R, Ralph, me, Tommy and Tennessee Ernie Ford.

The gathering for lunch at Hollywood’s Brown Derby Restaurant was in 1958. Top row L-R Tommy Collins, Ken Nelson, Hank Thompson. Seated L-R Minnie Pearl, Unknown, Faron Young and Merle Travis.

The luncheon was also attended by Capitol Record's president Glen Wallachs. L-R Glen,Tommy, me, Faron.

Hal Cook and Tex Ritter

Ken Nelson, The Fisherman.

1961-1970

The period from 1961 to 1970 was unquestionably my most active, both family and career-wise. My children were growing up; the catalogs of Central Songs and Snyder Music were growing; my artist roster was growing, and I was elected President of the Country Music Association. Seemingly, I was spending more and more time in Nashville.

Steve Sholes, who was the head of the A&R Department of Victor Records, was elected Chairman of the Board and I became President of Country Music Association (CMA) for two terms 1961 and 1962. Though we were working for competitive labels, we became close friends and worked well together. Steve was a warm, intelligent, cheerful man. He was the father of five (5) daughters and I had a friend in Hollywood, Jimmy Joyce, a studio singer, who had five (5) sons. Each would have liked to have at least one of the other sex. I used to kid them both about making at trade!

Along with our outstanding Board of Directors, and our Secretary, Jo Walker, whom we voted to become Executive Secretary in 1962, we accomplished a great deal. One of the first things we did was to vote for a salary raise for Jo. We instigated the "Walkway of the Stars" and Steve was the driving force behind the creation and building of the Country Music Hall of Fame.

Steve and I also made the decision to ask members of the industry, such as record companies, music publishers, and trade magazines, to make a pledge of $10,000 to stabilize our finances. When we approached our companies, they both turned us down. Steve and I got together and decided to tell our respective companies a "little white lie." We told them the other company had agreed to the pledge. Both companies then made the pledge! Several companies also pledged and of course, Central Songs was one of the first.

The following was my acceptance speech when I took over the presidency of CMA's first President, Connie B. Gay.

ACCEPTANCE SPEECH PRESIDENT OF CMA

Thank you, Connie.

Distinguished guests, Members of the Country Music Association, Ladies and Gentlemen:

I am both honored and proud to have been chosen as president of the Country Music Association. I accept the responsibility and can assure you that my heart and soul is with each and every one of you.

I feel certain that, with the outstanding and dedicated men and women we have on our Board of Directors and as Officers of the CMA, we will not only continue to keep apace with the splendid progress CMA has made thus far, but within the next two years we will progress beyond our wildest expectations. I say this, because I know the caliber of the men and women behind the organization, and because of the wonderful. cooperation CMA is receiving from radio and television stations, the trade magazines, advertising agencies, recording companies, music publishers, BMI, WSM and "The *Grand Ol' Opry*," and many others far too numerous to mention.

As my first official act as President of CMA, I want to take this opportunity, on behalf of the Association, to congratulate WSM and "The *Grand Ol' Opry*," on its 35th Anniversary!

As my second official act, I want to thank, on behalf of CMA, the retiring officers and members of the board for the unlimited time and effort they have given to the association.

I want to thank two, in particular, our retiring President, Connie B. Gay, and the former Chairman of the Board, Wesley Rose, without whose leadership and guidance the Country Music Association would not be on the solid foundation it is today.

I am happy to say that Connie has been elected to serve on the Board of Directors, representing the Radio and TV interests. I am sad to say that, because of business commitments that will take him around the world, Wesley Rose will not be able to serve this year. But I do know that, if we need him, if we have to call on him he will help us in any way he can, and the same is true of the other officers and retiring board members.

I'd like to ask these retiring board members and officers to stand up, so that we can show our appreciation:

Joe Allison
Eddie Arnold
Cracker Jim Brooker
Dee Kilpatrick
And Cindy Walker

The members who will continue to serve as officers and board members are as follows:

Steve Sholes — representing the recording industries, and who has been elected chairman of the board.

Our dear friend from Canada, Harold Moon — of BMI Canada, First Vice President.

Don Pierce — Starday Records, Nashville, Secretary

Paul Ackerman — of "*Billboard* ," New York City, trade magazine.

Dub Allbritten — of Nashville, Representing Managers.

Bob Cooper — of WSM, representing radio and television.

Jim Denny — of Cedarwood Music Company, of Nashville, representing music publishers.

Len Ellis — of Gary, Indiana, representing disc jockeys.

Pee Wee King — of Louisville, Kentucky, representing artists.

Joe Lucas—of Hickory Records, Nashville, representing the recording industry.

And last, but not least, Mac Wiseman, our former treasurer, who has been elected as a member of the Board to represent artists.

Will all of these people stand so that we can show our appreciation for what you have done in the past year, and for accepting the responsibility for next year!

The newly elected officers are as follows:

Bob Austin, CASHBOX, New York City

Mrs. Dorothy Gable, Litton Music Publishers, Knoxville, Tennessee, Vice President

For Treasurer, Bill Denny, Cedarwood Music Publishers of Nashville.

Assistant Treasurer, Miss Frances Williams, BMI, Nashville. Assistant Secretary,

Shelby Singleton, Mercury, Shreveport.

Let's have them stand and give them a hand.

And now we come to the newly elected members of the Board of Directors:

Hap Peebles of Wichita, Kansas, representing artists, managers, bookers, promoters, and ballroom operators.

Dal Stallard, Radio Station KCKN, Kansas City, Disc Jockey.

Roy Horton, Southern Music, New York City, Music Publisher.

Harlan Howard and John Loudermilk of Nashville, representing composers.

Johnny Sippel of *BILLBOARD* MAGAZINE, New York City, representing trade papers.

And finally, our two Directors-At-Large, Owen

Bradley, of Decca Records, Nashville, Tennessee,

And Bob Pampe of Columbia Records, Canada.

I would also like to announce that the young lady who has been so devoted to the CMA and without whom we couldn't get along, Jo Walker, is now the Executive Secretary.

You see, ladies and gentlemen, with such outstanding people as these, from every phase of the industry, how in the world can the Country Music Association help but go forward and grow, and grow, and grow.

Thank you!

I had never driven a car, and I realized that June was being over-burdened, driving the children to school and their various functions and taxiing me to and from the airport. I decided it was about time I learned to drive. I bought a car, took lessons for a year, and in 1961 at the age of 50, got my driver's license in Nashville.

The first time I was driving with June, I almost backed into a street light pole, and ever since then, whenever we go someplace together, she always does the driving. I didn't mind because she is an excellent driver, and was amused by her insistence. However, I did drive with the children. In all my years of driving, I've never had an accident, and only got one speeding ticket.

This same year, Central Songs had 6 BMI publishers' awards topped only by Acuff-Rose. Harlan Howard, who Buzz Carlton kicked out of Central's office, got the Writer's Award for 10 songs. Also this year, I released four (4) albums, produced by my Assistant Paul Wyatt, two by T. Texas Tyler, one by Al Dexter of "Pistol Packin' Mama" fame and a religious album with harpsichordist Rita Faye and the June Nelson singers.

It was either Chet or Owen who recommended that I invest in oil wells with them, and Owen's brother, Harold, Jim Reeves and a couple of other people. Because of my past experience, I was a bit reluctant but they assured me that the East Central Developing Company of Flora, Illinois was a reputable firm, owned and managed by Alex Zanetis. Alex was an aspiring songwriter with whom Chet and Owen were well acquainted. We each invested $1,500 in two wells; the Lynn Pearce Lease, and the Sam Howell Lease. But you can bet your boots, I didn't tell our President, Glenn Wallichs, about these wells. Both wells paid off handsomely until they went dry, a few years later.

June 2, 1961 was a sad day for the Nelson Family. June's Father, a wonderful, caring man, Dr. Fred Felcher, at the age of 73, died of a heart attack in his office, while treating a patient. He was of inestimable help in the embryonic stage of Central Songs and was our first President. He signed all the checks and correspondence until we moved to Hollywood, and Cliffie took over. Mrs. Felcher, June, and I and especially the children missed him.

Sometime in the 1950's we bought a weekend house at Lake Malibu. It was on leased land. We paid $4,500 for it and after three or four years, sold it for $9,000 and bought a house in Ventura County on Oxnard Shores, about a block away from the Pacific Ocean. We wanted an oceanfront house. We found one in Ventura, kept it for a couple of years, and then bought an oceanfront lot. We built a two-story house on it, that June designed, another one of her many talents. She insisted that the house be built on pilings with a fence in front of it. We were the only house on the Ventura Beach, that was over a mile long, on pilings and with a fence in front of it.

At the end of my first term, as President of CMA, this was my President's Report –1961:

> Ladies and Gentlemen and Fellow Members—today we celebrate the third birthday of the CMA, and we are proud to say that as young as we are, today we are acknowledged and recognized as an outstanding and permanent part of the music industry. Our membership has risen to close to 700 individuals and organizational members. Our organizational membership includes practically every major company of any importance in the music industry.
>
> The Board of Directors and Officers met four times during the past year—in New York City, Miami, and twice in Nashville. I think it is important to let you know that these officers and directors travel at their own expense.
>
> In the past year, we have achieved many of our goals. It is difficult to tell which is the most important so I will tell you about them in the order of their sequence.
>
> Last January, your CMA Board held its meeting in New York City. While there, we arranged a luncheon with top executives of the nation's leading radio and TV advertising agencies. Because of this luncheon, many sponsors and advertisers are using and exploring the potentials of Country Music.
>
> One of the important fund raising activities of the Country Music Association in this past year was a highly successful CMA produced Country Music Show, which was held in Miami, Florida.
>
> The American Federation of Musicians, as you may or may not know, has a fund, which is dispersed throughout America, and is used solely for the purpose of providing

the public with concerts without admission charges. The musicians used on such concerts are paid for by the trust fund of the AFM. Your CMA wrote to each local, pointing out the nationwide popularity of Country Music, and that it would be in the public interest to give free Country Music concerts. Because of our efforts, many locals are now giving such concerts.

The most outstanding is Local 47 in Los Angeles, California. Their Country Music concert was successful beyond all their expectations. As a result, they have given it national publicity in the musicians' magazine, and are going to give two Country Music concerts each year, instead of one.

Through the efforts of your CMA, there has been, and is, increased activities in Country Music on a worldwide scale, especially Canada, Europe, and Japan. Two of our members, Don Pierce and Wesley Rose, spent several weeks on the continent, were welcomed with open arms, and were highly successful in furthering the cause of Country Music there.

We now have thirty-five CMA members in Canada and members in each of the following countries – Australia, Austria, Belgium, England, Japan, New Zealand, Switzerland, Scotland, and West Berlin, Germany.

Jim Denny and Lucky Moeller informed us that there is an increasing demand for personal appearances of American Country Artists in these countries, and that the demand is growing rapidly. Since August of this year, they have had an American Country Music show booked in various spots, almost continuously, and they already have booked for 1962, shows for every month of the year. They report that wherever music is being furnished in Europe for listening pleasure, radio, jukeboxes, and so forth, Country Music has increased 35 percent—and is expected to rise to 65 percent.

The number of American Country records being released in these countries has doubled, and they are recording our songs in their own languages. Almost all of these nations have magazines devoted entirely to Country Music.

In the past year, we have had visitors from Japan and Europe. Their only purpose in coming here was to learn about our music and our artists. In fact, Mr. David Barnes, who owns and publishes THE COUNTRY AND WESTERN RECORD REVIEW magazine of England, has come all the way to Nashville to be with us during the Festival.

The most important and useful publication put out by the Country Music Association this year was your Association's brochure, which tells the story of CMA We have had numerous requests from various organizations for additional copies of this brochure to help them in promoting their own activities in Country Music. Ten thousand of these have been distributed throughout the industry.

The past year has seen a big improvement in the format and content of CMA's CLOSE-UP magazine. Four thousand copies of CLOSE-UP are printed and distributed monthly to all members, radio stations, record dealers, advertising agencies, and many foreign lands. We have had an increasing amount of space devoted to us by the trade papers: *BILLBOARD* ,CASH BOX, MUSIC REPORTER, MUSIC VENDOR, SPONSOR, and many national magazines.

Your CMA is being consulted by business firms, advertising agencies, and radio stations. They are asking our advice and help in establishing Country Music formats and shows. More and more radio stations are becoming aware of the potential of Country Music. Many are programming it for the first time; many are becoming full-time Country Music stations.

One station in particular, KSAY in San Francisco, asked for our help in changing over to an all-Country Music station. One of our members, Joe Allison, at his own expense, spent two full days in helping them make the changeover. Many stations have asked CMA for sales aid kits to show prospective sponsors. We are now in the process of assembling such a kit, and will have it ready shortly. Because of the increase in Country Music radio stations, there are now two companies devoted entirely to making Country Music jingles exclusively for sponsors and advertisers on these stations.

Your Association has proclaimed one week each year to be set aside as Country Music Week. This week will run concurrently with the WSM Country Music Festival. A Bill to this effect will be introduced by Congressman Ross Bass of Tennessee. We have had wonderful cooperation in regard to this. All of the trade papers, most of the major record companies, music publishers, and artists have cooperated 100 percent.

Your CMA has pressed and mailed to every radio station in the U.S. and Canada transcriptions of spot announcements, announcing COUNTRY MUSIC WEEK. Many major record companies have had special country releases during this week. Most music publishers and record companies stamped their mail with the announcement. Trade magazines have been able to utilize this to everyone's advantage. Henceforth, COUNTRY MUSIC WEEK will be an annual affair.

Another achievement of your CMA in 1961 was the formation of the Country Music HALL OF FAME. The enthusiasm and interest generated by this was beyond our wildest dreams. We received immeasurable national and international publicity. The operation of the CMA Hall of Fame is based on the same principles as the baseball Hall of Fame. One hundred men and women are appointed from all over the nation who have been associated with Country Music for the past ten years or longer. They are asked to nominate their candidate. In order to be placed in the Hall of Fame, a candidate must receive 75 percent or more of all the votes. This first year, only deceased candidates were nominated. The selectees will have a bronze plaque cast in their likeness. The plaques will be placed temporarily in the Tennessee State Museum, until such time as a regular Hall is established. The announcement of the selectees and the unveiling of the plaques will take place at the CMA banquet at the Hillwood Country Club, Friday night, November 3.

Outstanding on our list of accomplishments for 1961 was the CMA Radio Survey. We mailed to every radio station in the U.S. and Canada a questionnaire asking if they played Country Music, and if so, how many hours a day. We received over 1,550 replies which was better than a 50 percent return — this in itself was quite phenomenal. Of these 1,550 replies, more than 1,300 stations stated they programmed Country Music. We received outstanding publicity on this survey. We had printed a list of all stations replying, and how many hours a day they played Country Music. This list was mailed to all record companies, music publishers, advertising agencies, and it is available to anyone who wants it. Because of our survey, most all of the record companies and music publishers have revised their mailing lists, and hundreds of radio stations, who never before received records are now being serviced regularly with country Music records.

> Tomorrow morning marks the beginning of the 10th WSM *Grand Ol' Opry* Country Music Festival. At the WSM Breakfast, to be held at the Maxwell House, an announcement will be made of an outstanding Country Music event, which will take place later this month. When you hear of this great event, remember it was brought about and made possible by your Country Music Association.
>
> In summing up, your CMA has brought Country Music to the prominent position it so well deserves. Radio and TV stations are using more and more of our music because sponsors and advertisers are finding that they reach a greater number of people, and get better results by doing so. Jukebox operators in such metropolitan areas as New York, Chicago, Los Angeles, Detroit, and Boston are putting more and more Country records on their machines and finding it highly profitable. Many recording companies, who never before did so, are now issuing Country records. Everyone connected with Country Music — artists, songwriters, promoters, recording companies, trade magazines, music publishers, radio and TV stations are enjoying a tremendous upsurge in prosperity.
>
> Country Music is growing by leaps and bounds, not only in the United States and Canada, but all over the free world, and will continue to do so as long as we, the members of CMA, continue to work and pull together.
>
> Thank you.

Alan Livingston was now President of Capitol and Voyle Gilmore was head of A&R. In 1962, realizing the importance of Nashville as the Country Music Recording Center, we opened a local office on 16th Avenue in music row. it was my responsibility. I put my assistant Paul Wyatt in charge of the office and as Record Producer. I don't remember why, but after about two years, he left the company.

I hired Marvin Hughes, who was an excellent producer and had produced for me when I couldn't get to Nashville. He hired as his secretary, and later married, Kathy Hughes, who was the widow of Randy Hughes, the pilot of the plane that crashed in 1963, costing the lives of Patsy Cline, Hawkshaw Hawkins and Cowboy Copas.

I was very pleased with him until I began getting complaints from some of the artists that he had a drinking problem and was becoming difficult to work with. I had to discharge him. I hated to do it, but I had no choice.

I then asked Harold Bradley, Owen's brother, who had been a guitarist on many of my sessions, if he would like to take the job. When I told him the salary would be $20,000 a year, which was a good wage at that time, he laughed and said, "Ken, I make more than twice that just sitting here in the studio, playing guitar!" Harold was elected President of the Nashville Musicians Union and in the late 1990's was elected Vice President of the American Federation of Musicians, the National Musicians Union.

In 1962, I signed both Harlan Howard and his then wife, Jan, as solo artists but got no action with either of them and had to release them in a couple of years. Harlan became one of the most prolific and hit writer of country songs. Jan signed with Decca and was fairly successful.

I also produced two religious albums by Roy Rogers and his wife, Dale Evans. I remember going to their home in Apple Valley to discuss the contents of their albums. It was quite an experience. They had adopted several children and while we were talking, the children and a couple of dogs kept running in and out of the house. No one paid any attention to them. For me it was a fun afternoon. Roy was inducted into the Hall of Fame in 1988 and passed away in 1998. Dale was very active in religious circles; she wrote the popular Hymn, "The Bible Tells Me So." She passed away in 2001.

I also produced a country album by the popular singer Kay Starr. It wasn't a smash, but it did well.

One day, I received a phone call from Murray Wilson. He said, "Ken, you did me a favor and now I want to do one for you. My son's have formed a sensational group called the Beach Boys, and I want you to sign them."

I asked Murray what favor I had done for him and he replied, "you recorded one of my songs." I had no recollection of him or the song, but I asked him what kind of group it was. Murray said it was pop rock. I told Murray I ordinarily didn't produce this type of artist, but if he gave me his phone number, I would have Nick Venet, our rock and roll producer, call him.

I gave Nick his phone number and told him I promised Mr. Wilson he would call him. Two weeks later Murray called me and said Venet hadn't called. I told him I gave him the phone number and that I would remind him again to call, which I did. Another two weeks went by and Murray phoned again to say Venet hadn't called. I was embarrassed and assured him Venet would call.

I confronted Nick and angrily said, "Damn it Nick. This is the third time I promised this man you would call him. Please do it!" He finally did and when Murray sent him a tape, he excitedly ran to Voyle, now A&R chief. He, too, was impressed and met with Murray and signed the Beach Boys. At the next A&R meeting, Voyle said because of Nick's delay in phoning Mr. Wilson when Ken urged him to do so, we could have lost the Beach Boys. He suggested all A&R men follow up on tips of this kind.

When the English firm EMI, now owner of Capitol, sent records of the Beatles to Voyle, he didn't think they were for the American market, and wouldn't release them. EMI permitted two minor record companies to release them. These companies had no distribution outlets and a poor promotion department. As a result, the records were practically unheard of! By this time the Beatles had become the sensation of England and EMI insisted that Capitol re-release these records and of course, the rest is history. They were all smash hits!

The Beatles and the Beach Boys were the most dominant groups of the 1960's and are still popular today!

The year 1961 was the year of a major family crisis. I don't recall ever having the feeling of jealousy until sometime after we moved to California. In my previous marriage, I was suspicious of my wife but never jealous, even though I caught her in uncompromising situations. June was becoming more and more aloof and withdrawn. It was probably because she was over-burdened, taking care of the children, doing the office work for Central and Snyder, which she grudgingly did and directing the Church choir.

It became obvious to me that June was not capable of showing affection and I didn't expect it. I never saw her kiss or hug the children, her mother, father or a friend. I began to notice that after church services, or a Church affair, she always seemed to be with the same man laughing and talking and as our sex life seemed to be lagging, I became suspicious and jealous. I began to question her: Where had she been? Who was she with? Where had they gone, and what did they do?

When I was in Nashville, I would telephone her twice a week and go through the same routine. I was becoming paranoiac and it all came to a head one night when we were invited to a birthday party, being held at the gentleman's house. I had a recording session and was late in getting to the party. When I walked in the front door, the first people I saw were June and this man dancing! I was completely upset and seething with jealousy. I could hardly contain myself; I did but I was miserable.

Jealousy is an abominable emotion. It overwhelms one and causes unorthodox behavior. Although I had never accused her of misconduct, my constant questioning and innuendoes were affecting June also. I realized that my behavior would eventually destroy our marriage, which I didn't want to happen because I loved June and the children.

I decided to move out of the house, and perhaps being by myself, I could find the basis of my jealousy and dispel it. In July of 1961, I rented a house a couple of blocks from our Church. The house had a swimming pool and June would frequently drop the children off to see me. I was always happy to be with them. We would visit awhile and if possible, the three of us would usually go swimming. I never questioned them about their Mother.

When I was in town, I would go back home at least once a week and with our secretary, Lorraine, take care of Central and Snyder business. When I was in Nashville, I would phone June every week. Although it was difficult to ask her only about the children, she would tell me about their health and activities but preferred to give me very little other information. I had never studied psychology, but I knew it involved a person's behavioral pattern that evolved from their early childhood, background and environment.

I concluded the only way I could get to the cause of and rid myself of these disruptive feelings was by self-analysis. Every night, after work, I would come home and write. I began with my childhood. It was apparent that I wanted love and attention, which my Mother was not capable of giving me. I also wanted to give love and affection, which my Mother was not capable of accepting from me.

When I was a teenager and learned that my Mother and Father were not married, I lost whatever self-esteem I might have had and felt unwanted, unloved, insecure, inadequate, and ashamed.

In exploring my relationship with women, I was shy and never had a girlfriend. June was the first and only girl I ever pursued. All of my sexual experiences, outside of my patronizing prostitutes, were instigated by women and I subconsciously thought all women were sexual aggressors. When I thought June was overly friendly with this one man, this subconscious thought came to the forefront and even though June and I had no sexual intimacy before our marriage, my feelings of insecurity and inadequacy made me fearful of losing her as well as fomenting my suspicions and jealousy.

I wrote constantly and in my self-analysis, I realized that as a baby and a child, I had been denied a Mother's love and affection, causing me to become subconsciously feeling unloved, unwanted, and unworthy. When I found out I was born out of wedlock, it only heightened these feelings and I was subconsciously always wanting love, affection and approval. I was still dependent on the Mother image. Have I transferred this dependency to June, still trying to gratify my infantile needs? What about June's background? What feelings and emotions developed in her? What was she wanting?

Although June was an only child, raised in a two-parent home, there was little or no show of love or affection in her home. She had never seen her parents embrace or kiss. Her mother had a hard, demanding voice, ruled the roost, and made her toe the mark. Always questioning June: Who was she with? Where did they go? What did they do?

June could never discuss any of her problems with her Mother. Was this the reason she couldn't discuss our problems with me? Because of my suspicions and jealousy, has June transferred her Mothers image to me?

June's Father was a warm, caring man, who adored June but rarely, openly showed it. Was this the reason June was not capable of accepting my show of love and affection, and retaliating in kind? Although I know June loved and was concerned about the children, was this the reason she couldn't be affectionate with them?

June's Mother's religion was of the Presbyterian faith and she was raised as a Christian. In her early teens, she found out her Father was Jewish and although she was not a prejudicial person, it shocked and dismayed her. As a result, she distanced herself from him.

We each reacted differently to our childhood. I wanted to give and get love and affection. June seemingly rejecting love and affection and wanting freedom. Just as I did, she brought all of her subconscious thoughts into our marriage.

Why did I want to marry her? I admired her; she was beautiful, intelligent, and talented. I wanted to give and get love and affection. I wanted a home, children and naturally a sex partner. Sex was never a dominant desire when I was courting June. I was simply in love and love is an emotion that needs fulfillment.

I never understood why June married me. Did she want security? A home of her own and the freedom to be herself? I know it wasn't for sex. Although she was a willing partner, she never showed any desire or enthusiasm for sex.

After we were married for five or six years, June remarked that the only reason I married her was for sex. I said, "of course, I married you for sex; sex is an integral part of marriage, but that's not the main reason. I married you because of your beauty, your intelligence, your talent and mostly because I love you. I did curtail my sexual activities, which didn't bother me."

Outside of mental sexual cheating, which I am sure most men do, I had never cheated on June. But during the months of our separation, I strayed from the fold and twice let a prostitute orally copulate me.

I was writing my self-analysis for six months. During this time, my daughter, Claudia, told me that when I was away from home, Mother was an entirely different person, more carefree. When I was at home, she was more rigid and not as relaxed. I felt I was now aware of the basis of our feelings and behavior. I was sure I could deal with them but I wanted June to become aware of the cause of our problems.

Several times I suggested we see a psychologist together. June always refused. I asked our Minister, Herb Schneider, who was aware that we had separated, to talk to June. He convinced her that it would be helpful for us to see a psychologist and recommended one that he was familiar with. We visited the psychologist once a week when I was home. Most of the psychologist's questions were aimed at me. June did very little talking and I didn't tell him about June's background. He kept suggesting that I was the basis of our problems.

About the fourth session, the psychologist asked me why I wanted June to come with me to see him. I said, "Because I love her. I love our children, and I want to preserve our marriage."

The psychologist replied "Those are not the reasons. You wanted her to come with you to prove you were right." This really upset and angered me but I restrained myself. Of course, I wanted her to become aware of the reasons for my behavior, and aware of her behavior, but the thought of proving I was right, never consciously entered my mind.

In February of 1962, after our sixth session, the psychologist said, "I'm sure you two are now ready to go home and be together." I was sure I was now devoid of my jealousy phobia but I was never so scared in my life. I thought, Oh God, if I go back and have those same miserable feelings, I'll lose my mind! June made no comment, but seemed pleased.

There was no doubt we both had a better understanding of ourselves and of each other. I moved back home and from that point on, outside of the normal family problems, we had a happy and successful marriage.

At the November 1962 CMA Convention and WSM Festival, I gave the following report on the activities and growth of CMA for the year.

THE PRESIDENT'S REPORT
CMA 1962

Ladies and gentlemen, and fellow members, this week marks the fourth anniversary of the founding of the Country Music Association, and all of us are proud of the growth, of the maturity, of the national acceptance, and the world-wide recognition we have attained in such a short period of time. All of us are proud of our progress and of the benefits derived by our efforts—not only to our individual and organizational members, but to the entire music and entertainment industry as a whole.

This past year has seen our membership increase by 240 new members. We now have 937 individual members and 27 organizational members, for a total of 964.

Your Board of Directors and Officers met four times—in Las Vegas, Nevada, at the World's Fair Sound of Music in Chicago, and twice in Nashville. Practically all of our objectives have been or are in the process of being accomplished. I will now review the happenings of the past year.

A year ago this month, through the joint efforts of CMA and WSM, the *Grand Ol' Opry* appeared at Carnegie Hall in New York City at a benefit performance. This show was an over-whelming success—there wasn't a vacant seat in the house! The only criticism heard was that the show ended too soon. The New York press was high in its praise of the artists and of Country Music. The entire expense of this show was paid for by WSM.

In February, through the joint efforts of Charles Bernard and Hubert Long, CMA sponsored and paid all the expenses of a Country Music show for the luncheon of the Radio and TV Executives Society of New York City. Ferlin

Husky donated his services. It, too, was an overwhelming success—so much so that they have asked us to provide another show next year.

In June, the Johnny Cash show played to an audience of 10,000 in the Hollywood Bowl in Los Angeles. The Hollywood Bowl officials have indicated to me that they will have a Country Music show every year from now on. The Los Angeles Musicians' Union held its annual free Country Music show in September, and it was bigger than ever. The Canadian Musicians' Union is now holding an annual free Country Music show. In Las Vegas, Nevada, there are now four clubs featuring Country Music exclusively.

Since its inception, CMA has had many requests from amateur songwriters asking how to go about getting their songs reviewed and published. Many of these people had been the victims of song sharks. This year, as a public service and in order to guide these novice writers, we asked Bill Anderson, in cooperation with BMI, to compile a pamphlet that would give them the guidance and information they were looking for. Bill came up with an excellent pamphlet called "What Every Song Writer Should Know." This pamphlet has been exceedingly successful. We have sent out thousands of copies, and we are receiving requests for it from Better Business Bureaus, all over the United States and Canada, who are making their own reprints. These pamphlets are furnished free to all who want them and are paid by entirely by your CMA.

You will, of course, recall our highly successful radio survey of last year. This year, we made a survey of only those stations who said they were playing Country Music full time – to find out if they were still using it. Out of 74 stations, only two said they had changed their format. However, since the original survey, 23 additional stations have become full-time Country Music stations, so today we have a total of 97 radio stations in the United States alone, playing Country Music full time. Some of these are 50,000 watters. Your CMA has been responsible for the improvement in the record servicing of many of these stations, and we have had numerous letters thanking us for our help. We are now in the process of printing a radio kit, which will be sent to all stations and advertising agencies to show them the advantages of and to help them promote and sell Country Music to their advertisers and sponsors.

It was only natural that we conduct a survey of television stations. Here again, we were highly gratified by the response. Out of 600 stations questioned, we received over 300 answers—a better than 50 percent response. Here are the results:

70 stations are using live Country talent

32 stations are using Country Music films only

28 stations use both film and live talent

This makes a total of 130 TV stations using either film or live Country Music. Eighty-three (83) of these stations said they use gospel and religious music. Eighty-eight (88) stations said they use no Country Music whatsoever, and 56 of these 88 said they would have no interest at all.

To the question, "Would you be interested and use well-produced Country Music films?" 57 indicated they were definitely interested, 39 said possibly and 16 said "No," however, these 16 are using live talent. Fifteen (15) said doubtful, three if sponsored, and two said if free.

Of the 12 Canadian replies, all of them said they use Country Music, mostly live. This survey clearly indicates that television stations are definitely interested in Country Music. All of this information has been made available to all who request it. We have made some progress in television. Outstanding was the appearance of Jimmy Dean on the TONIGHT SHOW. Because of his nation-wide acceptance, I understand ABC is planning a full-time show with Jimmy next year. However, we haven't even begun to scratch the surface of this great entertainment media, and I think we are all agreed that CMA should level its guns and make the invasion of television its number one project and objective for 1963.

Many members of CMA, particularly artists and writers, are faced with a problem that is common throughout the entertainment field. Actors, performers, musicians, writers, professional baseball and football players are all confronted with the problem of making a large peak income one year and then, through circumstances beyond their control, they earn practically nothing in following years Their income for the peak years is taxed at the normal tax rate, without taking into consideration the fact that they may never earn that much money again. This, of course, is unfair and has left many seemingly successful people destitute. Many tax relief bills have been drawn up and presented to Congress, but all of them have been found to be unacceptable.

Your CMA decided to find out what was being done about this, so we wrote every organization we could think of who was faced with the same problem—Screen Actors Guild; AFTRA, the American Federation of Musicians, AGVA, the baseball and football leagues, and others. We asked them if they were concerned about this problem, what they were doing about it, and how we could help.

We received a reply from everyone we wrote—all stating practically the same thing. They were concerned about it, all were working on it, but individually they didn't know how we could help—but said if we thought of anything, to let them know.

We realized the big problem here was that each organization was working individually – each was going off in a different direction. What was needed here was a collective and concentrated effort. So, our CMA attorney, Mr. Dick Frank, is now in the process of organizing a meeting of all the attorneys of these various organizations. This meeting will take place next year in Washington, DC. These attorneys will put their heads together and draw up a tax relief bill for the entire entertainment field—and one that they feel will be acceptable to Congress. Your CMA can take full credit when this is accomplished.

Our greatest accomplishment in the past year is the Country Music Association group insurance program for members and dependents. Many of our members, either through financial difficulties or just plain oversight, have failed to provide themselves or their families with life insurance or medical and hospitalization protection. There have been some cases among our members where a family has found themselves in extreme financial difficulties because of a serious illness and no insurance. In the past, I have.heard of cases where the head of the household was killed in an auto accident and left his family penniless. Most of our artist members are traveling by automobile constantly, and it is imperative that every one of them provide their families with adequate protection.

Realizing this was a problem, your CMA Board asked our attorney, Dick Frank, to look into the matter. He contacted the Insurance Planning and Service Company, Inc. of Nashville, presented the problem, and they took over from there. The first thing they asked us to do was to send a questionnaire to each member to see if there was enough interest to warrant going ahead. Over 300 members indicated definite interest. This was more than sufficient.

So, today, we have a group insurance program, designed especially for the Country Music Association members and dependents. There are three plans, and I urge each and every member, whether he has insurance or not, to look these plans over. I understand there is a premium savings of from 25 to 40 percent. We need at least 200 applications before the plan becomes effective and, in the best interest of all, we want to get this off the ground as quickly as possible. I want to point out that CMA does not make any money on this insurance plan whatsoever—it is purely to help our members.

Last July, Senator Estes Kefauver of Tennessee and Senator Joseph Pastore of Rhode Island spearheaded and were responsible for the U.S. Senate passing a resolution, declaring November 4 through 10 as National Country Music Week. Governor Burt Combs of Kentucky and Governor Buford Ellington of Tennessee have declared this week as Country Music Week in their respective states.

As we did last year, various artists made voice tracks announcing Country Music Week, and we had transcriptions pressed and sent to every radio station in the U.S. and Canada. We have been successful this year in getting TV recognition. Last Friday, Mitch Miller paid us tribute and featured Hank Williams' songs on his show. There will be mention on other shows. The most outstanding achievement, however, is the Tennessee Ernie Ford Show over the full ABC network. Good Ol Ern is shouting the praises of Country Music and is featuring a Country Music artist every day this week!

As our organization grows, so do the demands for our services. More and more every day, we are being asked for help and assistance from all phases of the business—radio stations, artists, publishers, record companies, advertising agencies, sponsors, and many others. All are aware of the purposes, of the merits, and of the invaluable assistance that CMA is able to give. This, of course, is our main objective, and it is gratifying to know that we are recognized as the focal point for all Country Music services and information.

Every penny spent in providing these services is borne solely by your CMA. Our only sources of revenue are the membership dues and the yearly CMA banquet which, incidentally, is a complete sellout this year.

We have, at this time, only one paid full-time employee, our Executive Secretary, Mrs. Jo Walker. The workload she carries is unbelievable, and it is getting to the point where it is impossible for one person to do. I know I speak for alll of us when I say we are all grateful for her loyalty and devotion to CMA. I want to point out again that every officer and board member pays all of his expenses when attending CMA meetings. We are expanding our activities—we are increasing our services—we are growing! At the present time, our treasury is in a fairly healthy state. However, if we are to continue to grow as we have in the past, we must start thinking seriously about other sources of income.

Another of our outstanding achievements is the Country Music Hall of Fame. It met with immediate success. This year's selection will be announced at the CMA banquet. We are now in the embryonic stages of planning a Country Music Hall of Fame building. In it will be our offices—it will house our plaques—and will be a Country Music Museum.

More and more of our artists are being called upon to entertain American troops stationed throughout the world. We have a group in Europe right now.

Through the efforts of CMA, many American record companies are now servicing European disc jockeys direct. We have persuaded all of the record companies to cooperate fully with RADIO FREE EUROPE.

All of this has resulted in an increase in the demand for Country Music radio shows, records, and artists.

The list of National sponsors who have turned to Country Music is increasing at a rapid pace. Here are just a few who have come into the fold: Armour & Company, Greyhound Bus Lines, Colgate, Johnson's Wax, Delco Batteries, Ford Motors, General Motors, General Mills, Pure Oil, Lipton Tea, Lever Brothers, Pittsburgh Paint, Sears Roebuck, and many others too numerous to mention. Manufacturers of every type of product are becoming more and more conscious of the advantages of using the music America loves most!

There were two big breakthroughs for Country Music this year. The first was the complete recognition by pop artists of Country Music songs, spearheaded by the great Ray Charles album. Never before in the music business have so many pop artists recorded so many Country songs, and I believe, now that they have discovered Country Music, they will continue to look to us even more. The other big breakthrough is the increasing demand for Country Music artists in the colleges. For this, of course, we can thank our good friends, Flatt & Scruggs, who have and are playing in colleges in practically every state in the Union.

There is no doubt that Nashville, Tennessee has become the Country Music Center of the World! All of the major recording companies now have their own buildings with full-staffed offices here. People in all phases of the entertainment and music business are jumping on the Country Music bandwagon. Your CMA is growing by leaps and bounds. However, with the international situation as uncertain as it is, CMA must be cautious, aware, alert—be ready for any eventuality.

Little did WSM realize 37 years ago, when it first organized the Grand Ol, Opry, that it would be responsible for so many people and businesses enjoying the unprecedented prosperity that we in Country Music are experiencing today.

And, in the words of my dear friend, Simon Crum, I would like to close by stating that—COUNTRY MUSIC IS HERE TO STAY!

Thank you!

Wesley Rose felt it would be advantageous to have a well-known name as President of CMA. He asked Gene Autry to succeed me. Gene was reluctant, saying that because of his many business interests, including a major league baseball team, a hotel, a TV station, and publishing company, he just wouldn't have time to devote the proper attention to the position.

Wesley pointed out that his name was known worldwide and it would give the organization more recognition and prestige. Our Executive Secretary, Jo Walker, Wesley and I assured him that it would be no burden because between the three of us, we would handle all presidential matters. He would be President in name only, and would not have to attend Board Meetings, unless it was convenient for him to do so.

Gene agreed to accept the position and was voted for unanimously. Wesley was elected Chairman of the Board. We kept Gene informed on all matters and it accomplished it's purpose. With the help of Jo, I wrote his Presidential report for 1963. Tex Ritter succeeded him as President.

Gene and I had become friends. His home was in Studio City and mine in Sherman Oaks. We lived less than two miles apart and June and I were occasionally invited to play bridge. The first time his wife, if I recall rightly, her name was Ina, a very lovely and dignified lady, called June and invited us to play, she merely said she would expect us at seven o'clock. The evening was one of June's most embarrassing. We didn't think the invitation included dinner and bridge so we ate dinner as usual. When we arrived, the dining room table was set and before dinner we had a cocktail. Gene and June were conversing and Gene started to talk about baseball, not knowing he was the owner of the Los Angeles Angels, she said, "Oh, I hate baseball. I played basketball in high school."

Gene, being the gentleman he was, dropped the subject. The fact that we had previously eaten dinner curtailed our appetites and the maid remarked, "My goodness, you folks didn't eat much!" We did manage to eat all of the dessert. The next time I saw Gene, I explained June's remark, not knowing he owned a baseball team. I also told him the reason for our delicate appetites—he laughed!

The next time we were invited, we arrived with a good appetite. Joe Johnson, who managed Gene's publishing and record company, was also a guest. We were more relaxed than during our first visit; it was a most enjoyable evening.

Gene gave June a cigarette lighter with his name engraved on it. The next time we were invited, we looked high and low for his lighter but couldn't find it. When June lit a cigarette with a different lighter, Gene said, "Oh, where's my lighter?" This also was embarrassing for June as she explained that she misplaced it. Naturally we found it the next day! You can be sure that on our subsequent visits, she had the lighter with her.

Gene was one of the first singing cowboy movie stars; he made the first film in 1934 and starred in almost a hundred other films. He was also a recording artist and songwriter, who wrote such hits as "Back In The Saddle Again," and "Here Comes Santa Claus, Down Santa Claus Lane."

His biggest record hit, "Rudolph the Red Nose Reindeer," written by Johnny Marks, has become a perennial favorite. He didn't particularly like the song and wasn't going to record it, but his wife, Ina, convinced him of its merits and as a result, "Rudolph Went Down In History"!

In 1969 he was inducted into the Country Music Hall of Fame. In 1988, the Gene Autry Western Heritage Museum in Los Angeles became a popular tourist attraction. Gene passed away in 1998 at the age of 91.

Cousin Herb Henson was the popular host of the Bakersfield television show `The Trading Post" on which many aspiring artists got their start. In 1963, I recorded a live album performance held at the Bakersfield Civic Auditorium to pay tribute to Cousin Herb's 10 years in television.

It was a star-studded affair with the exception of Johnny Bond, Merle Haggard and the Kentucky Colonels, all of the performers were Capitol Artists, Buddy Cagle, Glen Campbell, Roy Clark, Tommy Collins, Rose Maddox, Joe and Rose Lee Maphis, Bob Morris, Roy Nichols, Buck Owens,

Jean Shepard, and Merle Travis. Johnny Bond and the Kentucky Colonels gave me permission to include them in the album but Merle Haggard, didn't so I couldn't include him.

I was very impressed with Merle Haggard and after the show, not knowing he was recording for a local label, Tally Records, I asked him if he would like to sign with Capitol Records. He said "No." I was surprised and asked him "Why not?" He replied, "Fuzzy Owens and Lew Tally gave me my start and I'm going to stick with them." I was disappointed but I respected him for his decision.

With all that talent, the album should have been a blockbuster but its sales were minimal. I believe the title "Country Music Hootenanny" hurt it. I didn't like the title but I let the Art Department talk me into it. The title should have been, "The Country Music of Bakersfield" or California Country.

A few months later, I noticed some of Merle's Tally records listed on *Billboard*'s chart. I called Fuzzy Owens, his manager, and said, "Fuzzy let's get together and talk. I think Merle has the potential of becoming a major recording artist, but your company doesn't have the distribution or promotion capabilities to make this happen."

He came to my office, and I presume with Merle's consent, agreed that it would be in Merle's best interest to be with a major label. In 1965 Merle signed with Capitol and I purchased all of Tally's masters. Fuzzy said that he had sent me a dub of Merle sometime ago, but if he did I never heard it. I'm sure if I had heard it, I would have signed him.

Merle Haggard is living proof that with self-confidence and determination, a person can go from the depths of degradation to the pinnacle of success.

Merle was born in Bakersfield but was raised in Oildale about a mile from Bakersfield. He had a brother and sister. The family of five lived in a converted railroad boxcar. When Merle was 9 years old his father died. His teenage years were filled with a series of crimes and at the age of 20 a burglary that led to a three-year prison term in San Quentin, from 1957 to 1960.

He was later given a full pardon by the then Govenor of California Ronald Reagan. Prisoners were allowed to have guitars and could play them in the prison yard. So Merle was able to improve his musical talents by playing and singing songs he had written to the other prisoners. He managed to avoid prison pitfalls and in 1960 was released with the proviso of two years probation.

While in prison he made up his mind that he would never again become involved in criminal activity. After his release he worked in the oilfields of Oildale for a few months and then decided he wanted to pursue a musical career. He quit the oilfield and worked in Bakersfield nightclubs.

Lew Tally and Fuzzy Owens were both local musicians, who had played on some of my sessions and brought me Jean Shepard's and Ferlin Husky's hit, "A Dear John Letter." They formed Tally Records and in 1963 produced Merle's first recordings. When I signed Merle, Fuzzy said he wanted to be his producer. I agreed but after the first session, the recording engineer said, "Ken that man is impossible to work with; he's overbearing."

I was in the control booth and noticed that he was giving the mixer unnecessary direction, and almost telling him when to breathe. I also noticed that he was giving Merle too many suggestions. To me this was wrong! When I told Fuzzy I was going to produce Merle's sessions, he made no objection, when I told Merle, he didn't say anything but had a look of relief. Later as a matter of courtesy and good relationship, I listed Fuzzy as co-producer.

Merle was a pleasure to record, but the problem was his voice and songs were so intriguing, he was all I was listening to, until I'd wake-up to the fact that there were background musicians in the studio that I should be paying attention to also.

I produced Merle from 1965 until I retired in 1976. During that time, every record we released, with the exception of one, was in the Top 10 *Billboard* chart. Every other record during that period was either, number one, number two or number three. I produced or assembled over 30 albums, a couple with his then wife, Bonnie Owens, and many live performances.

Although I produced the original record of "Oakie From Muskogee," I wasn't in Muskogee when he recorded the live album, but I did assemble, equalize and write the liner notes for it. It was his biggest selling album. Some of the other live performances were in San Quentin Prison, Independence Hall in Philadelphia, an album in a California Church (I don't remember where), and his tribute to his idol, Bob Wills, with the original Texas Playboys.

This album was recorded at Merle's estate in Bakersfield. Two things I remember about his home, the swimming pool was in the shape of a guitar and he had Lionel toy train tracks running throughout the entire house.

He left Capitol in 1976 the same year I retired and continued his successful career, recording an additional fourteen number one records for MCA and EPIC for a combined total of thirty number one records! I believe this is a record in itself.

In 1970 Merle was selected the CMA Top Vocalist of the Year, also Entertainer of the Year, and with Willie Nelson, Top Duo of the Year in 1983. He was inducted in the Country Music Hall of Fame in 1994 and 7 years later, still actively performing, has released a new CD titled, "Roots."

As a teenager, my son Gregory, was involved in some of the usual teenage mischievous actions. We sent him to a private co-educational boarding school in Idyllwild in the San Jacinto Mountains. He was there less than a year before he was expelled after being caught in the girls' dormitory at night. I'm sure he meant no harm; he did it on a dare.

Gregory came home and entered Birmingham High School in the Valley. A year and a half before he was to graduate, he was expelled for setting a trash can on fire. He transferred to Grant High for a year and with a half year to go, decided to go to Summer School. June and Claudia were staying at our Oxnard Shores beach house for the Summer so he enrolled in Oxnard High and without further ado he graduated in 1968.

For his graduation present, we bought him a used automobile and like many teenagers, he was over-confident about his driving capabilities. He was speeding, lost control on a curve, hit a tree, and completely totaled the car! It had to be sold for junk. Luckily, no other car was involved; Gregory had no passengers and his injuries were minor.

Although June and I tried to convince him of the importance of a college education, he had made up his mind that he did not want to go to college. He went to work at a gas station in Studio City and rented a one-room apartment. After working a little less than a year, he came to me and said, "Dad, I can't stand to look at another gas pump or motor. I want to go to college."

I said, "Okay, but I insist that you include in your curriculum two courses; bookkeeping and business contracts—because for the rest of your life, Uncle Sam insists you send him an income tax form with a complete record of your salary and investment earnings. And for the rest of your life, you'll be involved in contracts of one kind or another."

He agreed and moved back with the family. Before he entered college, we sent him on a guided bus tour throughout the Southern States. We felt that it was necessary that he have some knowledge of the rest of the country. When he came home, he said "The trip was fantastic, but I'll never ride a bus again!"

That fall he enrolled in Northridge College in the Valley. After a year in Northridge, with good grades, we were shocked when he told us he now knew what he wanted to be. He wanted to enroll in the California Institute of the Arts and study to become a classical guitarist. We had previously bought him a guitar and knew that he didn't have the musical talent to pursue this as a lifetime career. We reluctantly gave our consent, realizing that if we didn't, he would probably hold it against us for the rest of his life. He did attain a certain degree of guitarism and performed at a noontime concert at the school. I'm sure the concert made him realize he wasn't cutout for a musical career.

He came to us shortly afterwards and said, "I now know what I want to be. I want to be an attorney." We were delighted. Before he could attend law school, he had to have a college degree. He re-enrolled in Northridge College, got his degree, and enrolled in Pepperdine College in Malibu and got his law degree.

In 1963, I was asked by the Instructor of Broadcasting to give a talk on producing and promoting records to his Broadcasting Survey Class at the Los Angeles City College.

SPEECH

Last Year millions of records and millions of albums were manufactured and sold in the United States. If they were laid end-to-end, it is estimated they would circle our globe three times!

I am an Executive Recording Producer, an Artist, and Repertoire Manager for Capitol records, which is a subsidiary of the largest recording company in the world, English Musical Industries of Essex, England. At the present, I am head of the Country and Western Division of Capitol. However, I have produced recordings of every type of music. I am here this afternoon to give you, a picture of what is involved in being a producer of phonograph recordings. After I have finished with my word description, I will be happy to answer, to the best of my ability, any questions you might have.

As a Producer, one of my most important functions is as a Talent Scout. It is up to me to discover and bring to the label, new talent. This is done in many ways: through television shows; an artist's manager or agent will contact me; I hear about someone in a night club act and go see them; artists mail in audition tapes and records; an artist will become dissatisfied with the company he is with and want to come join us.

I personally audition about 20 new potential artists every year. After I decide that I want an artist, it is up to me to negotiate the terms of the contract. I contact the legal department of our company and have the necessary documents drawn up, usually a new untried artist will be signed for a period of one year with six option year periods. He will start at a royalty rate of from 2-1/2 percent to 3 percent of retail selling price of his records. The top artists usually get 5 percent of the retail-selling price. However, the cost of all musicians and musical arrangements are deducted from the accrued royalties before they are paid to the artist. So in essence, the artist is paying for his own recording sessions.

When the artist is ready to record, it is my job to get with him so we can mutually agree on the time, the place, the songs to be recorded, and if he doesn't have his own orchestra, which many country artists do, which orchestra leader to engage and how many musicians are needed. After these things are decided, we meet with the orchestra leader and discuss the type of background and arrangements we feel would be best for the numbers to be recorded.

Another prime function of a producer is the auditioning of songs. It is my job to determine whether or not they are suitable for recording. I must okay every song recorded. Songs come from many sources—often the artist writes his own, authors and composers send them in to me, and I hold regular meetings with music publishers. I estimate I audition well over a hundred songs a year!

When everything is set with the artist, I book studio time, or if it is a location job, I go to the City and place involved and make the necessary arrangements. As an example, last year I recorded an album at the-State Fair in Texas and included all of the sounds pertinent to the fair. The year before I recorded an album at the Cheyenne Rodeo in Cheyenne, Wyoming and incorporated all of the sounds pertinent to a rodeo. I also recorded an album in a gambling house in Las Vegas, Nevada and included all the sounds normally heard in a gambling house. I have also recorded in several nightclubs.

But getting back to a normal session in our Hollywood studios, a normal session runs three hours. That is, the musicians union allows us to record four songs or masters in that length of time. If we go over, we have to pay overtime.

A musician makes $56.40 for a three-hour session and $17.50 for each additional half-hour. The orchestra leader makes double that amount. During the session, the producer and recording engineer, or mixer as we call him, work hand-in-hand in the recording, or control booth. The producer is responsible for the total sound that is the correct balance between the vocalist and the orchestra, the correct equalization, the right amount of echo of the record.

If there's a written arrangement, the producer reads the score along with the orchestra leader and cues the mixer as to what to expect so that he can get the proper perspective of the instruments. Finally, the producer is responsible for the emotional quality and feeling of the record. If the producer does not feel that the singer has given his best or that the orchestra could do better, he has them do it over and over until he feels it is a master or take. He gives the final okay.

I have had sessions where we didn't even get one song in the whole three hours. On the other hand, I have had sessions where we have gotten six songs because everything jelled. The artist and the orchestra were on the ball!

When the record is finished, the producer sets the date for the record to be released and put on sale to the public. This release date depends on many factors: How popular the artist is; how well his last record is selling; is the artist appearing on a National TV show, or appearing in a movie; has the song been recorded on another label; is the song from a movie or a Broadway show; what competition is on the release with him? These and many other factors determine the date of release.

A record on a rush release, will be on sale to the public in six to ten days. After the release date is set, the producer's job is still not finished. It is his responsibility to write a review of the record, to see that the label copy is correct and to meet with the production, sales and promotion departments to determine how many records should be pressed and how best to promote the record.

As you are probably well aware, our main avenue of promotion is through AM radio and the disc jockey, and as I am told that this is primarily a class in radio, I would like to digress a few minutes and give you a brief synopsis of this facet of the recording and music business.

Our promotion department sends out to almost 3,000 radio stations, free of charge, promotion records on practically every single record released. If the promotion department feels that a radio station is not important enough to receive free records, the station is allowed to subscribe to our record service. If the stations want just the single releases, it costs $5 a month. If they want albums also, the charge is $10 a month. This barely covers the cost of handling and mailing. We do this because radio is practically our only means of exposing a record to the public.

It may seem to you from this bit of information that radio stations get their music without paying for it. But this is not the case. They get the records free but not the music. They have to pay for the right to play or perform a song over their stations. Every song or piece of music published, except music in the public domain, is controlled by three performance rights societies: The American Society of Authors and Composers (ASCAP); Broadcast Music Inc. (BMI); and a minor society—SESAC. All music publishers and songwriters assign the right to perform their songs to one of these societies. The society in turn collects a percentage of the annual gross receipts of all radio and television stations and then distributes the money to the publishers and writers. This has become one of the publishers and writers' biggest source of revenue. So you can see why they are anxious to have songs recorded and played over radio and TV.

Up to this point, I have been speaking primarily of single 45 rpm records. These are the small disks, seven inches in diameter. 45 rpm means the record spins on the turntable at 45 revolutions per minute. I would like to tell you now about albums. The record of an album is twelve inches in diameter and spins at a speed of 33 1/3 revolutions per minute.

Our weekly producers meeting is attended by the President of the Company and representatives of the Legal, Finance, Sales and Promotion Departments. In addition to setting the weekly single's release, we discuss all problems pertinent to recording. If an artist's option is coming up for renewal, we have his sales figures available so we can determine whether to keep him or drop him. We discuss new trends in music. We exchange ideas, but our most important function at these meetings is the planning and approval of albums.

When an idea or concept for an album has been submitted, by the individual producer, the Committee has to approve it. Some of the questions that arise are: What is the cost? What is the sales potential? How is it to be merchandised and promoted? When is it to be released?

Our album program is projected one year in advance. Our top artists, such as the Kingston trio, Nat King Cole, Tennessee Ernie, and the Beach Boys, usually have three albums a year. Other artists have from one to two depending upon their sales and popularity.

After an album has been approved, it normally takes from two to three months before it is ready for release. This is because of the many things involved. The actual recording, the cover preparation, the label copy, the clearing of the music, the title of the album, the writing of the liner notes, and preparation of the merchandising and promotion materials.

We can, if necessary, have an album ready for release in seven weeks. If urgent, we can do it in three to four weeks! Here again, the producer is responsible for correlating all of these steps: Get with the artist, pick the songs and handle the recording sessions. After the recording is completed, the producer assembles the album; that is, programs it.

Then he has a meeting with the Art and Editorial Departments to decide: What the title of the album will be? What kind of picture will be used on the cover? What is to be said on the back of the album cover? The producer has complete responsibility and must approve all of these steps after they are completed.

The sales of single recordings today, which are pointed mostly to the teenage market, was a boon to us. But albums are becoming the mainstay of our business. We are not issuing many albums on tapes at this point; it is a very insignificant part of our business. We are not yet able to predict how important tape recordings will become in the near future.

I have given you a brief description of some of the main functions of an Executive Recording Producer. I am sure you have many questions to ask, so "shoot away" and I will answer them to the best of my ability.

My dissertation on producing and promoting records was well received and I answered questions for over a half-hour!

I felt it was important to include this speech in my autobiography because of the tremendous changes in the industry that have taken place since then until now. I doubt if A&R men, like me, exist today. Most name artists have complete control over their recording careers. Attorneys and agents do the negotiating of contracts, incredible advances are given, hours and sometimes days spent recording a record or CD; albums are practically out of existence.

I don't approve of some of these changes, but I can't fault them because like everything else, technology, business procedures, and music are constantly changing and will continue to do so. There were many records and albums that became well over million sellers, but if an artist had sales of a hundred thousand or even fifty thousand, they were considered profitable. With the advent of cassettes and CD's, practically all homes have the equipment to play them and the unlimited expansion of the teenage market, has resulted in millions and millions more sales.

Lew Quadling, the pianist for the 1930-40's big band era, Dick Jurgens orchestra, brought me a country song he had written and told me an interesting story about Irving Berlin, one of America's greatest song writers. Eddy Howard, the band vocalist, and Jurgens, had written lyrics to a melody he had composed.

In 1938, Lew took the song to Irving Berlin's publishing firm in hopes of getting it published. When he finished playing and singing it for the office manager, the door opened and in walked Irving Berlin, who had been in the next room and heard it. He looked at the lyrics and asked Lew to play it again. When he finished, Berlin said that's a beautiful melody, would you mind if I wrote the lyrics for it? Lew who had written the melody was flattered and knowing that Howard and Jurgens wouldn't object, said "I would be more than pleased!"

Berlin wrote a completely new lyric and published it, crediting Quadling, Howard and Jurgens as the writers, taking no writer's royalties. The song, "Careless" was a hit in 1939-40. The closing lines of the song are so typically Berlin, "Are you just careless, or Do you just care less for me?" Lew told me that his prize possession is a letter from Berlin praising the merits of the melody. He had it framed and it enjoys a conspicuous place in his home.

Berlin's hits are too numerous to mention, but two of his songs, "God Bless America," and "White Christmas" have become perennial favorites. Ever since I was a youngster, I have been hearing, playing and singing Irving Berlin's songs. Although I never met him, I have always held him in high esteem. He was born in Russia in 1888. His eight member family of Jewish faith, immigrated to America when Irving was 5 years olds.

In 1911 he had his first big hit, "Alexander's Ragtime Band," the following year he married but his wife, after only five months of marriage, died of typhoid fever. He wrote the song, "When I Lost You," telling how void life was without her.

In 1918, at the age of 30, during World War I, he was drafted and while in the Army, wrote and produced his first musical show "YIP YIP YANK HAP." The cast was comprised completely of Army personnel. The female roles were men with wigs and dresses. The show played 32 performances in New York and then toured Army bases.

Berlin met socialite Ellin Mackay and they fell in love. In 1925 he wrote the song, "Always" which I presumed was inspired by Ellin. In 1926 when he was 37 years old and Ellin was 22, they eloped. When her father, a staunch Roman Catholic, Owner of Postal Telegraph Service, Western Union's rival, heard of the marriage, he disinherited her. Irving is reputed to have said, "Oh that doesn't matter, I gave her a million dollars as a wedding present." In 1927 he wrote the song, "Blue Skies" telling of his happiness.

After Japan's sneak attack on Pearl Harbor on December 7, 1941, which killed 2400 men and cut the Pacific Fleet in half, America declared war against Japan and the other two members of the axis, Germany and Italy. Irving Berlin again came to the forefront by writing the musical, "This Is The Army." He included a song destined for posterity, "God Bless America," that he wrote for his first Army show in 1918, but didn't include it. He did include "Oh How I Hate to Get Up In The Morning," The show was a tremendous success and he went on a national tour with the proceeds going to Army Emergency relief. The show then went to England and was so well received it was sent around the world. It was a great morale booster, not only for the thousands of troupes who saw it but also for the people who paid to see it. The show earned millions of dollars for needy families who had lost loved ones.

One of my favorite, lesser-known Berlin songs is "Russian Lullaby," which shows concern for the country of his birth. The closing lines are "Rock-a-Bye My Baby; Someday There May Be A Land That's Free For You and Me; and A Russian Lullaby."

Irving and Ellin's marriage obviously was a successful one, lasting 62 years until Ellin's death in 1988. One year later, in 1989, Irving Berlin passed away at the age of 101.

Charles Lee Guy Ill, at the age of 16, was convicted of involuntary manslaughter, a crime he insists he did not commit. He knew who was responsible for the crime but for some unknown reason would not divulge the person's name. As a result, he was sent to California State Prison in Vacaville, where he spent several years. While there, he became friends with fellow prisoner, Spade Cooley.

Spade was a well-known novelty orchestra leader, members of his band said he had a bad temper. He also was obviously a jealous man, jealousy and a bad temper are a disastrous combination! For some reason or other he accused his wife of cheating on him, which all evidence did not corroborate, losing his temper he killed her, in a fit of rage, in the presence of his 14-year-old daughter!

Charles had learned to play guitar. Spade worked in the prison wood shop, making guitars. They'd get together and play duets. While incarcerated, Charles developed his talents as a singer and guitar player. In 1962 he sent me a tape. I was impressed and wrote the Superintendent Dr. William Keating, for permission to come and record Charles. He readily consented. Charles and I corresponded and between us selected songs for an album called "A Prisoner's Dream."

In December of 1962, I took recording equipment, an engineer, and guitarist Joe Maphis to enhance the background in addition to Charles' guitar. We finished the album in three days and had included the song "Cold Grey Bars" written by Spade Cooley. When I visited Spade in his cell, he seemed remorseful and concerned about what his friends and the public thought of him. A few years later, Spade died in prison.

In 1963 I released the album, "Charles Lee Guy III A Prisoner's Dream." That year he was paroled to relatives in North Carolina. In 1964 I recorded him in Nashville with Nashville musicians. I was pleased with the results and especially pleased when one of the songs, "Rich Man's Gold," hit the charts.

But lo and behold, disaster struck Charles again! A girl he had been dating was found in a cornfield, shot to death. Being the last person to see her alive,

Charles was arrested for interrogation, and although a lie detector test proved him innocent, the ensuing publicity caused irreparable damage to his career.

I was summoned to our president's office and told that in the best interests of the label, I should drop him. I had no choice. He later had another harrowing experience in Louisiana. Because of his previous record, he was falsely arrested on suspicion of arson by a sheriff who brutalized the inmates. He later escaped through the swamps with bloodhounds after him. He managed to elude them but was later recognized and imprisoned again.

Charles managed to get a letter off to the Justice Department, telling them of the inhumane, filthy conditions of the prison, and they decided to investigate. When the sheriff found out, knowing he had no case against Charles and realizing he would testify against him, he offered to release Charles if he promised to leave and not return to that Louisiana parish. Of course Charles agreed and was set free! After the Justice Department investigation, the sheriff was removed and prison conditions normalized.

With the exception of his recording career, Charles' life had a happy outcome. His album, *A Prisoner's Dream* was released in the 90s in Europe on a CD. He lives in North Carolina, has two grown sons, a daughter, two grandchildren, and his dog Spooky. We have corresponded for many years and still do!

Glen Campbell, a young guitarist, was born in Arkansas. He and his wife packed all of their belongings in their small trailer and moved to Los Angeles in 1960. I don't recall how he came to my attention, but after hearing him play I knew he was very talented and hired him as often as possible. He soon became much in demand as a studio musician, even recording with the Beach Boys.

After hearing him sing a couple of duets with Merle Haggard, I was sure he had the qualities of a soloist and signed him as a vocalist. I had released two or three of his records and when he was to appear on a TV show, I expected him to sing songs we had recorded, but no, he sang rock 'n' roll songs. I told him I was disappointed and that he was not a rock 'n' roll singer but he paid no attention. He soon made another TV appearance and again did not sing any of the songs we had recorded. I was really upset! I told him his records were not being played by DJs, were not selling, and he had missed the opportunity to promote them. I guess he was trying to keep in step with the rock 'n' roll trend.

Later, at a Thursday morning A&R meeting, our A&R Chief, Voyle Gilmore, who had suggested I drop Buck Owens, also suggested I drop Glen Campbell because of the lack of air-play and sales. I strongly objected, saying Glen was a very talented singer and musician and it would be a mistake to drop him. I also said it was possible that I was not the right producer for Glen and suggested he assign Glen to another producer. Voyle said okay and assigned him to Al De Lory, who had recently joined the label.

There is no doubt that Al De Lory was a guiding light and partly responsible for Glen's successful career and fame. He chose the right songs and the right musical background for such hits as "Gentle on My Mind," "By the Time I Get to Phoenix," "Wichita Lineman," "Rhinestone Cowboy," and many others.

Although Glen was basically a country singer, his songs were country-pop oriented. Every record and album he released usually made both charts. In 1968 he was voted male singer and entertainer of the year at the CMA awards. That same year and for the next four years, he had his own television show, *The Glen Campbell Good Time Hour*. Glen also co-starred with John Wayne in the movie *True Grit*. He was an avid golfer, and because of his popularity, the Los Angeles Pro Tournament was called the Glen Campbell Open. I remember visiting his newly-built home in the Hollywood hills and, sure enough, he had a well-manicured putting green. I don't know if he owned his own theatre in Branson, but I do know he performed there and also on the Grand Ol' Opry.

A little aside on a trip to Nashville, I was on a plane with country singer Mac Davis. We sat together and he told me his wife had left him after falling in love with Glen Campbell. Glen, at that time, was divorced. Mac said he still loved her and felt badly when they married. He also said he didn't think the marriage would last because all she wanted to do was spend money! I don't know the outcome of the marriage, but at the age of sixty-six Glen is still making personal appearances.

In 1964 Central and Snyder were forging ahead at a rapid pace, so we decided it was important to have an office in Nashville. We purchased a building on Music Row and hired Smiley Wilson as manager. We had had the building for about two years when Hill & Range, a top country music publisher who also dealt in real estate, wanted the building and made us an offer we couldn't refuse! They would trade us a building in Hollywood at the corner of Yucca and Franklin Avenue, which was two blocks from the Capitol Tower, for our Nashville building.

Cliffie, who had other interests, was happy to consummate the trade. The building had several rooms, providing him, his secretary, and Buzz Carlton, with private offices. Although Central now owned an office building, it did not alleviate the workload that June, Lorraine, and I were doing at home. We retained Smiley Wilson as our Nashville representative.

After eleven years as musical and choir director of Christ Memorial Church, June resigned. She felt that because of the overburden of Central, she was not giving the choir proper attention. A few months later, June's mother, Bernadine Willey Felcher, fell and broke her arm. She was hospitalized but never recovered. I don't recall the cause of death. After she passed away, June mellowed and became a willing helper. She and June had had a close relationship. We all attended her memorial service and funeral. We missed her.

It was in 1964 that the University of California, University extension, in cooperation with NARAS, presented a well attended special program, "The

Recording Arts at UCLA." I, along with Lou Busch, arranger and conductor, Marty Cooper and independent producer Neeley Plumb of RCA Victor, and Irving Townsend of Columbia Records were invited to speak at the symposium "Hits and Flops and Why." The following is a speech I gave, which was well received.

WHAT MAKES A HIT RECORDING

In striving to make a hit phonograph record, the thing uppermost in my mind is to endeavor to produce a record that has the greatest area of appeal to the greatest number of people—a record that the average person can relate to, and because it appeals to them in some emotional area, they want to hear and play over and over again. Here are some of the basic elements that I feel are necessary to achieve this. Many records become hits with only one of these elements:

1) A song that has a good, understandable storyline with a melody that is easy to remember and retain and that the average person can identify themselves with.

2) An artist whose style fits the particular song being recorded and who gives an exceptionally stylized emotional performance.

3) An instrumental background or arrangement that is interesting but yet does not detract from the artist or the song.

4) An outstanding rhythmical drive or beat.

5) A unique sound.

If you are fortunate enough to be able to combine all of these elements in one record, you may possibly have a smash hit! However, there is no set formula, as the public is extremely fickle. Just as you think you know what it wants, it changes its mind. But you do have a better chance of making a successful record if it contains one or more of these elements, and this, I believe, is true of any type or category of music.

I have been asked many times what I look for in an artist:

I look for natural ability and musical intelligence.
The artist's emotional makeup.
Physical ability.

Degree of self-confidence.

We are all endowed with musical intelligence to a higher or lesser degree. Musical intelligence is a person's ability to hear and sing a melody and be able to determine whether or not it is in pitch. The ability to keep time and feel the tempo and rhythm; ability to understand, feel, assimilate, and retain the specific type of music to which a person is accustomed.

I believe a person's natural ability and musical intelligence is determined by the same factors that determine a person's customs, way of life, character, and personality—namely, heredity and environment. That is why we find specific types of people from a specific area who can only understand and enjoy specific types of music, such as rhythm and blues, country and western, popular, classical, etc. Of course, this doesn't mean there aren't people who enjoy all types of music!

The physical aspect is a person's muscular ability to execute and perform what he thinks and feels musically. What kind of tones will his vocal chords produce? What is the extent of his vocal range? Is his body soundbox adequate? How is his coordination between mind, feeling, and performance?

The emotional aspect is an artist's ability to arouse various dormant and latent emotions in the listener. An artist's success or failure depends greatly on this aspect.

It is generally agreed that we are constantly transmitting our feelings and emotions to others even in everyday conversations. I have heard it said many times that to be truly great, an artist must be neurotic. I don't believe this! I have known and dealt with many well-adjusted artists who were great in their fields; on the other hand, I have to admit that I have also been involved with neurotic artists. All in all, I have found that beneath their neurotic feelings, they are really warm, wonderful people struggling for a normal life, struggling to overcome their fears, frustrations, and anxieties, struggling for acceptance by their fellow man, but because of their backgrounds they don't know how to achieve these things and it is only through their singing and performances that they are able to express and convey to others their subconscious and true feelings and emotions.

One of the first things I try to determine is *Why does an artist want to perform? What is his motivation?* Through the years, I have found the following reasons:

to express himself—emotional release;
enjoys the physical vibrations of singing or performing;
likes people and feels he is giving of himself;
he is an exhibitionist—extremely egotistical; and
money.

Usually if an artist has only one or two of these motivations, he has neurotic tendencies and is difficult to work with. The ideal artist is one who has a well-balanced combination of all these motivations.

Some artists have an innate sense of what the public will accept from them. They have complete confidence in their abilities and are capable of choosing songs that are best suited to their particular styles and talents. They can plan their own musical backgrounds, and they know how to get the most of performing a song. They need very little direction. Generally speaking, this is the most successful type of artist. The other extreme is the artist who lacks confidence and needs help every step of the way.

As a record producer, I must keep my fingers on the pulse of whatever segment of the record-buying public I am aiming at. I must know not only the musical capabilities of an artist but in order to bring out the best of his talents, I must be aware of and understand his emotional make-up as well.

The Academy of Country Music was formed in Hollywood in 1964 to promote the growing number and popularity of country artists now emanating from and being produced on the West Coast. Tex Williams was the first president.

On the Academy's first two award shows in 1965 and 1966, I was awarded best producer status, which were metal cowboy hats. Central Songs was named best publisher. I was dubious of the organization because I thought they were trying to emulate the Grand Ol' Opry and the CMA shows. Both organizations now have yearly award TV shows that include all artists. CMA's show is in the fall; the Academy's show is in the spring. Both shows are very popular and have high TV ratings.

In 1965 Central had a surprise number one hit, written by Neal Merritt and recorded by Columbia's Little Jimmy Dickens, "May the Bluebird of Happiness Fly Up Your Nose!" The song also made number fifteen on the pop chart.

During the same year I added Bonnie Owens and Red Simpson to my roster; their singles and albums did well. Bonnie didn't seem to be relaxed in the studio; I'm sure if she had had more confidence in herself, she would have reached star status.

Red, who lived in Bakersfield, wrote several songs with Buck Owens and had two highly successful albums about truck drivers. We made an album about policemen, "The Man Behind The Badge," that I had high hopes for, but it didn't live up to my expectations. I'm sure it was because at the time there was a police scandal.

I made an album with Ken Curtis, better known as Festus on the TV series, *Gun Smoke*.

Peter and Gordon, a popular English duo who had gained some popularity here, were anxious to record an album of all country hits with Nashville musicians. It was a fun album to make because of their English accent; the album sold very well in England and Australia but had limited sales in the USA.

Capitol held its annual sales meeting in Puerto Rico. It was the most exotic place we had ever held a meeting. As usual I gave my annual sales pitch about the growth of country music.

In addition to her many other talents, June added golf. She became quite proficient and won many trophies. Not being athletic, I had no interest in the game until one day when June brought home a set of clubs for me and said, 'You're going to play golf!" I found myself enjoying the game, but in all the years we played together, I never once beat her. We used to gamble, betting ten cents a putt; occasionally I would win ten or twenty cents!

1965 was an exciting year for both of us. We decided to build a home. We found an ideal half acre lot nestled on the side of a mountain that overlooks the San Fernando Valley. It was in a cul-de-sac, at the end of Strawberry Drive in Encino. Once again June displayed her unique talent by designing a four thousand square foot dream house. The house and lot cost us one hundred thousand dollars, which was a goodly sum at that time however, we could well afford it because of our income from Central and Snyder.

It was an eight room house, and in addition we added an office with a lavatory for the publishing firms. It had a private entrance, so our go-between Buzz and our secretary Lorraine were free to come and go without disturbing us. The eight rooms included a kitchen, breakfast nook, a living room and family room, both with a fireplace, two bedrooms with a connecting bathroom, a sliding glass ceiling panel, and each with a walk-in closet.

Upon entering the guest lavatory, you were confronted with a dressing table on both sides with walled mirrors, then through an entrance were the toilet and urinal. In the hallway, before you entered the master bedroom, was a large linen closet. After entering the bedroom area, which took up the entire back end of the house, there was a vanity with mirrored wall and a small closet with two bi-fold, full length mirrored doors. Just before the bedroom entrance was a large walk-in closet. The bath area had his and her wash basins with mirrored walls, a shower, a Roman sunken bathtub, toilet, urinal, and a bidet. The bedroom's sliding glass doors opened directly to the swimming pool area, which was the full length of the house, overlooking the valley. There was rarely a day that went by without my getting out of bed, jumping in the pool, and swimming twenty or thirty laps.

When we built our beach house, I insisted on having urinals in the bathrooms for sanitary reasons. June decided to have a bidet in our new home. I don't understand why more homes and hotels don't have urinals. When Hubert Long came to visit me and saw the urinal, he had one installed in the apartment he was building. One of my artists, after visiting our house, had one installed in his home and jokingly told me, "Ken, every time I go to the bathroom I think of you!"

Three artists signed during this period. Their single records had poor acceptance, but their album sales were adequate. They were The Geezinalaw Brothers (a comedy duet) and Ned Miller (an outstanding song writer who recorded his biggest hit, "From a Jack to a King," on another label before he came to Capitol). I produced two albums of Miller's songs, as well as his songs with the Anita Kerr Singers; both had excellent sales! Ray Pillow, who this year was chosen by *Billboard's* Nineteenth Annual Country Music Awards as the Most Promising Male Vocalist of the year, became a regular on the *Grand Ol' Opry*.

Buck Owens and The Buckaroos won the Best Country Music Band of the year and Minnie Pearl won *Billboard's* Country Man of the Year award.

My daughter Claudia graduated from high school in 1966. June, Gregory, and I attended. As a graduation gift we bought her a car and had her take driving lessons. I wanted her to have freeway experience. In those days, Sunday morning freeway traffic was very light, so on Sunday mornings I would go with her for a freeway drive.

As we passed a road sign, I would ask, "What did that sign say?" This began to annoy her, and in an irritated voice, she said, "Oh, Daddy!" I decided to keep quiet. She obviously began to ignore the signs, and as a result we ended up in Ojai, which was far from our destination. I think she learned that paying attention to road signs is important.

We asked her what her car preference was and she said she wanted a Jeep, but after she drove one she decided it was too difficult to handle and chose the Volkswagen Bug.

In the Fall, Claudia was enrolled at California Lutheran University, a new school in Thousand Oaks. She wanted to become a teacher. The tuition then was three thousand dollars a year; we bought an insurance policy for two hundred dollars a year that guaranteed the yearly tuition would remain the same. We gave Claudia a monthly allowance, out of which she paid all of her expenses, rent, clothing, gas, etc. She came home on weekends.

The reason she chose Cal Lutheran was because Carmel "Candy" Maitland, with whom she had become friends, was a student there. She and three other girls, including Candy, shared a dormitory. Candy's father was Mike Maitland, at that time head of the sales department of Capitol. He and his wife owned a beach house close to ours; we became good friends and would visit each other frequently.

During her second year, Claudia had a terrifying experience. She was on a date with a fellow student whom she had dated a couple of times before, when their car was stopped by the police. She knew nothing about the young man and was shocked when they opened the trunk of the car and found a large amount of marijuana. His dormitory mates, knowing he was a dealer and afraid of becoming involved, had turned him in.

Poor Claudia—she was handcuffed, taken to the police station, and questioned. She told them she had dated the boy only a couple of times and knew nothing of his activities. She told them she was studying to become a schoolteacher. She was crying continuously and had almost reached the point of hysteria when they told her, "With this drug arrest on your record, you can never become a teacher."

After a thorough questioning and search, finding no evidence of dope or drugs, she was released. The young man was sent to prison. One of Claudia's roommates came and took her home.

One weekend when Claudia came home, I happened to walk in her bathroom, saw the sliding glass panel open, and smelled smoke. I confronted her and asked, "Are you smoking?' She said, "Yes." I realized that most of the students were probably smoking, and it was difficult not to be with the "in crowd," but knowing of the hazards, I hoped to convince her to quit before it became habitual.

I said, "Honey, you know I love you. I'm paying your college tuition, bought you a car, and give you a monthly allowance. I will buy you anything in the world that I can afford, but I will not buy you a stinking breath, yellow fingers, lung cancer, emphysema, heart trouble, and an expensive habit you will later want to break. Now if you want these things, you'll have to quit school, get a job, and buy them for yourself!"

She looked penitent but didn't respond. I wondered what she thought of my sermon, especially since June was practically a chain-smoker. I could never have carried out the threats and I imagine she continued smoking for a while, but I do know that by graduation, she did quit and hasn't smoked since. During her last year of college, being of an independent nature and wanting to earn her own way, she worked as a waitress in Du Par's Thousand Oaks restaurant. She graduated in 1970 and started teaching fourth grade immediately at Garden Grove elementary school in Simi Valley.

In cooperation with the National Academy of Recording Arts and Sciences, in the fall of 1966, I was again requested to speak at UCLA, to the

University Extension class on their program, "The Recording Arts: New Directions and Approaches." My subject was:

The Growing Country and Western Field

Country music has been a predominant type of music in America ever since the landing of the Pilgrims on Plymouth Rock. It had its origin in the folk songs that were brought over to this country by English immigrants who established their homes and families along the eastern seaboard and in the hills of Virginia, West Virginia, North and South Carolina, Tennessee, and other Central Southern States.

Their only form of entertainment was getting together, swapping stories, singing, and dancing. If there was some unusual event that took place in the community, such as a tragic death, an odd occurrence, an unrequited love affair, or a family feud, there was always some talented person who would set the story to music. Basically, country music today follows a similar pattern—the telling of a story.

Much of our pure American folk music comes from the families who did not migrate from the hills, who had no communication with the outside world, and who stayed put in the communities and homes their ancestors had established many generations before.

Another form of American folk music is the cowboy or western song. As America expanded and the cry was "Westward ho," many a brave, restless adventurer seeking new worlds to conquer migrated to Kansas, Oklahoma, or Texas and became a cowboy tending the vast cattle herds on the lone prairie. They too were faced with the problem of no entertainment. It was only natural that they should congregate around campfires, swap stories, and sing songs. And like their Eastern Hill cousins, there was always some talented cowboy who could set to music their experiences, their longings, their dreams and desires or any unusual event that had occurred.

It wasn't until long after World War I that the nation as a whole started to become aware of country music. Up until that time practically all country entertainers, or "hillbillies" as they were called then, performed only in and around their local communities. There were a very limited number of country entertainers on the great vaudeville circuits that were prevalent in the big metropolitan areas.

Phonograph recordings and radio, of course, changed the picture completely. Actually local radio stations were the first to recognize the fact that country, hillbilly, and rural music were the only types of music that a great percentage of the American public could enjoy, understand, and appreciate. It wasn't until the middle 1920s that the recording industry woke up to the fact that rural, country, and hillbilly music had a tremendous commercial potential.

The first company to recognize this potential was the OKEH Recording Company; at least they were the first to do anything about it. They took mobile recording equipment all through the South into remote rural areas and recorded the local talent. RCA Victor and Columbia Records soon followed in this venture. The first man to do mobile recording for OKEH Records was Ralph Peer, but within a short period of time he left OKEH and did the same thing for RCA Victor.

The first big country artist to gain recognition on phonograph records was a "city boy," Vernon Dalhart. He actually had studied opera but realized the potential of country music and made a fortune at it. The first genuine country artist to gain recognition was RCA Victor's Jimmie Rodgers, the "Singing Brakeman" who actually *was* a railroad employee from the State of Mississippi. He sold millions of records, and though he has been dead for many years, his recordings are still in great demand today.

It wasn't until after World War II that country and western music became national in scope. Prior to that, most country recordings were sold primarily south of the Mason-Dixon Line and in rural areas. Most of the country music performers performed only in the South.

The army had a great deal to do with bringing about the change. Many a city boy was exposed to country and western music for the first time because the Southern and rural hill boys brought their guitars and sang to them in the barracks.

The Special Services Division of the army was forced to put on country music shows because of the thousands and thousands of men from the South, the rural and hill areas, who could only appreciate this type of music. The city boy who had only been exposed to popular music and who used to laugh at country and rural music found himself liking and appreciating the simplicity, the sincerity, and the beauty of country music. When he returned home, he continued to want to hear country music.

However, one of the most important factors in the growth of country music nationally was the tremendous migration to the large cities, which took place after World War II. Entire families from the hill countries, the rural areas, and from the South moved to large metropolitan areas, brought their music with them, went to their local music stores, and demanded the recordings of their favorite artists. They also requested to hear them on local radio stations and forced promoters to bring live country music performers into the various cities.

Nashville, Tennessee, remains the focal point of the country music industry. The reason for this is because of the *Grand Ol' Opry* on radio station WSM. The *Grand Ol' Opry* is the oldest live radio show in the nation. It has been on the air continuously, featuring only country artists since 1925. A greater percentage of country artists live in Nashville. Most of the big country music publishers are based there and every major and many minor recording companies have offices and studios there.

There is a trade organization called The Country Music Association, which boasts a membership of over two thousand. It includes artists, musicians, writers, managers, promoters, publishers, trade magazines, advertising agencies, disc jockeys, radio stations, and every major recording company in the business. One of the Country Music Association's main purposes is to educate radio and TV sponsors to the fact that country music is an integral part of America.

They do this by putting on shows in the major markets, such as New York City, Chicago, Detroit, and just recently at the Coconut Grove here in Los Angeles. Today country artists perform to packed houses in every major city in such places as the Hollywood Bowl and Carnegie Hall. Television networks are finally becoming aware of the country music potential. More and more of the big TV shows are having country guest artists' appearances. As an example, sometime in December, Jackie Gleason will have an all-country show.

Every major city in the United States today has at least one radio station featuring country music exclusively. There are over four hundred radio stations playing country music full-time, and close to two thousand five hundred

> that program from one to eight hours daily. Popular singers, such as Andy Williams, Al Martino, Dean Martin, Perry Como, and many others are recording more and more country songs!
>
> It is becoming worldwide in scope. American country artists are constantly touring Canada, Europe, Japan, and Australia. It has definitely become a part of the American music scene. It is growing in volume and stature. It is a *big industry*, it is *big business*, and it's getting *bigger*!
>
> Outside of popular music, country music is listened to and enjoyed by more people than any other single type of music, and in the words of my old friend, Simon Crumb—"Country music is here to stay!"

In January of 1967, I hired Kelso Hurston as producer and manager of our Nashville office. I don't remember how long he was with us; I do recall he signed Billie Jo Spears, who had one successful record with us. She left our label in 1972 and had a fairly successful career with United Artists. Kelso also signed George Lindsey, who was Goober on *The Andy Griffith Show*. We had to drop him because of lack of sales.

In February of 1967 when I was going to Tokyo to record Buck Owens and the Buckaroos, live at the Kosei Nenkin Hall, knowing of June's fascination for Oriental objects of art and architecture, I asked her to come with me. I told her that after I finished my recording session with Buck, I would take a two-week vacation. She was thrilled; I booked our trip, which included a seven-day tour of Japan, three days in Taipei, Taiwan, and three days in Hong Kong. We left Los Angeles on February first and arrived in Tokyo the following day. The flight took fifteen hours; six hours to Honolulu, with a one-hour stopover, then nine hours on a Japanese airliner. It was very uncomfortable because the seats were obviously built for Japanese people, who have smaller body frames than we do!

When we landed in Tokyo, we were met at the airport by Warren Birkenhead and his wife, Mary. Warren was Capitol's, and I presume EMI's, Tokyo representative. I had met him a couple of times when he came to Hollywood on business. They drove us to our hotel, the Okura. Because of our exhausting trip, we agreed to meet the next day. Warren and Mary had lived in Tokyo since 1950 and were well acclimated to the thinking and culture of the Japanese.

The next day the Birkenheads took us to the American Club for lunch. The club was the center of social life for American residents; it had a library, a theatre, and other recreational facilities. That afternoon June and Mary, who really hit it off, went shopping in the Ginza, Tokyo's shopping and entertainment district. Warren and I went to his office. I got quite a surprise when suddenly the entire office force got up and did about ten minutes of calisthenics. Warren told me it was the Japanese custom for office workers to take an exercise break every morning and afternoon. That evening we all went to a *sukiyaki* house for dinner. Before entering the restaurant, you take off your shoes and put on slippers. All of the rooms are private and you are served by *geisha* girls. The food was tasty but there were no eating utensils, only chopsticks. I couldn't maneuver them so one of the *geisha* girls hand fed me! It was a fun experience that evening.

The next day, February third, I went to the airport to meet Buck and the boys upon their arrival. His records were very popular in Japan and we were met by a contingent of the press. The next two days were spent having press conferences, newspaper and radio interviews, taking pictures. We went to a *geisha* house and took photographs of Buck and the Boys with *geisha* girls and checked out the auditorium. I was relieved to learn my recording engineer spoke English and the recording equipment was tops. The performance played to a standing-room-only crowd and was a howling success!

The next day Buck and the Buckaroos went home so we were now free to start our vacation. We first went back to the art store and bought a hundred wood block Christmas cards and twelve wood block prints. We were taken up to the loft, shown beautiful painted screens that were about six feet high with four teak frame panels, and chose a scene that would be hand-painted on the screen. We were told it would take a month to paint and a month in shipping. We foolishly bought one, even though we felt we were being overcharged. We found out later this was true and we realized the folly of our compulsive buying when we totaled the final cost of the screen, including crating, shipping, customs duty, and hiring someone to deliver it to us from the airport. It was beautiful. We set it up in one of the living rooms, but I cannot recall what happened to it. We must have sold it when we moved. June had the prints framed with non-reflective glass. We have one in every room, even in the bathrooms!

After spending a day in Tokyo, we joined the eight-day Japan Sunrise Tour. Our itinerary included twelve cities, each one seemed more beautiful and interesting than the next. With the exception of the cold weather and rain we experienced during the tour, June was in seventh heaven, visiting the many wonders of Japan, the world's largest wooden building where the huge bronze statue of Buddha, cast in the year 1400, was housed, and the famous O'Hara and Folkcraft museums. One couldn't help but be impressed with the beautiful Japanese architecture, the old temples, castles, the Imari shrine, where we witnessed a *Shinto* dance, and the Imperial Palace, which we were not allowed to enter.

We took what, at that time, was the world's fastest train to Nagoya, where the Noritake China factory is located, to observe the making of the china. They make only bone china, which consists of ground-up bone, rock, and minerals. We watched the whole process. Most of the sets are for the Western market but June bought the Japanese home-style set, which consists of service for five. The salesman was delighted with her choice. The set cost eighteen dollars and the packing and shipping charges were almost the same.

One of the many boat cruises we took was to Mikimoto Pearl Island, where there is a cultured pearl hatchery. A grain of sand is implanted in an oyster's shell. The sand irritates the oyster, causing it to exude a liquid to cover it and this forms a pearl. June was anxious to purchase a necklace, but Mr. Li, a Hong Kong banker and a member of our group, told her it would be cheaper in Hong Kong. She had trouble restraining herself, but she did.

There were five couples in our group, three Chinese from Hong Kong, a couple from New Jersey, and us. We became quite friendly with Mr. Li and his wife; they gave us their phone number and we promised to call them when we got back to Hong Kong. One of our side trips took us to a mountaintop covered with snow. We Americans stayed in the bus while the Chinese, who had never seen snow, being thrilled at the sight, got out and had a ball throwing snowballs at each other like little kids. It was fun watching them!

Our Japanese tour ended in Osaka, where we boarded a Thai Airways plane for Taipei, Taiwan. The other couples went on to Hong Kong. We arrived in Taipei shortly after noon and were met by a representative of our travel agency, a beautiful, charming Chinese girl. She gave us each a rose and drove us to the Grand Hotel. The hotel has the reputation of being one of the finest in the world. We didn't doubt it. The room was by far the largest we had ever been in and was exquisitely furnished with Chinese furniture. June, being crazy about Chinese furniture, walked around the room, gasping in sheer joy. I, too, was impressed! Our evening meal of all Chinese food was excellent.

The United States has a large military installation here. We saw many top brass and their aides in the hotel. The next morning we toured the city and countryside of Taipei by private car. Our guide, Dorothy, was to leave for Canada in two months as one of twelve girls who had been chosen from a group of six hundred and fifty hopefuls to represent China at the Canadian World's Fair. She had asked to be our guide so she could practice her English. She spoke very well.

Here in Taipei, the main form of transportation was the bicycle among the bikes motor cars, pedi-cabs (bicycle-drawn rickshaws), ox-drawn carts, man-drawn carts, autobuses, trucks, and pedestrians. There was a real traffic problem. We had no desire to enter this frantic conglomeration without our private car and knowledgeable tour guide.

That evening we were scheduled for a Mongolian barbecue and a Chinese opera but the opera was cancelled. Our guide asked if we would like to go to a Chinese theatre restaurant; we made the mistake of saying, "Yes." The restaurant resembled the Lido in Las Vegas, on a smaller scale. It was packed with Chinese who were celebrating New Year's, which goes on for fifteen days. The food was of low quality, the floorshow was a troupe of not-too-attractive English girls with mediocre talent, as was the house band. We were glad when the evening was over!

The next morning we toured the National Palace Museum, which houses Chinese art treasures transported out of China by Chiang Kai-shek, a Chinese general and politician who was president of China from 1948-49. He was overthrown by Mao Tse-tung, a communist who became leader of the People's Republic of China. Chiang Kai-sheik fled to Taiwan and became its president.

Japanese architecture is very plain and beautiful. Chinese is the opposite—very ornate. Their artworks are a marvel to behold. We saw pieces of bronze and porcelain dated from 1100 B.C. to modern times, still in perfect condition. There is no doubt the Chinese were civilized centuries before Europe. We would like to have spent the whole day at the museum but our plane was leaving for Hong Kong that afternoon. We bid a sad farewell to the museum and the Grand Hotel.

We arrived at 4 P.M. on the island of Hong Kong, a part of the British Colony that included the Kowloon Peninsula and the New Territories. It is an area of about 390 square miles, with a population in excess of four million people. It reverted back to China in 1997.

We were met at the airport by our guide and were transported to our hotel, the Ambassador in Kowloon on the mainland. After unpacking, we went immediately to our tailor, William Woo. I don't recall how we heard of him but we had been patronizing him for a couple of years. He had a large clientele in California, coming over every year to set up a fitting room in a motel, tailor the clothes in his Hong Kong shop, and ship them back. The clothes always fit perfectly.

Here again we lost our minds. June ordered a black and white check wool suit, a cheongsam and jacket, a brocade type dinner suit, and a Thai silk dress. I ordered a dozen handmade to order silk shirts, a dozen ties, and two suits. We had dinner that night, which wasn't the greatest, at the hotel. Our room overlooked the island and harbor of Hong Kong, which is filled with boats of all types and sizes.

The next day was a full day of touring Kowloon and the "New Territories," where the farmers work and live. It borders Red China. We took pictures of the border. The scenery is beautiful; high mountains, a blue sea. Late that afternoon we had a fitting with Mr. Woo, then back to the hotel for dinner. We avoided spending any more money except for dinner—lunch was free.

The following day we toured Hong Kong Island, an area of only twenty-nine square miles, eleven miles long, five miles wide with a population of over a million. A mountain range divides the island with very little level ground. It is a city teeming with humanity, the vast majority being Chinese. The downtown business section with its skyscraper buildings faces Kowloon. Behind these buildings, rising up the mountainside, are a multitude of high-rise apartments interspersed with thousands of squatters. We drove through the old section of town, the sights and smells are beyond description, narrow streets with vegetables, meat, fruit stands. Everywhere one could put up a stand-barrow, so beauticians, bankers, letter writers, are all on the street; some of the letter writers had tables—some crates. We saw stores with valuables, art objects, hand-carved Chinese furniture, jade, ivory, gold jewelry.

Being American citizens we were not allowed to purchase anything from Red China, for which I was grateful. I'm sure if June had been allowed to make purchases, we would have been bankrupt!

We took a cable car up to the one thousand eight hundred foot peak. The ride was scary. It was in an almost vertical position all the way to the top. The combination of height, level, and speed got to me; it took quite a while to regain my equilibrium. Our guide met us at the top and drove us down the other side of the mountain to Repulse Bay, a beautiful beach resort with summer homes. We had lunch at a hotel on the beach that was built in the grand British style of the 1920s. After lunch we drove to Aberdeen which has the largest floating population in the world. Our guide told us thirty thousand people live on boats called sampans. They are jammed close together, generation after generation have lived on them. Merchants on sampans float among them selling food and other items. They even have floating schools. The people are very resourceful. The boats are crowded with women and children, cooking gear, etc. Some have crates, raising chickens for food. We saw both men and women with baskets hanging on the ends of a pole hung over their shoulders. They sell everything from food to furniture in this manner. The area is unbelievably squalid! The government is eliminating the area by building a number of apartment buildings to house the sampan people and filling in the area.

We had our third fittings at the tailor's that afternoon; obviously they had people working all night. That evening our guide took us back to Aberdeen for a Chinese dinner on a floating barge. We went from shore to barge via sampan. Two women ran the boat for speed. They lived on them; they were clean and neat. There were two wicker chairs for us, and a couple of children were tucked in the corner.

The barge was a huge floating oriental palace. Downstairs the Chinese ate and played mahjong. Upstairs was the main dining room for tourists. A young man sitting next to us, on shore leave from Vietnam, was quite drunk. He told us he had called his mother on the phone that afternoon and all she did was cry. June said, "I know, I'm a parent too!" He replied, "Yeah, your son's probably my age so you would know!" June would have had to be fourteen years old to give birth to our son to be his mother's age! The food was okay, but the young man's remark almost ruined June's evening!

Leaving Aberdeen our car had to inch its way through a mob scene, stopping many times. The boat people came ashore at night to shop and get the latest news from the stores and small stands that line the streets. It was an amazing sight!

The following morning, in an effort to stay out of stores and spend money, we took a tour of the harbor in a motorized junk. Twice we went into the floating population, composed of large junks and barges. Several times kids rowing sampans came to our boat begging for money. Two of the sampans had women onboard. They seemed quite determined and we gave each beggar about two dollars each. Generally speaking, we saw very little begging!

Hong Kong is the busiest port in Asia! There are not enough docking facilities to handle all the freighters that come from all over the world, so they moor in the middle and junks load and unload the freighters. From our boat, we got our only view of rooftop squatters; every large building houses a number of such huts. It was an enjoyable and educational tour.

That afternoon, we had our final fitting. Mr. Woo wanted us to take the clothing with us but that would have made our luggage overweight for flying, so he shipped it to us. That evening, the last of our tour....,was one of the most delightful. We went to dinner with Mr. and Mrs. Li, the couple we had met on our Japan tour. They wanted to take us for a snake dinner, which the Chinese are famous for. Mr. Li told us that some Chinese believe that snake blood is very healthy. A live snake is brought to the table, its stomach is slit open and they drink the blood. Another delicacy is snake bladder. This too must be fresh and the snake is served live, to be slit open.

I was glad to hear June tell him she just wouldn't be able to eat a snake dinner! He settled for a place that was famous for roast pigeon. It was out in the country of the New Territories. We parked the car in a lot, walked across railroad tracks, up a ramp that was lined with squatters' huts, then came the patio, where the Chinese play mahjong.

The restaurant was open air. June and I were the only Caucasians in the place. We noticed the floor was covered with cats as there were no windows; they were free to come and go. The Li's were quite amazed when we told them cats are not allowed in restaurants in the States. He said they eat pigeon bones and are there for handouts. June asked why so many had short tails and was told, "Chinese like to cut cat's tails."

We were served a platter of roast pigeon. The birds had been cut, lengthwise, down the middle. Mr. Li and June took a half, and Mrs. Li and I took a half. Mr. Li said to June, "Ooh, you've got the best part." She didn't know what he meant but soon found out. As she moved a wing, there was a long neck and a complete head. Not having the stomach for eating a bird's head, she cut it off and quickly gave it to a cat. Mrs. Li saw her and said, "I think Mrs. Nelson does not enjoy our pigeon." June told Mr. Li she enjoyed the pigeon but couldn't eat the head. Mrs Li devoured the head—eyeballs and all. To them it was the best part! We also had bean curd soup and chicken wrapped in paper, bones and all. From there we went back to a hotel in Kowloon and had another dinner—starting with shark fin soup. It was an evening we'll never forget! We were grateful to the Lis for showing us Chinese customs!

We spent the morning packing and discarding items we did not need, to avoid overweight baggage on the plane. Then we went to the Peninsula Hotel for lunch. We had crab and fish lip soup; it was delicious. Having a few hours to kill before plane time, we tried to avoid spending more money, but the bargains were so great that June weakened and bought a pearl necklace and a wristwatch for me; I still wear the watch.

Our plane was late in leaving Hong Kong, which caused us to miss our direct connecting flight to Los Angeles in Tokyo. We had to take a plane that landed in Honolulu for custom inspection, then go to San Francisco. After another hour's delay, we finally landed in Los Angeles—twenty-three hours after leaving Hong Kong! We had wired Gregory; he met a couple of very tired and weary parents at the airport!

March 31, 1967, Roy Horton, chairman of the board, and Paul Cohen, president of CMA, cut the ribbon officially opening the Country Music Hall of Fame. The opening was attended by countless country music celebrities and country music business leaders. Also in attendance were Tennessee Governor Buford Ellington, Congressman Richard Fulton, and Nashville Mayor Beverly Bailey. It was an unforgettable evening.

Two days later, Steve Sholes, who first suggested a Hall of Fame, was now president of the Country Music Foundation. Under his auspices The Hall of Fame was built. He proudly welcomed the first country music fans to purchase tickets to the Hall. Mr. and Mrs. Marvin Post and their three children, drove all the way from St. Paul, Minnesota, to tour the new museum.

For the second consecutive year, the Hollywood Academy of Country Music gave me the award for best C&W producer. In May I had numbers one, two, three, and five on the *Billboard* chart at the same time. Our president, Stan Gortikov, wrote me a congratulatory note and asked what I had against number four!

That year Central Song's big hit was "It's Such a Pretty World Today." The company was taking up more and more of our time!

On April 22, 1968 Country Music lost one of its most respected and beloved men—Steve Sholes, RCA Victor's vice-president in charge of A&R. I felt the loss personally, as I know many others did. Steve flew into Nashville, rented a car, and while driving to his hotel had a heart attack. He slammed into a wall and was fatally injured. It was providence that just the year before he had attended the opening of his pet project and had been inducted into the County Music Hall of Fame. Eddy Arnold, Chet Atkins, and I went to his hometown, Tenafly, New Jersey, and were three of his pallbearers.

This year, during his performance at the Hollywood Bowl, I presented Merle Haggard with a gold record, commemorating the sales of a million records of "Oakie from Muskogokee"—the Bowl was filled to capacity!

At Capitol Records 1968 sales meeting, I gave the following speech:

> I am happy to have this opportunity to personally thank each and every one of you on behalf of the country music department and our artists for the dominant part you have played in making Capitol, the leading country music label. In 1967 Capitol had nine number one country records on the *Billboard* charts. Our nearest competitors were Decca and Epic with four each. RCA Victor three, Columbia, Musicor, and Ashley, one each. In the album department, Capitol had seven number one country albums. Our nearest competitor was RCA Victor with four, Decca three and Columbia two. This shows without a doubt that Capitol not only has the best talent but also the best promotion and salesmen in the business!
>
> I don't have to tell you that country music is getting bigger and bigger every day! More radio stations are going full-time country; more people are listening to and buying country music than ever before. The demand for it is growing every day. We in the country music department are meeting that demand by infusing new blood into our talent roster and are developing new artists to the point where they become nationally known and have an automatic sale.
>
> Just as the development of new promotional and sales techniques must be uppermost in your mind, so must the development of new artists and new trends be uppermost in our minds. It is my firm belief that the year 1968 will see three or four new big country artists develop on the Capitol label—and I know that if we continue to get the great cooperation from our promotion and salesmen that we have had in the past, not only will we maintain our leadership in the country field, but we'll get so far ahead of competition that they'll never be able to catch up with us!
>
> Once again, on behalf of our artists and the country music department, I thank you!

June had become an excellent, avid golfer. Along with other prizes and trophies she had garnered, she won the 1969 Valencia Women's Club championship.

Our three publishing firms continued to grow and were taking up more and more of our time, especially in February and August when it was time to send the writers their royalty statements and checks. One day in 1969, June, my son Gregory, Lorraine Wilson, and I, were working in the office compiling royalty statements. In those days it was time-consuming because computers were not yet available.

June turned to me and said, "Ken, I didn't get married for this!" I laughed and said, "I know, honey. I'll see what I can do." Realizing the companies were overburdening both of us, I decided we should divest ourselves of them. I met with Cliffie and Lee, told them of the problem and they agreed we should put the companies up for sale.

Larry Greene, a copyright lawyer in New York, had been our attorney since the beginning of the business in 1948 when he wrote us about obtaining the British rights for our first publication, "The Gods Were Angry with Me," for the London firm of Campbell, Connelly.

When he came to our house several years later, he was astounded by our home operation. I called Larry and told him we wanted to sell the companies. Two or three weeks later, he called and said he had a buyer, Capitol Records. What a shock! He had offered the firm to Sam Trust, who was now in charge of Capitol's publishing firms. Having previously been with BMI, he knew of Central's catalog and earning power. Lee and Cliffie were equally shocked, as was I.

When Mr. Greene came to Hollywood to negotiate the sale, he told the financial negotiators there would be no audit of the companies. Their reply was, "If you think we're going to buy a company without an audit, you're crazy!" Larry replied, "Okay, but we will not divulge who the owners are."

Stan Gortikov, president of Capitol replied, "If you're worried about Ken Nelson, you needn't be. He's made the company millions of dollars!" Here I was feeling guilty all these years, and it had been known or surmised that I was part owner of Central Songs!

Having no idea what the companies were worth, we were pleasantly surprised when he told us the sale price was $1,700,000. Cliffie and I wanted to keep the building we owned in Hollywood. We were disappointed when he told us it was included in the negotiations. I'm sure that building is worth close to a million dollars today.

Cliffie, Lee and I held a meeting and decided to give Buzz Carlton, our go-between who was essential to our operation, a bonus of $100,000. He was upset and thought he should have twice that amount—we told him no way! He finally, grudgingly accepted the hundred thousand.

Dorothy, Cliffie's then wife, for some reason or other disliked Buzz and, knowing I had suggested the bonus, started to berate me. While I seldom lose my temper, I became angry and told her Buzz was invaluable to the company and it was none of her damn business what we gave Buzz!

We later apologized to each other for losing our tempers and remained good friends.

We also voted to give Lorraine Wilson a bonus; I don't recall the amount, but whatever it was, I'm sure it was inadequate.

We had agreed with our attorney, Larry Greene, on a fee of 10 percent of the sales price; however, when the sale was consummated, he only took a fee of 4 percent, saying Capitol had paid him a finder's fee of 6 percent. Larry, June, and I remained close friends, visiting each other until Larry's death in 2001. When my daughter was just a child, she said she fell in love with Larry because he was a gentle and kind man.

In April of 1970 President and Mrs. Nixon invited all members of the Country Music Association, their wives, and other Nashville dignitaries to the White House for an evening of entertainment featuring Johnny Cash. I think the performance was in the East Room. The audience included government officials and others. Johnny was enthusiastically received.

After the performance, the President, Mrs. Nixon, Johnny, and his wife, June, stood on the stage in a single line and each of us from Nashville and others shook hands with the president and Johnny and exchanged pleasantries with Mrs. Nixon and June. Following this we went to another room for a buffet and dancing to the music of the Marine Dance Orchestra. It was an enjoyable and memorable evening. If I recall, June, Johnny, and their recently born baby spent the night in the White House.

In 1953, I signed Freddie Hart. After releasing several records with no airplay and no sales, I had to let him go. He then signed with Columbia and Kapp records and did have limited success. In 1970 he signed with Buck Owens Productions, so here again he was a Capitol artist and BOOM! In 1971 had a million seller, "Easy Lovin'," which earned a gold record, made the pop chart, and was followed by five number one records. He stayed with Capitol until 1977. I guess I signed him at too young an age.

After the sale of Central Songs was finalized, June and I decided to celebrate and take a month's vacation in Hawaii. We took our golf clubs with us and played almost every day. We played golf on Mauna Kea, Maui, Kona, and Kauai. Kauai was our favorite island, and we left it with reluctance to spend some time in Honolulu. We booked a room at the Reef Hotel where we had stayed 10 or 12 years previously. It was so romantic; you looked out the window and saw the ocean and Diamond Head.

We were looking forward to recapturing that romantic sight, but alas—it was not to be! When we looked out the window, Diamond Head was now a ten-story open garage. We had dinner at the hotel, went out for a walk, and went to bed about 11:30 P.M. We kept being awakened by Don Ho—the popular Hawaiian singer who was entertaining in the nightclub below. We finally got to sleep around 3 o'clock but then around 5 A.M. a garbage truck came down the alley, banging garbage cans while emptying them. We looked at each other and said, "Let's get out of here; it's getting too much like New York!"

I called the airline and asked what time the next available flight was leaving for Los Angeles. They said 8 o'clock—we made it! Thus ended our recapturing the thrill and romance of our first visit to Hawaii.

Our daughter Claudia graduated from college that year but could not attend her own graduation because she was in the hospital having a cyst removed. Gregory and I went to the graduation while June was in the hospital comforting Claudia. We enjoyed the graduation, but it wasn't the same without Claudia. After she recuperated, she and four other girls rented a house but it became such a hassle and confusion she moved out and rented her own apartment. Immediately after graduation she acquired a position teaching at the Garden Grove School in Simi Valley and is still there in 2002.

Roy Clark, he and Buck Owens hosted one of TV's longest country shows "Hee-Haw." Roy was also the first artist to build his own theater in Branson Missouri.

CMA board meeting 1962. Top row L-R Greylan Landen, Don Pierce, Cal Young, Grant Turner, Bill Anderson, Hubert Long, Hap Peeples, Harlan Howard, Ray Odom, Jack Loetz, Harold Moon, Dorothy Gable, Dick Frank, Tex Ritter. Sitting – Francise Preston, Steve Sholes, Ken Nelson, Jo Walker, Chuck Bernard, and Ralph Emery.

Ken, Gene, Wesley and Steve

1963 turning the CMA Presidency over to Gene Autry.

Steve Sholes of RCA Victor, Ken Nelson of Capitol, Paul Cohen of Decca, Dee Kilpatrick. Dee was general manager of the "Grand Ole Opry" for a period of 3 years. He produced some of Capitols earliest recordings of Hank Thompson, Martha Carson and Leon Payne.

Wynn Stewart signing his contract in 1960.

In 1964 Charles Lee Guy a prisoner in Vacaville, California penitentiary, sent me a tape of his singing and playing. I went there and recorded him.

♥ **FREDDIE HART** ♥

Buck Owens arriving in Tokyo to record a live album, 1967.

KLAC
KEN NELSON PRESENTING
MERLE HAGGARD HIS GOLD RECORD
AT HOLLYWOOD BOWL 1968

In 1968 I presented Merle Haggard his first gold record at the Hollywood Bowl.

Attending a BMI award dinner, L-R Mrs. & Mr. Roy Acuff, Ken Nelson, Bob Ferguson, Mr. & Mrs. Ferlin Huskey.

Tex Ritter and Joe Allison.

The name of this trio slips my mind

1971-1980

In January of 1971, CMA held its annual board of directors meeting in Houston, Texas. I was to receive an award as producer of the single and album of the year 1970. I was in Houston, but at the same time I was to receive the award, I was recording an album with Ted Daffan. Wade Pepper, who was then president of CMA, accepted the award for me. Later that night at Ted Daffan's house party for the CMA officials, Wade presented me with the award.

In February of 1971, June and I took a six-week tour of Europe, for which I had booked an economy flight, but when we got to the airport, I decided to change to first class. It cost an additional $900.00 but it was well worth it. June was thrilled! Our tour included France, Switzerland, Italy, the Isle of Capri, Monte Carlo, Spain, Portugal, Gibraltar, and Morocco. We visited nineteen cities in all.

It was a ten-hour flight to London, where we changed planes for a one-hour flight to our first stop, Paris. On this flight we were the only ones in first class and did we get service, with three stewardesses and one steward! We arrived at ten A.M., checked into the Lido Hotel, unpacked our bags, and took a three-hour siesta.

Of course, you don't go to Paris without visiting Notre Dame, Napoleon's Tomb, dining at Maurice's, the Louvre and taking a night tour of the city. We had intended to spend the whole afternoon at the Louvre but overslept and didn't get there until almost closing time. We did see the Mona Lisa. Paris is an historical and fascinating city.

Our next city was Geneva, Switzerland. It took about seven hours to reach it via a fast, deluxe parlor chair train. We sat with two Frenchmen, who spoke English. Their conversation was most interesting, about everything from affairs of state to how the French love their dogs. We arrived at the Metropole Hotel at six-thirty P.M. The hotel is very old, very spacious with a large dining room where the food and service was excellent. We decided to have dinner there for our three-night stay.

The next day we went to one of the largest Swiss watch companies, Bucherer, and June could not resist buying a gold watch and bracelet for herself, a pearl and diamond ring for Claudia, and a watch and lighter for Greg. After her buying frenzy, we took a two-hour tour of the old and new ports of the city, UNESCO, the World Health Association, and the Red Cross. It's a fascinating city!

That evening while having a cocktail at the hotel, we were joined by Abdul Hammid, an Egyptian whom I had met the previous night in the lobby while smoking a cigar. He was there on UNESCO business. It was interesting to get his view of the world situation.

Then he said, "Let's not talk politics anymore. I want to get away from them for awhile."

We continued our conversation about families and experiences. He was quite fascinated when I told him I was a record producer of country music.

The next day we took a new Mercedes Benz to Chamonix, a small French town 3,500 feet high nestled in a valley between the French and Italian Alps. It had been snowing all day! When we arrived at Chamonix, we took the cable car to an altitude of 12,700 feet, three-quarters of the way up Mount Blanc, the highest mountain of the Alps. The cable car held fifty people, standing up, and it swayed like mad!

It took twenty minutes to get to the top. We had to walk down a long tunnel to an observation point. We couldn't see a thing because of the clouds. There was no heat in the cable car or tunnel; it was ten degrees below zero. We were all freezing!

There was a small cafe with a heater and we had to wait an hour and a half before descending. We all huddled around the heater and had a hot drink. On the descent, the clouds lifted and we could see the beauty of a glacier's high pointed rock cliff. We had lunch in the village with two men, one from Pakistan and the other from Indonesia. Coming from warm countries, they were both freezing on the way back to Geneva. This also being a big skiing center; we saw many ski lifts and slopes in use.

That evening at the hotel, we spent a pleasant evening with our new acquaintance, Abdul Hammid. The next day we said *adieu* to Geneva and left by train for Venice. We went through the Swiss Alps, through very long valleys, and mile-long tunnels that were cut through the Alps. There were little villages every few miles, each with its church and filled graveyard.

When we arrived in Venice at nine-thirty P.M., it was snowing with a bitter cold wind. We took a water taxi that had an inside cabin, down the Grand Canal to the Luna Hotel. The hotel faces the canal and is very old, but modernized. When we went to bed, June was aware of a scratchy throat and woke up with a terrible cold. That morning even though it was below freezing, we and another couple took the walking tour of historic St. Mark's Square, the cathedral, the Doges palace and prison, then to a glass factory and saw how

Venetian glass is made. In the showrooms, June had to resist the temptation to buy some crystal.

Half frozen, we went to Harry's bar for lunch. It had been recommended by a friend and was all he said it was! Back at the hotel, we took a water taxi to see the palace and inner gardens. Venice is three thousand years old, and some of the buildings look it!

By now June's cold was in full bloom, but our short visit to Venice was over. At five o'clock that afternoon we left for Florence and arrived at nine o'clock and took a taxi to the Baglioni Hotel. June had a bowl of soup and went directly to bed. I sat in the lobby, smoked one of my Havana cigars, then joined her. Our room was large and in the old style but not quite warm enough. June had been taking gobs of pills, and in the morning she felt better.

March 6, was our 26th wedding anniversary, and I had a dozen long-stemmed roses sent to the room. We took a morning tour to two ancient churches, the Medici's tomb where Michaelangelo had done the crypts and statues, then went to the gallery for a while. June was upset; the weather was so cold she couldn't shop and get a better feel of the city. The next day June's cold wasn't any better so we stayed in our room all morning. It being Sunday, all the museums were closed but in the afternoon we did go to an ancient monastery, still in use today. It was colder inside than outside, which was still below freezing.

Our next destination was Sorrento, an all-day train ride. We changed trains in Rome and Naples, where we passed by the ruins of Pompeii at the foot of Mount Vesuvius. We arrived in Sorrento at six P.M. and checked in at the Hotel Carlton. Our tour included a steamer to the Isle of Capri. It was difficult to understand why it was called the "playground of the rich." Everything looked decrepit and Roman ruins were everywhere. There were no beaches for swimming. Back in Sorrento, which is a resort town, all the restaurants were closed because this was not the tourist season. We had dinner at the hotel.

In the morning we left Sorrento by private car, with a driver, for Naples via the Amalfi Drive. It reminded us of our Route 1 near Big Sur. The scenery was spectacular; the road was a winding shelf far above the sea, carved out of the rock, built in 1825. Buildings were built to the very edge of the steep cliffs and in some cases were molded right into the rock. Anywhere there was a little soil, they had terraces to grow citrus and olive trees. They were all covered with arbors to protect them from the cold.

We arrived at our hotel, The Royal, around noon and checked into a nice, large, corner room on the bayfront. Our driver told us about a pizzeria a few blocks away; the pizza was out of this world. We had dinner at the hotel. In the morning, there was no heat in the room and the dining room was closed. The hotel workers were on strike so there were no hotel services anywhere in Naples.

A driver and guide took us through the old section of the city, where the buildings are 3,000 years old and the street can accommodate only one car. This section was founded by the Greeks before the Romans took over. We then went to the new section, which is mostly post-war. Naples was the filthiest city I had ever been in. It looked as if they throw their garbage out the windows; beggars and toughs roamed the streets; children hawked wares, and poverty abounded. The day we arrived, we read in the paper that due to the cold weather, rats as big as cats had come into the city the night before by the hundreds in search of food! I'm sure they didn't go hungry! Before our driver left us, we asked if the rats had come again last night. He said, "Yes!"

Since the hotel employees were on strike, it meant we had to walk three or four blocks to a restaurant, which June wasn't about to do for fear of the rats and the riffraff. So I walked to the pizzeria, without any incident, and we had dinner in our room. We had another one and three-quarter days in Naples with nothing to do. We played a lot of gin rummy. We had planned to go to Pisa, explore the Leaning Tower of Pisa, and to visit the ruins of Pompeii. But as all the museum attendants were on strike, those plans were squelched. Oh well, we did pass and saw them from our train window.

On Saturday, March 13, before leaving Naples we went to Marina's for one more of their delicious pizzas. What we liked most about Naples was leaving it! We left Naples at 3:30 P.M., arrived in Rome at 7:00 P.M. and checked into the Hotel Majestic.

In the morning, by motor coach, we toured the Pantheon, the Forum, the Roman Baths, and St. Peter's Basilica. Because the museum employees were still on strike, we could only get into St. Peter's Basilica, it was owned by the Vatican. All employees of Catholic museums and churches worked for them and not for the state. We joined the church services at high mass for a while. They had an excellent men's choir and organist. The church is fantastic! Afterwards we roamed around St. Peter's Square, and at noon sharp the Pope appeared at his window, blessed the crowd, and gave a short speech.

In the afternoon we toured Roman ruins. The Italians are very proud of their works of art, which seem to be mostly in churches and seemingly thousands of Roman statues. The Coliseum was supposed to be awash with cats, but we only saw two. We were having the first rain of our trip and they were in hiding. The oldest thing in Rome is a transplanted Egyptian obelisk, 3,500 years old and still in beautiful shape. It's very thought-provoking when you realize how far civilization has progressed in over two thousand years.

Monday morning, we went to the Vatican museum and the Sistine Chapel, the museum had countless antique priceless treasures, the ceiling of the Sistine Chapel was a sight to behold! Pope Julius, II commissioned Michelangelo to paint the ceiling of the chapel in 1505. There is no doubt that he was one of the world's most outstanding artists! On a scaffolding, high above the floor, he painted figures of Biblical men and women and Biblical scenes. He finished the project in four years.

We were supposed to go to Tivoli, but because of a mix-up we took the tour of the Appian Way, then the catacombs. The Roman catacombs hadn't been used since the 9th century and were just recently re-discovered. They have five levels that run underground for eleven miles. It was interesting but rather eerie.

From Rome we went to Monte Carlo but only spent one night and morning there. After dinner that evening, we visited the famous casino, but didn't gamble. I didn't want to emulate the 1892 song, "The Man Who Broke the Bank at Monte Carlo.

In the morning, before leaving for Barcelona, we took a quick tour of the City at 11:00 A.M., boarding the train and arriving in Barcelona at 8:30 P.M.. We checked into the Hotel Ritz. Here again we only had one day before leaving for Madrid. We took a quick tour of the city in the morning, left by train at 1:25 P.M., arrived in Madrid at 10:00 P.M. Thus ended the first leg of our tour.

The second phase was the American Express Iberian Tour, which included Spain, Portugal, and Morocco. Our first day in Madrid, we toured the Royal Palace and University City, spent most of the day just roaming around. In the evening our tour guide took us on a drive past splashing fountains and illuminated landmarks. Very impressive!

The next day we were driven to El Escorial to see a monastery with fifteen cloisters, an area within a monastery or church to which the religious are normally restricted, then to a church in the shape of a Greek cross. We drove to Toledo, visited El Greco's 16th century house, the cathedral, and the Alcazar, a castle built in 1615, then did a little shopping before returning to Madrid.

Spent one day in Cordova and one in Granada, toured the Cordova cathedral. Our day in Granada was mostly sightseeing, including the Alhambra, the 1612 Palace of the Moorish kings. We couldn't understand why our tour had three days in Costa Del Sol; there wasn't much planned. After a ride over the western slopes of the Sierra Nevada Mountains down to the Mediterranean coast of Malaga, a province of Spain in the Andalusia area, we had a short tour of the city and returned to the hotel. Nothing was planned for the afternoon or the next two days.

After our boring stay in Costa Del Sol, we were driven to the port of Algeciras, boarded a boat and crossed the Straits of Gibraltar, disembarked at Ceuta, had lunch, then drove to the Moroccan port of Tangier. We spent the afternoon sightseeing the Medina and the old Sultan's Palace. Nothing to do in the evening but gab.

The next city was Fez, a city in North Central Morocco, where we toured the Kavaouyine University, the Andalusian mosque, and the Kasbah. Dinner that evening was of Moroccan specialties; it was delicious!

Next day we went on to Marrakech, a city in central Morocco in the foothills of the Grand Atlas Mountains. We spent the evening strolling in Place Djemaa el-F'na, a huge market square. Our morning sightseeing included the Minaret of Kowtoubia, a tall slender tower from which to summon the faithful to prayer, the Medina, the Jewish Quarter and the Kasbah. If I recall rightly, this is the city where a very large area at the entrance of the Kasbah was an on-going entertainment center filled with acrobats, jugglers, magicians, musicians, a vocal quartet whose singers were all blind, crippled and blind beggars, everyone begging for money. I did donate to the blind quartet and to a couple of blind or crippled beggars. Our tour guide warned us not to leave the group while in the Kasbah, because if you strayed and got lost, your life could be in danger!

June and a couple of other women decided to stay in the bus. The Kasbah was a bit eerie with narrow streets, countless shops, meat sold in open air markets, and, to us, some strange looking characters. We made sure to stick close together.

On our way to the next destination, the capital of Morocco, Rabat, we stopped in Casablanca at a very picturesque seashore restaurant for lunch, then on to Rabat for a Moroccan Moorish barbecue. During our one-day stay in Rabat, our sightseeing included the Tower of Hassan, the Royal Mosque, the old section of the city and the palace of former Moroccan kings. In touring the Moorish Palace we found it unique and beautiful. It had a haven for the king's many wives and concubines. I'm not sure whether it was here or at the old Sultan's palace in Tangier where our guide told us if a wife or concubine ceased to please him, he had her thrown off the cliff on which the palace was located!

Before leaving, Rabat, our last stop in Morocco, we had breakfast then drove along the Atlantic Coast past the towns of Sale, Kenitra, and through the Forest of Mamora to Tangier in time for lunch. After lunch we cruised across the Straits of Gibraltar to Algeciras, a city and port of Spain.

Our morning was spent relaxing; in the afternoon we went to Jerez de la Frontera to sample sherry wine and to see a *bodega*, a place for maturing wine, then on to Seville. Dinner at our hotel was followed by a party at a cabaret. Our morning tour included the Giralda Belfry, the Alcazar, the gothic cathedral, and the ancient gypsy quarter of Santa Cruz. We loafed the rest of the day. In the morning we drove across the border to Portugal, stopped for lunch, then via Setubal on to Lisbon.

Our morning sightseeing included St. George's Castle, a bull-fight ring, the Tower of Belem, and the very interesting museum of royal coaches, some dating back centuries. After lunch on the Portuguese Riviera we went on to Sintra, well-known for its Moorish castle and royal palace then back to Lisbon. It was the last day of our tour and we did nothing but roam around the city, that night we attended our farewell dinner party.

In the morning, we left for home sweet home! We were becoming bored and had seen enough castles, palaces, and cathedrals to last us a lifetime. We arrived home the same day and that night, with a sigh of relief, sunk into our own beds. The next day back to work and much to do!

Bhaskar Menon, a native of India, had been sent by EMI to different countries around the world to establish or put in order foreign branches. He now came to Hollywood to be our permanent president. At one of our first staff meetings, he asked me to sit next to him. He was affable, intelligent, and very inquisitive about country music. He was well-liked.

I needed a replacement for our Nashville office, and on Cliffie Stone's recommendation I hired George Richey. One of the artists George signed was Charlie McCoy, a harmonica player. Outside of guitarists, I had no faith in other instrumental recordings and I kept putting off releasing Charlie's first session. In the meantime George decided to leave Capitol and asked me if he could buy back the masters. I consented. He sold them to Monument Records and POW, his first release "Today I Started Loving You Again" was a fairly good-sized hit and for the next couple of years his records were on the charts and good sellers. I don't know if George became a producer for Monument but I do know he married Tammy Wynette, and became her manager!

Because of the hot weather in the summer and the smog in the Valley, which seemed to be getting more intense, June and I decided to sell our Encino home and make our permanent home in the cooler, smog-free Ventura County area. Although we had a weekend and summer house on the beach in Ventura, it wouldn't do as a permanent residence. After looking at houses and lots in Thousand Oaks and Camarillo, we bought a two-acre lot in Ojai for $15,000.00, intending to build our own home. It was a beautiful area but we found out the summer weather was just as hot or hotter than the Valley. I foolishly sold the lot for what we paid for it. I found out later it was resold for $50,000.00

One day when I came home from work, June seemed unusually exuberant and told me of the perfect lot she had found in Camarillo. Wouldn't you know? It was an acre lot on a hill in the middle of the Saticoy Country Golf Club, with fairways on both sides, a private street with a gated entrance, and a view of the Ocean. The cost was $20,000.00, one thousand more than the cost of our first home in Studio City. Of course, we had to become members of the Saticoy Country Golf Club, and June was in golfer's seventh heaven! It was an ideal setting. We played golf whenever we wanted, made many friends, and it gave us a good social life.

I loved our Encino house and thought June would use the same plans for our new 3,600 square foot home, but she decided to have fewer but larger rooms. There are only five rooms: a kitchen with breakfast area, a large den that could be converted into a bedroom, guest and master bedrooms with dressing area and two walk-in closets, a huge living room with the dining area at one end, an atrium, and two bathrooms.

We engaged the services of an architect whom one of our golfmates at the club recommended. We found out too late that he was more into commercial buildings rather than homes. I felt he could have suggested some significant changes to improve June's plans but he didn't. The problem is you don't see this until the house is finished. I am happy with the house and its spacious rooms, but I still preferred the Encino house.

I don't recall the exact date, but this was the year that Gene Vincent, who is in the Rock and Roll Hall of Fame and has become a legend, passed away at the age of 36.

Much occurred this year in October. Mauri Lathower, a long-time employee of Capitol, was promoted to head of the artist and repertoire department. It was quite coincidental that his wife was a former singer on the *Supper Time Frolic*, when I was musical director of WJJD and sang on some of the first transcriptions that I produced for Capitol.

It was the 46th anniversary of the Grand Ol' Opry and Governor Winfield Dunn proclaimed October Country Music Month for the state of Tennessee. He invited all of us who had participated in the Music City Pro-Celebrity Golf Tournament and their guests to the governor's residence for a cocktail buffet. Two of the pros, as I recall, were Mason Rudolph and Lee Trevino. Trevino had a wonderful sense of humor. It was an affair to remember.

Wade Pepper was unquestionably tops in artist and record promotions. We had worked together many years and through his efforts my job was made a lot easier. I admired him greatly. He was sincere and dedicated to any task he undertook. Our friendship remains to this day. We both received one of *Billboard's* annual Country Music Awards: Wade as Best Country Music Record promoter, and myself as best country music record executive of 1971. I received another great honor this year; Connie B. Gay, CMA's first president, presented me with the Founding President's Award for my outstanding service and achievements to the Country Music Association.

The year ended on a sorrowful note. On December 23, Glenn Wallichs, who along with Johnny Mercer and Buddy De Sylva, had founded Capitol Records, passed away. He was a stalwart of the recording industry, a man of principle, integrity and compassion, especially towards his employees. He was held in high esteem by all who knew him. I admired him greatly. I never forgot the time I was apologizing for getting him involved in a crooked oil deal. He put his hand on my shoulder and said, "Ken, I'm over twenty-one!"

Part II

On the 24th of January 1972, I was appointed colonel, Aide de Camp Governor's Staff by Tennessee Governor Winfield Dunn. Unlike Colonel Tom Parker, who was appointed colonel by Governor Jimmie Davis of Louisiana, I never adopted the title.

I was also appointed one of the trustees of the Country Music Foundation for 1972 and 1973.

In a previous chapter I wrote of my association with Gene Austin and his publishing firm when I was seventeen years old. Gene was one of the first singers to record electronically. His easy, relaxed style was new to the public and between 1925 and 1934 he was one of Victor Record's most successful artists, selling millions of records. The last time I saw Gene, he was performing in a club in Palm Springs. He asked the audience for requests. I kept requesting all the songs his firm had published. He finally stood up and said, "Is Ken Nelson in the audience?" We met later and had a wonderful reunion. Gene is not remembered as well as he should be, but I will never forget him. Gene passed away in 1972 at the age of 71.

At a music symposium at either the University of Southern California (USC) or University of California at Los Angeles (UCLA), I don't recall which, I gave the following speech:

THE GREAT NASHVILLE SOUND

What is the Nashville sound? This is a question I have been asked many, many times. From the way people ask the question, it is quite obvious to me that they think it is some great technical secret discovered and used exclusively in Nashville. Nothing could be further from the truth!

Others use the same kind of recording machines, the same type of microphones, the identical amplifiers, and the same kind of recording tape. The studios are similar to those in New York, Hollywood, or any other city, and the engineers or mixers seem to do exactly the same things. If this is so, why then, this difference in sound? Well, I say people are asking the wrong question, because you can get a similar sound in practically any standard recording studio in the world. The difference is the people, the musicianship, and the feeling put into the record.

It all started when Radio Station WSM decided to organize a country music program. They called it the Grand Ol' Opry. It soon became the most listened-to country radio program in the United States. All of the top country singers and musicians migrated there and established their homes. Nashville soon became the country music center of the world. Music publishers, booking agents, song writers, and recording companies soon followed. Almost all of the country music industry was centered in one place. This meant that artists could obtain the services of the best songwriters and the best musicians. There was a closeness, a friendliness, an understanding, and more of a desire to help the other fellow than anywhere else in the music world that still is evident today. There are no strangers in Nashville! When an artist, no matter how big or small, comes to town to record, the music publishers and songwriters will bring him their best songs to choose from. When he walks into a recording studio, he immediately feels the friendliness and the desire of everyone to co-operate. There is a completely relaxed feeling. The session starts with introducing the artist, if he is not known. Everyone exchanges "howdys" and engages in queries about each other's family and general small talk of the day. In a few minutes, the artist will sing the song he is going to record to the musicians and vocal group, so that they may learn it. There is no sheet music used whatsoever. Each musician contributes his own individual ideas to the arrangement and takes pride in his work. On the playback each person will listen carefully to his individual part, and if he feels he can improve on what he has done, he will say so, his only thought is doing the best he can so that the artist will have a successful record. The engineers or mixers contribute in the same way, every man in the studio feels as if this recording were his very own. This, to me, is the "Nashville Sound."

However, in closing, I'd like to say many great country artists and musicians have developed on the West Coast, all the way from the great state of Washington to San Diego, and especially in the Bakersfield, California area. They have the same feeling of pride in their work as their Nashville brothers. The West Coast has been and is very country-music conscious. Many artists live and record in Hollywood.

I played two records—one from Nashville and one from Hollywood. I asked the audience if they could tell which was recorded where. Most of the audience thought the record produced in Nashville was recorded in Hollywood and the Hollywood record produced in Nashville.

In 1972 President Richard Nixon issued a proclamation declaring October as Country Music Month. In December, Bill Lowery invited me to the Lowery Publishing Group's Golden Clef Awards in Atlanta, an award Bill had instituted in 1969 because he believed that if singers get awards, songwriters who write the most popular and best selling songs should also be honored. I was surprised when Bill called me to the podium and presented me with the first Golden Clef Award ever given to a non-writer. He also had Santa Claus give me a set of golf clubs.

CMA's second quarterly 1973 board of directors meeting was held in New York. The meeting was given front page coverage in the *New York Times*. Radio Station WHN, the first and only full time country music station in New York, hosted a luncheon for CMA. It was attended by nearly 600 music industry representatives, advertising agencies, and representatives of the press. After the luncheon, we put on a show, "The Sound of Country Music," written by Bob Tuberty, produced by Frank Jones, and narrated by Tex Ritter. It featured Merle Haggard with Bonnie Owens and The Strangers, Danny Davis and The Nashville Brass, and Demetriss Tapp.

Bob Eubanks was the master of ceremonies when Merle was the headliner at the Hollywood Bowl before an audience of about 12,000. Marty Robbins and harmonica wizard Charlie McCoy also appeared. Roger Miller was on the stage but did not perform. I interrupted Merle's performance to present him with a platinum record to commemorate the sale of a million albums of *Oakie From Muskogee*. When Merle closed the show singing "Oakie," he brought the audience to its feet. Earlier this year, I presented Merle with a gold record commemorating the sale of over a million dollars worth of his album, *The Best of Merle Haggard*, which I had assembled in 1968. In 1972 I assembled and released another million seller, "The Best of The Best of Merle Haggard."

I had been with Capitol Records for 28 years. During that time I had produced transcriptions, records, and albums by over 200 artists and even though I would miss all the wonderful people I had been associated with during my career, I felt it was time for me to retire. However, I continued to produce Merle Haggard, we both left Capitol in 1976. When I left Capitol I was not given a bonus or severance pay. If it hadn't been for Central Songs and Snyder Music, my family and I wouldn't have had the standard of living we enjoyed.

Frank Jones was a prominent figure on the Nashville scene. He was director of marketing for Columbia Records, had served as chairman of the board of the Country Music Foundation for six years, also as its president. He was a board member of the Country Music Association, served two years as president of the National Academy of Recording Arts and Sciences in Nashville and as a board member and trustee of National NARAS. The last eight years he had produced many CMA presentations, including the show for CMA's annual banquet. Frank Jones and his family moved to the Los Angeles area, Frank would assume the vice-presidency, producer, and marketing of Capitol's country music department. He would work with Wade Pepper, vice president of country music sales and promotion.

One day when June was playing in a golf tournament, Claudia and I decided to go whale-watching. It's a thrilling sight to watch them jump in and out of the water. Our boat docked at the Channel Islands for a spell. We strolled a bit, then sat down to enjoy the scenery. While we were seated, Claudia told me she had found the man of her dreams, they were going to be married the next year, and we would meet him shortly. I was both thrilled and happy for her.

We hadn't allowed her to date until she was sixteen; had insisted we meet her dates and were told where they were going and that she should be home at a specific time. One fellow student she had dated was of Chinese descent. He was a perfect gentleman, telling us where they were going and bringing her home on time. We didn't object to her dating him, but I pointed out the difference in our customs and way of life and asked, "If you two become serious about each other, would his family accept you?" I think she thought I was telling her to stop dating him, which I wasn't, but she did.

When we met Amiel, Claudia's husband-to-be, we were both impressed and delighted. He was handsome, well-mannered, owned his own furniture upholstering and repair business in Thousand Oaks, and occasionally when he came to visit us would bring June a bouquet of flowers.

In June of 1974, Claudia and Amiel were married. The wedding and reception were held at the Santa Barbara Biltmore Hotel. I, the proud father, walked Claudia down the aisle. Lynn Mann, a former college classmate, was maid of honor. A friend of Ameil's was best man. We had no relatives in California and only one other family member, our son Gregory. Amiel had quite a large family; all tolled there were over a hundred in attendance, mostly friends. The hotel provided a bar and catered the food. We hired a dance orchestra. All-in-all, it was a memorable wedding. I don't know where they spent their wedding night, but the next day they left for the Mediterranean cruise we had given them as a wedding gift. Shortly after they came home from the cruise, they purchased a home on Lake Sherwood. Claudia continued teaching school. I loaned Amiel $25,000.00 for a down payment to purchase a building in Thousand Oaks that the Edison electric company was abandoning. He paid the loan off in a short period of time.

A year after Claudia's marriage, our son Gregory announced that he and his girlfriend, Melissa, a very lovely girl, were getting married.

We attended the wedding rehearsal and later a get-acquainted dinner. Our families seemed quite compatible. The wedding took place in Newport Beach. We were sure Greg had made a wise choice. I have no idea why or who was at fault but in less than a year, they were divorced. Greg never discussed it with us.

The following year, 1976, Claudia's marriage began to falter. Amiel, her husband, became involved with friends who encouraged him to take dope. He became addicted and tried to get Claudia involved. She, of course, was not that stupid. She tried to steer him onto the right path, but to no avail. He was neglecting his business and his addiction was costly. Claudia gave him an ultimatum—"either me or dope." The straw that broke the camel's back was when he went to a customer's house to give an estimate on re-upholstering her furniture. She left Amiel alone in the house and he stole some antiques and jewelry. When he brought them home, Claudia knew they were stolen. She moved out of the house, got an apartment, and filed for divorce. The man of her dreams had become the nightmare of her dreams.

Her divorce became final in 1978. She was awarded the Lake Sherwood house but sold it because of the high payments. June wanted her to buy a condominium, but being the independent person she is, she wanted her own house and bought a house in Moorpark for $69,000.00. We loaned her $10,000.00 for the down payment. When I saw the house, I was appalled. I said, "Claudia, you mean you paid $69,000 for this matchbox?" It was a three bedroom house with small rooms. If you put your arm out the window on either side, you could almost touch your neighbor's house. I was still living in the dark ages, comparing it with the two-story, three bedroom, thirty foot living room house on a quarter acre lot with fruit trees, which we had purchased in Studio City for $19,000.00 dollars in 1948, and the Sherman Oaks house in 1958 on three lots and with a swimming pool for $36,000.00. It is incredible the way real estate values have increased. In the year 2002, Claudia was still living in her Moorpark home, the same model houses on either side have sold for $250,000.00 each.

Ever since I can remember, my goal in life was to play the piano and become a successful songwriter, but fate decreed otherwise. I became a successful record producer but I never felt successful because to me a successful person is one who has achieved the goal of his heart's desire. I had written well over a hundred songs, had a few published and recorded, but never had a hit. I could write my melodies on manuscript paper but didn't have the knowledge to make the piano arrangements. I had been taking piano lessons. In 1978 I enrolled in a Ventura College Music Theory class. My grades were all A plus. After two years I became quite adept in making piano arrangements Melodies continue to come to me and I have written over an additional two hundred songs. I still write but only as a hobby.

Gregory had graduated from law school and was taking the bar exam. For sometime he had been dating Patricia (Patty) Kausen, a brilliant, charming young lady. We had taken them to dinner a couple of times. She impressed us. We learned that she had a brother and that when she was seven years old, her father had died of a brain tumor. Three years later her mother had married David Nyguist, the principal of a high school in Glendale. He was a wonderful father and treated Patty and her brother as if they were his own children. Gregory had proposed to Patty, but she refused to marry him until he passed the bar exam. After three times he passed, and on June 24, 1979, they were married at Forest Lawn in the same church her mother had been married. They spent their honeymoon on Catalina Island.

Gregory wanted to have his own law practice. He took out a loan for $20,000.00 from the Bank of A. Levy, for which I put up two ten thousand dollar bonds as security. He opened his law office in Ventura, was punctual with his payments, and had the loan paid off at the designated time.

The compact disk CDs were introduced to the public in 1980. They were a boon to the recording industry. Soon millions of households had the equipment to play them. The teenage market boomed, a hit recording or album could sell in the millions.

I had severed all connections with the music industry, but did keep in contact with many of my artists and the friends I had made in the business. June and I were enjoying retirement, we played golf every week. I played with her at least twice a week. She played in tournaments and on ladies day at the Club. Although I was a hacker and never beat her, I enjoyed the game. We often traveled throughout the state to play different courses.

June was never very enthusiastic about sexual intercourse. I often had the feeling she was just accommodating me. One night as I was making advances, she said, "Ken, I can no longer tolerate sex. Our sex life is over."

I replied, "Honey, you know I love you, but my biological sex clock is still ticking. And as sex is an integral part of life and marriage, you leave me the following choices: divorce, which I'm sure neither of us wants; masturbation, which I'm too old to enjoy; get a mistress, which would be expensive; patronize prostitutes; or we can continue our normal marriage."

June chose the latter. As we aged, our sex appetite diminished, and even though June was still a beautiful, attractive woman, I was able to limit my sex activity. Every time she accommodated me, I had a tinge of guilt. I also had the feelings she enjoyed knowing she was still a desirable woman.

Claudia's ex-husband, Amiel, had become a confirmed dope addict. In April of 1980, while on a high, he drove his car off a six hundred foot cliff. He broke his leg in two places and a one-inch tree limb was impaled in his arm. It took a rescue team an hour to get him out. In August of that year, he was arrested for setting his upholstering shop on fire. Two weeks previously he had purchased a $100,000.00 fire insurance policy on the building. It sustained $50,000.00 in damages. He set the fire after attending a party and his date was still with him. He threatened to harm her if she told anyone. How dope befuddles the mind. At his trial, she testified that he had set the fire. He was sentenced to a long prison term.

Why can't some people, and especially some teenagers, understand that taking that first experimental dose often leads to addiction and the ruination of their lives?

L-R , Lee Gillette, Hubert Long, Me, Bill Lowery at a Grand Ol' Opry celebration.

June and I in Cordova Spain, 1971.

California Governor Ronald Reagan and Buck Owens.

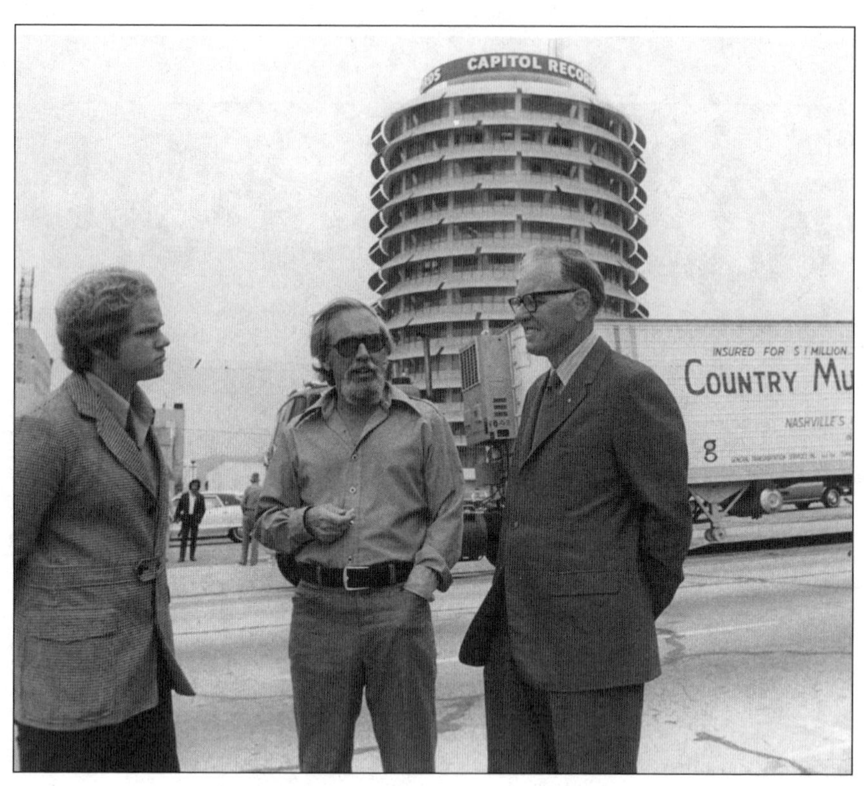

Steve Stone, Mauri Lathower, and Ken Nelson.

June and me attending our son's marriage to Patricia Kausen, in 1979

1981-1990

From here on until the inevitable, my life has been filled with both sadness and happiness. The decade began normally, but on August 20, 1981, Lee Gillette passed away at the age of 69. We had worked together and been the closest of friends since 1932. He was without question one of the great record producers of his time. Lee came to Capitol in 1944 as head of the transcription and the then-called hillbilly departments. Johnny Mercer signed Tex Ritter and produced Capitol's first country record, then Lee took over. Lee brought to the label such stars as Tennessee Ernie Ford, Tex Williams, Hank Thompson, Merle Travis, Cliffie Stone, Jimmy Wakely, and Martha Carson.

In 1951, I took over the country department and Lee was producing popular music exclusively. He produced almost all of Nat "King" Cole's records, Dean Martin, Kay Starr, Stan Kenton, Jan Garber, Ray Anthony, Alvino Ray, and many others. With few exceptions, he had a close relationship with his artists, especially with Nat "King" Cole. I met Nat a couple of times at Lee's house. He had a soft, unassuming personality. You couldn't help but like him. He talked of politics and the Dodgers baseball team; he was an avid fan. He was addicted to cigarettes and in 1965, at the height of his career, he died of lung cancer at the age of 46. His voice is truly "Unforgettable." Lee took Nat's death very hard and seemed to lose some of his enthusiasm as a producer. He retired from Capitol about the same time I did. Like me, he had no pension or retirement benefits, but because of Central Songs and Snyder Music he was able to maintain his normal lifestyle.

Lee was not an alcoholic but was a heavy drinker, and as a result he acquired cirrhosis of the liver. When it came to the point where he had to be hospitalized, he was put in the intensive care unit. When I went to visit him, I was told only relatives were allowed to see him. I explained that we had been lifelong friends and was told I could spend only ten minutes with him. He was glad to see me and tried desperately to tell me something but couldn't speak. After about fifteen minutes, I told him I had to leave but would come to see him again in a couple of days. Three days later when I came to visit him, I was told he had passed away that morning. What a shock! I can't express my feelings. His memorial service was attended by over 300 people, artists, musicians, composers, people he had worked with and friends. After the pastor's opening scripture, I gave the following speech about Lee's early life.

> Leland James Gillette was born in Indianapolis, Indiana on October 30, 1912. He was an only child. When he was eight years old, his folks moved to Peoria, Illinois where his father was head accountant at a leading hotel. A few years later, they moved to Chicago.
>
> I first met Lee around 1931. We were both playing in the same orchestra—or rather we were both playing in different small orchestras. He played guitar and I played tenor banjo. However, the banjo was much more popular in those days and I was getting all the jobs. So Lee decided to take up drums.
>
> It was then that we joined forces and formed a group, a five-piece orchestra, called the Campus Kids. We used to play high school dances in the afternoon for $.50 apiece, and night dances for $1.00 or $2.00 apiece. At that time, he was also writing a radio column for a local newspaper. He was always a radio enthusiast.
>
> This was at the height of the Great Depression and I had no money and no place to go. So Lee suggested that I come and live at his home. His mother, who incidentally was a pianist and had perfect pitch, consented and charged me $4.00 a week for room and board. Through Lee's efforts at getting dance jobs, we worked about three or four nights a week, I was able to pay my room and board. With our saxophone player, Jim Crotty, we formed a vocal trio and started singing over radio station KYW. We didn't get paid—not even our transportation.
>
> Lee's mother had an old violin and I decided I wanted to learn to play it. I was an early riser and Lee was a late riser. When we had a morning rehearsal at the studio, it was difficult to get him up on time, so I would go into the bedroom and practice the violin beside his bed. (Laughter) Well, he'd get so mad he wouldn't speak to me! And when we rode downtown on the Illinois Central, we would ride in different cars.
>
> About 6 months singing for free on KYW, I decided I wanted to become a soloist. I left the trio and that's when

Hal Derwin joined the Campus Kids. After I left, the group became very successful. They got the first liquor commercial on radio in 1933 and got paid for it! They then started to sing with Harry Sosnick's orchestra at the Drake Hotel. Later Lee joined a road show called "Swing Baby Swing" as a drummer. There he met a lovely young girl who sang with a group called the Ozark Sisters. Her name was Edith Bergdahl. They were married on March 22, 1937 in Episalanti, Michigan. They had two children: Phillip born in 1940 and David born in 1941. Phillip has two children: One is Chris and the other is Maritza.

After the show closed, they came back to Chicago and Lee got the Campus Kids together again—without me of course, as I had then become a radio announcer with Station WAAF. The group joined the *Fibber McGee and Molly* show in Chicago in 1939. The show moved to Hollywood. They contracted to have each show recorded by a man named Glenn Wallichs and after each show, Lee would go to pick up the recordings. Lee and Glenn soon became friends.

When the Campus Kids left the *Fibber McGee and Molly* show, they joined Buddy Rogers' Orchestra. When they left that band, the group disbanded and Lee came back to Chicago without a job. I was still working at WAAF and at that time the station was looking for another announcer. Lee auditioned and got the job! We worked there together a couple of years and then I moved to WJJD as program director and music director. It had a very popular country program which reached all over the nation called the *Suppertime Frolic*. In those days it was done with live talent. Lee soon joined me at WJJD and in 1942, when I was drafted into the army, he took over as program director and musical director.

I was discharged from the army in April 1944. I was going to move to California but the station manager asked me to stay and take charge of a new radio medium called FM radio. I stayed.

Around July of that year, Glenn Wallichs came to Chicago and looked up his friend, Lee Gillette. Glenn asked Lee what he was doing. When Lee told him he said, "You're just the man I'm looking for!" and asked him if he would consider moving to California and joining his new company, Capitol Records.

Lee jumped at the chance and the family moved out here. He was put in charge of the country and western, and the transcription departments. It soon became apparent that Glenn had picked the right man. He signed such artists as: Tex Williams, Jimmy Wakely, Tennessee Ernie Ford, Merle Travis and many, many others! He produced hit after hit in the country field.

On one occasion Lee came to Chicago to produce an album by a group called "Uncle Henry's Kentucky Mountaineers." He had booked the studio and the group. The day before the session, he received a call from Glenn Wallichs, saying he must meet him in New York the following day. Lee told me that I had to do the session because it couldn't be canceled. I protested, saying, "Lee, I've never done anything like this before!"

He said, "Don't worry about it. Just do it."

So I did it. It turned out okay.

I continued to do sessions for Capitol in Chicago. It soon became evident that Lee was becoming overburdened with two departments to manage—country western and transcriptions. He went to Glenn and Jim Conkling, who was then head of A&R and asked them if they would consider hiring me to take over the transcription department. They consented and my wife June and I were thrilled at the prospect of moving to California!

Mr. Wallichs and Mr. Conkling soon realized that Lee had tremendous potential as a pop A&R man and assigned him exclusively to that department. He was a genius, whose record in that field is unequaled. I was put in charge of country and western. Lee and I have worked together all of our lives. He has touched, helped, influenced, and enhanced the lives of many, many people. He loved people. He loved music. He loved life.

And although this phase of his life is over, his spirit and presence will always be felt by everyone who knew him.

End of Speech

Another outstanding Capitol producer, Dave Cavanaugh, passed away that same year on December 31 at the age of 62. He had been with the label 30 years and produced many top artists, such as Peggy Lee and Frank Sinatra. I remember him telling me about the time he went to Cuba to record an album by Nat "King" Cole. It was during the time Castro and his rebels were fighting to overthrow the Cuban government. He was stopped and questioned a couple of times by rebels. Dave said it scared the hell out of him.

Watching the passing of Lee and learning of the death of Dave, and some of my other acquaintances, I figured now that I was 70 years old it was about time I had another physical exam. As I had frequent heart palpitations, I went to a cardiologist whose name oddly was Dr. Hart. He immediately put me on heart medication, which I am still taking today.

My wife, June, had been elected tournament chairman of the Saticoy Country Club's Womens' Golf Club, and had set specific goals for the club, but after repetitive opposition by the president to her goals, she sent this letter to the Board:

> Dear Friends: We intended to have our tournaments as fair as possible and encourage participation by all members. Three words—fairness, competition, enjoyment—let's get out there and have fun. This is the creed I set for myself as tournament chairman. I have earnestly strived to achieve these goals in everything I have done. However, our president does not share these same views and has interfered and thwarted many of my objectives. Under the current circumstances, I find I cannot compromise my principles and self-worth by continuing this charade. The president has made it impossible to work with her. We simply do not see things the same way. Had it not been for the board's vote of confidence, I would have resigned some time ago, but now I regretfully submit my resignation. My decision is irrevocable.

This letter was submitted to the board in March of 1982. Ironically, two months later in June, June, who was very popular with the club members, who called her "Junepoo," was elected president. I had a "Junepoo" license plate made for her car and attached it while she was playing bridge at the club. I never saw her so tickled pink as when she saw the plate. She really got a kick out of it! The car was a 1980 Mercedes Benz, which I still retain with the same license plate.

On the twenty eighth of June that same year, June and I were overcome with exhilaration. We had become the proud and doting grandparents of a beautiful, adorable, redheaded baby girl, Tiffany Ann Nelson. Holding her in my arms was almost as thrilling as the first time I held my own two babies, Gregory and Claudia.

We decided, now that our family was expanding, it was about time to have our wills drawn up. Although our son, Gregory, was a lawyer, he didn't specialize in wills so he recommended an attorney. As June had inherited a rather sizeable estate from her parents, it necessitated keeping two sets of books—one for her estate and one for mine, which was community property. Although June made her own investments, we always discussed and agreed on the investments for both estates, then acted accordingly. We decided on the demise of one spouse, both of the estates would be inherited by the survivor.

In our gated community, called Fairway Hills, there were twenty-one homes. We have a homeowners association. When the secretary/treasurer sold her home and moved, the president asked me if I would take over the voluntary job. I accepted. It didn't entail too much work, just paying bills. There were no dues, so when our bank account was low, a request was sent to each owner to submit an equal amount of money to last a year or two. I would make up a financial statement every year and mail each owner a copy. I enjoyed the responsibility.

We continued to play golf and have dinner at the club every Sunday. June would play with the ladies on Tuesdays and Thursdays, and every now and then we would play different courses in the area. In 1983, June won the Ladies Club Championship.

Usually on Saturday our daughter, whom June called "Muffy," would join us and we'd go to the Pierpont Inn, a restaurant at the oceanfront for a late lunch.

Life was sailing along smoothly but I became concerned when June started getting up at night around three A.M., going into the breakfast nook, lighting up a cigarette, and doing a crossword puzzle. I would join her and ask if she was feeling all right. She always answered "Yes, I was just a little restless and wanted a cigarette." This really worried me. She had almost become a chain smoker.

I used to jokingly say to her, "Honey, if you don't quit, you're going to kick the bucket before I do and leave me all the money!" I never dreamed such a thing could happen because of the thirteen year difference in our ages. She and a golf friend did try to quit smoking but gave up trying after a couple of days.

June 2, 1984, was another joyous day. Our grandson Gregory Kenneth Nelson, Jr. was born! We were now the proud grandparents of a boy and a girl! However, our exuberance was short lived. June was not feeling quite up to par, and on June 7th, she saw her doctor. He sent her to a chest specialist for extra tests. After an X-ray examination, it was determined she had lung cancer that would metastasize and spread to other parts of her body. He assigned her to a lady oncologist, Dr. McIntyre, who specialized in cancer and whom June saw every week.

June maintained her regular golf, bridge, club meetings, our Saturday luncheons with Claudia and our Sunday golf games but in August she began to slow down, still playing but less and less. On Friday, August 24th, we were playing at the club, but after nine holes, she was exhausted so we quit. As tired as she was, she beat me by one stroke. This was the last game she ever played.

She began to have difficulty swallowing. X-rays showed the cancer cells had reached her esophagus. She began to get weaker and weaker. June would always drive whenever we went anywhere together, but now she had no choice but to let me drive. Beginning in September I drove her to her doctor's appointments for twelve days for radiation treatments. It was determined the cancer had reached her brain. Dr. McIntyre wanted to hospitalize her; however, neither June nor I wanted that. I explained that I was a medic in the Army, trained as a nurse assistant. I had taken care of sick and injured soldiers, giving them shots and medication, so I was perfectly capable of taking care of June at home. She agreed. I rented a portable toilet and borrowed an electric bed from a friend so she could put herself in a sitting position to read or watch television. By the beginning of October I had to help her get out of bed to go to the toilet. When she wanted to shower, I had to go into the shower with her, which was something I had always wanted to do, but she would never let me. It was a difficult task because she had a beautiful body. I had to overcome my male instinct and desires. I think being naked in the shower is one of the major thrills of marriage.

June's addiction to cigarettes was the cause of her cancer. She still wanted to smoke but I couldn't let her. I cut drinking straws in half. She would puff on them as though smoking. I think that partially appeased her craving.

She was now to the point where she was so weak I had to hand feed her. Sometimes when she refused food, I would threaten to put her in the hospital, where they would force feed her. She would eat a little.

Her friends from the club would come and visit her. The cleaning lady came on Tuesdays and I would go grocery shopping and get her prescription medication. On other days when I had other errands, Claudia or my next-door neighbor would stay with June. Claudia came every Saturday and go to the Pierpont Inn to get June's favorite dish, scallops.

One day as I was feeding June, she gave me one of the great thrills of my life, she voluntarily kissed me on my cheek, something she had never done during our courtship or our entire years of marriage. I still thrill when I think of it! As it was no longer feasible for June to ride in the car, Dr. McIntyre would occasionally come to the house. She complimented me on the way I was taking care of June. On the 15th of October, Dr. McIntyre told me June might not recover.

I kept hoping against hope that she would recover, but on Sunday, October 28th at 6:18 A.M., as I was feeding her breakfast, she gasped and died. The feelings I had are indescribable: shock, panic, disbelief. I finally got hold of myself and called Dr. McIntyre and the Neptune Society, the cremation service we had both signed with. June had indicated she wanted her ashes strewn over the mountains; no memorial service was held. On November 5, 1984, her ashes were disseminated in the Angeles National Forest over the big Tujunga Canyon area.

I had feelings of guilt because I didn't give June artificial respiration but I was in a state of shock and just not thinking. Dr. McIntyre and my daughter assured me it would have been ineffective because the cancer was so widespread. That still didn't alleviate my feelings of guilt. My life would never be the same. My consolation was my son Gregory, his wife Patty, my two grandchildren, and my daughter, Claudia. We spent Thanksgiving and Christmas together that year, but it just wasn't the same without June.

I was now living alone but kept busy. I made my bed every morning, changed the bed sheets every week, and laundered them, the linens, and my clothing every three weeks. I did calisthenics every morning for forty-five minutes, except on Sunday when I only did thirty minutes, made my breakfast and lunch, cooked my dinner three times a week, and if I wasn't having dinner with my daughter, at my son's house, or the Club, I would have frozen dinners. I did the grocery shopping every Tuesday, played golf every Sunday, and occasionally during the week I was taking piano lessons and practicing daily.

When June's parents passed away, she had inherited their house, cash, and other items. She sold the house, the saleable items, and along with the cash they left, opened her own bank account and an account with the same investment firm in which we had our community property account. She kept her own set of books. I didn't consider her accounts as community property, but any investment she made, with my consent, from our joint bank account was community property. I decided to maintain the two sets of books, the June F. Nelson Trust and the Kenneth F. Nelson Trust.

I still have and wear the lounging jacket, the bathrobe, the shirts she made for me. The last gift she bought me was a bottle of after shaving lotion, which I have kept unopened.

In 1985 Claudia and I planned to take an Oriental tour, during her summer vacation. It included China, Hong Kong, Bangkok, Singapore, and Tokyo. Never having traveled with her, I was concerned as to whether or not I would be a compatible traveling companion, so I told her to bring a friend. She chose another teacher from her school, with whom she had become quite friendly. It was a mistake. She didn't turn out to be the person Claudia thought she was. She was overbearing, unpleasant, and unappreciative. For some reason or other she seemed to dislike me. Claudia severed their friendship after the tour.

On June 30 we started our month long Oriental trip, with our tour group, by flying to Manila, changing planes and on to Hong Kong, where we boarded a train for Canton, the first of our five city tour of China. We had been given a card printed in both Chinese and English, to show the taxi driver the name of our hotel, The White Swan. At the hotel, we were met by our first tour guide, a middle-aged American, who spoke Chinese. He was to stay with us until we went to Shanghai. After dinner, which we all had together, I'm sure most of us hit the hay, immediately for a much needed rest. The next day we toured the city, the following day we visited the Canton handicraft center and the jade factory. W e enjoyed our short stay at the Chinese style hotel; the food and service were excellent. After three days, we left for Guilin via China Airlines on a prop plane. The plane had no air conditioning unit, each passenger was provided with a self air conditioner—a fan!

Guilin is a city on the banks of the Gui River, with a population of 370,000. I don't recall the name of our hotel because after touring the city, we spent much of our time sightseeing on the river. Our boat had two decks, the top deck was for the crew and the lower deck for tourists. It had eight tables that seated six people each, on both sides, next to windows. The Gui River is interestingly scenic. On the banks were houses built on platforms that extended into the river. We saw boats laden with food, clothing and household goods, plying their trade. A really interesting sight was women washing clothes in the river, next to a herd of water buffalo! Lunch was served on board. Lunch was a pigeon with the head on it. It was tasty. We didn't eat the head. Nor did we participate in the Chinese custom of drinking turtle blood, which several of the Chinese couples in our group were drinking. They consider it a health drink!

After three or four days we said goodbye to Guilin and our tour guide. I was leery of him because at every meal he would sit next to Claudia and her friend. Claudia was the most attractive woman in the group and he knew she was single. My fatherly protective and male instinct told me he was trying to strike up an intimate relationship with her. I'm sure she was flattered by the attention. My suspicions were really aroused when at the dinner party of our last evening in Guilin, they both left the party early after dinner. I called Claudia's room and her roommate said she wasn't there. I didn't question Claudia or tell her of my concern until after we got home.

We were met in Shanghai by two pleasant English-speaking young Chinese, Dai and Lei, who were our guides for the remainder of the China tour. Shanghai is a modern city with a population of 9,500,000. It is the largest city in China. We toured the city for several days visiting a large department store and a rug factory, where women were making handmade rugs.

June would have been fascinated by the Chinese architecture, especially the jade Buddha temple. Buddhism is a prominent religion of China and Buddha statues, many of them made of bronze, are seen throughout the country. When June and I returned from our Japan tour, she bought a bronze Buddha lamp. I know it was expensive; she wouldn't tell me what she paid for it. I tried several times to trick her into telling me the cost, but without success!

One of the highlights of our Shanghai tour was an acrobatic show. There were four men and a girl in each of the four groups that performed on a revolving stage in the center of the audience. Their suppleness was fantastic!

China has many historic cities but I think Xian, a city of the Wei, is one of the most historic. Its history dates back to 2000 B.C. Around 200 B.C. the Emperor Qin was born. At the age of 13, he started to construct a museum of thousands of life-size terracotta soldiers, archers, cavalrymen, and charioteers in horse-drawn chariots to protect him in his afterlife. The soldiers were both young and old. No two faces were alike. The Terracotta Army is in pits sixteen feet deep, forgotten until 1974 when workers digging a well uncovered the first pit. More pits have been discovered. Rank after rank of the Terracotta Army is an awesome sight and shows the ingenuity of the Chinese of that period. I had my Polaroid camera with me but we were not allowed to take pictures. We did buy a photo.

I always had my Polaroid camera with me and if I saw a lady with a baby or young child, I would take their picture and give it to them. I would usually then be surrounded by people wanting me to take their picture. I had to turn them down because I didn't want to run out of film!

We visited the temple which displayed the writings of Confucius and the Wild Goose Pagoda that had the Buddha scriptures.

We went to a theatre to see a Chinese drama. We couldn't understand what they were saying, but their actions fairly well conveyed what was going on.

We flew from Shanghai to the capital of China, Beijing, China's second largest and most interesting city. We stayed at the Great Wall Hotel. During our several days tour and our stay in Beijing, we visited the zoo to see the pandas. We were quite surprised to see pandas that were all brown. They are called lesser pandas, and are kept in a separate area, away from the black and white pandas.

The Ming Tombs are where all but one of the emperors of the Ming Dynasty, the rulers of China from 1368 to 1644, were buried. To get to the tombs, you walk down a long avenue lined on both sides with marble camels, elephants, lions, and horses. At the end of the walk is a life-size statute of an elephant and a huge statue of an emperor.

We had pictures taken of me and Claudia in Tiananmen Square, then visited the Forbidden City that housed the imperial families from 1421 to 1912. No commoner was allowed to enter the city. In 1925 a Palace Museum was started and opened to the public in 1949. The museum was most enlightening. We wanted, but were not allowed, to take pictures.

One of the most beautiful and unique buildings in Beijing is the Temple of Heaven where China's emperors worshipped. It became a public park after the communists took over in 1949. The entrance to the Emperor's Summer Palace shows the vivid imagination of the Chinese architects.

We rode the bus to Badaling Pass where we had the most exhilarating experience of our trip. We climbed the Great Wall of China and got a certificate stating so. The Great Wall was started B.C., took hundreds of years to complete, stretches over 4,000 miles, and was built to keep out the hordes of Huns and Mongols that were invading China. We took pictures of the wall from the top of the pass, the scenery was beautiful but it boggles the mind when you realize this wall was started almost 3,000 years ago; it extends over 4,000 miles through mountainous country; it shows the ingenuity and patience of the Chinese people.

Our final dinner in Beijing was Peking Duck, a special Chinese dish consisting of roasted duck meat, strips of crispy duck skin topped with scallions and sauce wrapped in thin pancakes; it was delicious!

The next day we boarded the plane for Hong Kong. The first sight that greeted our eyes as we disembarked to pickup our luggage was a huge McDonald's sign, "Welcome to Hong Kong and McDonald's"! During our short stay in Hong Kong, we toured the crowded streets, took a sampan boat ride, a ferry boat around the harbor and went up the Victoria Peak and saw the awesome panoramic view of the harbor and city.

Our China tour ended in Hong Kong, we had a farewell party on the eve of our departure. With the exception of Claudia, her friend, me and another couple, Charlotte and Ryan Conlon, the rest of the group were headed home. We five were going on another tour to Bangkok and Singapore.

Bangkok, the capital and largest city of Thailand, which is a monarchy formerly known as Siam, is located on the Chao Phraya River. It's a very modern city with all the problems of any large city—traffic congestion, crowded living conditions, and slums. It also has a large number of minorities including Americans. The native language is Thai, but English, which is taught in many schools, is commonly spoken. Bangkok is the government administration center of Thailand and is also the cultural and commercial center of southeast Asia.

We were met at the airport by our guide, Tim, a very personable young man who spoke perfect English. He took us to our hotel, The Regent, one of Bangkok's finest. While we were there, our then American secretary of state, George P. Schultz, was also a guest. We saw his security men meticulously scan every item in the lobby even the plants. We thought they might question us, but they didn't. I'm sure they knew all about us!

Our stay in Bangkok was most interesting. Buddhism is the dominant religion and there are many temples and Buddha statues throughout the City. The most impressive were the Temple of the Emerald Buddha and Watpho, which houses a massive statue of a reclining Buddha. The Royal Palace is an architectural wonder; it defies description and is a popular tourist attraction! I don't think anyone lives in it because the king and his family reside in the Chitladda Palace.

On one of our walking tours of the city we ran into a line of children being led around a building, marching and dancing. They were about the same age as the children Claudia teaches in her second grade class. I guess her teacher instinct took hold and she joined them; the children loved it!

We took a ferry boat ride through the floating market where all types of goods and food are sold from boats.

Thailand has many jungles, forests, and swamps, inhabited by many species of animals: tigers, leopards, Siamese cats, gaura (a large wild ox with short curved horns), water buffalo, gibbons, rhinoceroses, crocodiles, and a countless number of snakes, many poisonous. Elephants are trained to be workers, moving logs in the forests.

We went to the Ducit Park Zoo where many of these animals are on display, at Bangkok's Rose Garden there are several elephants with their masters. Tourists were offered tickets for an elephant ride; we were too chicken to ride one!

Secretary of State Schultz left Bangkok the day before we did. We happened to be in the lobby when his security men checked him out. All of the hotel employees had formed an exit aisle and applauded him as he walked to the door with a big smile. That evening we had a Thai dinner and attended a theatre to see Thai or Siamese classical dancing. Their costumes and dancing are truly unique and most entertaining.

Singapore, a very modern city, is the capital city on the main island of a group of islands off the southern tip of the Malay Peninsula and is one of the busiest seaports in the world. It was formerly a British colony; in 1965 it became a republic. Most of its population is Chinese; minorities include Malaysians and immigrants from India. It has a diversity of religions including Buddhism, Hinduism, Islam, and Christianity. Chinese and English are the dominant language. It has one of the world's lowest crime rates. Our short stay in Singapore was at the Dynasty Hotel. The city has many skyscrapers, among them—if my memory serves me right—is the world's tallest hotel. We toured the slumless, very clean city; visited the Tiger Palm Garden, which is dominated by statues; took a ferry boat ride around the harbor and took a dinner cruise.

Our Asian tour was at an end; our final stop was Tokyo. We toured the city for a couple of days, had a farewell drink with our tour companions, Ryan and Charlotte Conlon, with whom we had become friends. We still correspond with each other and as we live in different parts of the country, we took different planes home. We had to change planes in San Francisco; finally arriving in Los Angeles.

Up to this point our tour had run smoothly, but wouldn't you know it—Claudia's luggage was lost! The airline gave her $400.00 to compensate for the loss, but that wasn't enough to cover the cost of the contents or the clothing and other items she had bought.

On March 13, 1986, my third grandson, Charles Federick Nelson, was born. Like his sister, Tiffany, and my daughter Claudia, he was a redhead. When he was 12 years old, I bought him a set of golf clubs; by the age of 13, he was beating the daylights out of me.

In 1987, Claudia and I booked a Russia, Siberia, Mongolia tour. It was quite obvious after our Asian tour that we would be compatible traveling companions. We decided to request twin bed hotel rooms; it worked out fine and we got along like two peas in a pod.

We were the only members of the tour group from the West Coast. We flew to New York to catch a Finn Air flight to Helsinki and transfer to a flight to Moscow. In the Moscow airport, we were to join our tour group then transfer to the special private trans-Siberian train that was to be our home during our trip through Siberia. But our flight was two hours late in arriving and the train had already departed!

What to do? It was nighttime, we spoke no Russian, knew of no hotels. Claudia panicked and wanted to go home. I didn't relish the situation either, but luckily we heard a Russian lady, probably an airport employee, speaking English to a couple of people. We told her of our plight, and she suggested a hotel where English was spoken. She was sure they would have the route of the train and be able to arrange for us to connect with it at some point.

After we purchased some Russian roubles, she then courteously took us to a taxi and told the driver, who didn't speak English, which hotel to take us to. Being night, the streets were deserted. We had a wild ride to the hotel. Claudia says it was a two-hour ride. I know she was scared and I didn't feel too secure either.

Russia was still under Communist control, and when we arrived at the hotel, a soldier was standing guard at the entrance. We learned later that all hotels in Moscow require that you enter and exit through the same door with a soldier standing guard.

After checking into the hotel, we explained our situation to the clerk. He told us to see Fenapontova Svetlana in the morning and she would be able to help us. We spent a restless night and after breakfast, we met with Miss Svetlana.

She was an attractive young lady who spoke almost perfect English. She was very accommodating and seemed anxious to help us. She found that although the train made several short stops, none were long enough for us to board the train. Novosibirsk, an industrial city, with an airport and a population of over a million, was the first city the train would stop at for three days. Miss Svetlana made our plane reservations and wired the train to expect us, but the train would not arrive in Novosibirsk for four days. Having no guide, we were reluctant to explore Moscow on our own, so we spent the next three days in the hotel. It had good accommodations and food. We became quite friendly with Miss Svetlana and told her how grateful we were for her help. I had her give me her name and address. We still send her a Christmas card every year.

We paid our hotel bill with either an American Express check or our Bank of America Visa card. I don't remember which; both were accepted throughout our trip. We had purchased enough roubles to pay for incidentals. We were now on our way to Siberia, a cold, barren country where Russia, at one time, exiled criminals and political prisoners.

Our train would be in Novosibirsk, a city on the Og River with a population of 1,500,000 for 3 days. Our group had transferred to a hotel. When we arrived, they were on a boat trip. We checked into the hotel and that evening we were greeted by our tour guides, Steve and Marylyn, a married American couple, who spoke Russian and our group, who said they were relieved to see us because they thought something might have happened to us! Dinner was at a local restaurant where regional specialties were served. The rest of the evening was spent pleasantly getting acquainted with our traveling companions.

The following day we toured the city. There wasn't too much to see. I took pictures of Claudia at the huge farmers' market. That evening, after dinner, we went to an acrobatic circus. Here too the stage was round with the audience surrounding it.

The next morning we finally boarded the traveling hotel that was to be our home for the next 6 days. It was truly a luxury hotel on wheels. The compartments were rather small with bunk beds but that was of no consequence because most of our time was spent in the club car, where our guides gave daily lectures on Russia and Siberia, or watching the landscape from the huge windows in the aisle of our compartments.

Claudia had to share a compartment; I didn't. The food and service were superb; caviar was served with every dinner. I liked caviar. Claudia didn't. You could ring for service at any hour of the night and be promptly served.

We made several brief stops in Tashet, Kansk, and Achinsk. At Irkutsk, a major cultural city, our group of 20 people, transferred to a hotel and we toured the city. I continued to give away pictures I had taken with my Polaroid camera of people and children. The recipients were thrilled! I took a picture of two children and gave them a package of gum. I couldn't understand why their mother made them give it back. I felt sorry for them. She did take the picture.

The next day was spent taking a bus tour through Siberian forests and small villages to Lake Baikal, the clearest, deepest, fresh water lake in the world. We had lunch at a lakeside restaurant, visited a natural history museum. We returned to the hotel by hydrofoil, a boat that sometimes is out of the water and in the air. It was a thrilling experience! We had dinner at the hotel. Tomorrow morning, we would re-board our hotel on wheels for the last time; say goodbye to Siberia and hello to Mongolia! We had our last dinner on the train and spent the rest of the evening in the club car chit-chatting.

Mongolia had been under Communist domination from 1924 until 1991. In 1992, a democratic constitution was adopted, establishing the separation of church and state. They were now able to openly practice their religion, Lamaist Buddhaism, which the Communists had tried to suppress.

Mongolia's economy is dependent upon the export of the livestock bred on its vast prairie land. Cattle, sheep, goats and most important of all, horses, which provide transportation, food, milk, blankets, and rope made from their long hair. On our arrival in Ulan Bator, Mongolia's capital and largest city, we cleared customs then boarded a plane for a short trip to Kujirt and Karakorum, to visit a horse ranch. We watched them round up a herd of horses. We were surprised to learn that one of their best customers was France, the French imported them for their meat.

Mongolia's farmers and ranchers live in *yurts*, a well-insulated circular domed tent, with a stove in the middle and a regular size door entrance. We visited a horse rancher's family in their yurt. The hostess offered us goat cheese. Claudia couldn't eat it. I managed to. It wasn't very tasty. We took pictures of the family with their two children. They were thrilled when we gave them copies. We spent the night in a yurt tourist camp. Our yurt was comfortable and neatly furnished with twin beds; community toilets and showers were outside.

In the morning, we boarded a bus to Karakorum, the capital of Mongolia's 13th century conqueror and founder of the empire, Ghengis Khan. En route we saw many yurts but they were great distances apart. We saw herds of wild camels, one group had two very rare albinos. We took pictures. We also saw herds of sheep, cattle, and horses. We visited the site of the 16th century Erdeni Dzu Lamaist monastery, then returned to Ulan Bator and checked into our hotel.

The next day, June 6, was Claudia's 39th birthday. After visiting Revolutionary Square and Gan Dan, the only Lamaist Buddhist Temple, holding worship services during the Communist suppression, we spent the rest of the day shopping. We purchased several postcards and were really surprised when we bought stamps, two of them had scenes from the Walt Disney Mickey Mouse cartoon film, Fantasia. I found out later, Disney had granted Mongolia permission to use the pictures. That evening we had a birthday party for Claudia. The hotel furnished a birthday cake.

A bus trip to the Gobi Desert was planned for our last day in Mongolia, but Claudia and I had no desire to go, so we spent our last day in Ulan Bator exploring the city and its outstanding museums, the state public library with some 3,000,000 volumes, the Fine Arts museum, the Museum displaying relics of the Lamaist religion. All were impressive but the most outstanding of all was the museum with complete skeletons of all the huge dinosaurs and all the other animals, birds and reptiles, unearthed in the Gobi Desert. We weren't allowed to take pictures and were disappointed when told they had run out of brochures showing pictures and describing the museum.

We had our last dinner in Mongolia and spent our final evening with our group. From what they told us about their trip to the Gobi, I think we had the better day. In the morning Claudia and I flew to Leningrad.

Before 1914 Leningrad was known as St. Petersburg, named for Peter The Great, Russia's czar from 1682 to 1725. In 1914 it was renamed Petrograd. Then after the death of Vladimir Ilyich Lenin, the Communist Revolutionary leader, it was renamed Leningrad to honor him. When we were there in 1987, the City was still called Leningrad but in 1991 it reverted back to its original name, St. Petersburg. Henceforth, I will combine the two names.

Leningrad/St. Petersburg withstood a 900 day Nazi siege during World War II. It's the cultural and industrial center of the Soviet Union. It has beautiful parks with picturesque fountains and many museums. The most famous museum is the Hermitage of world-wide renown, with its 3,000,000 exhibits housed in five buildings. I don't know how he did it, but our guide got our group in after closing hours. We had the whole museum to ourselves. It would take two or three days to see all the exhibits.

We were only there a couple of hours. The beauty of the rooms and paintings are indescribable. I don't remember the name of our hotel, but it was tops. We toured the city, we were amazed at the number of historical and art museums. It also had six musical shows including a drama and a puppet show, each with its own individual theatre.

The other museums we visited during our stay were both the Winter and Summer Palaces of Peter the Great. The Peter and Paul Fortress, which was a political prison when Russia was ruled by czars. The Peter and Paul Cathedral, a prime example of Russian architecture, located on the same grounds as the Fortress, is the only wooden structure to survive from the city's early days. It's now the House Museum of Peter the Great, in its rooms are displayed authentic items, such as tools and documents of that era. The lady attendant in one of the rooms said in broken English, "I think we should be friends." I replied, "We are friends."

On our last night after dinner we took a trip along the Neva River, in a comfortable motorship. We were serenaded by an orchestra playing Russian folk songs. Leningrad/St. Petersburg is a most intriguing city. I wish we could have spent more time there, but we had to move on to our next destination, Moscow, for a short stay of two days.

Moscow is the capital and Russia's largest city. It is the educational and cultural center of Russia. It has over 75 institutions of higher learning, and a library which has one of the largest collections in the world. It is the home of the famous Bolshoi Ballet, the Moscow Symphony Orchestra, and the

Pushkin Museum of Fine Arts. The citizens of Moscow are predominantly Russian Orthodox but there are communities of Jews, Roman Catholics, Protestants, and Muslims.

When we were there, Russia was still under strict Communist rule, so when we checked into our first class hotel, the Lodi, there was a guard at the door and everybody had to enter and exit through the same door.

During our short stay, we toured the city. It has many parks and gardens, picturesque churches, and buildings. When we visited Red Square, we took pictures of each other. We also took pictures of the long double line of people in front of the building that housed the tomb of the Communist Leader Lenin, waiting to see his embalmed body. We didn't join the line.

On one side of Red Square is the huge state-owned well-stocked department store, GUM. We went through the entire crowded store but didn't buy anything. The three places we didn't get to visit were the Pushkin Museum of Fine Arts, the state-owned Library, and the Kremlin, where government offices are located. We wanted to see the Bolshoi Ballet but it wasn't performing when we were there. However, on our last night in Moscow, we attended a balalaika concert. It was most enjoyable. We were on the last leg of our journey and flew to Helsinki for our Finnair First Class, non-stop flight to Los Angeles.

Helsinki is the capital and Finland's largest city. Its population is less than 500,000. Finnish and Swedish are the main languages, the predominant religion is Evangelical Lutheran. We were only there for one day, so we just walked around the city. It has many parks and gardens. It is Finland's cultural center and boasts many libraries, museums, an opera house, and a music theatre. We visited the monument of the world renowned Finnish composer Jean Sibelius, who passed away in 1957 at the age of 92.

During our walk along the picturesque shoreline, we stopped at an ice cream stand and bought cones. I can truly say it was the most delicious ice cream I have ever tasted. After doing some window shopping, we called it a day. I was kind of glad. We only spent two nights and a day in Helsinki. The hotel and food were the most expensive of our tour. A piece of apple pie was $12.00.

In the morning we boarded our Finnair plane for home. When the Finns say First Class, they mean First Class. We were made to feel that we were the most important people in the world, the attention, the service, the food were all indescribable!

Back home we fell into our normal routine. I practiced piano, played golf, paid bills, did the grocery shopping, and kept my doctor and dentist appointments. Her summer vacation over, Claudia resumed teaching. On Tuesdays after school she would come to my house and do the bookkeeping for my investments, so when I kicked the bucket she would have complete knowledge of the estate.

On Saturdays we'd go to lunch, then visit my grandchildren. During Claudia's 1988 summer vacation, we decided to take another tour but not together. Besides teaching school, she was a lecturer for Weight Watchers. She became friends with a member of one of her classes and they decided to visit the British Isles, London, Ireland, and Scotland. I went to Scandinavia, to the capitals of Denmark, Sweden, and Norway. Grandpa and Grandma Nelson were immigrants from Norway and I wanted to see the home of my ancestors.

I only stayed four days in each city. The first was Copenhagen, Denmark. Its population is about 450,000. The predominant religion of all Scandinavians is Evangelical Lutheran. Denmark's most notable citizen was Hans Christian Andersen. At the age of 14, he ran away to Copenhagen, to get away from an unpleasant home environment, where he acquired an education and became one of the world's most known authors. He is best known for his more than 150 childrens fairy tales, such as "The Little Mermaid," "The Emperor's New Clothes," "The Ugly Duckling," "The Red Shoes," "The Snow Queen," and many more. His fairy tales have been translated into more than 80 languages. He passed away in 1875 at the age of 70.

During World War II from 1940 to 1945, the city was occupied by German troops. I visited the Parliament and Supreme Court building, the Royal Veterinary and Agricultural University, the Church of Our Lady and the Museum of Northern Antiques, but the most enjoyable were my two visits to the Tivoli Gardens, Copenhagen's famous amusement park.

My second city was Stockholm, Sweden's capital. Its population is about 680,000. It is a beautiful city with many parks and waterways. It is the city where the Nobel Foundation is located. The Foundation oversees the awarding of the Nobel Prizes. Alfred Bernard Nobel was an Inventor; one of his inventions was dynamite. He died in 1896 at the age of 63 and left most of his fortune to establish prizes for people who worked in the interests of humanity, such as world peace, medicine, and literature.

Stockholm is both an educational and cultural center, with schools of medicine, economics, music, and physical education. The city supports the Philharmonic Orchestra, the Royal Dramatic Theatre, and the Royal Ballet. Besides visiting some of these institutions, I spent much of my time just walking around the city and enjoying the parks and waterways.

Now on to the land of the Vikings, Norway, which I consider the country of my ancestors. Although my mother's ancestors came from the small country of Luxembourg, I considered myself of Norwegian descent because I have all of the Nelson family traits.

Norway Vikings, during the 9th and 10th centuries, fiercely raided the British Isles and what is now known as France, Germany, and Russia. They were led by Erik the Red, so-called because of his red hair. He is credited with discovering, naming, and colonizing Greenland. His son, Leif Erickson, is credited with being on the North American Continent, around 1001—long before Columbus. Because of the abundance of grapes, he named it Vineland.

Three other well-known Norwegians were the composer Edward Grieg, who died in 1907 at the age of 64, the poet and dramatist Henrik Ibsen, who passed away in 1906 at the age of 78, and Vidkun Quisling, a Norwegian politician who collaborated with Germany during the occupation of Norway by the Nazis during World War II. After the war in 1945 he was executed as a traitor. The name Quisling is now a word synonymous with traitor or collaborator.

The last four days of my trip were spent in Oslo, the capital and Norway's largest city with a population of about 460,000. It's on the Aker River, which is the beginning of the fjords, which extends about 125 miles inland. Oslo has many parks and statues. Its buildings are mostly of modern design. It is the cultural center of Norway. In the City are the University of Oslo, which includes the museum of Ethnography, the study and systematic recording of human culture, the museum of Paleontology, the science dealing with the life of past geographical periods and the museum of Mineralogy. There are also colleges of architecture, theology, veterinary medicine, fine arts, and music.

There are several other museums; it would take about a month to visit all of them. I did visit about six of them; to me the most interesting was the Historic Museum, it held Viking antiques and one of the huge Viking warships, the ships that carried the Vikings to the countries of their conquests. The ships were powered by about twenty oarsmen. Other places of interest were the Royal Palace, the Parliament building, the Norwegian Nobel Institute, which helps select the winner of the Nobel Peace Prize, and the National Archives.

I spent most of my last day on a bus viewing the magnificent Norwegian fjords, the next day back home via Finnair.

After my trip to Scandinavia, I decided to contact my half-brother, Peter Nelson, who still lived in Caledonia. I have a picture of him, with his baby sister on his lap, taken when he was six years old. I wrote him a long letter telling who I was, about my family, my livelihood and that during the great Depression of 1933 when my mother was in the hospital, and I was out of work. I had decided to visit my father and ask for help. Father greeted me very coolly, Grandpa and Aunt Lillian greeted me with open arms and affection. They helped me financially for three months until I got a job. Peter never answered my letter.

The last thing I did of any consequence in this period was attend the American Numismatic Association's seminar in Anchorage, Alaska, on "How To Grade U.S. Coins." I had joined the association in 1964 and am still a member. I had become an avid collector after I bought my son a penny coin album so he would have a hobby. Every-day when I came home, I'd throw my change on a table for Greg to look over. One day while looking over my change, he excitedly hollered, "Daddy, Daddy, you know what you got? A 1918 over 17 quarter!" I looked in a catalog and in good condition it was worth $250.00. That did it! I started collecting seriously. I purchased every coin the U.S. mint issued since 1957, including proof and uncirculated sets, silver dollars, commemoratives, gold and platinum sets.

In addition, I purchased every type of coin minted since the first coins were issued in 1794. I started albums of cents, two cent coins, nickels, dimes, quarters, half dollars and silver dollars. In 1969 we were going to build a home in Encino and I foolishly gave the albums to a coin dealer to auction. I received about $50,000.00. Today those albums would be worth twice that amount.

I kept the type set and all of the government issues. I still purchase every coin issued by the government. Gregory became a collector of stamps and first issue books. I too became a philatelist and have collected every first day issue stamp since 1974.

ALL GOOD WISHES TO KEN NELSON
HAROLD HENSLEY AND PRESIDENT REAGAN

President Reagan occasionally had country music entertainment at his Santa Barbara ranch. Here he is at the ranch with my favorite country music violinist, Harold Hensley.

The Forbidden City, Beijing.

I was surrounded by people wanting me to take their picture with my polaroid camera.

Elephants you can ride-Bangkok.

Water buffalo in China's Li River.

Claudia and me in Tienanmen Square, Beijing China, 1985.

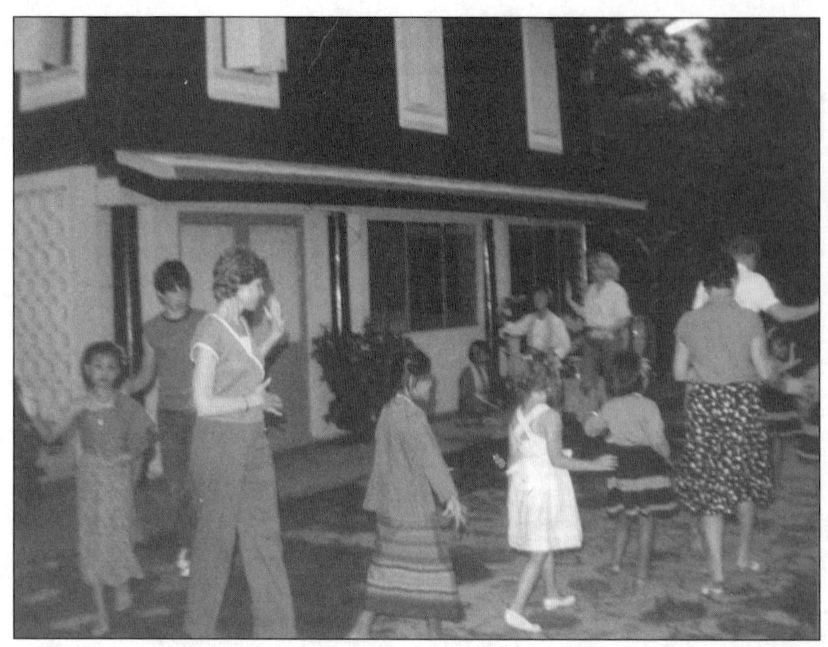

Claudia dancing with school children in Bangkok.

Claudia and me on The Great Wall.

Mongolian mother and child, 1987.

Me with Mongolian family.

Our very neat and comfortable sleeping quarters, the Mongolian yurt

June 6, 1987 celebrating Claudia's birthday in Mongolia.

My son Gregory's family 1989. Patty, Tiffany, Greg, Charles, Gregory Jr.

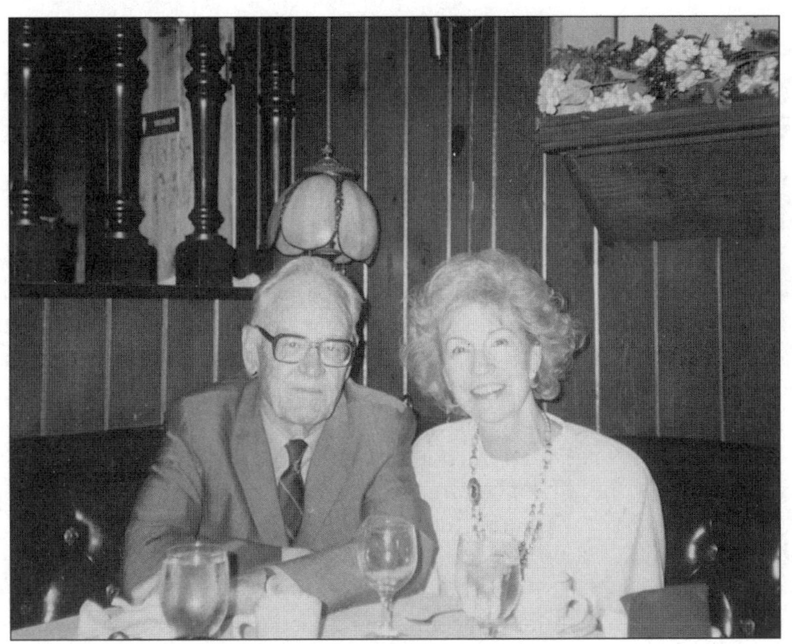

In 1988 Jo Walker visited Hollywood.

1991-2000

This period, the declining years of my life, was one of tragedy, sorrow, and happiness.

On January 29, 1991, the second greatest tragedy of my life occurred. My son, Gregory, passed away at the age of 46. His death was caused by skin cancer, melanoma.

Gregory had a happy childhood and, as any normal child, got into mischief. We would discipline but never berate him. One incident I vividly remember, when he was five or six years old, he and his neighborhood friend took a bucket of white paint and a brush from a garage and painted several neighborhood fences. We made them clean the fences as best they could, but June and I had to finish the clean up.

During his teenage years, he got into some trouble but nothing real serious. I remember the time when he was fifteen or sixteen; I caught him and his friend, Ted Ripley, drinking beer. I couldn't say anything because I was a beer drinker myself. I let June handle that one.

Greg was somewhat like his mother. He showed little or no affection to Claudia or me although he was somewhat affectionate with June. He was a good father and did show affection for his three children. On his deathbed, he told his wife, Patty to tell Claudia and me that he loved us. We both loved him. It was such a tragedy that a young, successful attorney should pass away at the age of 46.

About two years after Greg's passing, his wife Patricia (Patty) a very intelligent woman who had a position as an insurance adjuster, remarried, a man she knew from her high school days, Steve Keefer. Steve was the Southern California representative of a plumbing supply company. Claudia and I attended their wedding. He was very personable. We both liked him. The children readily accepted him; he was a good father.

I was now 80 years old. My hearing was diminishing so I had to get hearing aids. Was the cause of diminution the result of my radio announcing days plus my 28 years producing records or just the normal progression of aging?

Beside Gregory, during this era, so many of my friends, artists, whom I considered friends, business associates and acquaintances, stepped outside of the boundary of life.

Chet Atkins and I had been friends since 1951. We had kept in touch with each other all these years. At the age of 69, he was still performing. In 1993 he wrote me that his tour was bringing him to the Ventura Theatre, which is about 10 miles from my home. I went to his afternoon rehearsal. The show played to a packed house. Many people without advance tickets couldn't get in. His performance was inspiring. I didn't realize Chet could sing.

After the show, we spent a little reminiscing time together, talked of our families, then bid each other *adieu*—'til we meet again.

My mother's surname was Roster. At the age of 9, she took me to her brother's, my Uncle Mike's, farm in Freeburg, Minnesota, which was in the area where many of the Rosters and their relatives lived. I was accepted as part of the family.

I have a picture of the family clan, taken at the farm, sitting in the front row, next to me were my cousins Alvina, Agnes, and two other children—about our age. There was a total of 25 relatives including Mother, Aunt Annie, Cousin Cecelia, age 16, and Cousin Leonard, who was found dead of a heart attack in the farm barn at the age of 19. With the exception of Aunt Catherine, I hadn't seen or heard from any other Roster since that picture was taken in 1920. I had fondly remembered the farm and my cousins Alvina and Agnes. In 1993, I decided to go to Freeburg and see the farm and look up any Rosters that might be in the area.

The Mississippi River runs between Minnesota and Wisconsin. Freeburg and Caledonia are across the river from La Crosse, Wisconsin. I took a plane to La Crosse, and checked into the Radisson Hotel, which is at a bend of the river, rented a car and drove to Freeburg. I had vividly remembered the three-mile buggy ride to town with Aunt Anne and was sure I knew how to get to the farm. When I got to the town, the store was gone but I did recognize the road leading to the farm. As I drove up the road, I stopped at each farmhouse and asked if they knew the Rosters. Nobody remembered them. There was one house where no one was home. I kept going up the road but couldn't find the farm. After going to the end of the road, I thought this was futile and I turned back.

On the way back, there was a couple standing in the yard of the house where nobody had been home. I stopped and asked them if they knew the Rosters. They said, "Oh yes, we used to play with them when we were kids." After explaining who I was, I asked if they knew the whereabouts of any Rosters. They told me Cecelia lived in Caledonia. If I stopped at the hardware store they could give me her address. They also told me I should have turned onto the road about a mile from there to get to the farm. I went back, turned into the road, and sure enough at the end there was the farm. It wasn't the same—the house, the outhouse, the chicken coop, and the bullpen were gone. The only remaining buildings were the barn, the stone springhouse and a mobile home, no one was home.

I then drove to Caledonia, which is only a few miles from Freeburg. I was born there and in 1933 I had visited my father and grandfather so I was somewhat familiar with the town. As I passed the old lumberyard, there was a huge sign "NELSON CONSTRUCTION COMPANY." I was tempted to go in and visit my half-brother, who had ignored my letter, but I resisted the temptation. I went directly to the hardware store. They gave me Cecelia's address.

Cecelia owned her home, a two-story house and kept it neat as a pin. She lived alone, still had a speech impediment, but was easy to understand. She had never married, had worked in Catholic priest's parishes all her life and was now retired. She seemed as thrilled to see me, as I was her. After hugging, we sat in the parlor and talked. She amazed me. She brought out an album that had pictures of me, taken at Uncle Mike's farm in 1920, and pictures taken when Mother and I were in Brownsville and Minneapolis. She gave me those and the picture of the family gathering at the farm. What really threw me for a loop was when she showed me the *WJJD Magazine*, which had my picture sitting at the piano when I was musical director of the station. Mother must have sent it to her.

During the pleasant two hours we spent together, I learned a lot of family history. She told me Cousin Alvina's married name was Klug. She was a widow, lived alone in La Crescent, Minnesota and had 6 children—3 boys, Michael, Peter, and Dale; 3 daughters, Rita, Mary, and a girl who was in a home for the retarded here in Caledonia. I also learned that Cousin Agnes and her 2nd husband, who was 8 years her junior, lived in Columbus, Ohio. Her son from her first marriage, Robert Weier, and his wife, Lois, lived in Grove City, Ohio. Cecelia didn't offer an explanation why Agnes and her first husband had separated, and I didn't ask. She gave me the addresses of both cousins and after hugging goodbye, I promised to come see her the next year.

La Crescent is directly across the river from La Crosse and on the way back to my hotel, so I decided to visit Alvina. I arrived at her house just as she was leaving for church. I told her who I was and offered to drive her to church. She said it was within walking distance but accepted my offer. On the way, she told me she had thought of me often and was glad to see me. I told her how I remembered my visit to the farm, my three cousins Alvina, Agnes, and Cecelia, and that I was determined to go to Freeburg and look up any Roster that might be around. I explained how I found the farm and got Cecelia's address. I told her I would like to, but couldn't come visit her tomorrow because I had to fly home. But I would come visit next year and also visit Cousin Agnes in Ohio. After telling her how thrilling it was becoming reacquainted with two cousins of my childhood days, and that it brought back pleasant memories, I dropped her off at her church and went back to my hotel.

Not having traveled by train since I came to California and having time on my hands, I decided to see the country by Amtrak. My trip would include Minnesota, Illinois, and Longview, Washington. I would wait until next year to visit Cousin Agnes in Ohio. I paid for a sleeping room on the train but it was over a set of the wheels, when I tried to sleep that night, the click, click, click of the wheels made it impossible. I got up dressed, packed my bag, told the conductor the room was too noisy, and to find me a seat that wasn't over the wheels. The seats were reclining, very comfortable, and I slept like a log only waking up a couple of times when the train made stops.

Next year, as promised, I visited Cecelia in Caledonia and Alvina who also owned her home and lived alone in La Crescent. I spent a couple of hours with Cecelia. Alvina showed me pictures of her children and their families; gave me the phone number of her son, Michael Klug, who lived in La Crosse with his family; he was a financial advisor, would come to see her three or four times a week. He took care of her financial affairs; in the summer mowed the lawn, in the winter shoveled the snow. I surmised that Alvina didn't relish being hugged or kissed, but I did it anyway. When I got back to the hotel, I phoned Michael, Alvina had told him about me. He seemed anxious to meet me. He suggested that he come to the hotel about 9 A.M. and we have breakfast together. I told him I would look forward to it. He came exactly at 9 A.M. I liked him immediately. He told me he and his wife, Michelle, had three children. His brother Peter and his family lived in Sun Prairie, Wisconsin. His brother Dale lived in Sacramento, California. His sister Rita, Mrs. Diekroeger, in West Salem, Wisconsin. His sister Mary, Mrs. Horihan, in Canton, Georgia. It never occurred to me that I had so many second cousins. I'll find out later how many third cousins I have.

From La Crosse I paid a short visit to my friends, Reg and Tina McHugh in Glen Ellyn, Illinois. My final destination was Longview, Washington, where I visited June's first cousin, Veriane Potter, a relative of June's mother's side of the family. Veriane's husband, Glenn Potter, was deceased. They had five children and four grandchildren. Her children were all grown and had flown the coop. She now lived alone. She gave me two surprises: First, when she was seventeen, she and her mother, June's aunt, had attended our wedding. Second was really a surprise. She remembered a song I had written, 'Why Didn't I Listen to Mother?" Three or four years after my visit, she remarried and is now Mrs. Alfred Runnels. The train trip home was scenic, especially along the coast. Dinners were excellent.

When my granddaughter, Tiffany, entered her teenage years in 1995, she decided she wanted to learn to play the piano. I consented to be her teacher. Once a week I would pick her up after school and bring her to my house for her lesson. After about three months, her interest began to wane and the lessons stopped. I surmised there were other teenage activities that were more important.

In October 1996, my trip to Wisconsin and Minnesota to visit my cousins was now a yearly event. As there was no direct flight to La Crosse, I had to change planes in Minneapolis. My two Minnesota cousins were as happy to see me as I was them. In La Crosse that evening cousin Michael picked me up at my hotel, his wife Michelle, was with him; the three of us went to a restaurant and had an excellent dinner. Michelle was a charming lady. I learned more about the family. Michael said his brother Peter was anxious to meet me and would try to do so on my next visit.

I flew back to Minneapolis and boarded a train for two cities I had never visited, Seattle, Washington and Portland, Oregon. I spent three pleasant days in each city, exploring the city and its environs. When I boarded the train in Portland for home, seated across the aisle from me was a mother and her daughter. We soon became acquainted. They were Mrs. Diana Price and her daughter, Deborah of Kennewick, Washington on their way to visit Mrs. Price's sister in Santa Paula. Deborah was ten years old, active, precocious, and very intelligent. We spent much of the trip together playing UNO and just talking. Every member of the Price family's given name began with the letter "D": Mother Diana, Father Douglas, Sister Dana, Brothers, Daniel, David, Dustin. We decided that since Santa Paula was only twelve miles from my home, whenever they came to California to visit her aunt (Mrs. Price's sister), we could get together. I adopted her as my surrogate granddaughter and even though my name didn't begin with the letter "D," she adopted me as her surrogate grandfather. We do get together when they come to Santa Paula.

Mrs. Henry Cannon was an intelligent, dignified charming lady whom you would never suspect as being the great comedienne Minnie Pearl, who for years greeted the audiences of the Grand Ol' Opry in her bumpkin dress, hat with the price tag on it, and her famous "Howdee" greeting. The audience loved her. She was loved and admired by all who knew her. Minnie was inducted into the Country Music Hall of Fame in 1975. She passed away March 4, 1996, at the age of 84.

In April my cousin Cecelia passed away at the age of 93. Had I been informed in time, I would have attended the funeral. I'll miss visiting her. She was a sweet, adorable person whom I'll never forget.

I first met Elaine Keen and Reg McHugh about 1940. Reg and I became close friends. He chose me as best man when he and Elaine were married in 1942. I chose him as best man when June and I were married in 1945. Our families formed an immediate relationship, which my daughter and I still maintain.

In June of '96 it was with a heavy heart that I boarded a plane to attend Elaine's funeral. I had no desire to view her in the casket. I wanted to remember her as I knew her, outgoing, fun-loving, and vivacious. Along with her three sons, Keen, Kim and Mark, were two grandsons, Chad McHugh and Greg Jones. I too was a pallbearer.

The Crystal Palace, a major tourist attraction of Bakersfield, California was built in 1996 by Buck Owens Productions. The Palace houses a Country Music Museum, a restaurant and a nightclub which features country artists. Buck invited me to the opening night, which was October 23, 1996. It was attended by the mayor and other city dignitaries. Buck and the Buckaroos furnished the entertainment. He still appears there on Friday and Saturday nights. Buck called me to the stage and introduced me as the man responsible for his recording career. It was a gala evening.

During the interim of my signing him in 1952 and his demise forty-four years later, Faron Young had a successful career as a recording artist, entertainer, movie star, and businessman. He was divorced from his wife, Hilda, the mother of his four children. He had a history of alcohol abuse, had emphysema and prostate problems. On December 10, 1996, Faron committed suicide by shooting himself in the head. Four years later, in 2000, he was inducted into the Country Music Hall of Fame.

Ever since I was a child I had wanted to play the piano, so when I retired I started taking piano lessons. As I had no formal musical education, I couldn't make full piano copies of the songs I wrote. I enrolled in the Ventura College Music Class. I had become quite adept at sight-reading, playing and making piano copies. I had attained my lifelong ambition but age and Mother Nature had other plans. I was now 86 years old. About five years ago my hearing was deteriorating and I was now wearing hearing aids. This year my piano sounded so out of tune I called the piano tuner. We discovered it wasn't the piano—it was me that was out of tune. I no longer hear the right pitch or tone. I can no longer sing in tune. New melodies and musical themes still come to me, but I don't bother to write them down. I can't listen to music. I live in a music-less world.

Even though I wear digital hearing aids, if a person's voice is above a certain pitch and they talk too fast, I have difficulty understanding them. This is the case with many women. It also prevents me from enjoying some movies and TV shows.

During Claudia's Christmas vacation we took a ten-day tour of the continent "Down Under." Our itinerary included Sydney, Canberra and Melbourne. The original natives of Australia were Aborigines but like our American Indians, with the advent of immigration, they became the minority. In 1788 the British started to send their criminals to Australia. When they stopped this practice in 1849, immigration flourished. Some of the many indigenous animals and birds of Australia are the platypus, kangaroo, wallaby, dingo, koala, wombat, opossum, emu, and reptiles.

Sydney is the country's largest city with a population of about 4,000,000. We toured the city, took a Captain Cook's cruise, visited the wild animal park, went to the outback and took pictures of wild kangaroos. Sydney's opera house is known world-wide. There is no doubt that it is the most unique building in the world. We didn't enter it but we took pictures.

Canberra is the capital of Australia. All of the foreign embassies are located there. We only spent one day there so we didn't get to go to any museums or art galleries, but the city is an art gallery within itself because all of the embassy buildings are built in the architectural style of their country. Flowers are everywhere throughout the city. Claudia and I both agreed it was one of the most beautiful cities we've ever been to.

Melbourne is an economic and industrial center. It is Australia's second largest city. In 1850 when gold was found in the area, the population increased rapidly. Today, it has a varied population of about 3,500,000. When Australia won its independence from Great Britain in 1901, it became the capital until 1927, when it was moved to Canberra.

We did the usual sightseeing, river cruise, visited the wild animal sanctuary. The unusual thing we did was to visit Gola country and see the huge realistic statue of the master bandit Ned Kelly pointing a revolver. He caused terror and havoc during the gold rush era. We went to a sheep ranch and watched them shear sheep. It was interesting to know that Australia produces 25 percent of the world's wool. The most entrancing sight of all was, just before sunset, watching the penguins waddle ashore on Phillip Island. We spent Christmas in our hotel with our group, two days later we said goodbye to the land down under and flew home.

In 1998 some of the truly greats of country music were greeted by Saint Peter at the Golden Gate. Owen Bradley entered the gate on January 7th at the age of 83. He was a major factor in Nashville becoming the Country Music capital of the world.

On January 17, Cliffie Stone, my close friend and business partner, entered the Golden Gate at the age of 81. Through his TV show, *Hometown Jamboree* Cliffie was a major factor in the growth of country music on the West Coast. He discovered and nurtured many young artists. In 1945 he helped Lee Gillette establish the roster of country artists for Capitol Records.

Carl Perkins wrote and recorded the first big rock and roll hit "Blue Suede Shoes." He and Elvis Presley were contemporaries, both starting their recording careers with Sun Records of Memphis, Tennessee. Carl was a member of the Rock and Roll Hall of Fame; he met St. Peter on January 19 at the age of 66.

Although I had watched and enjoyed his performances many times I never met Grandpa Jones. Grandpa had been a staple of the Grand Ol' Opry for at least a half century. On February 19 he entered the Gate of Paradise at the age of 85.

Tammy Wynette, known as the First Lady of Country Music, entered the Portals of Heaven at the age of 56. She had many number one hits, the most notable "Stand by Your Man." I had never met Tammy but I had known her husband and manager, George Richey, before they were married. On the recommendation of Cliffie Stone, I hired and sent him to Nashville to manage our office and be the producer for Capitol. I don't recall why he resigned.

During the Great Depression of 1933, the Maddox family, including four boys and a girl, moved from Alabama to California. When the girl, Rose, was twelve years old, a musical family act was formed called The Maddox Brothers and Rose. It was an outstanding entertaining act, but never attained the recognition or success it deserved. When the group disbanded in 1959, I signed Rose. Her records had consistently good sales and airplay. Because of an illness, I reluctantly released her from her contract. On April 15, 1998, at the age of 73, Rose left for the Golden Gate.

Jack McFadden began his career as talent manager and booking agent in Bakersfield. The first act he booked was the Maddox Brothers and Rose. In 1963 and for the next thirty years, he was the agent for Buck Owens. Jack eventually moved to Nashville and opened his talent agency office there. He added many artists to his talent roster including Sonny James and Freddie Hart. I still carry the silver dollar he gave me many years ago, as a good luck charm. Jack was booked to enter the Golden Gate on June 15.

Whenever I went to the home of "The King of the Cowboys," Roy Rogers, and his wife, Dale Evans, to discuss the content of the religious albums, I was to produce for Capitol, Roy was never home. I never got to know him. The only times we talked were before and after a recording session. I found him to be mild-mannered and likeable. Roy reached the end of the trail on earth when he entered the Golden Gate on July 6 at the age of 87.

Gene Autry had an incredible career that started when he took the advice of Will Rogers, who after hearing him sing told him he should be in show business. He started singing on radio, was the first singing cowboy movie star, and signed a contract with Columbia Records, his sales were tops. Gene's enterprises flourished, he owned radio and TV stations, real estate, hotels, record and music publishing companies. The two things he was most proud of were his ownership of the Angels baseball team, and the $54,000,000 Gene Autry Cowboy Museum that he built in the Los Angeles Griffith Park, a major tourist attraction.

Knowing of Gene's hopes of the Angels winning a World Series, I felt saddened when he didn't live to see the Angels win the World Series in 2002. But Mother Nature deemed otherwise and on October 2 at the age of 91, Gene entered the Golden Gate.

I was thrilled when at the Motion Picture Academy Awards in March of 1998, Carrol McHugh and her partner, Donna Dewey, were presented with

Oscars for their documentary film, *The Story of Healing*. I first met Carrol, an intelligent lady with an engaging personality, at my friend Reg McHugh's home. She is the wife of Reg's son, Kim McHugh, whom I have known since he was a child. I never had the pleasure of meeting Donna.

I daily feed squirrels, rabbits, quail, bluebirds, pigeons, sparrows, and many birds I don't recognize, in my back yard. On my patio, I have three humming bird feeders that I fill two times a day. Because of the humming birds, I had a most unusual and rare experience.

After I put my cat out for his evening jaunt, I left the front door slightly ajar so he could come in. One evening, what I thought was a humming bird flew into the house. I opened the door and tried to shoo it out but to no avail. It finally landed on a table, and when I picked it up to put it outside, it bit me. It wasn't a humming bird—it was a bat! I had to go to the hospital for several days to get shots to guard against rabies. I'm sure the bat was avenging the whole bat community because of a song I wrote with my co-writer, Billy Fairman, "You've Got Bats in Your Belfry." It was recorded in 1948 by Tex Ritter.

My fall trip in September included Nashville, Atlanta, Chicago, and Minnesota. I hadn't been to Nashville for a number of years and the city had changed somewhat. I visited the impressive building Capitol Records had built just before it was ready for occupancy. I understand they later sold it. In Atlanta, I visited my friends Wade and Mary Jane Pepper, and Bill and Billie Lowery. Bill had sold his Lowery Music Company to Sony Music Company. In Glen Ellyn, I spent time with my friend, Reg McHugh and then on to Minnesota to visit my recently found relatives.

Hal Cook and I started our careers with Capitol Records in 1948. Hal soon showed his ability as an astute businessman and in 1952 became vice-president in charge of sales. He left Capitol in 1955 to become head of marketing for Columbia Records. In 1962 *Billboard Magazine*, recognizing his business acumen, convinced him to become their publisher. Sensing the worldwide interest in music, he developed the International Music Conference, a gathering of major music industry executives in various countries.

Because of his recognizing the popularity and potential of country music, Hal was elected to the board of the Country Music Association and in 1966 he became chairman of the board.

When I took over Capitol Record's transcription department in 1948, my secretary's first name was Caroline. I don't recall her last name but I know it wasn't Cook. I presume their romance and courtship evolved from their meetings at Capitol. She later became Mrs. Hal Cook. On January 22, 1999, Hal passed away at the age of 80.

I first met Joe Peter when I was enrolled in the fifth grade class of Carter Practice Grammar School. We only lived a couple of blocks from each other so we would walk home together. We became fast friends. We were both 14 years old when we graduated from grammar school in 1925. Both of us had learned to play musical instruments—Joe the violin and saxophone and I the tenor banjo. During our teenage years we played together in several orchestras. Joe went on to become a professional musician. I became a radio announcer. We had very little contact with each other until a few years ago. Whenever I was in Chicago, I made it a point to visit Joe and his wife, Charlotte, in their suburban home in Park Ridge. My childhood and close friend, Joe Peter, passed away on January 29, 1999, at the age of 88.

Along with members of the McHugh family, Claudia and I attended Reg's 80th birthday party at the Circus Circus Hotel in Las Vegas. While in Vegas, I noticed the Jordanaires were playing at the Golden Nugget. Claudia and I went to see them. I was a little disappointed when Gordon Stoker was not in the group. He is still a member but was back in Nashville nursing a cold. Ray Walker and Neal Matthews were as thrilled to see me as I was them. After the show we talked and took pictures. Our trip to Las Vegas was a double payoff of Reg's birthday party and seeing the Jordanaires.

On September 15 I was inducted into the Rock-A-Billy Hall of Fame. There was no formal presentation. I was sent a framed certificate stating so. Rock-a-Billy is a combination of Country songs with a rock beat. I produced records of this type but my most noted were by Gene Vincent and Wanda Jackson.

When I read the obituary of my half-brother, Peter A. Nelson, it dawned on me that I had a half sister, three nephews and two nieces. I was an uncle! Peter was a well-respected member of the Caledonia community, serving on many local committees. He obviously had musical talent. He served as choir director of his Church. In 1950 he purchased my grandfather's and father's business, The Nelson Lumber Company, which he sold in 1963 and founded the Nelson Construction Company of Caledonia. In 1990, his son, my nephew David, and a partner bought the company. A few years ago, hoping for the same warm response I received from Grandpa Nelson and Aunt Lillian, I wrote Peter, explained who I was, told him about my career, my family, and that I would love to come to Caledonia and meet him. I never received a response. Thinking the letter may have gotten lost in the mail, I wrote again. Still no response. I was disappointed. On November 30, 1999, Peter Nelson passed away at the age of 73.

Having lived most of the last century, I have seen the world grow from the horse and buggy stage to the technological world it is today. It's quite apparent that change is constant, man's computer, his brain, will make sure of that. What wonders will the new century bring?

I started the first day of the new year following my usual routine, then turned on the TV and watched the Rose Parade and the Rose Bowl football game between Wisconsin and Stanford Universities. It was an exciting game;

Wisconsin won 17 to 9. After dinner I watched a video movie and then off to slumberland.

The demise of many of my friends and acquaintances continues.

Leonard Sipes, accepted the name Tommy Collins, suggested by Ferlin Husky. When I signed Tommy in 1953 Buck Owens was the guitar player in his band. Tommy was well on his way to becoming a successful songwriter and recording star but in 1961 he decided to quit the entertainment field and become a minister. In 1964 he gave up his ministry and tried to regain his status as an entertainer and recording artist but to no avail. He moved to Nashville and became a very successful song writer. He was inducted into the Nashville Song Writers Hall of Fame. Tommy passed away March 14, 2000, at the age of 69.

I had just been to Las Vegas a few weeks ago and visited the Jordanaires, who were appearing there. Neal Matthews was a member of the group when I signed them in 1953. He and I did a little reminiscing. It was quite a shock when I read in the *Los Angeles Times* that Neal Matthews, Jr. passed away April 23, 2000, at the age of 70.

During the 1950s Bill Woods owned The Blackboard, a Bakersfield Night Club that featured country artists and music. Bill also played in and led the band there. Every country artist or musician of any note, when in Bakersfield, performed or played there. Bill became a disc jockey and hosted a TV series. He furthered the careers of practically every artist that emanated from Bakersfield. Bill Woods passed away April 30, 2000, at the age of 76.

It seems as though all I've been writing about is the passing of my friends, so it's a relief to write about a couple of diverse memories.

In June my granddaughter, Tiffany, graduated from high school. Her mother Patty, stepfather, Steve Keefer, Claudia and I attended the ceremonies which were held in the school stadium. The stadium was packed with parents, relatives, and friends. The graduating class was at least two or three hundred. It was a real thrill to hear Tiffany's name called and see her walk on stage and accept her diploma. Tiffany hadn't yet decided what career she wanted to pursue but I'm sure she will. She enrolled in the local two-year Ventura college and after graduating there will choose the school where she will finish her four years of college education.

In October I flew to Chicago to visit the suburb of Glen Ellyn to visit my friend, Reg McHugh. I checked into the Holiday Inn, called Reg to let him know I had arrived, and he told me he would pick me up this evening as we were going to have dinner at Joe and Ethel Owen's house. They only lived a couple of miles from my hotel. Joe Owens and Reg had been friends since 1937. It was fun reminiscing that night. Joe was an attorney but was always interested in music. He challenged me thinking he could remember more songs than I. Of course, he didn't have a chance because of my musical background. He finally admitted defeat. The next day Reg drove me through the Chicago loop and then continued on to the Northwestern University campus in Evanston, where he had taught. On the way home, he became lost, and it took us an extra hour to get back to town. Reg and I had dinner together, then said our goodbyes, as I was leaving on the morrow for La Crosse.

In one of my conversations with the lady hotel manager, the subject of music came up. She asked if I had ever heard of Art Van Damme. I said, "Heard of him?" The first hit record I produced was "Buttons and Bows" with the Dinning Sisters and the Art Van Damme Quintet. The very first album I produced was an Art Van Damme Quintet album. She was quite surprised and told me he was her grandfather and gave me his address; he now lives in California.

My October trip to La Crosse to visit my cousins had become an annual event. The visits weren't quite the same since cousin Cecelia had passed on. I spent some time with cousin Alvina Roster Klug and had dinner with her sons, Michael and Peter, and their wives, Michele and Emily. during the course of the evening, Peter told me that he and my nephew David Nelson were good friends. When he told David about me he expressed a desire to meet me. I told Peter to tell him I was anxious to meet him but our meeting would have to be postponed until next year because I was flying home tomorrow. I was excited and looking forward to meeting members of my present Nelson family.

Soon after my return home, Jimmie Davis passed away. It's incredible that one man could be successful in so many varied careers. Jimmie was an outstanding entertainer, a prolific songwriter—he wrote the international hit, "You Are My Sunshine." He was a recording star, a movie actor, a professor of teaching at Dodd College, a school for women. Jimmie who served 2 terms as governor of the state of Louisiana.

On November 5, 2000, after having lived a full century plus one year, Jimmie Davis passed away.

Bill Lowery, Me, Jerry Reed in Atlanta 1992.

Cousin Cecelia Roster.

Cousin Alvina Roster Klug.

Me happily posing with Alvina's sons, my second cousins, Michael, Peter and their wives Michelle and Emily.

My lifelong friend Joe Peter. Both of us at the age 85.

Cousin Agnes and Husband Gene Thomason. They live in Columbus, Ohio.

My surrogate granddaughter Deborah Price of Kennewick, Washington.

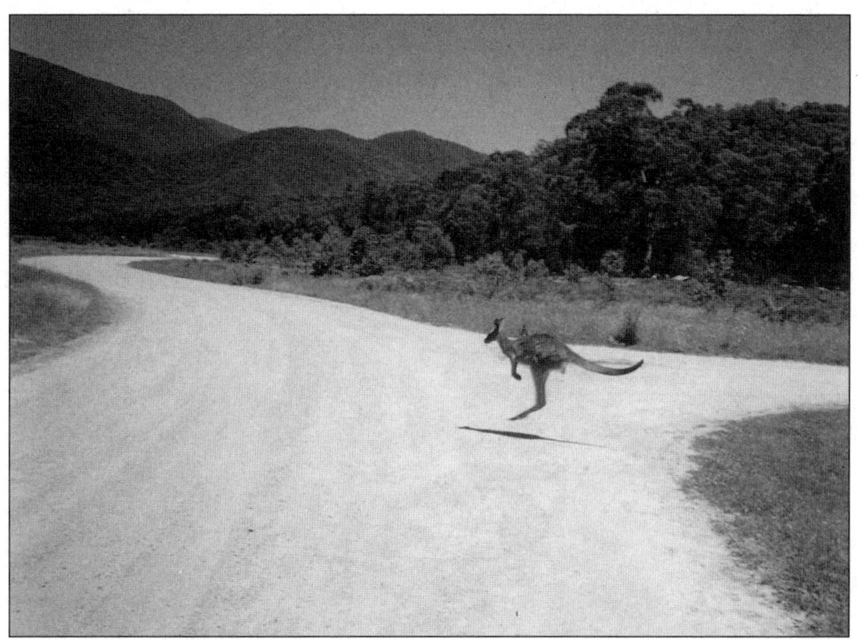

During Claudia's Christmas vacation in 1997 we went to The Land Down Under. We took this picture of a native.

The Statue of Ned Kelly, the notorious bandit of Australia's gold country.

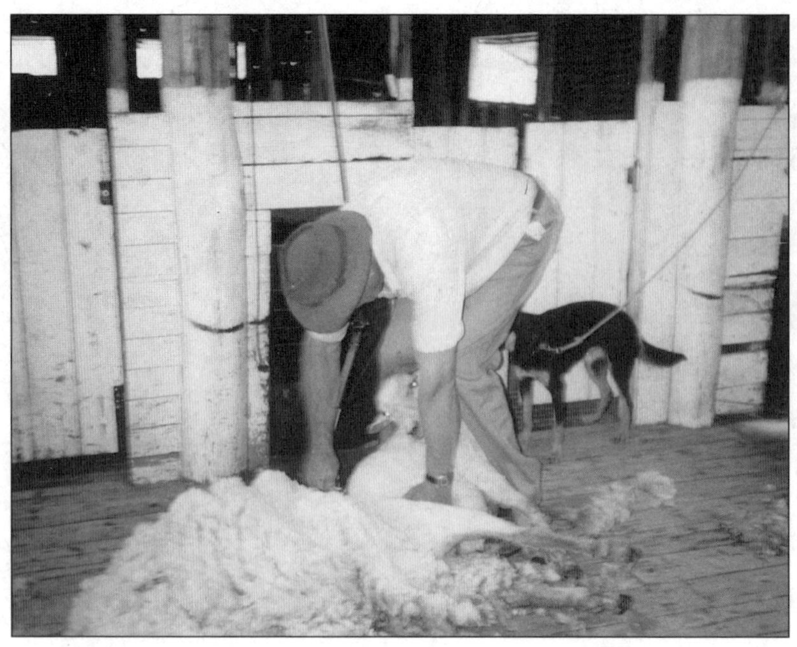

Shearing sheep, Australia provides 25% of the world's wool.

The world famous unique Opera House in Sydney.

Celebrating my long time friend Reg McHugh's 80th Birthday in Las Vegas. 1999. L-R Reg's daughter Sue, sons Keen, Kim, me, Reg, and Carrol, Kim's wife.

A 1999 photo L-R Granddaughter Tiffany, me, Claudia, Grandsons Gregory Jr., and Charles.

U.S. Navy Captain, Diane Diekman, a country music fan, was writing a book about Faron Young. She came to my home to interview me. In 1999 she brought her two adopted daughters to my home, April and Amanda. They adopted me as their grandfather. Now I have four granddaughters.

Photo of me in my later years.

2001

2001 was quite an eventful year! Not only for me—but for America as well.

On January 19th I arrived at the ninety-year milestone. I was receiving congratulatory letters, from many of the artists, friends and acquaintances that I had kept in touch with over the years. I couldn't figure out how they knew it was my 90th birthday until Claudia, my daughter, confessed she had written them and told them of the coming eventful day!

Regretfully I continue to write about my friends and acquaintances who have gone to the Great Beyond, but everyone I have or will write about has had some meaning in my life.

Ted Toll began his lifetime show business in Chicago, when he, Lee Gillette, and I were teenagers. While attending Bowen High School, he formed a dance band. I was the banjo player. We used to play afternoon high school dances in the gym for 50¢. When we had a night job, we got $2.00. I still have the printed announcement dated May 12, 1933, announcing the Keyhole Kapers to be held at the famous Granada Cafe, featuring two orchestras, Herby Mintz and Ted Toll. The Campus Kids, a vocal trio formed by Gillette, Jim Cortty and me, were also featured. Ted later became the feature editor of the Jazz magazine *Down Beat*.

He then became the producer of the *Don Mcneill Breakfast Club*. During World War II he enlisted in the Marine Corps and became a first lieutenant as an intelligence officer. After the War, Ted and his family moved to Hollywood, where he resumed his career as a producer and writer of radio, stage and TV shows. One of the TV shows he produced was *The Adventures Of Ozzie And Harriet*. He became an active member of Pacific Pioneer Broadcasters, an organization of people involved in radio and television. Gillette and I were charter members. In 1962 the family moved to Thousand Oaks, where Ted became an active member of the community. Three years ago he moved to Portland, Oregon where he passed away February 13 at the age of eighty-nine.

Dale Evans started her career as a singer in big band orchestras, then graduated to a nationally broadcast radio show. She was brought to the attention of Republic Pictures, whose star attraction was Roy Rogers, "King of the Cowboys." She signed a contract with them.

In 1944, she was Roy's leading lady in the movie, *The Cowboy and the Senorita*. After making several movies together, they fell in love and were married in 1947. Their career as a duo, Roy Rodgers and Dale Evans, skyrocketed! They co-starred in 35 westerns and in the *Roy Rogers* and *Happy Trails* TV shows. They wrote the theme song, "Happy Trails," and were recording stars. They eventually moved to Apple Valley and opened a museum in Victorville. They were true patrons of religion. Dale wrote religious songs and books. She also hosted a religious program. After 51 years of marriage, Roy reached the end of the trail. Three years later on February 8, 2001, at the age of 88, Mrs. Roy Rogers (aka Dale Evans) joined him at the end of the Happy Trail.

It was just five months ago that I spent a couple of pleasant days with my long-time friend, Reg McHugh. So it was quite a shock when his son, Kim, phoned me on March 11th and told me his father had passed away and his funeral would be on the 16th. I told him my daughter and I would be there. We arrived in Glen Ellyn, two days later and renewed acquaintances with members of the McHugh family: Daughter Sue, Sister Joan, and Sons Keen, Kim, and Mark. The wake was held at Leonard Memorial Home. I did not approach the casket. I wanted to remember Reg as I had known him. I can still hear him singing his two favorite songs, "Ace in the Hole" and "A Shanty in Old Shanty Town." Relatives and friends filled St. Petronille's Church where a mass was held for him and his eulogy, given by his son Kim, who gave a vivid description of his father's eventful and fruitful life. Because of the inclement weather, it was impossible to go to the cemetery for the actual burial. The words on his grave marker are:

Husband
Father
Coach
Grandfather
Friend
"Our Ace In The Hole"

Reginald G. McHugh passed away March 10 at the age of 82. His song has ended but his memory lingers on.

The British Archives of Country Music is a non-profit organization devoted to the preservation of country music for future generations. The Archives has one of the largest collections of country music memorabilia from all over the world—USA, Europe, Australia, Africa and Asia. In addition, to its library of over a half million records, it houses sheet music, biographies, photographs, reference books, magazines, videos, and CDs. Name the country music record from any country, you'll find it in the Archives.

The Archives are located in Kent, England. They were started by David Barnes, an avid country music fan. Dave and his wife, Sue, came to visit me a few years ago. We have been corresponding friends ever since. Dave is the manager of the Archives and editor of its magazine, *Just For the Record.*" He sends me a copy of each edition. He surprised me when he sent me a CD of the very first recording I had produced, "Uncle Henry's Kentucky Mountaineers."

Around June 12th I received a letter from Dave congratulating me on being inducted into the Country Music Hall of Fame. I couldn't understand how he could be so misinformed. I had been nominated several times but never made the grade. I was pleasantly surprised, thrilled and excited when a few days later I was informed by the Hall of Fame that I was one of the 12 inductees to be inducted on the fourth of October in the new $37,000,000.00 Hall of Fame building that opened in May and it was decided to make the first induction ceremonies in the new hall a memorable event by inducting ten nominees who had previously been nominated at least three times and Bill Anderson and Sam Phillips who would have normally been inducted. The other ten including me were: The Delmore Brothers, The Everly Brothers, Don Gibson, Homer and Jethro, Waylon Jennings, the Jordanaires, Don Law, the Louvin Brothers, and Webb Pierce. A couple of weeks after receiving the notice of my induction, the thrill and excitement were somewhat tempered by the demise of my friend, Chet Atkins.

There is nothing I can say about Chet Atkins that hasn't already been said. He was one of the world's great guitarists. He could play all types of music: classical, pop, country, rock and roll. Chet was a "producer" in RCA's Nashville studio. He later was elected a vice-president and manager of Nashville's Office and Studio. Our friendship dates back to 1951 when he played guitar on some of my first Nashville sessions. In 1973 he was inducted into the Country Music Hall of Fame. In 1993 he received the Grammy Lifetime Achievement Award. Chet sent me a congratulatory letter on my 90th birthday. I believe it was the last letter he ever wrote. I cherish that letter. Six months later on June 30th at the age of 77, Chester "Chet" Atkins, one of the most unassuming persons I have ever known, passed away.

After serving 25 years as voluntary secretary/treasurer of our homeowners association, I resigned. I no longer wanted the responsibility because now that I was 90 years old, I wanted to devote all of my time finishing my autobiography before my appointment with St. Peter!

September 11, 2001, was probably the worst "day of infamy" in the history of America when four planes were hijacked by terrorists. One plane crashed before hitting its target—the White House! The other three hit their targets—the Pentagon—and the 110 story twin towers of the World Trade Center in New York City. The death toll was estimated to be well over 4,000 including airplane crews and passengers, the people in the Pentagon, and the twin towers of the World Trade Center and rescue workers, including firemen and policemen. The nation was in total shock and disbelief! "How could this happen in America?" There was some discussion as to whether or not in the wake of this tragic event, the Hall of Fame inductions should be held. It was decided to carry on with all normal activities.

When I received the invitation to attend the induction ceremonies, it stated "black tie." When I tried on my tux, which I hadn't worn for years, it didn't fit. I didn't want to go to all the trouble of having it altered because in all probability, this would be the only time I would ever wear it. I wore my dark green suit, shirt and tie. All the inductees wore tuxes but there were many men in the audience in dark suits so I didn't feel out of place.

On October 2nd my daughter, Claudia, and I arrived in Nashville to attend the induction ceremonies to be held October 4th in the new Country Music Hall of Fame and Museum Building. I couldn't believe my eyes when I saw this beautiful edifice. I thought of Steve Sholes, who had first suggested a Hall of Fame and how overjoyed he would have been to attend these ceremonies.

The morning after the day of our arrival, I took Claudia on a tour of the city which had been my second home for twenty-five years. We visited Music City, so named because it is the center of the country music industry, with most all companies affiliated with country music, record company offices and studios, music publishers, talent agencies, and trade publications also located there. We then went to the Ryman Auditorium where the Grand Ol Opry held sway for33 years before moving to Opryland in 1974. The Ryman Auditorium was originally a church, built in 1881. It still has the original church pews. Live performances are still held in the auditorium and it is a popular tourist attraction.

In the afternoon, I taped an interview for CMA's oral history program. When Daniel Cooper, the content curator, asked me to do the interview, I agreed to do it but reluctantly because I am not a very good interviewee or ad libber. The interview lasted about two hours, I haven't heard it but I think it was okay because Claudia was with me and that made me feel more at ease. Later she reminded me that I had forgotten to mention that I was president of the County Music Association (CMA) for two terms. We spent the rest of the afternoon touring the museum. It sure brought back many memories!

When we came to Elvis Presley's Cadillac, which had been donated to the old museum, I recalled that I had objected to it being in the museum because I thought some people might be tempted to take some part of the car as a souvenir. I was wrong! I was happy to see it was still intact, without a scratch on it. I wondered how large a staff, and how many people were now employed by CMA and the Hall of Fame, because when I was president of CMA in 1961-62, we had one employee, Jo Walker.

That evening, we had dinner at the hotel. I called some friends and read my acceptance speech a few times. We watched a little TV, then prepared for the big day ahead and a big day it was! We spent the morning and part of the afternoon just "lollygagging" around! At 5:30 P.M. we checked in at the welcome desk of the Hall of Fame, and then were escorted to the Hall of Fame rotunda, where the attending inductees greeted each other and pictures were taken. We then were escorted to the Ford Theatre for a question and answer period with the press. CMA chairman and popular syndicated radio personality, Lon Helton, was the host and moderator for the press meeting.

At 7:00 P.M. all of us attending inductees and our guests joined the other 350 guests in the Hall of Fame's Grand Conservatory for dinner and to see a short film synopsis of the inductees' careers and to hear the acceptance speeches of the attending inductees. I felt quite honored when Claudia and I were seated at the table of Nashville's Mayor Bill Purcell and his wife and Rabbi Kenneth Kantor and his wife. Ed Benson, the executive director of CMA, and Kyle Young, Director of Country Music Hall of Fame, gave the welcoming speeches and Rabbi Kenneth Kantor gave the invocation. During dinner a film was shown of the plaques of members of the Hall of Fame. The master of ceremonies for the evening was the popular entertainer and recording artist, Marty Stuart.

The first inductee film shown was that of the Delmore Brothers, Alton and Rabin. I believe they were the first recording country duet. When I was the musical director of WJJD, Our station was the only one outside of the WLS *Saturday Night Barn Dance* that featured country music. Ours, a daily show called *The Suppertime Frolic*, was very popular. It featured Uncle Henry's Kentucky Mountaineers and great artists. When he left the station, the program was taken over by Randy Blake and featured all country artists recordings. It was up to me to purchase records for the program. Of all the dozens of country artists recordings, I purchased the Delmore Brothers on King Records, were the only country duet I recall.

On December 4, 1952, Rabin Delmore passed away at the age of 46. His Hall of Fame plaque was accepted by his niece, Billy Ann. Twelve years later on June 8, 1964, at the age of 56, Alton joined his brother; his son, Alvin Delmore, accepted his plaque.

In 1952 at the behest of Wesley Rose, I signed the Louvin Brothers, Ira and Charlie. Their unique sound and style was quickly accepted by both country and gospel fans. In 1955 they joined the Grand Ol Opry. In 1964 I released solo records by both Ira and Charlie. I was happy to see the Louvin Brothers inducted into the Hall of Fame, however, I was saddened that Ira was not here to accept this honor. He had died in an automobile accident on June 20, 1965 at the age of 41. His plaque was accepted by his son, Terry

Louvin. Charlie continued on the Grand Ol Opry and had a successful recording career. After paying tribute to his brother, Ira, in his acceptance speech, he accepted his Hall of Fame plaque.

I was next on the program and after showing artist highlights of my career, this was my acceptance speech that I had rehearsed several times, confident that I would remember it.

> I have been privileged to watch the Country Music Association grow from its embryonic stage to the great organization it is today. I am both humbled and proud to be the recipient of this prestigious award, but it must be shared with the artists, musicians, songwriters, and the recording engineers, such as John Kraus, Hugh Davies, John Palladino, and Nashville's own Mort Thomason, and last but not least an outstanding promotion man, Wade Pepper. These are the people who have made this award possible and on their behalf I accept this great honor. Thank you.

With the exception of a couple of mental pauses, everything was okay until I got to the recording engineers. I forgot to mention John Palladino and when I mentioned Nashville's own Mort Thomason, he was given a standing ovation. This interrupted my train of thought and I forgot to mention Capitol Record's outstanding country promotion man Wade Pepper. I later apologized to John and Wade for my forgetfulness.

In his book *The Scene from Nashville*, Ralph Emery referred to four producers: Owen Bradley of Decca Records, Chet Atkins of Victor Records, Don Law of Columbia Records, and Ken Nelson of Capitol Records, as the Four Horsemen. There is little doubt that these four men were an important factor in Nashville becoming the country music center of the World! Chet was inducted in the Hall of Fame in 1973 and Owen in 1974. Although both Don and I were nominated several times, we were not publicly known. We were the men behind the scenes.

I had never met Don but I admired his work. He produced some of the era's great artists: Little Jimmie Dickens, Carl Smith, Lefty Frizzell, Marty Robbins, Ray Price, Johnny Horton, Jimmy Dean and Johnny Cash. On December 20, 1982 Don passed away at the age of 80. His plaque was accepted by his son, Don Law.

As the writer of many hits, including "I Can't Stop Loving You," "Oh, Lonesome Me," and "Sweet Dreams," Don Gibson was inducted into the Nashville Song Writers Hall of Fame and as a successful recording artist, he was now inducted into the Country Music Hall of Fame. He was unable to attend the induction ceremonies. His plaque was accepted by Peggy Lamb.

Homer and Jethro, the country comedy duo, were not brothers. Henry Haynes was "Homer," Kenneth Burns was "Jethro." As youngsters in Knoxville, Tennessee, they formulated their act "Homer and Jethro." They became widely known for their comedy versions of popular songs. They recorded for RCA Victor and made appearances in nightclubs in Las Vegas as well as being featured on many television shows. I met them in Miami, Florida when they appeared with Buck Owens on the Jackie Gleason Show. On August 7, 1971, Homer (Henry Haynes) passed away at the age of 51 one. After his partner's death, Burns (Jethro) continued to tour, to record, as well as to teach mandolin until he died eighteen years later on December 4, 1989, at the age of 69. Henry (Homer) Haynes' plaque was accepted by his son, Fred Haynes. Kenneth (Jethro) Burns's plaque was accepted by his son, Johnny Burns.

Although I had seen, heard and known of Bill Anderson for many years, I had never met him until we inductees were taken to the Hall of Fame rotunda to have our photographs taken with the other inductees. After meeting him, it was easy to see why he was so popular—he had an engaging personality!

While attending the University of Georgia, Bill had worked as a disc jockey, sportswriter, and performer. His talent as a songwriter became quite apparent when he recorded his song, "City Lights" for a small label and when Ray Price recorded it, it became a hit. Many of his songs were recorded by such artists as Connie Smith, Lefty Frizzel, Roy Clark, and others. Bill signed with Decca Records and had many number one and Top ten hits. He joined the Grand Ol' Opry in 1961 and had his own syndicated television show. He hosted network programs on ABC and TNN. His many outstanding activities in country music earned "Whisperin" Bill Anderson his place in The Hall of Fame. After his acceptance speech, he happily accepted his plaque.

Webb Pierce was another artist I never met but I sure knew who he was—a member of the *Louisiana Hayride*. Webb Pierce's career started as a Clerk in the Shreveport, Louisiana, Sears Roebuck store. He graduated to become a honky-tonk singing star on radio station KWKH, *Louisiana Hayride* and signed with Decca Records. During the 1950s he had more number one hits than any other country artist. He became a member of the Grand Ol' Opry and moved to Nashville. Webb was known not only for his distinctive tenor voice, but also as one of country music's most colorful entertainers. Webb Pierce passed away February 24, 1991, at the age of 70. His plaque was accepted by his widow, Audrey Pierce.

I was one of the first producers to use the Jordanaires as a vocal background beginning in 1953. We made several successful religious albums but recognizing their talent as background singers, I encouraged them to pursue that as their career. They did and became the most recorded backgrounds for all types of artists, country, pop, rock and roll, and blues.

The Jordanaires, Hoyt Hawkins, Neal Matthews, Gordon Stoker, and Ray Walker, and I started our careers about the same time and I was happy to be inducted into the Hall of Fame with them. However, there was a sad note. Neal Matthews, Jr. and Hoyt Hawkins passed away, Hoyt on October 23, 1982, at the age of 55; Neal on April 21, 2000, at the age of 71. Hoyt's plaque was accepted by his widow, Dot Hawkins. Neal's widow, Cherise Matthews, accepted his.

As a child, Waylon Jennings, sang on the local radio station of his hometown, Littlefield, Texas. He later moved to Lubbock, Texas, and became a disc jockey. He learned to play bass and toured with Buddy Holly's band. He was supposed to be on Buddy Holly's fatal 1959 flight, but fate intervened. He had given up his seat to J.P. Richardson. In 1965 he signed with RCA Victor Records and became one of their most consistent hit makers. He also had hits with other artists: His wife, Jessi Colter, Willie Nelson, Jerry Reed, and Hank Williams, Jr. Waylon, with his long black hair and black suit and hat, was an eye-catching person. I spent a pleasant hour with him when he came to my office at the behest of my secretary, Betty Seigfried, who knew him. Waylon did not attend the induction ceremonies. His son, Buddy Jennings, accepted his plaque.

Sam Phillips, whom I had just met, was a loquacious man. He had an interesting personality. We had much in common and became quite friendly. Sam was born in Florence, Alabama, the hometown of W.C. Handy, sometimes called the "Father of the Blues." Sam grew up during the Depression period listening to African American singers, church choirs, and country music. The Grand Ol' Opry was one of his favorite programs. While still a teenager, he worked as a radio announcer and engineer. He first produced records for a rhythm and blues label and was highly successful with B.B. King, Howlin' Wolf, and others. After moving to Memphis, with a font of untapped talent, he opened his own studio, the Sun Record Company, with rock and roll, rockabilly stars such as Elvis Presley, Carl Perkins, Jerry Lee Lewis, and Roy Orbison. There is no doubt that Sam Phillips, Sun Records, played a part in changing the major music culture of the world.

In accepting his plaque, he gave an inspiring speech. Sam and I are now members of two Halls of Fame, the Rock-a-Billy Hall of Fame, and the Country Music Hall of Fame.

The last of the inductees were the Everly Brothers, Phil and Don. When Chet Atkins and I attended Merle Travis Day in his hometown of Rosewood, Kentucky, one of the acts performing there were two youngsters—the Everly Brothers. They really impressed me. I said to Chet, "I'd like to sign those kids." Chet replied, "You're too late, Ken. They're already signed.'

As children, the Everly Brothers, Phil and Don, performed with their parents. After graduating high school, their combination of rock 'n' roll and country caught the ear of Archie Bleyer, the owner of Cadence Records and he signed them. In 1957 their hit, "Bye Bye Love" dominated both charts, making number one in pop and country. This was followed by hits such as "All I Have to Do Is Dream" and "Wake Up, Little Susie." They became favorites here and abroad. In 1960, they signed with Warner Brothers Records. For some reason or other in 1973 they disbanded their duo but ten years later in 1983 they resumed their career as duet and recording artists. Don was not able to attend the induction ceremonies. Phil gave the acceptance speech and accepted both plaques.

The induction ceremonies were brought to an end with Mayor Bill Purcell coming on stage and joining the audience in singing, "America the Beautiful." Claudia and I then mingled with the crowd, where I met and introduced her to many of my friends and acquaintances.

The following day, Friday, we flew to La Crosse but had to leave Sunday because Claudia had to be back at her school on Monday. After checking into our hotel, I called my nephew David Nelson. He said he would be at our hotel about 1:30 P.M. the next afternoon. I then phoned Cousin Michael Klug. He told me he had made dinner reservations for the next night and would pick us up about six o'clock. After I phoned David and Mike, we took a cab across the river to visit cousin Alvina Roster Klug in La Crescent. I'm sure she was as happy to see us as we were to see her. We spent a couple of pleasant hours with her showing us family pictures and telling us about the family. Claudia was impressed by her spirit and agility. We had dinner at the hotel, watched television the rest of the evening, anxiously awaiting the next day. In the morning, we took a walk in the beautiful park on the banks of the Mississippi River. We took pictures of a riverboat and a huge statue of Hiawatha.

At last the big moment arrived! After being ignored by my father and brother, I met my nephew David. Claudia and I were sitting in the lobby facing the entrance. When he walked in, I recognized him immediately. After greeting each other, we spent the afternoon in a room overlooking the river, telling each other about our families. He told us of his wife, Sandy, and their three sons, Lucas, Brad, and Dorian, and that his sister, Cindy Sanders, who lived in Fairfield, California, would like to meet me. He gave me her phone number and address. We told him of my wife and son's death. He also told us that he and a partner now owned the Nelson Construction Company. When we said goodbye, I had a happy heart. I told Dave I wanted Claudia to see Caledonia and that we would visit him there next year. One couldn't help but like David Nelson. He was a most likeable, ingratiating person.

A few minutes before six o'clock, Michael, his wife, Michelle, Cousin Peter Klug and his wife, Emily, picked us up at our hotel. After introductions, we drove to a restaurant out of town where Emily's mother was waiting for us. It turned out to be a compatible evening. Michelle, Emily and Claudia were all teachers so they had something to talk about. Emily's mother was a professional piano player, so we had much to talk about. I told Peter how grateful I was and thanked him for being responsible for getting me and my nephew David Nelson together. It was a most enjoyable evening—good friends, good food, good company—but it ended too soon! After saying goodbye to Emily's mother, Mike drove the rest of us to our hotel. I told them we would be back next year. After saying goodnight and goodbye, it was the end of a perfect day. In fact, it was the end of three perfect days. On Sunday morning we flew home.

About three weeks after returning home, I received the video of the induction ceremonies. Outside of my hearing and eyes, I never had any major health problems. I exercise 30 - 45 minutes a day and still play golf, so I never gave age any serious thought. But when I saw myself on TV, I was shocked. I walked like an old man and my acceptance speech was not as fluent as it should have been. It made me realize old age is catching up with me. It didn't bother me, but I have become more cautious and careful in my activities.

Claudia and I spent Thanksgiving Day at the home of my daughter-in-law, Patty, her husband Steve Keefer, and my three grandchildren.

Soon after Thanksgiving there was a sad note. On December 4 Grady Martin passed away at the age of 72. Grady was a Nashville studio guitarist. He was very creative. He played on most of my Nashville sessions. I venture to say there was not one single pop or country artist who recorded in Nashville that didn't have Grady on their sessions, including Bing Crosby, Elvis Presley, Buddy Holly, and Joan Baez. In 1980 he had joined Willie Nelson's band and was with him until 1994 when ill health forced him to leave. In 2000 he was given a Career Achievement Award at the Ryman Auditorium. I had worked many years with Grady and considered him a friend.

On Christmas Eve my family came to my house for dinner and to exchange presents. It was a merry and happy ending to my first ninety years!

2002

I started my 91st year by renewing my driver's license. I passed the test with flying colors! Phew!

So many of my friends and acquaintances continue to leave me. Waylon Jennings, one of my fellow inductees, did not come to the ceremonies. I can understand why. A few weeks later on February 13, at the age of 65, Waylon Jennings passed away.

There is no doubt that Harlan Howard was the most prolific and successful country songwriter of his time. He is a member of the Country Music Song Writers Hall of Fame. In 1999 he was inducted into the Country Music Hall of Fame. Ever since 1956 when he came to the studio to hear Wynn Stewart record the first song of his to be recorded, "You Took Her Off My Hands—Now Take Her Off My Mind." Harlan and I have been friends and kept in touch with each other. Many of his songs hit the pop charts and were recorded by all types of artists. Congratulating me on my 90th birthday was the last letter I received from Harlan. On March 4, 2002, Harlan Howard passed away at the age of 74. I will miss him.

The Hall of Fame medallions are not given to the inductees at the induction ceremonies but are given in special medallion presentations, usually held in May of the following year.

On May 5, Claudia and I flew to Nashville to attend the medallion ceremonies to be held the next day, Sunday, May 6th. A limousine was waiting to take us to our hotel. We had dinner, watched television and then to sleep. The next day we had a leisurely breakfast and lunch. I telephoned some friends and memorized my acceptance speech. A few minutes before 5 P.M. a limousine came to take us to the ceremonies in the Hall of Fame rotunda. I didn't know we would walk to the entrance on a red carpet and be interviewed by television reporters! I hadn't prepared a speech for the grand entrance. All I said was, "I am honored. I've had a great life. Country music has been good to me."

Before the ceremonies, a reception was held on the terrace for the board of directors, members of the Hall of Fame, and friends. I renewed many acquaintances and introduced Claudia to Eddy Arnold, whom I hadn't seen since Steve Shole's funeral, to Don Pierce, Dolly Parton, Bud Wendell, and others.

After the reception we went to the Hall of Fame rotunda for the medallion ceremonies. The master and mistress of ceremonies were Little Jimmie Dickens and Brenda Lee. The six inductees attending the ceremonies were: Bill Anderson, Gordon Stoker, and Ray Walker of the Jordanaires, Charlie Louvin of the Louvin Brothers, Ken Nelson, and Sam Phillips. I had written, rehearsed and memorized the following acceptance speech:

Being a new member of the Country Music Hall of Fame I find it difficult to express my feelings and emotions in being in the company of all these illustrious and famous men and women. With humility and pride, I receive this keepsake to commemorate the occasion. Thank You.

But alas and alack, no acceptance speeches were given. If I had known this, I would have used the speech on the television reporter interview on my walk up the red carpet. After the ceremonies all Hall of Fame members who were present came on stage and a group picture was taken. The music of Jimmy Martin and his Nitty Gritty Dirt Band was the finale of the program. Then we all went to dinner.

The next day we flew to LaCrosse, Wisconsin. We decided this was a good time to visit our relatives so Claudia took the week off. We informed my nephew, David, and Cousin Michael we were coming. When we arrived at the hotel, I phoned Michael. He told me that tomorrow afternoon at 2 o'clock at the little theatre, his daughter Eva would be performing in the play, "Mr. Poppers Penguins," and after the play we would go to his house and meet the rest of the group, then go to dinner. I told Mike we wouldn't miss the play for the world! He told me he would meet us at 1:30 P.M. in front of the theater, which was within walking distance from the hotel.

After speaking with Mike, I phoned my nephew, David Nelson, and told him we would rent a car and come to Caledonia Wednesday morning and take him to lunch.

Tuesday afternoon we met Mike and Emily, Cousin Peter's wife, at the theatre. The full-house audience loved the play and so did we. Eva is an excellent actress! After saying goodbye to her actor friends, she joined us. When we arrived at the house, other members of our party were there. The group members were: Michael, Michelle, Eva, Peter, Emily, Emily's mother, Helen Hoskins, Claudia and me. The group was enhanced when Cousin Rita and her husband John Diekroeger, joined the group. After visiting about an hour, the party left for dinner.

Before saying adieu to another pleasant and memorable evening with my cousins and cousins-in-law, Emily's mother gave us two CDs of her piano playing which we later enjoyed.

The next morning we rented a car to drive to Caledonia, Minnesota, my birthplace, to have lunch with my nephew David Nelson, but as La Crescent was on the way, we stopped and visited with Alvina for awhile. The Caledonia graveyard is on the outskirts of the city so we stopped and viewed many of the gravesites of the Nelsons and Rosters. On the way to town, we got lost and stopped at a store to ask directions. After continuing on, suddenly appeared "The Nelson Construction Company" sign!

David was waiting for us. He took us into his office and introduced us to his secretary. She said she knew who I was and knew the Rosters. Dave then took us into the huge former lumberyard building. I remembered it so vividly because when I was 19 years old, it was in there that I had met my father and Grandpa Nelson. It now housed building materials. David then introduced us to his two sons—Lucas and Brad. The youngest was going to have lunch with us. Brad had to work.

I was quite surprised when Dave drove us to Freeburg, the place of many of my childhood memories. He said the restaurant was one of the best in the area. The food and service were excellent! Family talk dominated lunch conversation.

Before going back to his office where our rental car was parked, Dave drove us through Caledonia and Claudia got to see Cecelia's house. After telling David how happy I was that we had gotten together, we got in our rental car and headed for LaCrosse, Wisconsin.

I was with a happy heart, knowing I was a member of two families and Claudia had the knowledge of my family history. After dinner, we spent the evening watching television. Our plane didn't leave for home until Friday so we had nothing to do on Thursday. So we thought.

Thursday morning I got up, put on my exercise shorts, put a bath towel on the rug, laid down on my back and started my daily exercise routine. After about two minutes, my body became limp. I couldn't stop moving my arms or legs. Claudia realized I was having a stroke. She called the front desk. They sent up a wheelchair and provided transportation to the hospital, where it was confirmed that I had had a slight stroke. Claudia told the doctor we had plane tickets for our return home to California tomorrow and asked if we could go. The doctor gave me some medication and said they would run some tests and let us know. During the day, I was examined by three different doctors. About 3:30 P.M. we were told it was okay to go home but to be careful and pick-up a prescription at Walgreen's Drugstore that they had phoned in, and to see my doctor immediately upon return. Not having had anything to eat all day, we stopped at the hospital cafeteria and had a bite. The hotel sent their bus to bring us back to the hotel. On the way back, we stopped and picked up my prescription.

The stroke was a precursor of my old age miseries. After dinner Claudia phoned the airline and requested a wheelchair for when we arrived in

Minneapolis where we had to change planes for Los Angeles. The rest of the evening, we watched TV. Friday morning I didn't do my daily exercises. When we arrived in Minneapolis, a wheelchair and driver were waiting for me. It was quite a distance between the two airlines. I couldn't have made it by walking. It was a fun ride. I really enjoyed it! Airlines provide wheelchairs free of charge but I gave the driver $20.00.

On the way home, we discussed the events of the six days and we were glad that the stroke had happened after the medallion ceremonies and our visits with my Roster cousins and my nephew, David. It only goes to show there is always something to be thankful for.

When we arrived in Los Angeles, I was feeling better and regained my strength, so I was able to walk to our transportation home. We hadn't told any of our relatives about my stroke. When we got home, I called my medical advisor, Dr. Jeffrey Allan, and told him what had happened. I made an appointment for Monday after Claudia's school class. Dr. Allan has been my medical advisor since 1994. When my previous doctor retired, his first action was to have me stop taking Coumadin, a blood thinning medication, because I was urinating blood. Dr. Allan's first action when we met on Monday, was to put me back on Coumadin, but in much smaller dosage than I had previously taken. After a thorough examination, Dr. Allan determined that there was no major damage and that I could resume my normal activities.

The next big event was on May 16th when my granddaughter, Tiffany, graduated from Ventura Junior College. There were over 350 students in her graduating class. She hadn't made up her mind what career she wanted to follow. Through the efforts of her stepfather, Steve Keefer, a former military man, she was granted a scholarship to San Diego State College.

The next big event was in June when my grandson, Gregory Nelson Junior, graduated from Buenaventura High School. Greg is an energetic, ambitious young man. He was already working in a clothing store. He wanted to continue his education and enrolled in Ventura Junior College. I was very proud of both my grandchildren, Tiffany and Gregory.

Another big event happened in June. My niece, Cindy Nelson Sanders, who lives in Fairfield, California and represents Claire's Accessory Company for the Northwest area, called me to let me know she was coming to Oxnard to attend a business conference. She said she would be staying at the Oxnard Embassy Suites where the conference was being held. She told me the dates she would be available to meet with Claudia and me and would love to come to Somis, which is in the Oxnard area.

I was really thrilled! At last, I was going to meet my niece, another member of the Nelson family. Claudia and I picked Cindy up at the agreed-upon date and brought her to my house. We found her charming, knowledgeable and interesting with a lovely personality. We spent a couple of hours at my home, showing her pictures that Aunt Lillian Nelson had sent me They were pictures of my father, Grandpa Nelson, and my brother, Cindy's father. There was a picture of Cindy's father when he was six years old, holding his baby sister on his lap. I also showed Cindy pictures of my career.

My friendly neighbor, Don Howard, was kind enough to let me sign his name on dinner checks at the club and I would reimburse him later. So we took Cindy to dinner at the club. During dinner, Cindy told us about her 9-year-old daughter, Danielle, and we talked about some of our family history and my career. After spending a pleasant evening, we took Cindy back to the hotel and vowed to keep in contact with each other. Uncle Ken Nelson had the thrill of hugging and kissing his new-found niece!

When I first went to Nashville in 1951, I had met Joe Allison, a disc jockey on WSM. Joe took me in hand and introduced me to many of the top country music Nashvillians. We became friends and have maintained our friendship through the years.

Joe has many talents. One of which few people knew about was that he was a cartoonist. I have a cartoon he drew of me and one he drew of Tex Ritter. As a songwriter, he wrote one of Tex Ritter's first hits, 'When You Leave, Don't Slam The Door." Later he moved to the San Fernando Valley, which is close to Hollywood. He co-wrote three of Central Songs million-seller hits, such as "He'll Have To Go," "He'll Have To Stay," and Tommy Sands, "Teenage Crush." He also wrote Faron Young's big hit, "Live Fast, Love Hard and Die Young." Cliffie hired Joe as Central's professional manager. After working for Central for a couple of years, I hired Joe to replace George Richey, whom I had previously hired as manager and producer of Capitol's Nashville office. For a period of time, Joe managed our Nashville office. When he retired from Capitol, he went into the business of buying and selling antiques. I lost another good friend, Joe Allison, at the age of 77.

This was the year the Los Angeles Angels, the baseball team previously owned by Gene Autry, won the World Series. Gene Autry was an avid baseball fan but as owner of the Angels he never saw them win a pennant. It's too bad Gene passed away before seeing them win the World Series.

I never met Horace Logan, but I certainly knew of him. He was the impresario of the well-known Shreveport *Louisiana Hay Ride*, and it was on this program that I first heard Web Pierce and Faron Young. Horace passed away October 16th at the age of 86.

I was more than thrilled when I learned that Sonny James was given the honors he so rightly deserved. He received the Country Radio Broadcasters Prestigious Career Achievement Award, and the Golden Voice Award. Sonny was the only artist during my era (pop or country) who had 16 consecutive number one hits. Therefore, I feel certain he will be inducted into the Country Music Hall of Fame.

In the beginning of December, I received a letter from David Roger's wife that he had passed away. David and I had corresponded for many, many years. Ever since I auditioned him and turned him down, he gave up the idea of a vocal career and became a driver on a Nashville city bus. He was courteous, kind, and helpful to the passengers and they loved him. He would occasionally send me little books on golfing and historic facts and jokes. I would visit him every time I went to Nashville, but on the 4th of December, I lost another good friend.

The usual Nelson family Christmas Eve was spent at my home, and thus the year ended on a happy note.

HARLAN HOWARD

photo: Señor McGuire

2003

This was the year that my old age miseries really took effect. Not only did I have the miseries but in addition many of my friends and acquaintances continued to pass on.

June Carter Cash, Johnny's wife passed away May 16th at the age of 73. I remember June so vividly because in 1970 all of the CMA members were invited to an evening of entertainment at the White House with June and Johnny Cash. After their performance, they stood on the stage with President Nixon and his wife. Members of the audience passed single file and shook hands with each of them. When June saw me, she shouted out, "Ken!" The evening ended with June telling me about their baby who was also sleeping in the White House that night. June was certainly an inspiration to Johnny.

At the beginning of June 2003 I noticed scabs on my forehead and head. I went to my dermatologist, Doctor Thacher. After examining me, he handed me a brochure about herpes, commonly called shingles. He insisted I go to an ophthalmologist, Doctor Brinkenhoff, who was in the same building. He called him and told him he was sending me over and to look at me immediately. Dr. Brinkenhoff did see me immediately and gave me a prescription for eye drops and told me to come back in three weeks.

The following week I had severe attacks of excruciating pain on the right side of my face. The pain was so intense the only way I could relieve it was to lay on the floor and scream.

These attacks started to come at frequent intervals, even at night after I fell asleep. I would lie in bed and scream. One thing I felt so badly about was when my granddaughter, Tiffany, came to visit me and I had one of these horrible attacks. Tiffany wanted to call 911, but I told her to call my daughter, Claudia, who came and took me to the hospital. At the hospital they examined me, gave me a pain killer and a prescription, and after three or four hours, sent me home.

The following day I went to see my doctor. He gave me a prescription for a pain killer and told me it could cause listlessness, sleepiness, and exhaustion.

And it sure did, for about a month. When I stopped taking the pills, I regained some of my energy but still had the shingles!

If you get herpes (shingles) on any part of your body, except the face, they will disappear within a period of two to three months. If you get them on either side of your face they will affect your vision on that side and you have the after effects, pain, tenderness, and impaired vision for the rest of your life. There is no cure.

Mother Nature brought on another old age misery. My foot was infected and it was difficult walking. I went to a podiatrist, Doctor Leibold. The foot cleared up but Mother Nature still wasn't done with me!

Since 1948 I have only had peripheral vision in my left eye. The shingles, which are on the right side of my face, have infected my right eye. I have difficulty reading and writing. My vision is becoming debilitated. I can no longer drive.

I was living alone but, again, fate took a hand. In the year 2003, after 33 years of teaching, my daughter, who lives in Moorpark, eighteen miles away from me, had decided to retire. She planned to be a substitute teacher and continue to work for Weight Watchers. Her date of retirement coincided with the beginning of my old age miseries. She was able to meet my needs—such as driving me to my doctors, dentist, the market, and other appointments.

Later, when I could no longer read or write, she wrote the checks and helped me sign them to pay my obligations. Without her help, I could never have been able to finish my autobiography. She would also read to me the stock market reports and my favorite comic, "Alley Oop." There are not enough words in the dictionary to express my obligations and gratitude to my wonderful daughter who is always helpful, cheerful, and patient.

Sam Phillips was a fellow inductee when I was inducted into the Country Music Hall of Fame in 2001. I really liked Sam and felt we would become very close friends, but it was not to be. He passed away at the age of 80 on July 7th, 2003.

On Sunday morning, October 27th, 2003, during the Great California Fire, the sheriff came to my house. He told me I had to evacuate immediately! I looked outside and the whole north side—a mile away—was on fire. The flames were heading toward my home!

I called my daughter and told her to come and get me. I quickly put all my important papers in my fireproof cabinets and threw other important things in a plastic bag to take with me. The sheriff took me to the bottom of the hill and I waited for my daughter there. After waiting for a long time, all of a sudden my daughter-in-law and my grandson, Gregory, appeared and drove me to their home. Patty told me that Claudia had called her and said she couldn't get through because of the fire. They had closed the road from her house in Moorpark to mine. I spent the rest of the day and had dinner with my entire family. They wanted me to stay the night, but I said if I could not get back to my home, I would rent a motel room. I wanted to come back and check on my house.

When I got to my home, I breathed a sigh of relief. The fire no longer posed a threat to the neighborhood and it was safe to go back home! I had been concerned about my cat, K.C., and I was relieved to know he was safe. I hadn't had time to find him and take him with me when I had to evacuate.

When we moved to Studio City, California in 1948, the San Fernando Valley was still pristine. Tex Ritter and his wife, Dorothy, had a ranch in the valley. One of our first invitations was to his ranch. Dorothy was a gracious hostess. They had met when Tex was a film star and she was his leading lady. She also starred with Buck Jones. June and Dorothy became good friends. We used to visit their ranch frequently when my children were around five or six years old. They would play with Tommy and John, the Ritters' children. Dorothy passed away November 13, 2003, at the age of 88, two months after the death of her famous television actor son, John Ritter. She is survived by her other son, Tom.

Wesley West was given the name "Speedy" West because he was the first steel guitarist to use pedals which enabled him to give a cleaner performance. He was much in demand with both pop and country artists. I used him on hundreds of Capitol sessions. "Speedy" West and Guitarist Jimmy Bryant, made a great team together! I made a couple of albums with them which were best sellers. Jimmy passed away quite some time ago. Speedy was not only one of my favorite musicians, but was also one of my favorite people. On November 16, 2003, Wesley "Speedy" West passed away at the age of 79.

Don Gibson, one of my fellow Hall of Fame inductees, had not been present at the induction ceremonies. He was obviously not feeling well. Don was a member of two Halls of Fame—the Nashville Songwriters Hall of Fame and the Country Music Hall of Fame. Although I recorded many of his songs, I never had the pleasure of meeting him. Don Gibson passed away November 19, 2003, at the age of 75.

Another artist I had never met, but had seen and enjoyed many times on the Grand Ol Opry, was Bill Carlisle. At the age of 90, I was the oldest living person to be inducted into the Country Music Hall of Fame. In 2002 Bill Carlisle took that title away from me at the age of 93. The following year on December 18, 2003, Bill Carlisle passed away at the age of 94.

Mother Nature wasn't through with me yet! In late November, my voice became inaudible. My medical advisor, Doctor Allan, sent me to Doctor Bayer, an ear, nose, and throat specialist. He determined that I had a growth on my vocal chords and that I would have to go through seven weeks, five days a week of radiation. I did not want my daughter to have the responsibility of taking me to my radiation treatments for seven weeks! I decided to hire a taxi cab service.

Fortunately Dr. Lum the radiologist told me about the American Cancer Society. The Society provides volunteer drivers who will pick you up and wait until the radiation treatment is over and bring you home. The volunteer drivers were always on time, courteous, and pleasant. So I decided to donate a hundred dollars a week for the seven weeks with the American Cancer Society volunteer drivers.

The radiation period was extended for a week because of the Christmas holidays, which meant an extra week of radiation. I had a happy Christmas Eve when my family came over to my home for our usual Christmas Eve gathering.

I met my nephew David for the first time.

In The Rotunda of the Hall of Fame, L-R – Tammy Genovese, Kyle Young, The Seven of the Inductees who were present at the Induction ceremonies, Gordon Stoker of the Jordanaires, Ken Nelson, Jordanaire Ray Walker, Sam Phillips, Bill Anderson, Phil Everly of the Everly Brothers, Charly Louvin of the Louvin Brothers, Lon Helton and Ed Benson.

Giving my acceptance speech at the Inductees Ceremonies.

The present Jordanaires with me and Sam Phillips, Curtis Young, Gordon Stoker, me, Ray Walker, Louis Nunley and Sam.

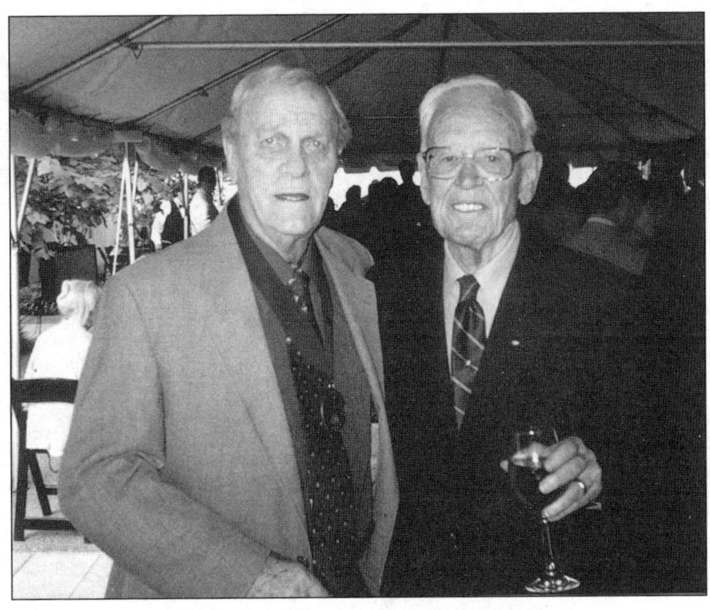

Eddie Arnold and me at the Medallion Ceremony 2002.

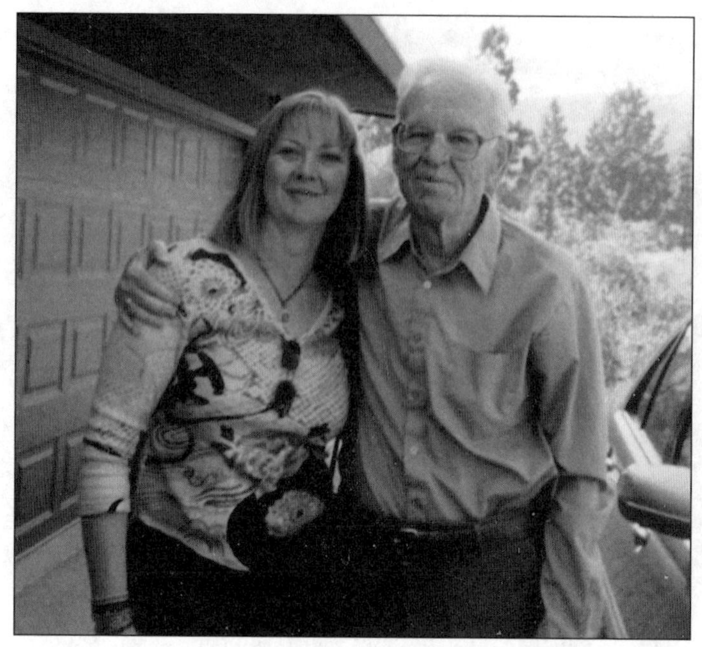

Meeting my niece Cindy Nelson Sanders for the first time in 2002.

Me, Little Jimmy dickens and Brenda Lee.

Me and Sam Phillips at the Medallion Ceremony.

Members of my new found family The Nelson's, as they are related to my nephew David Nelson. Front row, son Lucas, Granddaughter Kayla, Mother, niece Dannelle, sister, who is my niece, Cindy, Nephew Andy, sister-in-law Jeanne. Back Row, son Chris, grandson Michael, daughter-in-law Julie, son Bradley, Dave's wife Sandy and my two nephews Dave and Doug.

2004

I have written about the beginning of my life. Now I am going to write about the coming finale.

What a relief when the radiation period was over. I could sleep later in the morning and I regained the ability to talk. But the old age miseries were still with me. The shingles are supposed to last for only a three or four month period, but they are still with me after almost a year. Why do they spend billions of dollars sending a camera to Mars when they can't even find a cure for shingles, which affects thousands of people? My head and forehead itch, and I have the chills. My eye is in constant pain and my sight has become more and more blurred. I can only read or write with a magnifying glass.

My equilibrium and my short-term memory, which is getting shorter every day, and arthritis, have been added to my old age miseries. I have trouble sleeping. I now know what the saying "weak in the knees" means.

Life did not seem worth living. I had thoughts of suicide. Why delay the inevitable? I realized this would be an embarrassment for my daughter, grandchildren, and my newfound family and relatives. I thought of my many friends and acquaintances who had suffered pain and long hours of confinement, who had probably suffered as much or more than I and had the courage to wait until they were called by Mother Nature. So I dismissed the thought of suicide and decided to wait my turn.

I have been living alone since June passed away in 1984. I really miss her, but my children and grandchildren partially filled the void. During her summer vacations, Claudia and I traveled to various eastern countries and also went to Australia.

I believe anyone who lives alone should have some animal for companionship and to take care of. I went to the Humane Society and got a cat. It is quite obvious he had been abused. All four of his paws were declawed. When I got him home he immediately went into hiding in the sunken area above the closets in my den. He would come down only at night to eat and relieve himself. Every day I would take a ladder and climb up to pet him, to develop his confidence. After seven months of hiding, he finally got the courage to come down and live a normal life. His previous owner had called him by the initials KC, which I didn't particularly like, but I didn't change it because I didn't want to give him more problems.

After I contracted shingles, my life became routine. I still have a maid come every week for the house cleaning, and a gardener for the yard work. I have now become a walking drug store. I take nine prescription medications internally a day plus eight various vitamin pills. In addition, I put nine drops of prescription medication in my right eye for a total of eighteen prescriptions each day!

When I get up in the morning I make my bed and then start ingesting my daily medications, feed my cat, KC, and let him out. He stays out for about a half an hour and comes back in. I then start my daily routine of thirty to forty five minutes of exercise. Except on Sunday, which I call my "goof-off day" and I only exercise for about ten to fifteen minutes. I make my breakfast but I sure miss not being able to read the morning paper. I check my three humming bird feeders to make sure they are full.

There are many types of birds who live in my area, quail, pigeons, bluebirds, owls, sparrows, and swallows, who build their mud nests around my house. We also have squirrels and rabbits. I buy wild bird seed, sunflower seeds and peanuts. I distribute them around my house. I'm sure they all await my presence. What surprised me was watching the squirrels eat the birdseed, the bluebirds eating the peanuts, and the orioles drinking the humming bird syrup.

I live on top of a hill and have to walk down to the street to pick up the morning newspapers and deposit the outgoing mail, that my daughter has prepared for me in the mailbox. After breakfast and feeding the birds, I take a morning nap. When I wake up, I clean the kitchen. On Monday and Friday, if there are no doctors' appointments, I shave and take a shower. On Saturday I turn on the dishwasher. I do my own laundry. I change the bed linens every Thursday and launder them every three weeks. I also launder my clothes every three weeks.

Claudia makes my doctors' appointments during the week, according to her teaching and social schedule. If the appointments are in the late afternoon, we go to dinner. If the appointments are in the morning, we do my weekly shopping. When we go to the market, Claudia lets me "drive" the shopping cart. I help her fill it, but as I can't read labels, she checks the date on the perishable goods.

These are the other activities Claudia performs for me: she checks my prescription drugs and if needed gets them refilled, drives me to all medical and dental appointments, drives me to the barber shop and waits, while I drive her crazy. Some of the other activities that Claudia performs are she reads my mail to me, makes out the checks for payment of bills, guides my hand to sign the checks, addresses envelopes for my birthday and anniversary cards, keeps my ledgers and bookkeeping up-to-date. Before we start one of the most important activities, the continuation of writing my autobiography, she checks my hearing aids and, if the batteries are run down, she replaces them. As I dictate my autobiography, she writes, then helps me revise, edit, look up words in the dictionary, and then takes the script to Glenda Croumie's Somis Secretarial Service to be typed and printed. My daughter is now living two lives—her own and mine!

After my afternoon nap, I continue my daily routine of taking prescription drugs and putting eye drops in my eye. I check and refill the humming bird feeders. I walk down and get the mail, which I cannot read. I try to think of what to write and jot it down the best I can.

My evening, which I look forward to, begins at five o'clock. I feed my cat and let him out. I have one beer every day while listening to the financial report and the news. Then I have dinner. If I'm not having a microwave dinner, I make my own. After dinner I have several spoonfuls of ice cream and KC comes back in. I then go into my bedroom with five ounces of candy, consisting of Hershey Bar and Mints. KC jumps on my lap to be brushed and petted, while I watch and listen to my two favorite programs, *Jeopardy* and *Wheel of Fortune*, even though the figures are blurred. After I watch the two programs, KC goes out again. On Sunday and Wednesday I watch *60 Minutes*. After I floss and brush my teeth, I let KC in. I sure miss not being able to read the paper before going to sleep. At 9:00 or 9:15 P.M. I put my last eye drop of the day in and so to bed.

I have a sad event to tell about, the death of my childhood friend, Joe Peter's sister Anne (Peter) Southworth. The Peter family consisted of Mr. and Mrs. Peter, Joe, Anne, and Dolly. They treated me as if I was one of their own. I had kept in touch with Joe until his death in 2000 and continued correspondence with Anne and Dolly all these years. Anne (Peter) Southworth passed away April 6, 2004, at the age of 94.

I had decided to end my book but two more serious events happened. The first was the death of President Ronald Reagan, whose honesty and forthrightness I had admired for many years. In reading about his life, I couldn't believe how our lives paralleled each others. We were both born in 1911, I on January 19th and Reagan on February 6th. We spent our childhood in Illinois, he in Dixon and I in Chicago. At an early age, he became a drum major in the YMCA band and I became a tenor banjo player and singer in orchestras. After my ninth grade in school, I started working for music publishers while Reagan went to high school and college. In 1933, we both were working as radio announcers. He in Des Moines, Iowa at WHO and I in Chicago at WAAF. In 1940 he moved to California and started his acting career. In 1941 I became musical director of WJJD in Chicago.

Both of our first marriages ended in divorce, but both of our second marriages were happy and enduring. In 1947 Reagan showed his political acumen when he became president of the Screen Actors Guild. In 1948 my family and I moved to California when I was hired to take over the transcription department of Capitol Records. In 1951 I was put in charge of the country music department, and later became a vice-president of Capitol.

In 1966 Reagan served two terms as governor of California. I am sure he enjoyed country music because I have pictures of him with some of my artists. In 1961, I was elected president of the Country Music Association for two terms.

In 1976 I retired, and in 1980 Ronald Reagan was elected president of the United States. He was beloved, admired, and respected and will go down in history as one of the great men of our time.

In 1994 he contracted Alzheimer's. He was under the care of his beloved wife, Nancy Reagan, until his death on June 5, 2004. One of the most amazing things about our parallel lives is that he was buried in Simi Valley in Ventura County and I, who have lived in Ventura County for many years, will be cremated and have my ashes strewn over the Ventura County mountains.

The second serious event was the demise of my close friend Bill Lowery at the age of 79. I had first met Bill in 1953 when he was an announcer at a radio station in Atlanta, Georgia. I went there to record a religious group, the Statesman Quartet. Bill sang me a religious song and recitation he had written called, "I Have but One Goal." I was impressed and recorded him. The record was a big seller in the religious field. I also encouraged Bill to start a publishing and artist agency in Atlanta. He published two of my biggest hits: Sonny James, "Young Love" and Gene Vincent's "Be Bop A Lula." Bill and I had kept in close touch with each other all these years. Again, I was saddened by the loss of a dear friend on June 8, 2004—three days after President Reagan passed away.

After finishing my autobiography, I had intended to place in an album in sequential order, all of my momentous, letters, newspaper articles and the dozens of photographs of artists I have produced. I have already made albums of photos of my many friends and co-workers, but I have not yet had time make an album of the photographs of my newfound Nelson and Roster family relatives. I have been neglecting my coin collection, which is quite extensive. It is comprised of every coin issued by the U.S. Government since it first started issuing coins in 1793. It also contains every commemorative coin, mint and proof sets issued since 1958. Claudia expressed an interest in continuing the coin collection. I had hoped to do all of this before leaving this world because it would be a tremendous amount of work for Claudia.

There is a ray of hope that I may be able to accomplish all of this. My ophthalmologist and optometrist told me, when the shingles clear up, I may be able to have a cornea transplant and I will be able to see clearly again.

I am not a psychologist or philosopher, but these are some of my observations of life. Religion is a necessary evil. It is necessary because it gives people hope and faith. It is evil because millions of people have died because men of one religion are trying to convince men of another religion that their religion is the true religion. Ever since the 11th and 12th century when Christian powers undertook the Crusades to win the Holy Land from the Moslems, religious wars have continued. In the 16th century in Paris, the Protestants were being slaughtered by Catholics. Christians against Christians, and even as late as 2000 in Ireland, Catholics and Protestants were killing one another. Today Israelis and Palestinians are avenging each other. Don't they know vengeance begets vengeance? Men will always have a divergence of opinion in religion and politics so there will always be wars. Ever since man first appeared on earth, men have been inventing items to make living easier but also continue to invent weapons to make killing each other easier. Today we have nuclear bombs that can wipe out an entire city. Where will it end? Was Shakespeare right when he said, "What fools these mortals be?"

Here are some of my thoughts about life:

> Man did not invent the computer. He was born with a computer—his brain, which absorbs, retains, and disseminates a limited amount of information. However, he did invent the mechanical computer in 1945, which can absorb, retain, and disseminate an unlimited amount of information.
>
> When we bring children into the world, we fail to realize that they will have to run the Gauntlet of Life. The trials and tribulations, the emotional, the mental, the physical, the medical and the miseries of old age. We should try to become aware of and recognize our passions, feelings, emotions, desires, and try not to let them interfere with our ability to think clearly and intelligently. Live for today, but keep your eye on tomorrow. The course of a child's life is determined by the environment they were raised in, as is the development of their emotions and the ability of their brain (computer) to assimilate, retain, and disseminate their teachings and experiences.
>
> On the subject of marriage, I believe a successful marriage is comprised of emotional compatibility, intellectual compatibility, philosophical compatibility, sexual compatibility, and of course, love and respect for each other. This does not mean that these requirements must be a perfect match.

It depends on to what degree each mate can tolerate the range of these areas in the other mate.

Women carry the burden of the world. When a girl becomes a teenager, her problems begin. She has a menstrual period every month, which goes on for at least forty years. Then she goes through the change of life. Women bear and raise children and yet in many cultures they are considered inferior. In one culture, some men felt they proved their manhood by having their wives give birth to boys. If the wives gave birth to girls, they would drown the baby girls. In some societies, women dare not show their faces and no part of a body is exposed while in public. If a woman commits adultery, she is stoned to death in the public square. Yet the man who was responsible goes unpunished!

Here in America, women were subservient to men until recent times. Even though they were teachers in all public schools, men refused to trust their ability in business and politics. It wasn't until 1920 that women finally got the right to vote and took their rightful place in the world. They have become business executives, heads of corporations, politicians, mayors, governors of state and congresswomen. However, many women are still being subjected to spousal and sexual abuse. In many cases they are still dominated by men.

Here are some of my letters to the editor that were published.

There is something radically wrong with our values when a man in shorts, prancing around a basketball court, earns $120,000,000 million and we bicker over giving a man or a woman maybe supporting a family a minimum hourly wage of $5.00.

It seems a bit incongruous that we spend billions of dollars trying to prevent Saddam Hussein from developing, manufacturing, and storing lethal chemical weapons, and yet the tobacco cartel, which kills tens of thousands of people worldwide each year, has free reign.

Some of the sitcoms and soap operas seen on television, and many of today's movies, such as: "Dangerous Beauty," seem to be aggressively competing with the pornographic movie industry and will probably eventually put them out of business.

> In 1948 when I wrote music to the Pledge of Allegiance, I wondered how many people knew what the pledge really meant. So this is what I wrote as a foreword: The Pledge of Allegiance to the flag is a pledge to the ideals of our forefathers; the men who fought and died in the building of this great nation. It is a pledge to fulfill our duties and obligations as citizens of the United States and to uphold the principles of our constitution. As Franklin Delano Roosevelt explained, "It is a pledge to maintain the four great freedoms cherished by all Americans; freedom of speech, freedom of religion, freedom from want and freedom from fear."

In 1998, *Dear Abby* published my foreword on Independence Day in her column.

With a few exceptions I have had a good and fulfilling life. When it will end! I don't know. When it does end, I do know life will go on without me.

The following are country artists I have produced

Roy Acuff
Alicia Adams
Ira Allen
Bobby Austin
Bobby Bare
Molly Bee
Wayne Berry
Janie Black
Jeanne Black
Blue Sky Boys
Hylo Brown
Al Brumley
Jimmy Bryant
Gary Buck
The Buckaroos
James Burton & Ralph Mooney
Ty Butler
Buddy Cagle
Glen Campbell
Thumbs Carlisle
Don Carroll
Jenks Carmen
Cindy Carson
Martha Carson
Chaparral Brothers
Leon Chappel
Roy Clark
Tommy Collins
Ken Curtis (Festus of Gunsmoke)
Dave Davenport
Duane Dee
Dub Dickerson
Al Dexter and Jimmy Dolan the Dillards
Eddie Downs
Johnny Draper
Bill Dudley
Bobby Durham
Roland Eaton
Bobby Edwards
Stony Edwards
The Eligibles
John Fallin
Farmer Boys
Rita Faye
Werly Fairburn
Dallas Frazier
Geezinslaw Brothers
Bobbie Gentry
Bobby George

Gosdin Brothers
Rudy Gray
Charles Lee Guy
Merle Haggard
Denny Hall
Walter Hensley
Dickie Harrell
Freddie Hart
Dwayne Hickman
Roy Hogsed
Harlan Howard
Jan Howard
Jimmy Heap
Cousin Herb Henson
Marvin Huges
Tommy Hunter
Ferlin Husky
David Ingles
Wanda Jackson
Peter James
Sonny James
Jim and Jessie
Red Johnson
The Jordanaires
Karl and Harty
Gail Kelly
Karen Kelly
Milt Kilpatrick
Rodney Lay
The Louvin Brothers
Norma Lee
Lemonade Charade
Pat Levely
Margare Lewis
Billy Liebert
Big Bill Lister
Kenny Loran
Bobbie Louis
Bill Lowery
Bob Luman
Rose Maddox
Joe Maphis and RoseLee Maphis
Grady Martin
Curt Massey
Curt Massey and Martha Tilton
Leon McAuliff
Nell McBride
Darrel McCall
Marvin McCullough
Skeets McDonald
Neal Merritt
Dick Miles
Ned Miller
Beth Moore
Merrill Moore
Bob Morris
Johnny and Jonie Mosby
Mafe Nutter
Gene O'quin
Bonnie Owens
Buck Owens
Leon Payne
Ray Pennington
Peter and Gordon
Ray Pillow
Gene Price
Jimmy Pruett
Donna Ramsay
Susan Raye
Jerry Reed
Dell Reeves
Jeannie Ciriley
Richard and Jim
Tex Ritter
Ole Rasmussen
Roy Rogers and Dale Evans
Dave Ronson
Johnny Rose
Bob Roubian
Denny Saeger
Carole Sands
Johnny Seay
Lloyd Schoonmaker
Jean Shephard
Red Simpson
Chester Smith

Billie Jo Spears
Statesmen Quartet
Ray Stevens
Wynn Stewart
Cliffie Stone
Billy Strange
The Style Masters
Earl Sinks
Cathie Taylor
Earl Taylor
Mary Taylor
Len Tanner
Hank Thompson
Merle Travis
T. Texas Tyler
Uncle Henry's Kentucky Mountaineers
Don Ulrich
The Vulcans
The Victors
Buddy Wayne
Speedy West
Tabby West
Bob White
Tex Williams
Mac Wiseman
Jimmy Wolford
Jimmy Work
Faron Young
The Zircons

Pop artists I have produced:

Ray Anthony
Bob Bain
Lou Busch—Joe Fingers Carr
Dinning Sisters
Art Van Damme
Esquerita,
Stan Freeburg
Billy May
Nelson Riddle
Kay Starr
Tommy Sands
Gene Vincent

Transcription artists I produced:

Claude Gordon
Frank DeVol
Rex Maupin
Les Baxter
Louis Castelluci
Calvary Quartet
Clark Dennis
Ernie Felice
Shug Fisher
Spike Haskell
Bob Grabeau
Wally Fowler
Nelson Hall Orchestra
Buddy Cole
Danny Kuaana Orchestra
Norma Zimmer and Bill Reeve
Eddie Lemar Orchestra
Mellow Men Quartet
Andy Parker and The Plainsmen
Del Porter and Tooters
The Starlighters
Sunset Trio
Ray Turner
Wesley Tuttle
Hal Derwin
Richard Cannon

Index

A
Acuff, Roy, 47, 116,168, 237
Academy of Country Music, 213, 226
American Cancer Society, 330
Anderson, Bill, 312, 316,321
Andrew Jackson Hotel, 100
A.F.T.R.A. - American Federation of Television and Radio Artists, 74
Alameida, Laurindo, 125
Allan, Buddy, 152
Allan, Dr. Jeffrey, 323, 329
Allison, Joe, 100, 147,160,162, 237, 324
Amiel, 250, 251, 252
American Federation of Muscicians, 84
American Society of Authors and Publishers (ASCAP), 60, 62, 91, 142
Anderson, Bill, 312, 316, 332
Anderson, Hans Christian, 275
Anthony, Ray, 258
Arnold, Eddy, 144, 226, 321, 333
Atcher, Bob, 64, 66
Atkins, Chet, 81, 102, 113, 124, 156, 165, 226, 289, 312, 315, 317
Atlas, Ralph, 66
Atomic Bomb, 79
Austin, Bloom and Koehler, 30
Austin, Gene, 30, 31, 33, 35
Austin, Gene, Inc., 31, 32
Autry, Gene, 132, 197-198, 233, 295, 324
Axton, Mae, 142

B
Barnes, Dave, 312
Basic Training, 69
Baxter, Les, 92
Beach Boys, 187-188
Beatles, 150, 187-188
Beginning of the Old Age Miseries, 322-323, 327
Berlin, Irving, 207-208
Ben, Bernie, 50
Benson, Ed, 314
Billboard Chart, 84, 246
Birkenhead, Warren & Mary, 220-221
Black Monday, Tragic Tuesday, 39
Blake, Randy, 82, 314
Blanchard, Lowell, 51
Bleyer, Archie, 32, 47, 317
Block, Martin, 63
Bloom, Marty, 17, 30-33, 35-36
BMI, Broadcast Music, Inc., 60, 62-63, 84, 104, 142
Borrelli, Judge, 38
Bradley, Harold, 124, 156, 186
Bradley, Owen, 102, 124, 294, 315
British Archives, 311
Brown Derby, Lunch at, 174-175
Brown, Hylo, 126
Bryant, Jimmy, 329
Buckaroos, 150, 152, 215
Burke, Johnny, 47

Busch, Lou - aka - Joe Fingers Carr, 126

C
Cable Piano Company, 55, 72-73
Cagle, Buddy, 199
Camp Barkeley - Abilene Texas, 67-69
Campbell, Glen, 199, 209-210
Campus Kids, 50, 56-57
Capital Records, vii, 72, 87, 98, 103, 132-133, 161, 214, 228, 249
Capone, Al, 30
Caraway, Miles, 107
Carlisle, Bill, 329
Carlton, Buzz, 89-90, 228
Carr, Joe Fingers, 126
Carson, Martha, 99, 134, 156-157, 164, 258
Carter Practice Elementary School, 14, 45, 140
Cash, Johnny, 229, 327
Castle Chick, 35,-36
Century Songs, Inc., 83, 103-104
Chappel, Leon, 99, 104
Chase, Eddie, 63
Chicago Musicians Union, 56
Chicago Symphony Orchestra, 55
Chicago Tribune, 20, 90
Christ Memorial, Unitarian, 116, 132
Clark, Roy, 152, 162-163, 199, 231, 316
Cline, Patsy, 118
Cohen, Paul, 226, 233
Coin Collection, 277
Cole, Buddy, 92
Collie, Biff, 146
Collins, Tommy, 106, 116, 119, 149, 169, 174, 199, 298
Columbia Records, 65
Conkling, Jim, 86-88, 101, 161
Conlon, Ryan and Char Lotte, 268-269
Continental Bank, 27
Coogan, Jackie, 117
Cook County Jail, 38
Cook, Hal, 87, 101, 175, 296
Cooley, Spade, 208
Coolidge, Calvin President, 34
Cosse, X 156-157
Country Music Association, vii, 144-145, 177, 226, 312-313, 332
Country Music Disc Jockey Association, 144
Country Music Hall of Fame, 226, 312-313, 332
Cowan, Louis B., 139, 140-141
Crane Company, 28-29
Creighton, Harry, 55, 62
Crosby, Bing, 91
Crotty, Jim, 49-51, 61

D
Darin, Bobby, 158
Dave Davis, 36-37, 39
Davis, Jimmie, 161, 299
Davis, Mac, 210
Davis, Oscar, 144
Davis, Sheriff Tex, 136
Dean, Eddie, 101
Delmore Brothers, 312, 314
DeLory, Al, 204, 210
Dennis, Clark, 92
Derwin, Hal, 52, 56, 260
DeVol, Frank, 42
DeSylva, Buddy, 72
Dewey, Thomas, 90
Dexter, Dave, 136
DiCandriano, Princess, 92
Diekman, Diana, 308
Dinkler, Mr., 138-139
Dinning Sisters, 84, 299
Disc Jockey (DJ), 63
Dubin, Al, 32

E
East Central Developing Oil Company, 181
East, St. Louis, 40

Eighteenth Amendment, 49
Ellington, Duke, 87
Ellison, Bob, 65-66
Emery, Ralph, 315
Engeman, Karl, 161
English Music Industry (EMI), 130, 187
Esch's (Aunt) Farm, 3-4
Esquerita, 156
Evans, Dale, 311
Eubanks, Bob, 249
Everly Brothers, 312, 317

F
Fairman, Billy, 85
Fairway Hills, 263
Farnon, Christine, 145-146
Faye, Rita, 181
Felcher, Bernadine Mrs., 74-75, 80-81, 210
Felcher, Fred (Dr.), 74-76, 80-81, 83-86, 90, 103, 181-182
Felcher, June, 73-75, 95
First Royalty Check, 63
Fitzimmons General Hospital 69-71, 94
Ford, Tennessee Ernie, 91, 157
Foster, Steven, 60
Fowler, Wally, 72
Frazier, Dallas, 126
Freeberg, Stan, 101-102
Freeway Music, 132

G
Gay, Connie B., 144, 246
Germany, 67
Gibson, Don, 312, 315, 329
Gillette, Edie, 72, 76, 87
Gillette, Lee, 22, 49-52, 56-57, 59-61, 63, 67, 71-72, 81, 86-88, 92, 98, 109, 111, 124, 142, 145, 157, 254, 258
Gilmore, Voyle, 112, 156-157, 186-187, 209
Gold Star Music Publishing Co., 40, 42
Goodman, Wendell, 131
Gortikov, Stan, 226, 228
Grand Ol' Opry, 246
Green ,Dr., 75,79-80,84
Green, Larry, 228-229
Green, Mort, 21-22
Guy, Charles Lee, 208-209, 234

H
Haggard, Merle, 119, 151, 198-199, 200, 209, 227, 236, 240
Hall of Fame Medallion, 320
Halsey, Jim, 112-113, 162
Harre, Art, 52, 57, 60, 64, 67
Harrell, Dickie "BEBOP", 138
Hart, Freddie, 126, 229, 235, 295
Hawkins, Hawk Shaw, 118
Heap, Jimmy, 101, 111
Heiftz, Jascha, 69
Helton, Lon, 314
Hensley, Harold, 101, 278
Henson, Cousin Herb, 198
Herston, Kelso, 220
Hill Billy Music, 54, 98-99
Hill & Range, 210
Hitler, Adolph, 79
Hoffman, (Mr. & Mrs.), 5
Hollander, Al, 64, 67
Hollywood Walk of Fame, 145
Home of the Friendless, 1
Homer and Jethro, 316
Hoover, Herbert, 34
Horton, Roy, 226
Howard, Don, 324
Howard, Harlan, 131, 151, 180-181, 184, 187, 232, 320, 326
Howard, Jan, 132, 187
Hughes, Marvin, 132, 156, 158, 186
Hughes, Randy, 118
Hunt, PeeWee, 92
Huskey, Ferlin, 116-118, 121, 126, 134, 191, 199, 237, 298

I
Induction Into Army, 67

J
Jackson Park Hotel, 48-49
James, Sonny, 104, 113, 115, 166, 324
Jackson, Wanda, 113, 130-131, 162, 173, 297
Jean, Billie, 105
Jelly Roll Morton, 18
Jennings, Waylon, 312, 317, 320
Joe Morris Music Co., 34, 40
Joe - World War I Vet, 7
Johnson, Joe, 132, 198
Jones, Frank, 249-250
Jones, George, 125
Jordanaires, 120, 121-122, 169, 297-298, 312, 316-317, 312, 332, 333
Joyce, Jimmy, 177

K
Karl and Harty, 64, 81, 85, 124
Kausen, Patricia (Patty), 251-252, 328
Kaye, Sammy, 66
Keefer, Steve, 288, 319
Kennedy, Jim, 89, 115
Kennedy, Ona, 89,
Kern, Jerome, 66
Killen, Buddy, 141
Kilpatrick, Dee, 99, 144, 233
Kirkham, Millie, 126
King Oliver, 118
Klug, Michael & Peter, 290-292, 299, 318, 321
Koehler, Ted, 30, 31
Kraus, John, 112
KRKS - Radio Station, 142-144
KYW, 6, 50-3, 56, 61, 64

L
Lake Malibu, 182
Lamb, Charlie, 144
Lane, Frankie, 47
Lathower, Mauri, 246, 256
Law, Don, 125, 312, 315
Lee, Brenda, 312, 334
Lewis, Joe, 69
Lewis, Ted, 30
Li, Mr. & Mrs., 225
Liebert, Billy, 101
Little Jimmi Dickens, 321, 334
Livingston, Allan, 154, 160, 186
Logan, Horace, 324
Lombardo, Guy, 51
Long, Hubert, 104, 144, 161, 215, 254
Louvin Brothers, 104, 108, 167, 312, 314, 321, 332
Lowery, Bill, 114-115, 129, 137, 149, 249, 254, 296, 300, 340

M
Maddox, Rose, 158, 160, 199, 295
Magnetic Tape, 91
Maitland, Mike, 216
Mallie, Tommie, 47
Marks. Johnny, 198
Martin, Grady, 319
Mary, 64
Mature, Victor, 126
Maupin, Rex, 50, 84
May, Billy, 101-102
McCoy, Charlie, 245
McDonald, Skeets, 131, 134
McFadden, Jack, 150, 295
McHugh, Kim and Carrol, 295
McHugh, Reg & Tina, 62-63, 75-76, 97, 123, 292, 297-299, 307, 311
McIntyre, Dr., 263-264
McLemore, Ed, 137
Melrose Brothers Music Co., 18-19, 29, 50
Melrose, Lester, 18-19
Melrose, Walter, 18-19, 30
Menon, Bhaskar, 245
Mercer, Johnny, 72, 104, 258
Miller, Ned, 215
Monte, Herb, 89

Moon, Harold, 144
Moore, Merrill, 104, 115
Morris, Rod, 114
Mother, Susan Nelson, 3, 19, 22, 24, 26, 42, 86, 103-104, 116, 123
Mullen, John, 91
Mussolini, Benito, 79
"My Brothers Will", 72
"Myra"-First Wife, 57-59

N
NARAS - National Academy of Recording Arts and Sciences, 112, 144-146, 210
Nashville, 99, 313, 315
Nelson, Charles, Frederick - Grandson, 270, 309
Nelson, Cindy - Niece, 334
Nelson, Claudia - Daughter, 85, 215-216, 230, 250, 251-252, 265, 270, 274, 307, 310, 320, 327-328, 337-338
Nelson, Conrad - Father, 1, 42-43, 90-91
Nelson, David - Nephew, 297, 299, 318, 321-322, 331, 336
Nelson, Grandma, 3, 43-44
Nelson, Gregory - Son, 80, 103, 160, 200-201, 215, 250-252, 286, 288
Nelson, Gregory Jr. - Grandson, 263, 307, 323, 328
Nelson, H.P. - Grandpa, 3, 42-44, 90
Nelson, Lillian - Aunt, 43-44, 90
June - Wife, 76-77, 79-81, 122, 130, 210, 214, 220, 227-229, 239, 245, 252, 262-265
Nelson, Kenneth Francis, 1, 67, 177, 188-191, 249
Nelson, Peter - Brother, 276, 297
Nelson, Tiffany Ann - Granddaughter, 262, 291, 298, 307, 323, 327
Newman, Charles, 47, 50-51
Nixon, President, 229, 249
Nobel Foundation, 275
Nuwana, 72-74

O
Olsen's Orchestra, George, 26, 33
O.P.A. - Office Of Price Administration, 67
Price, Deborah, 212
Oriental Trip, 265-269, 279-283, 285
Ovens, Don, 147-148
O.W.I. - Office Of War Information, 67
Owens, Bonnie, 117, 200, 214, 249
Owens, Buck, 119, 126, 149-153, 160, 163, 199, 209, 214-215, 220, 229, 231, 236, 255, 293, 295, 298, 316
Owens, Fuzzy, 199-200

P
Pagent of Progress, 16
Palladino, John, 87, 93
Palmer House, 8
Parker, Colonel Tom, 147
Paul, Les, 64
Pearl Harbor, 66
Pearl, Minnie, 292
Peeples, Hap, 118
Pepper, Wade, 115, 239, 246, 296, 315
Peter, Joe, 15, 37, 57, 296-297, 302, 339
Petrillo, James C., 56, 82, 84
Pierce, Webb, 104, 312, 316
Phonograph Records, 18, 31, 65, 82
Phillips, Sam, 312, 317, 321, 328, 335
Piggly Wiggly, 78
Pillow, Ray, 215
Pledge of Allegiance, 85
Potter, Vivian, 291
Prairie Theatre - Amature Night, 21
Presley, Elvis, 129, 149, 313
Price, Deborah, 304
Purcell, Bill, 314, 318

Q
QRS Piano Player Rolls, 18
Quadling, Lew, 206-207

R
Radio, 19-20, 22, 23, 25-26, 38, 71-72, 91
RCA, 38-39
Reagan, Ronald, President, 152, 199, 255, 278, 334, 340
Reed, Jerry, 114, 129, 300, 317
Rich, Don, 150, 152
Richey, George, 245, 295
Riddle, Nelson, 130, 145, 148
Ritter, Tex, 75, 85, 96, 99, 109, 130, 175, 197, 232, 237, 249, 258, 296, 324, 329
Rock-a-Billy Hall of Fame, 297
Rogers, David, 324-325
Rogers, Roy, 187, 295
Roosevelt, President, 49, 60, 66, 74, 343
Rose, Fred, 47, 51, 66, 108, 113,k 128-129
Rose, Wesley, 50, 116, 144, 197, 314
Roster Family, 1, 4-5, 8, 12-13, 289-292, 300-301, 303, 318
Russia, Siberia, Mongolia Tour, 270-274

S
Saint Anselems Church, 7
Sam's Club, 49-50
Sands, Tommy, 130, 136, 146-148, 174, 324
Saticoy Country Club, 262
Scandanavian Tour, 275
Schneider, Herb, 154
Schultz, George P., 268-269
Scott, Francis M. (Scotty), 146
Shepard, Jean, 113, 117-118, 170, 199
Sherwood Music School, 73
Sholes, Steve, 177, 226, 233
Simmons, Eddie, 53, 55, 57
Simpson, Red, 151, 214
Sinatra, Nancy, 148-149
Sippi, Dr., 71
Smith, Al, 34
Smith, Carl, 126
Smith, Lyle, 26, 33
Snow In The Valley, 90
Snyder Music Co., 91, 122
South Town Syncopaters, 22
Speeches, 127-128, 133-136, 154-156, 179-182, 191-197, 202-206, 211-213, 217-220, 227, 247, 259-261
Starved Rock, 77-78
S.S. Kresge, 41
Stapp, Jack, 105, 138-141
Starlighters, 87
Starr, Kay, 187, 258
Stevens, Ray, 114, 149
Stewart, Wynn, 131-132, 234, 320
Stitzel, Mel, 50
Stone, Cliffie, 83, 89-90, 99, 101, 132, 144, 146, 245, 258, 294-295
Stryker, Fred, 113-114
Stuart, Marty, 314
Studio City Home, 88-89, 129
Supper Time Frolic, 64-65, 81-82

T
Talbot, Eddie, 40, 42
Tally, Lew, 199
Tanner, Elmo, 51
Television, 38, 60
"That's My Desire", 47-48
Thomason, Mort, 121, 315
Thompson, Hank, 99, 101, 105-106, 111-112, 117, 131, 134, 162, 170-171, 174, 233, 258
Tilden Tech High School, 23
Toll, Ted, 49, 310
Transcriptions, 72, 84, 91, 93, 96
Travis, Merle, 72, 81, 99, 106, 111, 124, 174, 199, 258, 261, 317
Tree Music, 140-141
Trianon Ballroom, 18

Truman, Harry S. - President, 79, 82, 90
Tubb, Ernest, 144

U

V
Vallee, Rudy, 41
Van Damme, Art, 84, 299
Venet, Nick, 138, 187
Ventura College, 293
Ventura Homes, 182
Victor Records, 65, 93
Vincent, Gene, 130, 136-138, 156, 171-173, 246, 297, 340

W
WAAF Radio Station, 52-56, 58, 64, 73
WAC's Camp, 68
Walker, Jo, 145, 177, 197, 287, 314
Wall, Maurie, 37-38
Wallichs, Glenn, 72, 81, 86, 102-103, 107, 160, 246
Warren, Harry, 32-33
Welk, Lawrence, 63
Wells, Kitty, 105
West, Speedy, 117, 329
White City, 17, 56
Whiteman, Paul, 18, 41
Williams, Hank, 105-106
Williams, Tex, 99, 111, 213, 258, 261
Wilson, Lorraine - Stu, 153, 157, 188
Wilson, Meredith, 159
Wilson, Murray, 187
Wilson, Smiley, 210
WIND- Radio Station, 65
Wiseman, Mac, 144, 180
WJJD - Radio Station, 64-67, 71-72, 82
WLS Barn Dance, 53
Woo, William, 223-225
Woodlawn Business Men's Association, 56
Woods, Bill, 298
Woods Theatre Building, 35, 39, 47
World War, 67, 69
Wyatt, Paul, 181, 186

X

Y
Young, Faron, 104-108, 134, 170, 174, 293, 308, 324
Young, Joe, 47
Young, Kyle, 314
Young, Victor-WGN, 76